IR35: Personal Service

IR35: Personal Service Companies

Anne Redston

**professional
information**

40 Bernard Street
London
WC1N 1LD
Tel: +44(0)20 7920 8991
Fax: +44(0)20 7920 8992
E-mail: info@abgpublications.co.uk
Website: www.abgweb.com

British Library Cataloguing-in-Publication Data

A catalogue record for this book is available from the British Library.

Typeset by Mac Style, Scarborough, N. Yorkshire
Printed by Creative Print and Design, Wales

Contents

Acknowledgements   xxi
Tables of Cases   xxiii
Tables of Statutes   xxvii
Table of Statutory Instruments   xxxi
Table of Manuals and Handbooks   xxxiii
Abbreviations   xxxvii

1 Introduction   1

2 Purpose and developement of IR35   3
  2.1   **Introduction**   3
  2.2   **Background to IR35**   3
     2.2.1   The personal service company   3
     2.2.2   Changing employment patterns   3
     2.2.3   Growing government concerns   5
  2.3   **The legislative process**   7
     2.3.1   IR35   7
     2.3.2   The April paper   7
     2.3.3   Problems with the April paper   8
     2.3.4   The September Press Release   9
     2.3.5   Tax legislation   9
     2.3.6   National Insurance legislation and regulations   9
     2.3.7   Frequently Asked Questions   10
  2.4   **Conclusion**   10

3 Tax planning and IR35   11
  3.1   **General**   11
  3.2   **Paying dividends rather than salary**   12
     3.2.1   Outline   12
     3.2.2   Corporate tax rates   12
     3.2.3   National Insurance   14
     3.2.4   Other advantages of using dividends rather than salary   18
  3.3   **Small salary payment**   18
  3.4   **Payments to family members**   19
     3.4.1   Outline   19
     3.4.2   Revenue attacks   19
     3.4.3   Worked examples   20

3.5		**Expenses and capital allowances**	23
	3.5.1	Expenses	23
	3.5.2	Capital allowances	24
3.6		**Pensions**	24
	3.6.1	General	24
	3.6.2	Tax advantages	24
	3.6.3	Personal pensions	25
	3.6.4	Stakeholder schemes	26
	3.6.5	Occupational schemes	26
3.7		**Interest relief**	27
	3.7.1	Outline	27
	3.7.2	Close companies	27
	3.7.3	Deduction for loan interest	28
3.8		**Retention of funds in the company**	29
3.9		**Capital gains tax advantages**	29
3.10		**Tax planning pitfalls**	29
	3.10.1	Introduction	29
	3.10.2	Non-repayable tax credits	30
	3.10.3	Illegal dividends	30
	3.10.4	Loans to participators	31

4 Scope of personal services legislation			33
4.1		**General**	33
	4.1.1	IR35 target constituency	33
	4.1.2	Sham companies	33
	4.1.3	Legislation	34
4.2		**Personal services provided on or after 6 April 2000**	34
	4.2.1	Personal services	34
	4.2.2	Provided on or after 6 April 2000	34
4.3		**Provide to a business . . .**	35
	4.3.1	Scope of definition	35
	4.3.2	. . . A business carried on by another person (the client)	35
4.4		**The worker would be regarded as an employee of the client**	36
4.5		**Intermediaries**	37
	4.5.1	Introduction	37
	4.5.2	Company	37
	4.5.3	Partnerships	41
	4.5.4	Individuals	42
	4.5.5	More than one intermediary	42
4.6		**Worker recieves payment or benefit not within Schedule E**	43
	4.6.1	Interpretation	43
	4.6.2	De minimis exemption	44
4.7		**Sole traders**	44

4.8		**National Insurance**	45
	4.8.1	Legislation	45
	4.8.2	Annual earnings period	45
	4.8.3	Aggregation of earnings	46
	4.8.4	Interpretating the scope of the Act	47

5 Hypothetical contracts and mutuality — 49

5.1		**Construction of the legislation**	49
	5.1.1	Tax	49
	5.1.2	National Insurance	50
	5.1.3	Caveat	50
5.2		**Contractual arrangements**	50
	5.2.1	Outline	50
	5.2.2	The contract is normally the starting point	51
	5.2.3	Implied terms, extensions and variations	51
	5.2.4	Where there is ambiguity, the contract normally decides status	53
	5.2.5	Reality differs from written contract	55
	5.2.6	No formal contract	55
	5.2.7	Summary	56
5.3		**Mutuality of obligation**	57
	5.3.1	Summary	57
	5.3.2	No mutuality and no employment	59
	5.3.3	Series of small contracts of employment	63
	5.3.4	Gradual change to the relationship to create mutuality	64
	5.3.5	Overriding umbrella contract	66
	5.3.6	Case law conclusion	68
	5.3.7	Revenue view of mutuality	69
	5.3.8	Application to personal services workers	70
5.4		**Contracts with clients**	71
5.5		**Contracts with agencies**	71
	5.5.1	Both contracts are included	71
	5.5.2	Different terms in agency/client and service company/agency contracts	71
5.6		**Agency as client?**	72
5.7		**Summary**	73

6 Employed or self-employed? — 75

6.1		**Introduction**	75
6.2		**Development and scope of legislation**	75
6.3		**Status tests and checklists**	76
	6.3.1	General	76
	6.3.2	Hierarchy of status tests	77

6.4	**The 'in business on your own account' test**	78
	6.4.1 The self-employed business	78
	6.4.2 Being in business is not a necessary condition for self-employment	78
	6.4.3 A third way	79
	6.4.4 The professional	80
	6.4.5 Conclusion	80
6.5	**Fundamental status tests**	80
	6.5.1 Introduction	80
	6.5.2 Right to send a substitute	81
	6.5.3 Significant financial risk and opportunity to profit from sound management	85
	6.5.4 Hiring of staff	87
6.6	**Important status tests**	88
	6.6.1 General	88
	6.6.2 Provision of equipment	89
	6.6.3 Control	90
	6.6.4 Length and number of engagements: factors personal to the worker	95
6.7	**Minor status tests**	97
	6.7.1 Summary	97
	6.7.2 Exclusivity	97
	6.7.3 Payment terms	98
	6.7.4 Right of dismissal	99
	6.7.5 Intention of the parties	100
	6.7.6 Business structure	100
	6.7.7 Part and parcel of the organisation	101
6.8	**Overall summary**	102
7	**Revenue view of employment status**	105
7.1	**Introduction**	105
7.2	**General**	105
7.3	**Overall approach**	106
	7.3.1 General	106
	7.3.2 Hierarchy of tests	106
	7.3.3 Employment as the default position	107
	7.3.4 Mutuality of obligation	108
7.4	**Particular status tests**	108
	7.4.1 Substitution	108
	7.4.2 Risk	110
	7.4.3 Profiting from sound management	111
	7.4.4 Hiring staff	111
	7.4.5 Provision of equipment	112

	7.4.6	Control	113
	7.4.7	Number and variety of engagements	114
	7.4.8	Regular or long engagements with the same client	115
	7.4.9	Payment terms	116
	7.4.10	Intention of the parties	117
	7.4.11	Business organisation	117
7.5	**Case studies**	117
7.6	**Standard contracts**	118
7.7	**Status reviews**	119
7.8	**Challenging the Revenue view**	120
	7.8.1	General	120
	7.8.2	Questions of law and fact	120
	7.8.3	Importance of agreeing the facts	121
	7.8.4	The legal process	122

8 Status cases and IR35   123
8.1	**Introduction**	123
8.2	**Recent court decisions I: the professional**	124
	8.2.1	Hall v Lorimer	124
	8.2.2	Key factors leading to the decision	125
	8.2.3	Conclusions	128
	8.2.4	Application of the case to personal service workers	128
8.3	**Recent court decisions II: the manual worker**	129
	8.3.1	Lee Ting Sang v Chung Chi-Keung	129
	8.3.2	Relevance for personal service workers	131
	8.3.3	Conclusion	131
8.4	**Recent court decisions III: the special case**	132
	8.4.1	Barnett v Brabyn	132
8.5	**Other useful cases**	133
	8.5.1	Comparison of cases	133
	8.5.2	Summary	135

9 Changing the contractual relationship   137
9.1	**Introduction**	137
9.2	**General**	137
9.3	**Substitution clause**	138
	9.3.1	Introduction	138
	9.3.2	Clause accepted by the client	138
	9.3.3	Appointment, permission and veto	138
	9.3.4	Responsibility for work and for payment	139
	9.3.5	Identifying the substitute	139
	9.3.6	The client contract	140
	9.3.7	Use of alternates	140
	9.3.8	Conclusion	140

9.4	**Project-based work**		140
	9.4.1	General	140
	9.4.2	Clause has to be genuine	141
	9.4.3	There has to be real risk	141
	9.4.4	Contract variations	141
	9.4.5	Other characteristics	142
9.5	**Hiring staff**		142
9.6	**Control**		143
	9.6.1	General	143
	9.6.2	Control over the specialist	143
	9.6.3	Control as to when, where and what	143
9.7	**Insurance**		144
	9.7.1	General	144
	9.7.2	Remedying defective work	144
9.8	**Providing own equipment**		145
9.9	**Pay and benefits**		145
	9.9.1	Holiday pay and benefits	145
	9.9.2	Hourly rates	146
9.10	**Intention of the parties**		146
9.11	**Tax clauses**		147
9.12	**Business structure**		148
9.13	**Exclusivity**		148
9.14	**Termination and notice**		149
9.15	**Off-the-peg solutions**		150
10	**Income and benefits from relevant engagements**		153
	10.1	**Introduction**	153
	10.2	**Receipts basis**	153
	10.3	**Apportionments of income**	154
	10.4	**A single employment**	155
	10.5	**Steps One and Two of the deemed Schedule E calculation**	156
		10.5.1 General	156
		10.5.2 Payments/benefits received by the worker from the intermediary	157
		10.5.3 Payments/benefits which are not taxable	157
		10.5.4 Payments/benefits from a third party already within Schedule E	157
		10.5.5 Interaction between IR35 and PAYE/P11D rules	160
	10.6	**Common benefits**	161
		10.6.1 Accommodation	161
		10.6.2 Assets	162
		10.6.3 Cars	164
		10.6.4 Chauffeur	166

10.6.5	Conferences	167
10.6.6	Entertaining	167
10.6.7	Fuel	170
10.6.8	Gifts	170
10.6.9	Loans	170
10.6.10	Relocations	171
10.6.11	Telephones	171
10.6.12	Travel and subsistence	171
10.7	**PAYE Settlement Agreements and Taxed Award Schemes**	172
11	**Expenses included in deemed payment**	**173**
11.1	**Introduction**	173
11.2	**The 5 per cent allowance**	173
11.2.1	General	173
11.2.2	What does the 5 per cent deduction cover?	173
11.2.3	Interaction with corporation tax	174
11.3	**Expenses in the deemed Schedule E calculation**	175
11.3.1	Step Three	175
11.3.2	Cash basis	176
11.3.3	Costs incurred by the employee/director rather than the intermediary	176
11.3.4	Partners	177
11.3.5	Apportioned costs	177
11.3.6	Expense disallowances	178
11.4	**Schedule E expenses**	179
11.4.1	Tax	179
11.4.2	National Insurance	179
11.5	**The general rule: s198(1)**	179
11.6	**Travel and subsistence expenses**	181
11.6.1	General	181
11.6.2	Legislation	182
11.6.3	Ordinary commuting	182
11.6.4	Private travel	187
11.6.5	Accommodation and subsistence	187
11.6.6	Working rule agreements	188
11.6.7	Planning for travel costs	188
11.6.8	Vehicle running costs and business mileage	189
11.7	**Personal Incidental Expenses**	190
11.8	**Training**	191
11.8.1	Training paid for by the worker	191
11.8.2	Training paid for by the client or agency	191
11.8.3	Limits of relief	192
11.8.4	Individual learning accounts	192

	11.8.5	Indicator of self-employment	193
11.9	**Professional subscriptions**		**194**
11.10	**Insurance**		**194**
11.11	**Capital allowances**		**195**
	11.11.1	Step Four	195
	11.11.2	Assets generally	196
	11.11.3	Cars, motor bikes and bicycles	197

12	**Completing the deemed Schedule E calculation**		**199**
	12.1	**Introduction**	**199**
	12.2	**Step Five**	**199**
		12.2.1 General	199
		12.2.2 NIC relief	199
		12.2.3 Timing of payments	200
		12.2.4 Net relevant earnings	200
		12.2.5 Calculating the maximum contribution	201
		12.2.6 Over-contribuions	202
	12.3	**Step Six**	**203**
		12.3.1 General	203
		12.3.2 Class 1 NICs	203
		12.3.3 Class 1A NICs	204
	12.4	**Step Seven**	**204**
		12.4.1 General	204
		12.4.2 Salary	205
		12.4.3 Benefits	205
		12.4.4 P11Ds	207
		12.4.5 Interaction with Step Three	207
	12.5	**Step Eight**	**208**
		12.5.1 Class 1 charge	208
		12.5.2 Calculation of NIC due	208
	12.6	**Step Nine**	**209**
	12.7	**Attributable earnings but no deemed Schedule E, or vice versa**	**209**
		12.7.1 Overseas interactions	209
		12.7.2 National Insurance deeming rules	209
	12.8	**Worked example**	**211**

13	**Corporation tax, dividends and VAT**		**215**
	13.1	**Introduction**	**215**
	13.2	**Recognition of income**	**216**
		13.2.1 Corporation tax basis	216
		13.2.2 Deemed Schedule E basis	216
	13.3	**Accounting year end other than 5 April**	**216**
	13.4	**Possible solutions to accounting year end date problem**	**218**

13.4.1	Summary	218
13.4.2	31 March deemed to be 5 April?	219
13.4.3	Provision for deemed payment?	219
13.4.4	Provision for actual payment?	220
13.4.5	Making a terminal loss claim	220
13.4.6	Change of accounting date to 5 April	221
13.5	**Withdrawal of funds**	222
13.5.1	Options available	222
13.5.2	Withdrawal of funds following deemed Schedule E calculation	223
13.5.3	Salary during the fiscal year	226
13.6	**Dividends**	228
13.6.1	Using dividends to extract profits	228
13.6.2	Claiming relief for double taxation	231
13.6.3	Restriction on dividends payable	233
13.7	**Corporation tax losses**	233
13.7.1	Expenses exceed 5 per cent of income	233
13.7.2	Using corporation tax losses	235
13.7.3	Management of corporation tax losses	235
13.7.4	Insolvency	236
13.8	**Cessation and liquidation**	236
13.8.1	Options available	236
13.8.2	Retaining the company	237
13.8.3	Closing down the company	237
13.8.4	Freelance	238
13.8.5	Travel costs	238
13.8.6	Timing	238
13.9	**Planning points**	239
13.10	**Value added tax**	239
14 Partnerships		241
14.1	**General**	241
14.2	**Exceptions**	241
14.2.1	No relevant engagements	241
14.2.2	The statutory exemptions	241
14.3	**Concession and practice**	244
14.3.1	Introduction	244
14.3.2	ESC A37: 'Tax treatment of directors' fees recieved by partnerships and other companies'	244
14.3.3	Revenue practice	245
14.3.4	National Insurance	246
14.4	**Workers within partnerships**	246

14.5	**The deemed income calculation**	**247**
	14.5.1 Introduction	247
	14.5.2 Step One	247
	14.5.3 Step Two	248
	14.5.4 Step Three	249
	14.5.5 Step Four	249
	14.5.6 Step Five	252
	14.5.7 Steps Six and Seven	252
	14.5.8 Steps Eight and Nine	252
14.6	**Interaction of deemed payment and partnership tax position**	**253**
	14.6.1 Deemed payment a requirement	253
	14.6.2 Timing of deemed payment	253
	14.6.3 Deduction in partnership computation for deemed payment	253
	14.6.4 Accounting dates	254
	14.6.5 Effects of deemed Schedule E payment on other partners	257
14.7	**National Insurance**	**258**
	14.7.1 Interaction with Classes 2 and 4	258
	14.7.2 Small earnings exception	258
14.8	**Payment of PAYE and NICs**	**259**
15	**Self-assessment and personal services**	**261**
15.1	**General**	**261**
15.2	**Outline of self-assessment for individuals and partners**	**261**
15.3	**Reporting personal services income via self-assessment**	**263**
	15.3.1 Notifying chargeability	263
	15.3.2 Salary and deemed Schedule E income [1.8]	263
	15.3.3 Benefits [1.12–1.23]	263
	15.3.4 Expenses and capital allowances [1.32–1.36]	264
	15.3.5 Reliefs [1.3.8 and 14]	265
	15.3.6 Dividends	266
	15.3.7 Student loan repayments	266
	15.3.8 Overseas income and residence status	266
	15.3.9 Self-employed individuals	268
	15.3.10 Partners	268
15.4	**Disclosure**	**268**
	15.4.1 General	268
	15.4.2 Personal services	269
15.5	**Changing the tax return**	**270**
	15.5.1 Methods of changing the return	270
	15.5.2 Amendments	271
	15.5.3 Error or mistake	271

	15.5.4	Enquiry	272
	15.5.5	Discovery	272
15.6	**Interest and penalties**	**274**
	15.6.1	Alternatives	274
	15.6.2	Tax paid late	274
	15.6.3	For late submission of returns	274
	15.6.4	For fraud or negligence	275
15.7	**Interim payments under self-assessment**	**275**
15.8	**Corporation tax self assessment**	**276**
	15.8.1	Outline of system	276
	15.8.2	Implications for personal services	277

16 Tax payments, penalties and investigations			**281**
16.1	**Introduction**	**281**
16.2	**PAYE and P11D administration**	**281**
	16.2.1	PAYE and NIC deductions	281
	16.2.2	P11Ds	282
	16.2.3	End of year returns	282
16.3	**Timing of deemed Schedule E payment**	**282**
	16.3.1	Relevant events	282
	16.3.2	Receipt of income after relevant event	283
16.4	**Payment of PAYE and Class 1 NICs**	**284**
	16.4.1	19 April payment deadline	284
	16.4.2	Concession on penalties	284
16.5	**Interest**	**286**
16.6	**Penalties**	**286**
	16.6.1	General	286
	16.6.2	Fixed penalties	286
	16.6.3	Fraud and negligence – generally	287
	16.6.4	Penalties for fraud or negligence	288
	16.6.5	Criminal penalties for fraud or negligence	289
16.7	**Reducing the penalties**	**290**
	16.7.1	Summary	290
	16.7.2	Benefit of the doubt	290
	16.7.3	Reasonable excuse	291
	16.7.4	Mitigation of penalties	292
16.8	**Assessment and collection**	**293**
	16.8.1	Time limits for collection	293
	16.8.2	Collection of unpaid tax and/or NICs from the worker
		or director	293
16.9	**Investigations**	**295**

17 Overseas implications – tax   297
  17.1 General   297
    17.1.1 Introduction   297
    17.1.2 Outline and scope   297
  17.2 Residence and personal services   298
  17.3 Definitions   299
  17.4 Outline of the rules   299
  17.5 Coming to the UK from overseas   300
    17.5.1 Residence   300
    17.5.2 Ordinary residence   302
    17.5.3 Examples of residence and ordinary residence
          determinations   304
  17.6 Counting the days   304
  17.7 Procedure for establishing residence status   305
    17.7.1 Introduction   305
    17.7.2 Form P86 – arrival questionnaire   305
    17.7.3 Self-assessment form   306
  17.8 Non-residents   306
    17.8.1 Outline   306
    17.8.2 'Merely incidental'   306
    17.8.3 Double tax treaties   308
    17.8.4 Apportionment of income   309
    17.8.5 Dual contracts for non-residents   310
    17.8.6 Tax allowances for non-residents   310
    17.8.7 Tax treatment of dividends received by non-resident
          personal services worker 310
  17.9 Working overseas   311
    17.9.1 Introduction   311
    17.9.2 Full time contract of service abroad   311
    17.9.3 Out of the UK for a whole tax year   313
    17.9.4 Permanent residence abroad   314
    17.9.5 Procudures for obtaining non-residence status   315
    17.9.6 Residence status abroad   315
  17.10 UK residents working abroad   315
    17.10.1 Tax basis   315
    17.10.2 Relief for overseas tax suffered   316
    17.10.3 Travel expenses   317
  17.11 Domicile   317
    17.11.1 Concept of domicile   317
    17.11.2 Domicile of origin   317
    17.11.3 Married women   318
    17.11.4 Domicile of choice   318
    17.11.5 Procedure for establishing a change of domicile   319

17.12 Consequences of being non-domiciled   320
   17.12.1 Tax advantages   320
   17.12.2 Personal services implications of being
         non-domiciled   320
   17.12.3 Foreign emoluments   320
   17.12.4 Travel expenses   322
17.13 Remittance basis   323
   17.13.1 Outline of issues   323
   17.13.2 Meaning of remittance   323
   17.13.3 Remittances out of mixed funds   324
   17.13.4 'Received in the United Kingdom' 326
   17.13.5 Deemed income calculation issues arising from
         remittance basis   327
   17.13.6 Republic of Ireland   327
17.14 Partners   328

18 Overseas implications – National Insurance   329
  18.1 Introduction   329
  18.2 Interaction with the personal services rules   329
  18.3 NICs and individuals working abroad   330
    18.3.1 Outline of existing NICs rules   330
    18.3.2 Personal serivce workers overseas 331
    18.3.3 EEA treaty arrangements   332
    18.3.4 Application to personal services workers 333
    18.3.5 Bilateral Social Security Treaty countries 334
  18.4 NICs and individuals coming to the UK to work   334
    18.4.1 Establishing whether the individual has a NIC liability   334
    18.4.2 EEA countries   335
    18.4.3 Bilateral Social Security Treaties 336
    18.4.4 Other countries   337
    18.4.5 Consequences of being within the PSC rules for tax
        but not for NIC   337

19 Offshore companies and partnerships   339
  19.1 Introduction   339
  19.2 Corporate tax residence in the UK   339
    19.2.1 Scope   339
    19.2.2 Management and control   339
    19.2.3 Application to personal service companies 341
  19.3 Non-resident companies with a UK trading presence   341
  19.4 Non-residents with no trading presence in UK   342

		19.4.1	PAYE	342
		19.4.2	National Insurance	343
	19.5	Speical rules for offshore personal services companies		343
		19.5.1	PAYE	343
		19.5.2	Interaction with s203C ICTA 1988	344
		19.5.3	National Insurance	344
	19.6	Enforcement		344
		19.6.1	Options	344
		19.6.2	Transferring responsibility to the worker	345
		19.6.3	Is the legislation ultra vires?	345
		19.6.4	Investigations and information	345
	19.7	Partnerships		346
		19.7.1	Residence	346
		19.7.2	PAYE and NIC obligations	347
	19.8	Summary		347
20	Particular businesses			349
	20.1	Introduction		349
	20.2	Actors and entertainers		349
		20.2.1	General	349
		20.2.2	Tax: employed or self-employed?	349
		20.2.3	National Insurance: employed or self-employed?	350
		20.2.4	Expenses and other reliefs	351
		20.2.5	Expenses disallowable in the deemed Schedule E computation	352
		20.2.6	Overseas issues	352
	20.3	Directors and temporary executives		354
		20.3.1	Social changes	354
		20.3.2	Employed or self-employed?	354
		20.3.3	Pre-IR35 status issues	356
		20.3.4	Lump sums from pension schemes	357
	20.4	IT contractors		358
		20.4.1	Political pressure	358
		20.4.2	Employed or self-employed?	358
		20.4.3	Expenses	359
	20.5	Musicians		361
		20.5.1	General	361
		20.5.2	Employed or self-employed?	362
		20.5.3	Royalty companies	363
		20.5.4	Other points	363
	20.6	Oil and gas workers		363
		20.6.1	General	363
		20.6.2	Employed or self-employed?	364

20.6.3	Residence status and personal services rules	364
20.6.4	Foreign tax and double tax relief	366
20.6.5	Reporting requirements	367
20.6.6	Travel expenses	367
20.7	**Sportspeople**	**368**
20.7.1	General	368
20.7.2	Employed or self-employed?	369
20.7.3	Overseas issues	370
20.7.4	Pension schemes	370
20.8	**Subcontractors**	**371**
20.8.1	Introduction	371
20.8.2	Recategorisation: the history	371
20.8.3	Employed or self-employed?	372
20.8.4	Use of partnerships	372
20.8.5	Subcontractor tax deductions and the deemed income calculation	373
20.9	**Teachers and lecturers**	**376**
20.9.1	Introduction	376
20.9.2	Employed or self-employed?	376
20.9.3	National Insurance position	378
20.9.4	Overseas issues	379
20.10	**TV and film industry workers**	**379**
20.10.1	Background	379
20.10.2	Employed or self-employed?	380
21	**Agencies, clients and umbrellas**	**381**
21.1	**Introduction**	**381**
21.2	**Agencies**	**381**
21.2.1	Areas unaffected by the personal services legislation	381
21.2.2	Contracts	382
21.2.3	Other consequences	383
21.2.4	Reporting to the Revenue	383
21.3	**Clients**	**384**
21.3.1	Outline	384
21.3.2	Overseas service companies	384
21.3.3	Third-party reporting	385
21.3.4	Freelance consultants	386
21.4	**Umbrella companies**	**386**
21.4.1	Structure	386
21.4.2	Umbrellas and IR35	386
21.4.3	Composites post-IR35	387

22 **National Minimum Wage, Working Families Tax Credits and Student Loans** — 389

  22.1 **Introduction** — 389

  22.2 **National Minimum Wage** — 389

    22.2.1 Outline — 389

    22.2.2 Definition of a worker for NMW purposes — 390

    22.2.3 Pay for NMW purposes — 392

    22.2.4 Position of the client — 392

    22.2.5 Enforcement — 393

    22.2.6 Conclusion — 395

  22.3 **Working Families Tax Credit** — 395

    22.3.1 Background — 395

    22.3.2 Earnings for WFTC — 396

    22.3.3 Capital for WFTC — 398

    22.3.4 Mechanism for receiving WFTC payments — 399

    22.3.5 Conclusion — 399

  22.4 **Student loan repayments** — 400

    22.4.1 Outline — 400

    22.4.2 Interaction with personal services legislation — 400

    22.4.3 Conclusion — 402

23 **Tax planning after IR35** — 403

  23.1 **Introduction** — 403

  23.2 **Status and contracts** — 403

  23.3 **Managing the deemed income calculation** — 404

    23.3.1 Dividends versus salary — 404

    23.3.2 Paying the tax and NICs — 404

    23.3.3 Keeping appropriate records — 404

  23.4 **Expense reliefs** — 405

  23.5 **Losses** — 406

  23.6 **Pensions** — 406

  23.7 **Overseas issues** — 407

  23.8 **Partnerships** — 408

  23.9 **Clients and agencies** — 409

  23.10 **Penalties and investigations** — 409

  23.11 **Other possibilities and risks** — 410

24 **Case studies** — 411

  24.1 **Introduction** — 411

  24.2 **Case studies for IT contractors with service companies** — 411

  24.3 **Case studies for subcontractors** — 419

Index — 425

Acknowledgements

My thanks to those who read and commented on various chapters of this book. Without their considerable assistance *IR35: Personal Service Companies* would have been easier to write but much less interesting. Any remaining mistakes or errors of judgement are my own. I particularly appreciated the help provided by Martin Benson, Colin Davis, Nigel Eastaway, Roy Faichney, Malcolm Gammie, Peter Gravestock, David Heaton, David Maclean, Divya Malde, Julian Taylor, Sarah Walker and John Whiting. I'd also like to thank Lissa Allcock, John Newth, Keren Newth, Annette Morris and my husband David Earle, for his inimitable combination of technical knowledge and imperturbable calm.

Anne Redston

May 2000

At the time of writing the Revenue's Employment Status Manual (ESM) was in preparation. This Manual includes the status sections from the Schedule E Manual (SE), as well as some additional sections, not all of which had been written at the time this book went to print. In particular, the section on personal service companies was incomplete. However, where text has moved to the ESM from the SE Manual both references are given. Where the wording has changed slightly, but the meaning is the same, the original text has been retained. There have been consequential changes to the paragraph numbers in the rest of the SE Manual, and again both are given where possible. The new numbers are given first, followed by the old numbers.

Table of Cases

(References are to paragraph)

Addison and Others *v* The London Philharmonic Orchestra Society Ltd
[1981] ICR 261 ....6.7.6, 7.4.2, 7.4.3, 9.8, 20.5.2
Airfix Footwear Ltd *v* Cope [1978] ICR 1210 ....5.3.1, 5.3.2, 5.3.4, 5.3.6–5.3.8,
7.3.4, 8.5.2
Akarimsons Ltd *v* Chapman [1997] SSCD 140 ....16.7.3
Anderson (Anderson's Executor) *v* CIR [1998] SSCD 43 ....17.11.4
Andrews *v* King [1991] 64 TC 332 ....6.5.4
Argent *v* Minister of Social Security [1968] 3 All ER 208 ....20.9.2
Attorney General *v* Prince Ernest Augustus of Hanover [1957]
1 All ER 49 ....4.8.4
Australian Mutual Provident Society *v* Chaplin and Another [1978]
18 Australian Law Reports 385 ....6.5.4
Bank Line Ltd *v* IRC [1974] 49 TC 307 ....13.7.3
Barnett *v* Brabyn [1996] 69 TC 133 ....8.4.1
Blackwell *v* Mills [1945] 26 TC 468..11.8.1
Blyth *v* Birmingham Waterworks Co [1856] 11 Ex 781............................16.6.3
Bond *v* CAV Ltd [1983] IRLR 360..5.2.3
Boyd Line Ltd *v* Pitts [1986] ICR 244 ....5.3.1, 5.3.5, 5.3.6
Brady *v* Group Lotus Car Companies plc and Another [1987]
60 TC 359 ....16.6.3
Brett *v* Brett [1826] 2 Add 210 ....4.8.4
Brown *v* Bullock [1961] 40 TC 1 ....11.5
BSM (1257) Ltd *v* Secretary of State for Social Services [1978]
ICR 894...5.2.4
Calcutta Jute Mills Co Ltd *v* Nicholson (1876) 1 Ex D 428; [1876]
1 TC 83 ....19.2.1
Carmichael and Another *v* National Power [1999] 4 All ER 897 ....5.2.6, 5.3.2
Cassidy *v* Ministry of Health [1951] 1 All ER 574 ....6.6.3, 6.7.7, 8.2.2
Chaplin *v* Australian Mutual Provident Society [1978] 18 ALR 385 ....5.2.2
Clark *v* Oceanic Contractors Incorporated [1982]
56 TC 183...19.3, 19.6.3, 20.6.2
Clark *v* Oxfordshire Health Authority [1997] EWCA 4792....5.3.1, 5.3.5, 5.3.6
Collins *v* Hertfordshire County Council [1947] 1 All ER 633....................6.6.3
Construction Industry Training Board *v* Labour Force Ltd
[1970] 3 All ER 220..5.6, 6.4.3
Copeman *v* William Flood and Sons Ltd [1940] 24 TC 53 ....3.4.2

Dale *v* IRC [1954] AC 11 ....20.3.4

Davies *v* Braithwaite [1933] 18 TC 198..6.6.4, 20.2.2

Davies *v* Presbyterian Church of Wales [1986] AC 508 ....7.8.2

De Beers Consolidated Mines *v* Howe [1906] 5 TC 198 ....19.2.2

Derry *v* Peek [1889] 14 AC 337 ....16.6.3

DPP *v* Schildcamp [1971] AC 123..4.8.4

Edwards *v* Bairstow [1956] AC 14..7.8.3

Ex parte Blain [1879] 12 Ch D 522 ....19.2.1

Express and Echo Publications Ltd *v* Tanton [1999]
    IRLR 367 ....6.5.2, 7.8.3, 9.3.3, 9.3.4, 9.3.5

Fall *v* Hitchen [1972] 49 TC 433 ....20.2.2, 20.5.2

Four Seasons (Inn on the Park) Ltd *v* Hamarat [1985]
    EAT 369...5.3.2, 5.3.6, 5.3.8, 7.3.4

Fuge *v* McCelland [1956] 36 TC 571..20.9.2

Gallagher *v* Jones [1993] 66 TC 77 ....13.2.1

Global Plant Ltd *v* Secretary of State for Health & Social Security
    [1971] 3 All ER 385 ....6.5.2, 6.5.3, 6.7.5, 9.4.1

Grant *v* South-West Trains [1998] IRLR 188 ....5.2.3

Hall *v* Lorimer [1993] 66 TC 349 ....6.3.1, 6.4.4, 6.5.2, 6.5.3, 6.6.2–6.6.4, 6.7.3,
    6.7.6, 6.7.7, 7.4.1–7.4.3, 7.4.5–7.4.7, 7.4.11, 7.6, 7.8.3, 8.1, 8.2.1, 8.2.2, 8.3.1,
    8.3.2, 8.5.1, 8.5.2, 9.3.5, 9.6.1, 9.8, 20.9.2, 20.10.2, 23.2

Hellyer Brothers Ltd *v* McLeod [1986] ICR 122 ....5.3.1, 5.3.4–5.3.6, 5.3.8

Henderson *v* Henderson [1965] 1 All ER 179 ....17.11.4

Henwood *v* Clarke (1997) STS 789 ....10.6.3

Herbert Smith *v* Honour [1999] STC 173 ....13.2.1

Hillyer *v* Leeke 51 TC 90...11.5

Hooper *v* British Railways Board [1998] IRLR 517 ....5.2.2

Hornal *v* Neuberger Products Ltd [1957] 1 QB 247 ....16.6.5

Horner *v* Hasted [1995] 67 TC 439..6.6.3

Horrigan *v* Lewisham London Borough Council [1978] ICR 15 EAT 5.2.3

Humberstone *v* Northern Timber Mills [1949] 70 CLR 6.6.2

Humbles *v* Brooks [1962] 40 TC 500 ....11.8.1

Ironmonger *v* Movefield Ltd [1988] IRLR 461 ....5.6, 6.4.3

Jowitt *v* London Symphony Orchestra Ltd [1990] EAT 301 ....6.7.2

Knights *v* Anglian Industrial Services [1996] EAT 640...............................5.6

Lee Ting Sang *v* Chung Chi-Keung [1990] 2 AC 374 ..6.5.3, 6.5.4, 6.6.3, 6.6.4,
    6.7.7, 7.8.1, 7.8.2, 7.8.4, 8.3.1, 8.3.2, 8.5.1, 20.8.3

Levene *v* CIR [1928] 13 TC 48 ....17.3, 17.5.1, 17.5.2

Lomax *v* Newton [1953] 34 TC 558..11.5

Lucas *v* Cattell [1972] 48 TC 353 ....10.6.11

MacFarlane and Skivington *v* Glasgow City Council [2000] EAT 1277 ..6.5.2,
    9.3.3

Market Investigations Ltd *v* The Minister of Social Security
    [1968] 2 QB 173; [1968] 3 All ER 732.... 5.3.3, 5.3.5, 5.3.6, 5.3.8, 6.3.1,
    6.4.3, 6.5.2, 6.5.3, 6.6.3, 6.7.2, 8.5.1

Massey *v* Crown Life Insurance Co [1978] ICR 590 ....5.2.4, 6.7.5
McCowen, Alec and Sam West *v* IRC (1993) 6.7.3, 20.2.3
McLeod *v* Heller Brothers Ltd [1987] IRLR 232 ....7.8.3
McManus *v* Griffiths [1997] 70 TC 218 ....6.5.2, 6.7.4, 7.8.2, 9.9.1, 9.14
McMeecham *v* Secretary of State for Employment [1997] IRLR 353 ....5.6
McMenamin *v* Diggles [1991] 64 TC 286 ..6.5.2, 6.5.3, 6.5.4, 6.6.3, 6.6.4, 7.4.1
Midland Sinfonia Concert Society Limited *v* The Secretary of State for Social
    Services [1981] ICR 454 ....7.4.2, 9.8, 20.5.2
Miners *v* Atkinson [1997] 68 TC 249 ....20.4.3
Mitchell *v* CIR [1951] 33 TC 53 ....17.6
Montreal Locomotive Works *v* Montreal and Attorney General
    for Canada [1947] 1 DLR 161 ....6.5.3
Morren *v* Swinton & Pendlebury Borough Council [1965] 1 WLR 576;
    [1965] 2 All ER 349 ....6.6.3, 6.7.4
Mrs F and S2 (Personal Representatives of F deceased) *v* CIR
    [2000] SSCD 1 ....17.11.4
N Ltd *v* HM Inspector of Taxes [1996] SSCD 346 ....16.6.5
Narich Pty Ltd *v* Commissioner of Payroll Tax [1984] ICR 286....6.6.3, 20.9.2
Nethermere (St Neots) Ltd *v* Gardiner [1983] ICR 319; [1984]
    IRLR 240 ....5.3.1, 5.3.2, 5.3.4, 5.3.6–5.3.8, 7.3.4, 7.4.8, 7.8.3
Neubergh *v* CIR [1977] 52 TC 79 ....17.6
Nuclear Electric plc *v* Bradley [1996] 68 TC 670 ....13.7.3
Nunn *v* Gray [1997] SSCD 175 ....16.7.3
O'Kelly *v* Trusthouse Forte plc [1983] 3 All ER 456 ....5.3.1–5.3.3, 5.3.6, 5.3.8,
    6.5.3, 6.7.3, 6.7.4, 7.3.4, 7.8.2, 7.8.3, 8.2.2, 8.5.1, 9.9.1
Owen *v* Burden [1971] 47 TC 476 ....10.6.5
Padmore *v* CIR [1989] 62 TC 352...19.7.1
Parikh *v* Sleeman [1990] 63 TC 75 ....11.8.1
Parsons *v* Albert J Parsons & Sons Ltd [1979] ICR 271......................22.2.2
Pepper *v* Hart [1992] 65 TC 421 ....5.2.4
Pleasants *v* Atkinson [1987] 60 TC 228 ....16.6.3
Plummer *v* CIR [1987] 60 TC 452 ....17.11.4
Queensland Stations Pty *v* Federal Commissioner of Taxation
    [1945] 70 CLR 539...6.6.3
R *v* Cunningham, Charlton, Wheeler & Kitchen [1996] STC 1481 ....16.6.5
R *v* Dimsey and Allen [1999] STC 846 ....16.6.5
R *v* Downes [1983] CLR 819...16.6.5
R *v* Hiscox [1978] 52 TC 497..16.6.5
R *v* Inspector of Taxes *ex parte* Fulford-Dobson [1987] 60 TC 168............17.6
Ready Mixed Concrete (South East) Ltd *v* Minister of Pensions and National
    Insurance [1968] 1 All ER 433........................6.5.2, 6.6.2, 6.6.3, 6.7.7, 9.3.4
Reed *v* Clark [1986] 58 TC 528 ....17.3, 17.9.3
Reid *v* CIR [1926] 10 TC 673 ....17.5.1

Roberts *v* Toyota (GB) EAT [1980] 614 ....5.2.3
Robson *v* Dixon [1972] 48 TC 527 ....17.8.2
Rochester (UK) Ltd and Another *v* Pickin [1998] SSCD 138 ......16.6.3, 16.8.1
RTZ Oil & Gas Ltd *v* Elliss [1987] 61 TC 132 ....6.7.6
Scottish Provident Institution *v* Allen [1901] 4 TC 409 ....17.13.3
Scottish Widows' Fund Life Assurance Society *v* Farmer [1909]
  5 TC 502 ....17.13.4
Shirlaw *v* Southern Foundries [1926] 2 KB 206...5.2.3
Sidey *v* Phillips [1987] STC 87 ....20.9.2
Specialeyes (Optical Services) Ltd (1991)
  (unreported, see *Taxation* 4 July) 5.3.2, 5.3.3, 8.5.1, 9.8
Stagecraft Ltd *v* Minister of National Insurance [1952] SC 288 ......6.6.3, 6.7.3
Steeden *v* Carver [1999] SSCD 283 ....16.7.3
Sterling Trust Ltd *v* IRC [1925] 12 TC 868...17.13.3
Stevenson, Jordan & Harrison *v* MacDonald & Evans [1952] RPC 10......6.7.7
Tudor and Onions *v* Ducker [1924] 8 TC 591 ....16.6.5
Udny *v* Udny [1869] LR 1 Sc; Div App 441 ....17.11.4
US *v* Silk [1946] 331 US..6.6.2
Walls *v* Sinnett [1986] 60 TC 150..8.1
Walsh *v* Randall [1940] 23 TC 55 ....17.13.4
Ward *v* Dunn [1979] 52 TC 517..11.5
Warner Holidays Ltd *v* Secretary of State for Social Services
  [1983] IRC 440..20.5.2
WF and RK Swan (Hellenic) Ltd *v* The Secretary of State for
  Social Services [1983] QBD...7.4.10
Wickens *v* Champion Employment [1984] ICR 365........5.3.8, 5.6, 6.4.2, 7.3.4
Wilkie *v* CIR [1951] 32 TC 495 ....17.6
Withers *v* Flackwell Heath Football Supporters' Club [1981] IRLR 307 ..5.2.5
Woodcock *v* CIR [1977] 51 TC 698 ....11.5
Young and Woods Ltd *v* West [1980] IRLR 201 ....5.2.5

Table of Statutes

(Statutes are in chronological order. References are to paragraph)

1911 Perjury Act (c.6)—
 s5 ....16.6.5
1913 Forgery Act (c.27)—
 s6 ....16.6.5
1948 Companies Act (c.38)—
 s332....................................4.8.4
1968 Provisional Collection of
 Taxes Act (c.2) 2.3.5
1969 Employers' Liability
 (Compulsory Insurance)
 Act (c. 57) 11.10
1970 Taxes Management Act
 (c.9)—
 s9(6)(a) 15.4.1
 s9A 15.5.4, 17.11.5
 (4) 15.5.2
 s12A 15.2
 s12AB(2) 15.5.2
 s16 ....10.5.4, 16.9, 20.10.2,
 21.2.4, 21.3.1
 s29 ....15.5.5
 (3) 15.5.5
 s33 ....15.5.3
 (2A)...............................15.5.3
 s33A 15.5.3
 ss34, 36 ....16.8.1
 s59A(3) 14.6.4
 s59D 3.2.4, 15.8.1
 s87A 15.8.1
 s93.................................15.6.3
 (7) 15.6.3
 s93A 15.6.3
 s95..................................15.6.4
 s98..................................21.2.4
 s98A 16.4.1, 16.6.4

 (2)(b) 16.6.2
 (4) 16.6.4
 s99.................................21.2.2
 s102................................16.7.4
 s118(2) 16.7.3
1973 Finance Act (c.51)—
 Sch 15, para 2 ....20.6.5
1978 Theft Act (c.31) 16.6.5
1983 Oil Taxation Act (c.56) ..16.9,
 20.6.5
1985 Companies Act (c.6)—
 s225................................13.4.6
 ss263–268, 277 ....3.10.3
 s334..................................3.8
1988 Income and Corporation
 Taxes Act (c.1) 16.6.5
 Pt XIV, Chs I, IV............12.2.2
 Pt XV, Ch 1A 3.4.2
 s9....................................13.2.1
 s13....................................3.2.2
 (1), (3) 3.2.2
 s13A 3.2.2
 (6) 3.2.2
 s13AA 3.2.2
 (4), (6) 3.2.2
 s19(1) 17.4, 17.8.1, 17.13.5,
 20.3.2, 20.6.3, 20.7.2
 s62....................................14.6.4
 s62A 14.6.4
 (9) 14.6.4
 s63A 14.6.4
 s65(6)–(9)......................17.13.4
 s68..................................17.13.6
 s74(1)(a) 3.5.1, 11.5
 s105................................13.8.6

s112 ....19.7.1
s132 ....17.8.1
  (5) 17.13.4
s134 ....5.6, 21.2.1
ss145–146 ....10.6.1
s154(1) 10.5.1, 14.5.3
s155ZA 10.6.1
  (3) 10.6.2
s156..............................10.6.2
  (2), (4), (7) 10.6.2
s156A 10.6.2
ss159, 159AB 10.6.3
s160 ....3.8
  (1C), (3) 10.6.9
s161 ....10.5.3, 10.6.9
  (1A)..............................10.6.9
s166..............................12.4.5
s192(1) 17.12.3, 17.13.6
  (2) 17.12.1
ss193–194 ....20.6.6
s195 ....17.12.4, 20.6.6
s198 ....11.3.4, 11.5, 13.5.3,
  17.10.3, 20.4.3, 20.6.6
  (1)..........11.4.1, 11.5, 11.8.1
  (1A) ..11.4.1, 11.6.1–11.6.3,
  11.6.8
    (b)(ii) 20.6.6
s198ff 10.5.5, 11.3.3, 11.3.5,
  14.5.4, 15.3.4
ss193–194 ....17.10.3
s200A 11.7, 12.2.4
s200AA 12.2.4, 12.4.5
s200B..................11.8.2, 12.2.4
s200C 11.8.2
ss200E, 200H 11.8.4
s201A 12.2.4, 20.2.4, 21.2.1
s201AA...............11.10, 20.4.3
s202B 10.2, 12.4.2, 22.3.2
  (1)(b) 22.2.5
  (c) 13.5.2
s203 ....10.5.4
s203C 9.11, 19.4.1, 19.5.1,
  19.5.2, 21.3.2

s203D 19.4.1, 19.5.2
s203ff 19.3, 19.7.2
s206A 10.7
s209(2)(b)......................3.10.3
s233 ....17.8.7
s314 ....20.6.2
s353ff 3.8
s359 ....11.11.3
s393 ....13.7.3
  (1) 13.7.2
s393A 13.4.5
  (1) 13.7.2
  (2A)...............13.4.5, 13.7.2
s403A 13.7.3
s413(3)(a), (7) 13.7.2
s414 ....3.7.2
  (1) 3.7.2
s416 ....3.2.2, 3.7.2, 17.12.3
s419(1), (4)....................3.10.3
s508A(1)(b) 3.2.2
ss555–557 ....20.2.6
s555 ....20.7.3
  (2) 20.2.6
  (7) 10.6.6
s559 ....20.8.5
s590(3) 20.3.4
s625 ....23.6
s635 ....20.3.4
s641 ....12.2.3, 23.6
s641A 12.2.3
s643 ....12.2.2
s646 ....12.2.5
  (2)........11.10, 12.2.4, 20.2.4
s830 ....20.6.3, 20.6.5
  (5) 20.6.3
s839 ....14.2.2
Sch 6 paras 6–9 ....10.6.3
Sch 8 para 7(5) 4.5.2
Sch 11A.........................10.6.10
Sch 12, para 2 ....17.12.3
Sch 12A..11.4.1, 11.6.1, 20.6.6
  para 2 ....11.6.3
  para 5 ....11.6.3

(1)(a) 11.6.3
(3) 11.6.3, 20.6.6
Sch 18 ....13.7.2
Finance Act (c.39)—
s66 ....19.2.1
1989 Finance Act (c.26)—
s43 ....13.4.4
1990 Capital Allowances Act
(c.1)—
s24 ....3.5.2
s27 ....11.11.1, 15.3.4
(1) 11.11.2
(2)(a)..11.11.1, 14.5.5, 14.6.3
(2A) 11.11.1, 11.11.3,
14.5.5, 14.6.3
s35(2) 11.11.3
s65(1) 14.5.5
s79 ....11.11.1
s140 ....14.6.3
1992 Social Security Contributions
and Benefits Act (c.4)—
Pts 1–V 5.1.2, 12.7.2, 18.2,
20.3.2
s1(6)(a) 19.5.3
s2 ....18.3.1
(b) 12.7.2
(1)(a)................5.2.2, 20.3.2
s6(1)(a) 18.2
s7 ....10.5.4
(2)(b) 19.4.2, 21.3.2
s11(4), (5) 14.7.2
ss115, 121C....................16.8.2
s122(a) 5.2.2
Sch 1, para 7 ....16.6.4
(3), (5) 16.6.2
Social Security
Administration Act (c.5)—
s114A 16.8.2
Taxation of Chargeable Gains
Act (c.12)—
Sch A1, para 11 ....3.8
1994 Finance Act (c.9)—
s86(3) 3.2.2

1998 Social Security Act (c.14)........
16.8.2
Finance Act (c.36)—
s42(1) 14.5.2
(2) 13.2.1
Sch 2, paras 17–19 ....15.8.1
Sch 18, paras 2, 3, 14, 24, 42ff,
46.................................15.8.1
para 51 ....15.8.2
paras 66–77, 89..........15.8.1
National Minimum Wage Act
(c.39)...............22.2.2–22.2.4
s49 ....22.2.2
s54 ....22.2.2
(3)(b) 22.2.4
1999 Social Security Contributions
(Transfer of Functions,
etc.) Act—
s8(1)(m) 5.1.2
Employment Relations Act—
s39 ....22.2.5
Welfare Reform and Pensions
Act 2.2.2, 2.2.3, 3.2.3,
4.8.4, 5.2.4
s75 ....4.8.1, 4.8.4
2000 Finance Act 16.6.5, 22.2.5
s143 ....22.2.5
Sch 12..........2.3.5, 4.1.3, 5.1.3,
5.2.3, 5.3.4, 8.2.1, 12.5.2,
13.6.1, 17.14, 19.5.1, 20.3.2,
20.5.2, 20.10.1, 21.3.2
para 1 ....5.6, 14.2.1
(c) 20.3.2
(1) 5.1.1
(a) 4.2.1, 4.3.1
(c)...............................6.2
(4) 4.4, 5.1.1, 5.2.3,
6.6.4, 7.8.2
para 2(b)..........4.6.1, 21.4.2
(i) 4.5.2
(1) 6.6.4
(2) 14.6.2, 16.3.1
paras 3–5 ....21.2.1

para 3 ....4.5.2, 21.4.2
(1)(b)(ii) 4.6.1, 9.15
(2) 4.5.2
para 4 ....14.2.2
(2) 14.2.2
(3) 14.4
para 5 ....4.5.4
para 6 ....20.2.6, 20.7.3
para 7 ......10.1, 10.4, 10.6.6,
11.2.1, 11.3.1, 12.2.2,
12.2.6, 12.4.5, 13.2.2,
13.4.4, 18.4.5, 21.4.3
para 8 ....20.8.5
para 9 ....10.3, 11.3.5
para 10(3)(b) 10.5.1
para 10(5)(a), (b) 10.2
para 11 ....10.6.6, 16.4.1
(2) 10.4, 10.6.3, 10.6.6,
11.6.3
(3) 17.2, 20.6.4
(b) 12.3.3
(4)(b) 11.3.3
(5) 14.6.5
(6) 19.5.1, 19.7.2
(7) 12.2.4

para 12(2) 13.8.6, 16.3.2
(3) 14.6.2
para 13 ....13.6.1, 22.4.2
(1), (c)................13.6.2
(3), (4) 13.6.2
(5)(a), (b), (c)........13.6.2
(6) 13.6.2
para 14(3) 4.5.5
para 15 ....4.5.5
para 16 ....4.5.5, 21.2.1
para 17 ....17.13.5
(2)......13.3, 14.6.3, 15.8.2
para 18(2) 11.3.6, 14.6.3
(3)..11.3.4, 11.3.6, 14.5.4,
14.6.3
para 19 ....4.5.2
(c) 14.2.2
(4) 4.5.2
para 21(4) 4.5.2, 14.2.2
para 22 ....4.2.2
(1) 12.2.5
(2) 4.2.2, 10.2
para 23 ....14.6.4
(3) 14.6.4
para 24 ....21.2.1

Table of Statutory Instruments

(References are to paragraph)

1978   Social Security (Adjudication) Amendment Regulations
           (1978/1689)—
       Reg 1(2) 20.5.2
       Reg 2 ....21.2.1
       Sch 1 ....12.7.2
           para 2..21.2.1
           para 4..20.9.2
       Sch 2 ....12.7.2
       Sch 3, para 2 ....21.2.1
           para 9..19.4.2, 21.3.2
1979   Social Security (Contributions) Regulations (1979/591)—
       Reg 19(4)(b) 10.5.4, 10.6.2
       Reg 19B 4.6.2, 14.3.4, 20.3.2
       Reg 26A(1), (2), (4)–(6) 14.7.2
       Reg 28A(1) 16.5
       Reg 119 ....18.4.4
           (b)...19.3
       Reg 120 ....18.3.1, 18.3.3
       Sch 1C para 10(a) 10.5.4
1987   Income Tax (Entertainers and Sportsmen)
           Regulations (1987/530) 20.2.6
       Family Credit (General) Regulations (1987/1973)—
       Sch 3, para 6 ....22.3.3
1993   Income Tax (Employments) Regulations (1993/744)—
       Regs 2, 28...10.5.4
       Reg 42 ....21.3.2
           (3) 16.8.2
       Reg 46 ....10.5.4, 15.3.3
       Reg 46AB..10.5.4
       Reg 49(5) 16.8.2
           (7) 16.8.1
       Reg 51 ....16.5
1998   Social Security (Categorisation of Earners) Amendment Regulations
           (1998/1728)...20.2.3
1999   Social Security (Categorisation of Earners) Amendment Regulations
           (1999/3)..20.2.3

National Minimum Wage Regulations (1999/584)—
Reg 2(a), (b) 22.2.2
Regs 5, 10...22.2.3
(1999/3219)—
Reg 8 ....22.3.4
2000   National Insurance Regulations (2000/727) 4.1.3, 4.8.1, 4.8.4, 11.6.8
Reg 1(3)...4.2.2
Reg 6 ....4.8.2, 5.1.2, 5.6, 20.3.2
   (1)(c) 12.7.2, 18.2
   (3)(b)..14.8, 18.2
   (4) 5.1.2
Reg 7 ....10.1, 11.4.2, 18.4.5
Reg 8 ....16.4.1
   (1) 12.5.1
   (2) 4.8.3, 22.4.2
   (3) 14.7.1
Reg 12 ....21.2.1
Education (Student Loans) (Repayment) Regulations (2000/944)—
Reg 15(5)(b) 22.4.2
Regs 21–26 ....22.4.2
Reg 27ff 22.4.2
Reg 41 ....16.6.4
Reg 42 ....16.6.4
   (5) 16.6.2
Reg 51 ....16.6.4

Table of Manuals and Handbooks

(References are to paragraph)

Double Tax Relief Manual 20.2.6
   905 ....20.2.6
   1936 ....20.9.4
Employer Compliance Manual
   13044...10.6.11
   13209...10.6.6
Employment Procedures Manual
   8089 ....17.7.2
   8321 ....20.6.4
   9178 ....21.3.2
Employment Status Manual 5.3.2
   0514 ....5.3.7
   1074 ....5.3.2
   4103 ....20.10.2
   4104 ....20.10.1
   4121 ....20.2.2
   4121–2 ....20.2.2
   4124 ....20.2.2
   4140 ....20.5.2
   4150 ....12.7.2
   4152 ....12.7.2
   4323ff 20.8.3
   4501ff 20.9.2
   4502 ....20.9.2
Enquiry Handbook
   640 ....15.6.3
Investigation Handbook...15.8.2
   2334 ....15.8.2
   5000 ....16.6.3
   5010 ....16.6.3
   5062 ....16.7.3
   5065 ....16.6.3
Inspector's Manual
   36 ....17.9.3
   40 ....17.5.1
   41 ....17.9.4, 17.9.5

50 ....17.6
601e 3.5.1, 11.3.5
710 ....11.6.8
1042 ....3.4.2
1567 ....17.13.3
1569 ....17.13.4
1810 ....20.2.2
5032 ....17.11.5

International Tax Handbook
1609 ....19.7.1
1612 ....19.7.1
1617ff 19.7.1

Oil Taxation Office Section 830 Manual
7.7.1 ....20.6.5

Schedule E Manual 5.3.2, 5.3.6, 5.3.7, 7.2, 7.3.4, 7.4.8, 7.4.9, 11.11.2
535–710 ....7.2
603 ....7.4.1
605 ....7.4.5
622 ....7.4.2
631 ....7.4.9
658 ....7.4.10
663 ....5.3.7, 7.3.4
667 ....5.3.2
675 ....7.4.9
685 ....7.4.11
690 ....7.4.8
1172 ....11.8.2
1182 ....10.6.8
1226 ....4.6.2, 14.3.1, 14.3.3, 14.3.4, 20.3.2
2254 ....10.6.1
3141 ....10.6.2
3454 ....10.6.3
3492 ....10.6.3
4031 ....11.5
4034 ....11.5
4038 ....11.5
4105 ....11.5
4376 ....20.4.3
4522 ....20.6.3
4615 ....17.10.3
4720 ....20.6.6
4806 ....11.11.2
4850 ....11.11.2

5013 ....17.12.3
5032 ....17.11.5
5052 ....17.8.2
7323 ....20.10.2
7324 ....20.10.1
7333 ....20.2.2
7335 ....20.2.2
7351 ....20.2.2
7364 ....20.5.2
7420 ....20.7.2
7420ff 20.7.2
7425 ....20.7.2
7745 ....20.6.4
7800 ....20.7.2
01220..11.8.2
01460..10.6.8
03001–3..14.3.1, 14.3.3, 14.3.4, 20.3.2
11352..10.6.1
21625..10.6.2
23304..10.6.3
23803..10.6.3
31645 ....11.5
31650 ....11.5
31661 ....11.5
32070..20.4.3
32435 ....11.5
32795..20.4.3
32800..20.4.3
33034..20.6.3
34060..17.10.3
35080..20.6.6
36560..11.11.2
36730..11.11.2
40203..17.8.2
41010..17.12.3
41060..17.11.5
64100ff 20.7.2
64120..20.7.2
64145..20.7.2
67125..20.6.4
68400..20.7.2

Abbreviations

Inland Revenue Manuals

AP	Assessment Procedures
CGM	Capital Gains Manual
DMG	Decision Maker's Guide to Working Families Tax Credits
DTRM	Double Tax Relief Manual
ECM	Employer Compliance Manual
EH	Enquiry handbook
EPM	Employment Procedures Manual
ESM	Employment Status Manual
IM	Inspector's Manual
IH	Investigation Handbook
ITH	International Tax Handbook
NAG	National Audit Group Instructions
RG	Residence Guide
SAT1 (1995)	The New Current Year Basis
SAT2	Self Assessment – The Legal Framework
SE	Schedule E Manual

Other Inland Revenue booklets

IR 20	*Residents And Non-Residents – Liability To Tax In The UK*
IR56	*Employed or Self-employed*
IR175	*Supplying Services through a limited company or partnership*
COP 14	Code of Practice into Company Tax Returns

Other abbreviations

CA	Contributions Agency
CT	corporation tax
CTSA	Corporation Tax Self Assessment
CTC	childcare tax credit
DPTC	Disabled Persons Tax Credit
EBT	employee benefit trust
ESC	Extra Statutory Concession
EPP	Executive Pension Plan
FAQ	Frequently Asked Question (per Revenue website)
FCA (Gen) Regs	Family Credit Act General Regulations
FICO	Inland Revenue's Financial Intermediaries and Claims Office
FII	Franked Investment Income
FRS 12	Financial Reporting Standard 12
ILAs	Individual Learning Accounts
NICO	National Insurance Contributions Office
NMWA	National Minimum Wage Act
NRE	net relevant earnings
OECD	Organisation for Economic Co-operation and Development

PCG	Professional Contractors Group
PII	professional indemnity insurance
RIA	Regulatory Impact Assessment
SA	self-assessment system
SCO	Special Compliance Office
SLR	Student loan repayments
SSAS	Small Self Administered Scheme
TAS	Taxed Award Scheme
UEL	The upper earnings limit for National Insurance
WFTC	Working Families Tax Credit
WFPA	Welfare Reform and Pensions Act
WRAs	Working Rule Agreements

1   Introduction

IR35 is conceptually simple, but operationally complex. It involves income tax, corporation tax, National Insurance, and partnership tax. Special rules for self-assessment, subcontractors, residence and domicile all play minor roles. At its heart lie the status tests, distilled for over a century and laced with uncertainty.

The fact that IR35 is difficult is not unusual: anti-avoidance laws are often hard to understand. This usually doesn't matter, because they operate as 'Stop' signs in the statute book, warning taxpayers against taking certain routes. IR35 is different. It is not trying to prevent people using personal service companies, it is seeking to increase their tax burden.

There is a simpler solution. If employees were no more heavily taxed than the self-employed, many anti-avoidance rules would fall away. If National Insurance was acknowledged as a tax, and levied fairly across the population, there would be no need for the personal services legislation.

In the Budget press release announcing IR35, the Chancellor said that it 'underlines the Government's commitment to achieving a tax system under which everyone pays their fair share'.

If we truly had a tax system where everyone paid 'their fair share', IR35 would have been unnecessary. It was introduced because employees were seeking the same tax treatment as the self-employed. The true anomaly in the UK system is the unfair tax burden on employment, not the existence of personal service companies.

Many thousands of people – tax advisers, agencies, accountants, IT consultants, oil workers, media moguls and footballers – are now going to have to understand these rules. Dawn Primarolo, the Paymaster General, is optimistic that they will succeed. In the House of Commons debate on IR35, she declared:

> 'I do not believe that it is beyond the intellectual capacity of those IT consultants who are still protesting to get to grips with these rules.' (*Hansard* 3 May 2000, Col. 214).

This book is a response to Dawn's challenge. It aims to help those facing IR35 understand how it works. However, it comes with a health warning. This is new legislation, and will change and develop as the years progress. Some of its implications will have slipped by unnoticed; others may prompt speedy amendments. *IR35: Personal Service Companies* is a first attempt at explaining what these new laws mean and describing their consequences. It is an initial assessment of the subject, not the last word.

2 Purpose and development of IR35

2.1 Introduction

Press Release IR35 was published in March 1999. It was headed 'Avoidance of tax in the provision of personal services', and was the very last Inland Revenue press release issued with the 1999 Budget papers. Since then it has developed into one of the most controversial tax changes ever proposed. This chapter explains why the rules were introduced, and considers how the legislation has evolved.

2.2 Background to IR35

2.2.1 The personal service company

The main shareholder of a personal service company (PSC) is also its director. Frequently he is its only shareholder and director, and there are no employees. Instead of working directly for clients, or taking up employment within other businesses, the individual operates via his company, which contracts with clients to supply the services of its director.

The service company invoices the client for the cost of supplying the director. The money received by the PSC is used to meet the expenses of the company, with the net profit paid out either as dividends on the director's shares, and/or as salary.

In the 1990s personal service companies became more common, partly as a result of changing employment patterns and partly because of the tax advantages, see Chapter 3.

2.2.2 Changing employment patterns

Under the traditional business model, individuals are recruited by employers, for whom they work for a period until moving on to join another organisation. This has changed, partly as a result of the recession of the late 1980s. Many skilled individuals were made redundant and, unable to find permanent employment elsewhere, began offering their services as consultants via their own service companies.

As the economy recovered, employers remained reluctant to increase head-count by taking on permanent staff. Instead, they used short-term contractors on a project-by-project basis. As each assignment ended, the workers were relocated or their contracts terminated. Service companies thus provided a flexible resource in a cost-conscious and ever-changing business environment. In areas such as IT, companies did not want to recruit and retain expensive, immobile workforces for what were essentially short or medium-term projects. Once again, contract staff were the answer.

The increasing regulatory burden was a further reason why employers were reluctant to take on permanent staff. Using contractors allowed them to avoid, not only employer's National Insurance, but also arguments over unfair dismissal, maternity rights, and racial/sexual discrimination.

From the worker's point of view, the PSC route allows greater flexibility, increased control over the type and variety of work, and more power to negotiate rates of pay and other conditions. A company gives the appearance of more substance than a sole trader business, as well as offering the attraction of limited liability. From the client's perspective, service companies provide protection from the PAYE and NIC liabilities which might arise if a sole trader was later recategorised as an employee.

Number of service companies

Not all contract staff have their own service companies. Some are employed directly by agencies who supply them to clients; others are taken on by employers directly, using fixed term contracts. But by the end of the millennium there were said to be roughly 66,000 personal service companies (WFPA, Regulatory Impact Assessment, para 15).

However, this was later admitted to be an underestimate. Dawn Primarolo said that:

> 'There are 90,000 individuals working through service companies. Their average annual earnings are £50,000 and they pay, on average 21% in tax and National Insurance. Compared to someone who would be doing exactly the same job . . . that person pays 35% tax and national insurance.' (*Hansard*, 6 June 2000)

This suggests a shortfall of £7,000 (£50,000 x 14%) per individual working through a service company. This would mean that IR35 could be expected to raise some £630m (90,000 x £7,000).

However there appear to be discrepancies between these figures and those provided in the Budget 2000 Red Book, which said that the extra tax to be levied under IR35 was £900m. If each individual is expected to pay an extra £7,000, the total number of people within IR35 would be 128,000.

Therefore, as at June 2000, government research suggested that between 90,000 and 128,000 companies will be brought within IR35. There will of course be other service company workers who remain outside the regime. This suggests that a significant number of PSCs are operating within the UK economy.

2.2.3 Growing government concerns

Proposals were brought forward in the early 1980s to close down the tax advantages of service companies, but these were rejected after widespread criticism. However in 1999 the concerns of the Department of Trade and Industry (DTI) and the Inland Revenue combined with those of the Labour Government to create a force for change.

The DTI saw service company arrangements as undermining the workers' employment protection. Budget Press Release IR35 expressed this as follows:

'Those who do participate (in the new arrangements) often have to pay a price in terms of loss of protection under employment law. They may find their terms and conditions altered – perhaps losing entitlement to sick pay or maternity leave. They may even lose their jobs without entitlement to notice or redundancy pay. They will usually have no right to any claim for unfair dismissal and may lose their entitlement to social security benefits through a failure to make adequate contributions.' (*Hansard* 3 May 2000, Col. 212–3)

Ministers also worried that the use of service companies was unfair to the rest of the population who paid tax and NICs on their earnings in the traditional way. Dawn Primarolo, speaking in the IR35 debate on 3 May 2000, said:

'We want to stop people who are really the same as employees from dressing up their working arrangements by setting themselves up as a service company to avoid paying the correct levels of properly due tax and National Insurance ... Such avoidance is simply not fair to the rest of us, and we should deal with it.'

Mr Timms, speaking for the Government in the debate on the Welfare Reform and Pension Bill on 3 November 1999, explained the financial consequences as follows:

'It is highly possible for a highly paid office worker earning perhaps £1,800 per week to pay no National Insurance contributions at all, while a nurse earning £300 a week pays £23.45 and her employer pays £26.53 in National Insurance. . . . this is obviously not right and we are sorting it out.' (*Hansard* 3 November 1999, Col. 404)

The Revenue for their part had been worried for some time about the rapid growth of personal service companies. The increasing artificiality of some arrangements convinced them that many service companies were being set solely or mainly for tax avoidance purposes. In particular, they were concerned about the creation of composites, Friday to Monday companies, and the use of 'long-term temps'.

Composites

Composites or 'umbrella' companies are corporates whose shareholders/ employees tend to have a skill in common. In a typical composite, a group of otherwise unconnected individuals form a company to supply services. Every shareholder has a different class of share, and the income each person generates pays the dividends on his own share class. In the late 1990s, when composites became commonplace, dividends were frequently paid monthly.

The Revenue saw composites as artificial structures formed largely to exploit the tax advantages of a PSC. Examples of composites unfavourably regarded by the Revenue included companies formed by train drivers and doctors' secretaries.

Friday to Monday companies

The tax and regulatory advantages of PSCs encouraged some employers to hive off parts of their work-force and re-engage them immediately as independent contractors each with their own service company. In some cases individuals were made redundant or given early retirement, only to return the following week as directors of a PSC. However their work, responsibilities and roles were substantially the same: what had changed was their employment rights and tax status.

The Friday to Monday problem was highlighted in IR35:

'There has for some time been general concern about the hiring of individuals through their own service companies so that they can exploit the fiscal advantages offered by a corporate structure. It is possible for someone to leave work as an employee on a Friday, only to return the following Monday to do exactly the same job as an indirectly engaged "consultant" paying substantially reduced tax and national insurance. The Government is going to bring forward legislation to tackle this sort of avoidance.'

The long-term temp

The Government also expressed concern about the 'long-term temp' – a person who worked in an organisation for some considerable time, but within the wrapper of the service company. In the House of Lords debate on the Welfare Reform and Pensions Act, Lord McIntosh of Haringey, for the government, said:

> 'Let us consider the case of two people sitting side by side in the computer department of a big company. One is an employee of the company, the other works for his own service company. They might both have been there for the same length of time; they are both part of the same team and work under the same team leader, doing the same type of work. It has been argued that because one worker has chosen to set up a service company he is somehow an entrepreneur and deserves to pay less tax and NIC . . . I do not think his colleague at the next desk would agree.' (*Hansard* 13 October 1999, Col. 478)

The existence of large numbers of long-term temps thus reinforced the Government's conviction that it would be unfair to the rest of the working population if they turned a blind eye to service companies.

2.3 The legislative process

2.3.1 IR35

Press Release IR35 was issued on 9 March 1999. Apart from outlining the issue, and mentioning Friday to Monday companies, it gave few other details. However, it did say that:

> 'The proposed changes are aimed only at engagements with essential characteristics of employment. They should affect only those cases where these characteristics are disguised through use of an intermediary – such as a service company or partnership. There is no intention to redefine the existing boundary between employment and self-employment . . . The Inland Revenue will over the next few months be working with representative bodies on aspects of the practical application of the new rules and on the production of guidance. Any groups interested in contributing to this process should write to . . . Personal Tax Division.'

2.3.2 The April paper

The first sign of government thinking emerged in April, when a paper was circulated to those bodies who had responded to the invitation to contribute contained in the Press Release. The April paper was heavily caveated, with the following warnings:

'This summary is for use as a basis for discussion but is not a consultation document. This summary should not be taken as indicative of the form new rules might eventually take and is not to be relied upon in individual circumstances where the underlying facts may differ.'

The proposals encompassed:

- All those who supply services through intermediaries, including companies, agencies and partnerships;

- Where the worker operates under the control of the client;

- As to the tasks undertaken or the manner in which they were controlled.

Where these conditions applied, the client was to deduct PAYE and NIC from amounts invoiced by the intermediary. This obligation could however be ignored if the client knew that 'substantially' all the monies related to the work done were being paid on to the worker as salary, and were thus subjected to PAYE and NIC in the intermediary. No definition was given of 'substantially'.

To make obtaining this information easier for the client, intermediaries could register on a national database; registration would count as confirmation that all relevant amounts would be paid on to the worker and subjected to PAYE and NICs. Clients could thus access the database before paying an invoice in order to find out whether they could pay it gross or whether they should first deduct tax and NIC.

2.3.3 Problems with the April paper

These proposals were heavily criticised. In particular:

- The certification scheme was denounced as bureaucratic and burdensome;

- The crude 'control' test would catch many people who would have been regarded as self-employed if they had operated as a sole trader instead of via an intermediary;

- Anyone familiar with NIC and the NIRS2 computer system wondered how it would cope with miscellaneous receipts deducted from invoices and paid over by clients without any link to the workers' NI numbers;

- The extent to which expenses could be deducted (if at all) was unclear;

- Tax and NIC had to be deducted by the client in all cases where the invoiced amount was greater than the salary paid, even if the recipient was a non-shareholding employee who received a market rate salary;

- There were fears that the UK economy would be damaged by a collapse of the contracting market and by economic migration to more benevolent regimes such as the Netherlands.

Although the April proposals had initially been sent to a mere handful of people, word of their content began to spread. The Revenue finally received over 1,700 responses, most of them uncomplimentary. The proposals were condemned as oppressive, disproportionate and damaging to the economy.

2.3.4 The September Press Release

After considerable debate, a revised scheme was finally published in outline on 23 September. Under these new proposals, three features of the April scheme were dropped:

- The intermediary, not the client, became responsible for compliance with the legislation. The need for a certification scheme thus disappeared;

- An exemption was announced for 'genuine' employees of a PSC or partnership who were not shareholders or partners. A de minimis exemption was to be granted for small shareholders;

- The control test was replaced by a fairer version using the existing Schedule D/E divide. The individual worker would only be within the new rules if he would have been an employee of his client had he not been operating within the 'wrapper' of a service company or partnership.

2.3.5 Tax legislation

Draft tax legislation was published in February 2000, and was then included as Schedule 12, Finance Act 2000. Although the Act did not become law until July, the legislation took effect from the beginning of the 2000/01 fiscal year, by virtue of the Provisional Collection of Taxes Act 1968.

2.3.6 National Insurance legislation and regulations

National Insurance legislation cannot generally be backdated in the same way as tax. The Government thus introduced enabling clauses into the Welfare Reform and Pensions Bill, which was going through Parliament at the end of 1999. These provisions were broad-brush powers which allowed detailed regulations on personal service companies to be written later.

The legislation was introduced in the House of Lords, where it was fiercely debated. At one point the Bill was thrown out by the Upper House and returned to the Commons. However it succeeded in becoming law just before the end of the Parliamentary session.

Draft NIC regulations were subsequently published in February 2000; final regulations were laid on 13 March 2000 and came into force on 6 April.

2.3.7 Frequently Asked Questions

The Revenue faced considerable criticism for the way the consultation process had been handled, particularly in its initial stages. Partly as a reaction to this, and partly as an acknowledgement that many of their fiercest critics were from the IT industry, the Revenue used their website to ensure that those involved were kept informed as the legislation developed.

Particularly novel were the regular bulletins of Frequently Asked Questions on IR35 (FAQs), which covered everything from partnerships to composites, from overseas companies to travel expenses. This welcome development allowed the Revenue to deal with issues and uncertainties as they arose.

2.4 Conclusion

A conclusion seems premature, as the history of IR35 has only just begun. But a few points are already apparent:

- The government has shown that it is not to be deflected from enforcing the personal services rules, despite continuing and vocal opposition. One of the key points at issue is that the personal service worker is taxed as a quasi-employee, but lacks the equivalent employee rights;

- The original concern about the lack of employment protection for workers using service companies has not been addressed in this legislation, but may be covered by later changes;

- The line between Schedule D and Schedule E is fundamental to IR35, and is likely to be further tested in the courts. This may also affect wider issues of employment law.

3 Tax planning and IR35

3.1 General

Personal service companies became popular partly because of their tax advantages. But the more popular they became, the greater the loss of tax to the Treasury. It was this, combined with the fact that 'such avoidance is simply not fair to the rest of us' (Dawn Primarolo, *Hansard* 3 May 2000, Col. 213) which lay behind Ministers' determination to press ahead with IR35.

The main focus of the Government's attacks was on the use of dividends to avoid National Insurance, but service companies have other tax advantages. They include:

(a) Paying salaries to family members to absorb their tax allowances and lower rate bands;

(b) Utilising the corporate tax rules for expenses and capital allowances rather than the less generous reliefs available to employees;

(c) Maximising pension contributions in ways which are inaccessible to individuals;

(d) Obtaining a tax deduction against other income for interest on funds borrowed to invest in the business;

(e) Retaining surplus funds in the company to take advantage of the low corporate tax rates;

(f) Access to a 10 per cent rate of capital gains tax on disposal of the company's shares.

This chapter explains some of the tax and National Insurance planning which lay behind the introduction of IR35. Personal service companies which fall wholly or partly outside the new legislation can still use these opportunities, as can small corporate businesses other than suppliers of personal services, see **4.2.1**. A number of pitfalls associated with these planning ideas, such as illegal dividends and the rules for directors' loans, are discussed at the end of the chapter.

Even where companies are caught by IR35, some tax advantages remain. Chapter 23 summarises those which survive, as well as highlighting others appropriate to the new era.

3.2 Paying dividends rather than salary

3.2.1 Outline

One of the most significant tax planning opportunities for small companies arises from the combination of low tax rates on company profits (see **3.2.2**) and the absence of National Insurance on dividends (see **3.2.3**). Considerable savings can be made if most of the company's profits are paid out as dividends rather than as salary.

Two recent tax changes have further increased the advantages of this route. ACT was abolished with effect from 6 April 1999, and four weeks earlier the March 1999 Budget announced a reduction in the corporate tax rates for small businesses. It is no coincidence that the same budget gave birth to IR35.

3.2.2 Corporate tax rates

Salaries are deductible from profits and so reduce the corporate tax due, while dividends are paid out of post-tax profits. The rate of tax on company profits is thus a factor in deciding whether to pay salaries or dividends.

If tax on profits is higher than tax on salary, salary should be paid to reduce profits; if corporate taxes are low, but taxes on salary are high, it is better to pay the corporate tax and distribute the net profit as a dividend. There is of course a third factor, the relative taxation of dividends and salary, which is discussed at **3.2.3** below.

The salary versus dividend comparison is weighted in favour of dividends for small companies, because they are unlikely to pay tax at more than 20 per cent; some may also benefit from the 10 per cent starting rate.

In general, as the company becomes more profitable, the dividend route becomes less efficient. This is because corporate tax rates increase once profits exceed £300,000. Service companies with higher levels of profits should model their tax position under both the salary and the dividend routes in order to determine the optimum cut-off point.

Starting rate

The 10 per cent starting rate was introduced with effect from 6 April 2000. It applies only to the first £10,000 of profits, with a marginal calculation operating between £10,000 and £50,000 (s13AA ICTA 1988). The simplest way of calculating tax on profits between £10,000 and £50,000 is to establish a rate of tax for profits in the marginal band so as to arrive at the right tax charge overall. For 2000/01 this is 22.5 per cent.

The effect of the marginal calculation is to tax profits below £50,000 in such a way that when profits reach £50,000 *total* profits are taxed at the small company rate. It is sometimes mistakenly thought that there is a 10 per cent band, as there is with income tax, but this is not the case.

The position is more complicated when the company has franked investment income.

Small companies' rate

The 20 per cent small companies' rate applies where profits do not exceed £300,000. For profits between £300,000 and £1,500,000 a marginal rate applies. This has the effect of taxing total profits at somewhere between 20 per cent and the full corporate rate of 30 per cent (s13 ICTA 1988).

As with the starting rate, the simplest way of dealing with this is to establish a tax rate for profits in the marginal band so as to get the correct answer overall. For 2000/01 this is 32.5 per cent, see Example 3A. Again, the position is more complicated when the company has franked investment income.

Example 3A

Tigger Limited's corporation tax profits for the accounting period ended 31 March 2000 are £350,000. Corporation tax payable is:

	£	Rate	£
£			
Profit up to marginal band	300,000	20%	60,000
Excess	50,000	32.5%	16,250
Total tax			76,250
Tax rate	76,250/350,000	21.78%	

Other points

(a) The £10,000, £50,000, £300,000 and £1.5m limits are reduced pro-rata if there are associated companies. Thus, if there are two companies in the group, each limit will be halved (s13(3) and s13AA(4) ICTA 1988). Associated companies are defined in s416 ICTA 1988;

(b) The limits are reduced where the accounting period in question is less than 12 months (s13A(6) and s13AA(6) ICTA 1988);

(c) Accounting periods straddling 1 April are treated as two separate periods, one ending on 31 March and one beginning on 1 April (s86(3) FA 1994).

Exclusions from the reliefs

Neither the starting rate nor the small companies' rate is available (s13(1) ICTA 1988) for:

(a) Non-resident companies. However a non-discrimination clause in a double taxation agreement may allow the UK branch or agency of a non-resident company to access the starting rate or small companies' rate (*CCAB TR500* 10 March 1983);

(b) Housing investment trusts (s508A(1)(b) ICTA 1988);

(c) Close investment-holding companies. This is not defined in the legislation (s13A ICTA 1988), which instead says that all companies are close investment holding companies unless throughout the accounting period they exist wholly or mainly for one of the following:

    (i)   The carrying on of trade(s) on a commercial basis;

    (ii) Letting of property other than to connected persons;

    (iii) Holding shares in, administering, or lending money to a company which is not a close investment holding company.

3.2.3 National Insurance

The real benefits of paying dividends rather than salary derive from the fact that no National Insurance contributions are due on dividends. Of the various tax advantages available to the service company, National Insurance avoidance was the main target of IR35. In the Revenue's first Frequently Asked Question (FAQ) 'What is IR35 about?' they said:

> 'Intermediaries such as service companies can be set up to provide the services of a single worker to a client in circumstances where, if it were not for the service company, the worker would be an employee of the client. The use of service companies in this way allows the client to make payments to the company rather than the individual, without deducting PAYE or NICs.
>
> The worker can then take the money out of the service company in the form of dividends instead of salary. Dividends are not liable to NICs so the worker will pay less in NICs than either a conventional employee or a self-employed person. The Chancellor believes that avoidance of PAYE and NICs in this way needs to be tackled in the interests of fairness.'

In 1999 the government estimated that the use of dividends rather than salary by service companies was costing the Treasury £220m per year in lost National Insurance. It was expected that this amount would increase further as more people took advantage of the opportunity (WRPA, RIA para 14). In March 2000 further research indicated that the number of service companies 'using the loophole' was actually twice the original estimate (*Hansard* 3 May, Col. 217). This would put the National Insurance loss up to £440m a year.

These savings come about because salary is subject to both employee and employer's NIC. Employee NIC is charged at 10 per cent on amounts between the employee's earnings threshold (£3,952 for 2000/01) and the upper earnings limit (£27,820 in 2000/01). Employer's NIC is charged at 12.2 per cent on all earnings above the employer's earning threshold (£4,385 in 2000/01). Since there is no cap on employer's NIC, its cost grows as salary increases.

The amount of NIC saved depends on the position of the individual, see Examples 3B and 3C below.

Taxation of dividends

Dividends received by an individual come with a 10 per cent tax credit. The dividend plus the tax credit constitute Franked Investment Income (FII). If the recipient is a non-taxpayer, the tax credit is not recoverable. FII received by a basic rate taxpayer is taxed at 10 per cent (the Schedule F lower rate) and thus the tax credit covers the liability.

Higher rate taxpayers pay tax on FII at 32.5 per cent, the 'Schedule F upper rate'. Taking into account the tax credit, this is equivalent to 25 per cent of the dividend.

Example 3B shows how this works, using a simple scenario where the director is already within the higher rate band, and including the employer's NIC saving.

Example 3B

Mike's company makes recordings of choral music. In the year to 31 March 2001 it has pre-tax profits of £10,000. Mike has other income which has brought him into the higher rate tax bracket; he has also paid the maximum Class 1 employee NIC liability. The company can either pay him salary or a dividend.

	Rate	£
Dividend		
CT profits		10,000
CT thereon	10.0%	(1,000)
Available to Mike		9,000
Dividend received		9,000
Add tax credit	1/9	1,000
		10,000
Tax thereon	25.0%	(3,250)
After tax income		6,750
Effective rate of tax	32.5%	
Bonus		
CT profits		10,000
Less bonus		(8,913)
Less employer's NIC		(1,087)
Profits subject to CT		0
Bonus received		8,913
Less income tax	40.0%	(3,565)
After tax income		5,348
Effective rate of tax	46.5%	

Example 3B shows that the use of dividends rather than salary can reduce the combined NIC and tax rate by 14 per cent where the shareholder/director is already within the 40 per cent tax bracket.

Where an individual is a both a basic rate taxpayer and below the upper threshold for employee NICs, paying a dividend rather than salary produces an even more tax-efficient result. This is because:

(a) Profits in a small company are usually taxed at no more than 20 per cent (see **3.2.2**); when these profits are paid out as dividends they suffer no further tax when received by a basic rate taxpayer. This is in contrast to salary which would have been taxed at 22 per cent;

(b) By paying a dividend, both employer's NIC (as in Example 3C) and employee NIC are saved.

These advantages are demonstrated in Example 3C.

Example 3C

Bill is the sole shareholder in his woodcarving business. His company has taxable profits of £10,000, and he can choose either to receive all profits as a dividend, or as salary. He is a basic rate taxpayer, with £6,000 of other income. The calculation is the same as in Example 3C, apart from the final stage, the tax and NICs on Bill's salary.

	Rate	*£*
Dividend		
Corporation tax:		
Profits		10,000
Corporation tax	10%	(1,000)
Net profit paid as dividend		9,000
Income tax		
Basic rate tax payable		nil
Cash received		9,000
Effective rate of tax	10%	
Bonus		
Profits before salary		10,000
Less salary		(8,913)
Less employer's NIC	12.2%	(1,087)
Profits subject to corporation tax		nil
Income tax		
Salary received		8,913
Employee's NIC	10%	(891)
Income tax	22%	(1,961)
Cash received		6,061
Effective rate of tax	39.4%	

By paying a dividend Bill has reduced his combined tax and NICs rate from almost 40 per cent to a mere 10 per cent.

3.2.4 Other advantages of using dividends rather than salary

A number of other advantages arise from paying dividends rather than salary:

* Dividends provide a cash flow advantage, because tax on salary is deducted weekly or monthly under PAYE, whereas tax on a dividend is paid on 31 January following the fiscal year of receipt;

* Corporation tax is also paid later than PAYE, being due nine months and one day after the end of the company's accounting period (s59D TMA 1970);

* Abolition of ACT in 1999 further increased the cash flow benefits of dividends compared to salary.

3.3 Small salary payment

It is, however, not advisable for all profits to be paid out as a dividend. If no salary at all is paid, the individual will have no contributions record. As a result he will have no state pension, and will fail to qualify for contributory benefits such as statutory sick pay.

For 2000/01 entitlement to contributory benefits can be achieved without incurring either employer or employee NICs: a salary of between £3,484 and £3,951 gives entitlement to benefits without suffering any National Insurance. For earnings between £3,952 to £4,385, only employee NICs are due. Above £4,385, both employer and employee NICs become payable.

When calculating the salary to be paid, it may be necessary to consider minimum wage requirements, see **22.2**. For the payment of salaries to other family members, see **3.4** below.

Contributions to personal pensions and retirement annuities depend on the existence of net relevant earnings (NRE), essentially salary and taxable benefits. If salary and benefits are low, NRE will be low, and an individual's pension contributions will therefore be limited. This issue is discussed at **3.6** below, along with consideration of other forms of pension which do not depend on NRE.

A higher salary should be considered where the individual has allowable expenses, such as interest, to deduct from his taxable income, as otherwise no tax relief may be obtained for the expense. This is because the tax credits on dividends are no longer repayable, see **3.10.2**.

3.4 Payments to family members

3.4.1 Outline

If the service company director has a spouse or partner whose taxable income is low, a salary from the company for administrative support provided will use up his or her available personal allowance and/or lower tax bands. Salary can also be paid to other family members in a similar position. The advantages of such payments are illustrated in Example 3D below. However, the Revenue may challenge the deductibility of the salary paid, see **3.4.2** below

3.4.2 Revenue attacks

Care needs to be taken that the spouse/partner does in fact do sufficient work to justify the salary, see *Copeman v William Flood and Sons Ltd* [1940] 24 TC 53 and IM 1042. In *Copeman* the director of a family company employed his two children on salaries of £2,600 each. However the daughter drew only £70 of remuneration and the son £277. The Revenue contended successfully that only £350 in the case of the son and £78 in respect of the daughter had been paid for the purposes of the trade.

It was argued in the company's defence that directors have discretion to spend the company's money. However the judge said that:

> 'It may very well be that there are sums which are paid to the directors as remuneration for their services in accordance with the Articles of Association and in accordance with a resolution of the company, but it does not necessarily follow in the least that they are sums which are wholly and exclusively laid out for the purposes of the trade.'

If, following *Copeman*, the salary is disallowed in the company, there will be double taxation if the spouse/partner has already been taxed on the earnings received. For this reason the Revenue do not use the disallowance threat lightly, but where the salary paid is:

- Insufficient to attract a tax charge; or

- Appears to have been pitched so as to gain entitlement to benefits without payment of NIC; or

- The work done is hard to identify,

the Revenue may challenge the deduction (IM 1042).

In addition to the above the Revenue may also seek to argue that the payment to family members is a settlement of monies on them, and thus effectively a payment into trust under Chapter IA Part XV ICTA 1988. In general, however, the Revenue are unlikely to take this point to the Commissioners.

3.4.3 Worked examples

In Example 3D below an average rate of tax and NIC of only 24.5 per cent is achieved on net profits of £96,680, by using two people's personal allowances and their lower rate bands, as well as dividends.

Example 3D

Tony and Cherie have a personal service company, through which Cherie provides legal advice. Tony is an employee of the company, writing up the books and making appointments. He works 26 hours a week for the company, and Cherie an average of 50, for 45 weeks a year. Cherie owns 65 shares in the company and Tony 35. In the year to 5 April 2001 the company's turnover is £100,000, ignoring VAT. They decide to pay themselves a salary which meets the minimum wage requirements, utilises most of their personal allowances, and ensures that both have entitlement to contributory benefits, but to take the balance in dividends. Their net take home pay is as follows:

		£	Notes	Rate	£
Company					
Turnover					100,000
Salaries					
Tony					(4,329)
Cherie					(8,325)
Employer's NIC					
Tony	XS over	4,385	1	12.2%	0
Cherie	XS over	4,385	1	12.2%	(481)
Other expenses					
Capital allowances					(750)
Travel & subsistence					(600)
PII cover					(1,000)
Other					(970)
Profits subject to CT					83,545
Less CT thereon				20%	(16,709)
Available for distribution					66,836
Dividend allocated	Cherie			65.0%	43,443
	Tony			35.0%	23,393

Notes

1. This is the annual employer's earnings threshold of £4,385, rather than the sum of the monthly or weekly limits, which are slightly different. Personal service workers are on an annual earnings period for NICs, see **4.8.2** and the annual threshold is thus used throughout this book.

	£	Rate	Tony	Cherie
Individuals				
Salary received			4,329	8,325
Employee NIC, XS over	3,952	10.0%	38	437
Net dividend received			23,393	43,443
Personal allowances			4,385	4,385
Income tax calculation				
Net dividend received			23,393	43,443
Tax credit			2,599	4,827
Gross dividend			25,992	48,270
Salary			4,329	8,325
			30,321	56,595
less PA			(4,385)	(4,385)
Taxable income			25,936	52,210
Taxable salary net of PA				3,940
Tax thereon		10.0%	1,520	152
		22.0%	2,420	532
Tax on salary			3,940	684
Dividend + tax credit, after any PA balance			25,936	48,270
10.0%	1,520	n/a	0	n/a
22.0%	24,416	n/a	24,460	n/a
32.5%	0	0	23,810	7,738
	25,936	0	48,270	7,738
less tax credit on div taxed @ HR				(2,381)
Tax on dividend			0	5,357

Take home cash	Tony	Cherie	Total
	£	£	£
Salary	4,329	8,325	12,654
Tax	0	(687)	(687)
Employee NIC	(38)	(437)	(475)
	4,291	7,201	11,492
Net dividend	23,393	43,443	66,836
less higher rate tax	0	(5,357)	(5,357)
	27,684	45,287	72,971

21

Total tax & NIC paid	£	£	£
Employer's NIC	0	481	481
Employee NIC	38	437	475
Income tax			
salary	0	687	687
dividend		5,357	5,357
Corporation tax			16,709
			23,709
Effective rate of tax on turnover			23.7%
Effective rate of tax on profit*			24.5%
*£100,000 less expenses of £3,320			

If, instead of taking most of their income as dividends, Tony and Cherie were to have taken it as salary, their tax would have increased by over 12 per cent from 24.5 per cent to 36.8 per cent, see Example 3E. Because of the number of variables in any given situation, the actual saving from paying dividends rather than salary will vary considerably.

The same set of facts is used again in Chapter 12 to show that the PSC rules would increase the tax still further, to 39.5 per cent, see Example 12.8.

Example 3E

The facts are in Example 3D, but Tony and Cherie take all their money as salary, with Tony earning £30,000 and Cherie the balance. The tax effects are as follows:

		£	Rate	£
Company				
Turnover				100,000
Salaries				
Tony				(30,000)
Cherie				(57,121)
Employer's NIC				
Tony	XS over	4,385	12.2%	(3,125)
Cherie	XS over	4,385	12.2%	(6,434)
Other expenses				
Capital allowances				(750)
Travel & subsistence				(600)
PII cover				(1,000)
Other				(970)
Profits subject to CT				0

Individuals		Rate	Tony £	Cherie £
Salary received			30,000	57,121
Employee NIC, XS on	3,952	10.0%	2,387	2,387
up to	27,820			
Income tax calculation	£	£	£	£
Salary			30,000	57,121
less PA			(4,385)	(4,385)
Taxable income			25,615	52,736
Tax thereon				
10.0%	1,520	152	1,520	152
22.0%	24,095	5,301	26,880	5,914
40.0%	0	0	24,336	9,734
Tax on salary	25,615	5,453	52,736	15,800

Take home cash	Tony £	Cherie £	Total £
Salary	30,000	57,121	87,121
Tax	(5,453)	(15,800)	(21,253)
Employee NIC	(2,387)	(2,387)	(4,774)
	22,160	38,934	61,094

Total tax & NIC paid	£	£	£
Employer's NIC	3,125	6,434	9,559
Employee NIC	2,387	2,387	4,774
Income tax	5,453	15,800	21,353
Corporation tax			0
			35,586

Effective rate of tax on turnover 35.6%
Effective rate of tax on profit* 36.8%
* £100,000 less expenses of £3,320

3.5 Expenses and capital allowances

3.5.1 Expenses

A company can deduct expenses from its taxable profits provided they are wholly and exclusively for the purposes of the business (s74(1)(a) ICTA 1988). Deductible expenses include items such as salary, training, travel, pension contributions and employer's National Insurance. The corporate tax rules for deductibility of expenses are far more generous than those available to employees, see **11.5**.

23

Despite the requirement that the costs be 'exclusively' for the business, in practice apportionment is permitted, see IM 601e. For instance, where a company is based in the home of the sole shareholder/director, it is normal for running costs such as light and heat to be split between business and private use. Car costs can also be apportioned.

3.5.2 Capital allowances

There are also tax reliefs for capital expenditure, again on a more generous basis than those available to employees, see **11.11**. The company can claim allowances if it 'has incurred capital expenditure on the provision of machinery or plant wholly and exclusively for the purposes of (its) trade' (s24 CAA 1990). Capital allowances can thus be claimed on computers, software, furniture and motor vehicles, subject to a private use restriction.

3.6 Pensions

3.6.1 General

The rules for pensions are complex, and a full discussion is outside the scope of this book. However, in assessing its options, the company should consider tax efficiency, administrative convenience, and the long term expectations of the directors.

Working through a personal service company allows access to more tax-efficient pensions vehicles than those available to individuals, including sole traders and partners. Many small companies use either a Small Self Administered Scheme (SSAS) or an Executive Pension Plan (EPP). Even where a personal pension vehicle is used, rather than a SSAS or an EPP, company contributions can achieve a useful NIC saving as compared to contributions made by an individual.

3.6.2 Tax advantages

Inland Revenue approved pension schemes have certain tax advantages:

- Contributions are deductible from profits for corporation tax purposes, and are free of NICs;

- No income tax or employee NICs are paid by the individual on any company contributions made;

- If contributions are made by an employee they are paid out of salary after deduction of both employer and employee NICs. They are, however, tax free and reduce the amount of income taxed at the individual's marginal rate;

- The pension fund itself is not taxed on either capital gains or income received. However, this advantage has been eroded since 2 July 1997 when pension funds were prevented from recovering the tax credit on UK dividends received;

- When the pension finally comes into payment, up to 25% of its value can be taken as a tax-free lump sum.

There are broadly speaking two types of UK approved schemes, personal pensions (see **3.6.3**) and occupational schemes (see **3.6.5**)

3.6.3 Personal pensions

A personal pension can be bought 'off the peg' from numerous financial institutions. Either the employer or the employee can make contributions. The administration involved is small.

Money saved in the personal pension is used on retirement to buy an annuity. There is also a drawdown option whereby the annuity can be deferred and income taken from the fund in the meantime.

Contributions to a personal pension are limited by:

- Net Relevant Earnings (NRE). This is broadly the individual's Schedule E salary plus any taxable benefits;

- Age at the beginning of the tax year. The older the individual, the higher the percentage of NRE that can be contributed. The figures are given in Table 3.1

- The earnings cap. This sets a maximum NRE figure above which earnings cannot be taken into account for pension provision purposes. For 2000/01 it is £91,800.

Table 3.1 NRE percentages for contributions to Personal Pension Schemes

Age	Percentage
< 36	17.5
36 to 45	20
46 to 50	25
51 to 55	30
56 to 60	35
61 or more	40

Pension contributions should be made by the company rather than the individual. This is because a company contribution saves employer's NIC on the full amount of the contribution. Depending on the individual's pay level, it may also save employee NIC. If the contribution were made by the director or employee, he would receive tax relief but no NICs relief.

In small companies there is a tension between the desire to pay dividends instead of salary so as reduce the cost of NICs, and the need for NRE which provide the basis for pension contributions. If the workers are mostly remunerated by way of dividends, they are likely to have low NRE. They can, however, use the SSAS or EPP routes, see **3.6.5**. And from 2001 stakeholder schemes (see **3.6.4** below) will provide another solution.

3.6.4 Stakeholder schemes

Stakeholder schemes are similar to personal pensions, and will be introduced from April 2001. They allow contributions up to £3,600, regardless of NRE. Contributions in excess of £3,600 must be supported by evidence of earnings, and are subject to the same limits as other personal pensions, see Table 3.1 above.

Stakeholder contributions above £3,600 which are supported by evidence of earnings can continue for four more years without any further evidence being required. Thus it may be possible to pay a significant salary level every fifth year, perhaps up to the earnings cap. This would create the maximum NRE for that year and establish entitlement to a high level of contributions over the next four years.

3.6.5 Occupational schemes

Occupational schemes can be either final salary and money purchase. Final salary schemes are more costly to administer than money purchase schemes, and have demanding regulatory requirements. They are thus usually not accessible to small businesses such as personal service companies, and are thus not discussed further in this chapter.

A money purchase (defined contribution) scheme is set up under trust. Employer contributions are not limited by the NRE rules, but are fully tax deductible as long as the funding of the scheme is only sufficient to allow the payment of employees' pensions at the maximum permitted level. This is two-thirds of the earnings cap (see **3.6.3**). For 2000/01 the maximum pension is thus £61,200. A company using a defined contribution scheme can thus frequently make higher contributions than would be permitted under the rules for personal pensions.

Employees may also make contributions, limited to 15 per cent of their net relevant earnings.

Two common forms of defined contribution schemes much used by service companies are the SSAS and the EPP.

Small Self-Administered Schemes

A SSAS can provide pension arrangements for up to eleven members. Unlike other occupational pension schemes, where investments in the sponsoring employer are limited to a maximum of 5 per cent of the pension fund, SSASs can operate almost as 'captive' funds, investing substantially in the sponsoring company. Significant tax planning opportunities are thus available.

Executive Pension Plans

EPPs provide benefits, usually to one member, by earmarking a policy purchased from an insurance company. The insurance company can loan back to the employer part of the assets held within the policy.

3.7 Interest relief

3.7.1 Outline

If the service company satisfies the definition of a close company, see **3.7.2**, and money is borrowed to invest in the company, tax relief may be available on the interest cost, see **3.7.3** below.

3.7.2 Close companies

Most personal service companies fit the definition of close companies found in s414 ICTA 1988. This is that the company is:

- Under the 'control' of five or fewer 'participators'; or

- Under the control of participators who are directors (s414(1) ICTA 1988); or

- Five or fewer participators, or participators who are directors, together possess or are entitled to acquire such rights as would entitle them to receive the greater part of the assets available for distribution if the company was wound up.

A participator is a person who has a share or interest in the capital or income of the company and includes:

- Any person possessing, or entitled to acquire, share capital or voting rights;

- Any loan creditor;

- Any person possessing, or entitled to acquire, a right to receive, or to participate in, distributions or any amount payable by the company (in cash or in kind) to loan creditors by way of premium on redemption; and

- Any person entitled to ensure that present or future income or assets of the company will be applied directly or indirectly for his benefit.

A person has 'control' of a company:

> 'If he exercises, or is able to exercise or is entitled to acquire, direct or indirect control over the company's affairs, and in particular, but without prejudice to the generality of the preceding words, if he possesses or is entitled to acquire the greater part of the share capital or issued share capital of the company or of the voting power in the company'

or if he is entitled to the greater part of the assets on its winding up (s416 ICTA 1988).

Most personal service companies fall within the definition because control is exercised by the shareholder/director who is clearly a participator, and by a small number of others, such as a spouse, partner, or other family members.

3.7.3 Deduction for loan interest

To succeed in obtaining a deduction, the company must be close throughout the accounting period, and must not be a close investment holding company (see **3.2.2**). In addition the shareholder must either:

- Have a 'material interest' in the company, which in this context means that he must own more than 5 per cent of the ordinary shares or be entitled to more than 5 per cent of the assets on a winding-up; or

- If the shareholding is less than 5 per cent, he must work for the greater part of his time in the management of the company or of an associated company.

In addition:

- The funds must be used either to buy shares in the company, or be lent to the close company for its business;

- The borrowing must be a loan, and not, for example, an overdraft or a credit card debt; and

- The interest paid must not exceed a commercial rate.

Care needs to be taken when an individual has both interest relief and receives most of his money as salary, see **3.3**.

28

3.8 Retention of funds in the company

Because the rates of corporation tax suffered on the profits of small companies are lower than many individuals' marginal tax rates, see **3.2.2** above, money not required can be retained in the PSC. The company thus becomes a tax-efficient money box.

The surplus funds can then be invested, either in cash or in other assets, though this may affect the company's status for business asset taper relief purposes, see Sch A1, para 11 TCGA 1992; CG 17919–17920.

Alternatively, it can be loaned to the directors, shareholders or employees, but subject to the following constraints:

- A loan to a director cannot be more than £5,000 (s334 Companies Act 1985);

- If the loan is made other than to a director, it can exceed £5,000. However a cheap or interest free loan in excess of £5,000 is taxable under s160 ICTA 1988 unless it is a 'qualifying' loan, see ss353ff ICTA 1988;

- Care is also needed not to fall within the close company loan rules, see **3.10.4**.

3.9 Capital gains tax advantages

Shares in a service company are likely to be a business asset for taper relief purposes. Tax on the shares when sold can thus be as little as 10 per cent. The tax planning possibilities offered by the business asset taper are however outside the scope of this book, but it should be remembered that shares can only reflect the intrinsic worth of the business. A service company with minimal assets which simply sells the services of its only director is unlikely to have created transferable value.

3.10 Tax planning pitfalls

3.10.1 Introduction

In addition to the many tax advantages offered by the service company, there are a number of dangers. These include non-repayable tax credits, illegal dividends, and close company loan provisions.

3.10.2 Non-repayable tax credits

Normally, when an expense reduces an individual's taxable income, he pays less tax. However, if he receives only dividends, this is no longer the case. From 6 April 1999, tax credits on dividends are not repayable.

Thus if the individual's taxable income consists entirely of dividends, and he also has deductions, such as interest (see **3.7**) to offset against his taxable income, there will be no repayment of the 10 per cent tax credit. If the individual has no other income against which the expense can be offset, the tax relief will be wasted. His salary payment may thus need to be adjusted in consequence, see **3.3**.

3.10.3 Illegal dividends

A dividend is only lawful if the company has sufficient distributable profits. If an interim distribution is made before the end of the financial year, it may exceed the profits later found to have been available. The company will thus have paid a dividend which is wholly or partly illegal (ss263–268 Companies Act 1985).

Illegal dividends are a particular risk for personal service companies, whose directors/shareholders commonly take quarterly or monthly distributions instead of salary. A check should thus be made before each withdrawal to see whether the dividend can legally be paid.

National Insurance implications

In February 1994 the Contributions Agency stated in a note to the ICAEW and other professional bodies that an unlawful dividend would be regarded as earnings for NIC purposes. However this view is questionable, since the fact that the dividend is illegal does not change its nature.

Loans to shareholders

Where an individual has received a dividend, and knows, or has reasonable grounds to believe, that it is illegal, the dividend is void for tax purposes. The company has not made a distribution as a matter of company law, and thus the dividend does not form part of the recipient's income for tax purposes. In other words, there has been no dividend and the cash still belongs to the company.

However, if the company is close (see **3.7.2**), a loan has been made to the shareholder which may cause a tax charge to arise under s419(1) ICTA 1988. The rules for calculating the charge are given at **3.10.4**.

Relief will however be available under s419(4) ICTA 1988, if the dividend is repaid to the company within nine months of the company's year end. Repayment is also a requirement of s277 Companies Act 1985 when a dividend has been received by someone who knows or has reasonable grounds to believe that it is unlawful.

Innocent receipt

Where the shareholder had no knowledge of the illegality of the dividend and no reasonable grounds to believe it to be illegal, the above paragraphs do not apply.

However this situation is unlikely to apply to a PSC, where there is substantial identity between the directors and shareholders. The Revenue view is that 'when dealing with private companies controlled by directors who are shareholders, such a member ought to know the status of the dividend and it is our view that s277 Companies Act 1985 will apply in the majority of such cases' (CT 2007a:28).

Where it can be successfully argued that the shareholder did not know the dividend was illegal, the dividend does not have to be repaid. It will then remain a distribution under s209(2)(b) ICTA 1988. If such a shareholder then repaid the company (despite not being liable to do so) this would be a transfer of his own income and would not affect the higher rate position. In other words, if he repays the money to the company, he still pays tax on it.

3.10.4 Loans to participators

As discussed above, most personal service companies will be 'close' for tax purposes. One of the significant consequences of close company status is that if the company loans money to a participator (see **3.7.2**), it may be required to pay tax equal to 25 per cent of the loan balance. The following rules apply:

- If the loan is repaid or written off *within* nine months of the end of the accounting period in which the loan was made, no tax is payable;

- If a loan is released, repaid or written off *after* nine months following the year end, the company can reclaim the tax charged, but it is only received by the company nine months after the end of the accounting period in which the loan, etc. was repaid, released or written off;

- If the amount is released or written off, it becomes taxable on the individual as if it were a dividend.

The effect of these provisions is to charge the company for the individual's use of the borrowed money, but only to the extent that he has not repaid the

31

amounts within the permitted nine months following the end of the accounting period. A similar nine month period is granted to the Revenue if the tax has later to be repaid to the company. Example 3F shows how this works in practice.

Example 3F

Olive is the shareholder and director of Train, a company providing video services to the TV industry. It is a close company with a 31 March year end. Train loaned Olive £100,000 on 15 May 1999. On 20 August 2000, Olive repaid £70,000 and on 20 September 2001, Train wrote off the balance of the loan.

Olive borrowed the funds in the year 1999/00. She repaid £70,000 within nine months of the end of the company's 1999/00 accounting period, so this eliminates any close company charge on £70,000. The tax due on the balance is as follows:

Train

1.1.01   Corporation tax due of (£100,000 − £70,000) = £30,000 @ 25% = £7,500 (Note 1)

31.12.02 The company is due a repayment of £30,000 × 25% = £7,500 (Note 2)

Olive

Her taxable income for 2001/02 is increased by £30,000 + £3,333 = £33,333
This is subject to the Schedule F upper rate:

	£	Rate	£
Income	33,333	32.5%	10,833
Less tax credit			3,333
Tax due			7,500

Notes

1. The loan outstanding at the end of March 2000 was £30,000. Tax is therefore due at 25 per cent on the normal payment date, nine months and one day after the end of the company's accounting period.
2. The loan was written off in September 2001. This is in the financial year ending 31 March 2002. Since tax has already become due, the repayment is not due until 9 months after the end of the accounting period, namely on 31 December 2002.

The close company provisions can catch small companies unaware. For example, an overdrawn current account amounts to a loan for the purposes of these rules. See also **3.10.3** above on the implications of illegal dividends.

4 Scope of personal services legislation

4.1 General

4.1.1 IR35 target constituency

IR35 is aimed at those who would have been employed by the client had they been engaged directly rather than via an intermediary. The Budget Press Release itself stated that:

> 'The proposed changes are aimed only at engagements with essential characteristics of employment. They should affect only those cases where these characteristics are disguised through use of an intermediary – such as a service company or partnership'.

This was reinforced by Dawn Primarolo in the IR35 debate:

> 'Some people have chosen to use service companies because they do not fit the definition of self-employment, but still want to benefit from the tax breaks available for self-employment. They are really only employees who want a better deal from the tax system than that to which their status entitles them. Those people will be targeted by the new rules.' (*Hansard* 3 May 2000, Pt 24, Col. 214)

This chapter looks at the scope of the personal services legislation for both tax and National Insurance. The two sets of rules are similar, although not identical. Any differences are commented on as appropriate throughout this book.

4.1.2 Sham companies

In the past the Revenue's only weapon against such service companies was to argue that the arrangements were a 'sham'; that the company was simply a façade, designed to look as if real legal rights and obligations had been created between the company and the client, whereas in reality it was the individual who had contracted with the client. However, the Revenue rarely succeeded, and then usually only if the procedures and/or documentation were defective.

Post-IR35, service company arrangements could still be a 'sham'. If they were, and the contract was really between the individual and the client, the individual could be reclassified as an employee. IR35 would not be applicable, as it deals only with genuine arrangements under which a worker provides services via an intermediary.

However, it is unlikely that the Revenue will seek to argue this difficult point in the future. They will instead apply IR35 to all intermediaries where the worker would have been an employee had the services been supplied directly.

4.1.3 Legislation

The scope of the personal services rules is defined by Schedule 12, Finance Act 2000. This establishes that to be within the new rules for tax purposes there must be:

(a) An engagement for personal services provided on or after 6 April 2000;

(b) Where the services are provided to a business carried on by another person ('the client');

(c) And the worker would be regarded as an employee of the client but for the interposition of . . .

(d) . . . at least one intermediary between the worker and the client. The intermediary must meet certain defined conditions; and

(e) The worker either receives a payment or benefit from the intermediary which is not chargeable under Schedule E, or has the right to such a payment.

The same criteria are included in the parallel National Insurance regulations (SI 2000 No 727). They are discussed in more detail below.

4.2 Personal services provided on or after 6 April 2000

4.2.1 Personal services

The legislation only covers the provision of personal services. Engagements for the provision of goods, rather than for services, are completely outside these rules. Companies and partnerships involved in manufacturing, selling or distribution are thus not within the scope of IR35 (Sch 12, para 1(1)(a) FA 2000).

4.2.2 Provided on or after 6 April 2000

The legislation's start date was 6 April 2000. Engagements which were partway through on that date are within IR35 in so far as the work done relates to the period after 6 April, see Sch 12, para 22 FA 2000.

Although generally the PSC rules are on a receipts basis, see **10.2**, an exception has been made for the commencement year. Money received before 6 April 2000 which relates to work done after that date is brought into the calculation of deemed income for the year 2000/01. This is to prevent people accelerating cash receipts so that they fall into the previous fiscal year and so are received before the start of the new regime (Sch 12, para 22(2)FA 2000; SI 2000 No 727 Reg 1(3)).

4.3 Provided to a business . . .

4.3.1 Scope of definition

The legislation is limited to the provision of services 'for the purposes of a business carried on by another person' (Sch 12, para 1(1)(a) FA 2000). It thus excludes any contracts made by an intermediary with an individual on a personal basis. An example would be a gardener with a one-man company who spends two days a week in what might otherwise be regarded as a relevant engagement with a local family.

This exemption has been granted for the pragmatic reason that most of these contracts will in any event fall outside the PSC rules on other grounds, usually because the worker will meet the tests of self-employment set out at **4.4.1** below and Chapter 6.

However this is not invariably the case, and this exemption may then be turned to advantage. For example, the provision of domestic help by nannies, cooks and chauffeurs could be structured via a personal services company so as to fall outside of the new legislation. The PSC would have access to the tax planning advantages set out in Chapter 3, and the individual could take this tax efficiency into account when agreeing payment terms.

This device would, however, not succeed where the cost of the chauffeur or nanny was reimbursed or paid for by the individual's employer, because the services would then be provided to the employer for the purposes of his business, and not to the householder.

Another example might be the provision of nursing services to a house-bound patient. Providing the contract was with the individual, and not, for example, his insurance company or the local health authority, the engagement would fall outside the personal services rules.

4.3.2 . . . A business carried on by another person (the client)

For the legislation to be effective the worker must be supplying services 'for the purposes of a business carried on by another person ('the client')'. It has been argued that:

- The worker is providing services for the purposes of furthering his own business, not the business of another, and thus the legislation does not apply. However this interpretation begs the question, since if the worker is 'in business on his own account', he should pass the status tests and fall outside IR35 in any event;

- The 'client' for whose business the worker is providing services is in fact the agency. This issue is explored in more detail at **5.6**.

4.4 The worker would be regarded as an employee of the client

It is necessary to consider whether, if the worker had contracted to supply personal services directly to the client, the contract between them would have been one of employment. In other words, would the worker have been regarded as an employee if there had been no intermediary?

In deciding whether the engagement would have the characteristics of employment it is necessary to look at the 'circumstances' under which the services are provided. This is defined in Sch 12, para 1(4) FA 2000 as including:

> 'The terms on which the services are provided, having regard to the terms of the contracts forming part of the arrangements under which the services were provided.'

The major point of reference is thus the contract or contracts under which the worker is providing services. Other surrounding facts may also be relevant – for example, whether the worker has other clients and a business organisation. How this part of the legislation should be interpreted in the light of normal contract law is discussed in Chapter 5.

It is well known that there is no statutory definition of 'employment'. However, the question has come before the Courts on numerous occasions. The approach taken has been to identify factors which help determine whether a particular contract is a 'contract of service' (employment) or a 'contract for services' (self-employment), or possibly a third type of contract, see 6.4.3. This may involve a review of whether mutuality of obligation subsists between the parties, see Chapter 5.

Typically the self-employed person has some or all of the following characteristics:

- Greater control over his work than an employee;

- The right to send a substitute;

- Runs some risk of making a loss if he does the job badly;

- Can make a profit if he works more efficiently;

- Supplies some of his own tools and equipment;

- No holiday or sick pay, and no notice period;

- Paid on invoice.

On the other hand, a typical employee is likely to provide the services personally, receive benefits such as holiday pay, take no financial risk and be subject to greater control and direction than the self-employed worker.

4.5 Intermediaries

4.5.1 Introduction

For a worker to be within IR35 there must be at least one 'relevant' intermediary between the worker and the client. Commonly this is a company or partnership, but it could be an individual. The legislation lays down specific tests for each.

4.5.2 Company

A company is a relevant intermediary for the purposes of the legislation if either or both of the following applies:

- The worker has an interest in more than 5 per cent of the company (the 'material interest' test). In deciding whether he has more than 5 per cent it is also necessary to look at amounts held by his associates, such as family members and business partners. Both 'material interest' and 'associate' are discussed in more detail below; or

- A payment or benefit which is not chargeable under Schedule E is received or receivable by the worker from the intermediary, and this payment or benefit 'can reasonably be taken to represent remuneration for services provided by the worker to the client' (Sch 12, para 3 FA 2000).

It is enough for either of the tests to be satisfied. So a composite company made up of 100 workers, each with a 1 per cent shareholding, will fall outside the material interest test because each individual's shareholding is less than 5 per cent. But the payments from the client to the company have to reach the workers, and it is probable that this will be in a form which 'can reasonably be taken to represent remuneration', and if so, the individuals will be within IR35.

A number of 'IR35 avoidance schemes' have been marketed on the basis that they provide money to the worker in a form which cannot 'reasonably be taken to represent remuneration'. However, the phrase is so widely drawn that it is likely to allow most, if not all, such arrangements to be successfully challenged, see **9.15**.

Associated companies

Companies are exempt from IR35 if the 'client' is an associated company. This is to prevent the rules applying where, for example, the owner/director of the holding company provides services to an underlying subsidiary, for which he received no specific remuneration. However, the subsidiary pays a dividend to the holding company and thence to the managing director.

Without this exemption, the holding company could be a relevant intermediary because:

• The director is a majority shareholder, and thus within the material interest test;

• He supplies personal services to another company (the subsidiary); and

• He receives a 'payment or other benefit not chargeable to tax under Schedule E' which could 'reasonably be taken to be remuneration' for the services provided to the subsidiaries, namely the dividend (Sch 12, para 2(b)(i) FA 2000).

However, he has not provided any services to a third-party client, and thus should not be within the rules. Example 4A sets out a structure which would be affected by the legislation, failing this exemption.

Example 4A

John is the major shareholder of a small plc., Hips and Haws (H&H). H&H is a holding company with two trading subsidiaries, Band Ltd (B) and Count Ltd (C). B manufactures musical instruments, and C sells them. The structure of the group is as follows:

Hips & Haws (holding co)

Band Ltd		Count Ltd
(Trading co)		(Trading co)

John is employed by H&H and his services are supplied to B Ltd and C Ltd by H&H. A management charge is made to the subsidiaries to cover the cost of his services. B and C pay their annual profits to H&H as dividends. In turn, H&H pays dividends to its shareholder. Without the exemption in para3(1), H&H would be an intermediary within IR35, and John would be subject to a deemed salary calculation. But John has supplied no third-party services; indeed the company's activities are manufacturing and selling, rather than providing personal services. It is thus appropriate that he should be removed from the scope of Schedule 12.

However, the group company exemption only applies if the both the 'intermediary' (H in Example 4A), and the 'client' (B or C) are under the control of the worker or the worker and another person (Sch 12, para 3(2) FA 2000). This prevents the setting up of 'captive composites' where the client outsources a department, gives the former employees shares in a company of which it is the majority shareholder, and pays them in dividends.

However, this restriction also means that the group exemption is not effective where the worker (together with another person) is not a majority shareholder in the holding company. Thus a director of H, with 10 per cent of the shares, who supplied services to B and C, could potentially be caught by the PSC rules.

However, it is understood that the Revenue do not intend the rules to operate in this scenario, and it is to be hoped that guidance will be given to that effect. The technical defence, if attacked, would be that the dividend paid from the holding company could not 'reasonably be regarded as remuneration' for the services provided by the director to the subsidiary, and was instead a commercial return on his investment in the business.

Material interest

Put simply, a person has a material interest in a company if he and his associates have any of the following:

(a) Control over more than 5 per cent of the share capital;

(b) Rights to receive more than 5 per cent of the dividends; or

(c) Rights to receive more than 5 per cent of the assets on a winding up.

The full definition (Sch 12, para 3 FA 2000) is extremely detailed, in order to counter avoidance devices such as indirect holdings and the use of rights or entitlements. It states that a material interest is:

(a) Beneficial ownership of, or the ability to control, directly or through the medium of other companies or by any other indirect means, more than 5 per cent of the ordinary share capital of the company; or

(b) Possession of, or entitlement to acquire, rights entitling the holder to receive more than 5 per cent of any distributions that may be made by the company; or

(c) Where the company is a close company, possession of, or entitlement to acquire, rights that would in the event of the winding up of the company, or in any other circumstances, entitle the holder to receive more than 5 per cent of the assets that would then be available for distribution among the participators. For the definition of participator, see **3.7.2.**

In the context of a personal services company, the material interest test is met if:

• The worker, either alone or with associates, has a material interest in the intermediary; or

• An associate of the worker, either with or without other associates, has a material interest in the intermediary.

Associates

An individual's associates include any of the following (Sch 12, para 19 FA 2000):

• Relatives. These are the person's husband, wife, parent or remoter forbear, child or remoter issue, brother or sister. A man and a woman living together as husband and wife are treated as if they were married (Sch 12, para 21(4) FA 2000), and thus will count as 'husband' or 'wife' for these purposes. Revenue booklet IR175 simply says that 'family includes unmarried partners' but in fact unmarried partners of the same sex are not 'treated as if they were married.' A Conservative party amendment to extend this part of the legislation to gay couples was rejected by the House of Commons in June 2000;

• Business partners of the individual;

• The trustees of any trust settled by the individual, and also the trustees of any trust settled by relatives, whether or not they are still alive;

• The trustees of a trust which holds shares in the personal service company, if the individual has an interest in the trust. However there is an exemption for shares held in an employee benefit trust (EBT). EBTs hold shares in the company for the benefit of employees, for instance as part of an employee share option scheme (Sch 8, para 7(5) ICTA 1988). The exemption exists because an EBT may well hold more than 5 per cent of the company's shares, and thus all employees with an interest in the EBT would automatically and unfairly fall within the PSC rules. However the exemption does not apply to an individual who has held, at any time on or after 14 March 1989, a material interest in the company without taking account of the EBT shares, see Sch 12, para 19(4) FA 2000.

• The personal representatives of a deceased person, if the service company's shares are held in his estate and the individual is a beneficiary.

4.5.3 Partnerships

The inclusion of partnerships in the new rules was surprising, since, unlike a company, a partnership has no separate legal identity under UK law. The Revenue had previously argued that they could look through the partnership and recategorise an individual partner if he did not pass the status tests in respect of an engagement.

This is still seems to be the view of some parts of the Revenue, see for example their *Television Industry Guidance Notes in respect of freelancers*, which says:

> 'In English Law, a Partnership does not exist as a separate legal entity. Therefore if you are engaging a partner as opposed to an employee of the Partnership any fee paid should be dealt with in accordance with the (rules for employees).'

However it is understood that the Revenue have in fact received legal advice which indicates that contracts between the client and the partnership, rather than between the client and the individual partner, cannot be looked through in this way.

So a contract with a partnership would be effective in protecting a partner from recategorisation as Schedule E, even though the nature of his engagement clearly failed the status tests. Partnerships therefore had to be brought within the personal services legislation, if only to prevent them replacing companies as the new tax-efficient IR35 avoidance vehicle.

However, had the full PSC rules been applied to all partnerships providing personal services, the consequences for legitimate businesses would have been extreme. Fortunately, the Revenue accepted that this was unnecessary, and have limited the scope of the new rules. FAQ General 6 stated that the Revenue:

> 'Do not want the new rules to place unnecessary burdens on partnerships . . . what they want to do is to distinguish between partnerships which can be

used by a worker to control the form in which income from relevant engagements is passed on to him or her, and partnerships which are legitimate businesses but may occasionally second a partner to work for a client in circumstances which might otherwise be caught by our legislation.'

As a result, most genuine profit-sharing partnerships are excluded from IR35. The ways in which partnerships can fall outside the rules, and what happens if they are caught, are discussed in Chapter 14.

It is worth noting that partnerships can be an intermediary, not only in respect of the partners, but also as regards employees of the partnership, see **14.4.**

4.5.4 Individuals

The legislation covers a third category of intermediary, the individual. Like partnerships, individuals have been included largely for anti-avoidance reasons. The purpose is to prevent a wife, say, contracting with a client company to provide her husband's IT services, and so avoiding the new rules. It is doubtful that such stratagems would in any event have been successful, even without the inclusion of individual intermediaries in the personal services legislation.

If a worker's services are supplied via an individual, then that person is a relevant intermediary if the worker receives a payment or benefits, other than under Sch E, which can 'reasonably be taken to represent remuneration for services provided' (Sch 12, para 5 FA 2000). The rules are also operative where the payment or benefits are receivable rather than actually received.

4.5.5 More than one intermediary

It is possible for there to be more than one intermediary between the client and the worker – for example, a client might contract with a composite company which was in turn owned by an number of service companies. Alternatively, and more commonly, an agency could be interposed between the service company and the client.

Where there is more than one intermediary, it is necessary to establish whether they are all 'relevant' and thus within the scope of the legislation. To be 'relevant', an intermediary must, among other tests, have made a payment *directly* to the worker. Agencies generally pay the service companies and not the workers, and will rarely be relevant intermediaries, see FAQ General 48 and **21.2.**

Where multiple intermediaries do fall within the PSC rules, then:

(a) The legislation applies separately to each of them (Sch 12, para 14(3) FA 2000);

(b) Where an amount is received by one intermediary and passed to a second, it is only included once in the deemed Schedule E calculation (Sch 12, para 15 FA 2000);

(c) Each intermediary is jointly and severally liable for the worker's PAYE and NIC deductions in relation to engagements for which they were intermediaries (Sch 12, para 16 FA 2000). Concern has been expressed that this places an impossible burden on some intermediaries in the chain, as they may not know whether or to what extent the tax and NICs have been paid. However, since the legislation only applies to relevant intermediaries, they are in practice likely to be connected to each other and thus to know the true position. This therefore appears to be a problem which is more apparent than real.

4.6 Worker receives payment or benefit not within Schedule E

4.6.1 Interpretation

The worker is within the personal services legislation if:

(a) A contract of employment would have existed between the worker and the client if there had been no intermediary; and

(b) The intermediary is 'relevant' within the meaning of the legislation; and

(c) The worker receives from the intermediary a payment or benefit not chargeable to tax under Schedule E; or

(d) He has rights *entitling* him to receive from the intermediary a payment or other benefit that is not chargeable under Schedule E (Sch 12, para 2(b) FA 2000).

Thus if the individual is, for example, paid in dividends, which are not chargeable under Schedule E, he is caught by (c) above; if he has the right to receive a dividend which has not been exercised, he is caught by (d).

The legislation extends the scope of the rule in order to minimise the chances of avoidance. The worker is still caught if:

• The payment or benefit is paid to an associate of the worker, or the associate has the rights which entitle him to the payment or benefit. This is to prevent the sums being diverted, say, to a spouse or family member. Associates are defined at **4.5.2**;

- The payment is made indirectly by the intermediary, or the worker has a right to receive some indirect form of payment;

- 'Rights to receive a payment or benefit' includes an entitlement which is triggered 'in any circumstances'. Thus if, for instance, the worker could only access the money if the company was wound up, he would still be caught.

It has been argued that an employee with a 1 per cent shareholding, who is paid a normal salary under Schedule E, will be within the PSC rules because he has an entitlement to a dividend, i.e. a payment or benefit not within Schedule E. However this is not the case. To be within the personal services rules the payment or benefit must 'reasonably be taken to be remuneration' for services provided to the client (Sch 12, para 3(1)(b)(ii)). This will not be the position with 'normal' employees.

4.6.2 De minimis exemption

There is an exemption from the personal services tax rules where the relevant engagement forms a small part of a larger Schedule D business, see ESC A37 and paragraph 1226 of the Revenue's Schedule E Manual. These exemptions cover both self-employed individuals and partners and are set out in full at **14.3**.

For National Insurance purposes there is a statutory exemption for partners who receive small amounts of employment income, on a similar basis as for tax, see **14.3.4** (SI 1979 No 591 Reg 19B).

4.7 Sole traders

An individual who does not operate via a company or partnership, but provides personal services as a sole trader, is not within IR35. Instead he is subject to the normal employment/self-employment tests set out above and in Chapter 6.

If he fails these tests, so that he is categorised as an employee of the client rather than as a self-employed consultant, he will be within Schedule E. The client is liable for tax and NIC in respect of past payments, and may have difficulty recovering this from the individual. In other words the burden is on the client, rather than on the worker.

As a result, clients may increasingly require consultants to be engaged via their own service companies rather than as individuals. This gives the client protection from assessments to PAYE and NIC if the individual's status has been misjudged. The personal service rules may thus have the ironic consequence of increasing the number of service companies rather than reducing them.

IR35 could also cause an increased Revenue focus on status tests and the Schedule D/E divide, and this may impact on sole traders as well as on those with service companies and partnerships.

4.8 National Insurance

4.8.1 Legislation

Section 75 of the Welfare Reform and Pensions Act 1999 contains the primary National Insurance legislation. The detailed regulations (SI 2000 No 727) are similar to the tax legislation, but there are divergences caused by the different structures of the tax and NICs systems. Two particular points fundamental to the operation of the NICs regulations on personal services are the annual earnings period and the aggregation of earnings rules.

4.8.2 Annual earnings period

For most employees, NIC is due as earnings are received, so that a monthly-paid employee has a monthly earnings period. The upper earnings limit is spread over these monthly payments, see Example 4B.

Example 4B

Desirée earns £4,000 a month and is employed as a dancer. She is not within the personal services regime. Her employee NICs are calculated as follows for the fiscal year 2000/01:

- The employee's earnings threshold ('EET') at which employee NICs begin to be paid, is £3,952 or £329 per month;

- The upper earnings limit ('UEL'), above which no employee NICs are payable, is £27,820 or £2,318 per month;

- Her monthly earnings subject to employee NICs are thus £1,989, being the difference between the lower and upper monthly limits;

- Each month she pays NICs of £199 (1,989 × 10%);

- The balance of her monthly salary, £2,011, is not subject to employee NICs.

However, different rules apply for directors, who have an annual earnings period. As a result, earnings up to the EET are received free of NICs; they then pay NIC as earnings are received, until they reach the UEL.

The NIC regulations for personal services apply an annual earnings period to all those within the personal services regime, 'whether or not the worker is a director of the company for the year' (SI 2000 No 727 Reg 6). It thus applies not only to service company directors, but to employees within the personal services rules. More controversially, it embraces partners to the extent that they have relevant engagements. Example 4C shows the effects.

Example 4C

In April 2001 Desirée sets up a personal service company and charges the theatre where she dances £5,000 a month. She pays herself a salary of £4,000. Her employee NICs position for 2001/02 is as follows, assuming the same rates and limits as in 2000/01:

1. In the first month she pays employee NICs on only £48 (4,000–3,952);

2. For the next five months she pays NICs on all her earnings at 10 per cent, at a cost of £400 per month;

3. In the seventh month £3,820 is subject to NICs, at a cost of £382, as she reaches the UEL;

4. For the remaining five months, no employee NICs are due;

5. There is no change to the payment of employer's NICs.

4.8.3 Aggregation of earnings

The annual earnings period does not apply only to the attributable earnings calculation. Other earnings 'paid to the worker by the intermediary in the year concerned to or for the benefit of the worker in respect of employed earner's employment' must be aggregated with the result of the attributable earnings calculation, and the total assessed on the basis of an annual earnings period (SI 2000 No 727 Reg 8(2)).

However the aggregation requirement only applies to earnings from the intermediary which relate to an employment. There is thus no requirement to aggregate the result of the deemed calculation with a partner's earnings from non-relevant engagements.

4.8.4 Interpreting the scope of the Act

A point of statutory construction has been raised in respect of the heading for s75 in the Welfare Reform and Pensions Act. The section is headed 'earnings of *workers* supplied by service companies'. This could be interpreted as suggesting that if a service company was not supplying 'workers' but merely 'services' it might fall outside the scope of the NIC rules.

The question of whether headings have any legal status, since they are not part of the legislation voted upon by Parliament, was covered by Sir Rupert Cross in his classic work '*Statutory Interpretation*'. In his view, headings have parliamentary authority because they are included in the Bill and form part of the text entered on the Parliamentary roll. They are thus 'appropriately consulted to resolve an ambiguity in the text'.

He quotes in his support the ancient case of *Brett v Brett* [1826] 3 Add 210, during which Sir John Nicholl said that:

> 'To arrive at the true meaning of any particular phrase in a statute, that particular phrase is not to be viewed, detached from its context in statute: it is to be viewed in connection with its whole context – meaning by this as well the title and preamble as . . . the enacting part of the statute.'

This approach was cited with approval in the more recent cases of *AG v Prince Ernest Augustus of Hanover* [1957] 1 All ER 49, and again in *DPP v Schildcamp* [1971] AC 1 23. This second case is of particular importance because of the House of Lords' conclusion that the scope of s332 Companies Act 1948 should be restricted by reference to its heading.

It would thus be possible to argue that the scope of the National Insurance Regulations could be similarly restricted by reference to the heading in the Welfare Reform and Pensions Act, so that they do not apply where 'services' rather than 'workers' were supplied. However the Revenue would no doubt argue that this is mere sophistry, and that the meaning of the words is clear from their context within the rest of the legislation.

5 Hypothetical contracts and mutuality

5.1 Construction of the legislation

5.1.1 Tax

The personal services tax legislation applies where an individual provides personal services to a client:

> 'Under arrangements involving a third party (the intermediary) and the circumstances are such that, if the services were being provided under a contract directly between the client and the worker, the worker would be regarded for income tax purposes as an employee of his client.' (Sch 12, para 1(1) FA 2000)

The personal services legislation is thus based on a *hypothetical contract* directly between the client and the worker. It will apply if the 'circumstances are such that' the worker would be an employee of the client under this hypothetical contract. The circumstances:

> 'Include the terms on which services are provided, having regard to the terms of the contracts forming part of the arrangements under which the services are provided.' (Sch 12, para 1(4) FA 2000)

There are two important points of construction here. The first is that the actual contractual arrangements between the client and the intermediary, or between client, agent and intermediary, are simply aids which assist in constructing the hypothetical contract between the worker and the client; they do not determine the matter.

The second point, which follows from the first, is that in interpreting this hypothetical contract, it is important to look at other factors in addition to the terms of the extant contracts. Other circumstances might include:

* The number of other engagements taken on by the worker; and

* The extent of his business organisation.

This would reflect the assurances given in the House of Commons during the debates on the Welfare Reform and Pensions Bill in 1999, that these wider issues would be taken into account when the personal services legislation was drafted, see **6.7.2**.

5.1.2 National Insurance

The NICs regulations are similar to the tax legislation. They apply where a worker supplies personal services:

> 'Under arrangements involving an intermediary, and the circumstances are such that, had the arrangements taken the form of a contract between the worker and the client, the worker would be regarded for the purposes of Parts I to V of the Contributions and Benefits Act as employed in employed earner's employment by the client.' (SI 2000 No 727 Reg 6).

The 'circumstances' are then commented on as follows:

> 'Any issue whether the circumstances are such as are mentioned in paragraph 1(c) is an issue relating to contributions that is prescribed for the purposes of section 8(1)(m) of the Social Security Contributions (Transfer of Functions, etc.) Act 1999 (decision by an officer of the Board.' (SI 2000 No 727 Reg 6(4))

In plain English, this means that the Inland Revenue will decide what 'circumstances' should be taken into account, with a right of appeal to the Tax Commissioners. There is thus no danger that the 'circumstances' will be decided differently for NICs and tax.

5.1.3 Caveat

This chapter looks at how the hypothetical contract between the client and the worker might be interpreted by a court. However, as Schedule 12, FA 2000 is new legislation, and the concept of a hypothetical contract has not been tested, what follows can only be a preliminary view.

5.2 Contractual arrangements

5.2.1 Outline

Having accepted that IR35 depends on a hypothetical contract, the terms of that contract will for the most part be deduced from:

- The actual contracts between worker and client, or those between worker/ agency and agency/client; and

- Any other relevant circumstances.

Because IR35 does not depend only on the written contracts, some basic principles of contract law may be applied in a different way. What follows looks at how contracts involving questions of status are normally interpreted. It then suggests the approach which might be taken under the personal services legislation.

5.2.2 The contract is normally the starting point

When considering whether a worker is employed or self-employed, the court usually begins by looking at his contract. The National Insurance legislation makes this explicit. An individual is an employed earner if he is working under:

> 'Any contract of service or apprenticeship, whether written or oral and whether expressed or implied.' (ss2(1)(a), 122(1) SSCBA 1992)

Under general law, where there is a written contract, the parties' subsequent conduct is not admissible in construing what the contract means (*Hooper v British Railways Board* [1998] IRLR 517). This was confirmed in the status case of *Chaplin v Australian Mutual Provident Society* [1978] 18 ALR 385, where Lord Fraser said:

> 'The first principle is that, subject to one exception, where there is a written contract between the parties whose relationship is in issue, a court is confined, in determining the nature of that relationship, to a consideration of the terms, express or implied, of that contract in the light of the circumstances surrounding the making of it, and it is not entitled to consider also the manner in which the parties subsequently acted in pursuance of such a contract. The one exception to that rule is that, where the subsequent conduct of the parties can be shown to have amounted to an agreed addition to, or modification of, the original written contract, such conduct may be considered and taken into account.'

This is, however, manifestly not the case when applying the personal services legislation. Here it is necessary to look at 'the terms on which the services were provided' and not simply the written contracts. These only form 'part of the arrangements under which the services are provided'. The court is thus unlikely to confine itself 'to a consideration of the terms' which are in the written contracts between the parties.

5.2.3 Implied terms, extensions and variations

A contract can be written, oral, or implied, and, if written, is likely to contain both express and implied terms. An express term is one which the parties specifically deal with and include in the contract. An implied term is a right or obligation which is left unexpressed. In the case of the hypothetical contract postulated by Schedule 12, there will be no distinction between express or implied terms – the terms of the hypothetical contract are those 'on which the services are provided' whether or not they are contained within the written contracts.

However, in constructing this hypothetical contract, one can presume that a court would start from the written contract and may be guided to some extent by existing practice concerning the addition of implied terms or other extensions.

Implied terms

Under normal contract law, an implied term is deemed to be inserted in a contract if:

- It represents the true intention of the parties as to what the terms of the contract should be. This is sometimes known as the 'officious bystander test', following McKinnon L.J. He said that an implied term:

  'Is something so obvious that it goes without saying; so that, if the parties were making their bargain, an officious bystander were to suggest some express provision for it in their agreement, they would testily suppress him with a common, "Oh, of course"' (*Shirlaw v Southern Foundries* [1926] 2 KB 206);

- It is customary in the particular business, or the usual and well-known practice of the employer. This must be 'reasonable, certain and notorious' (*Bond v CAV Ltd* [1983] IRLR 360);

- The contract will only work properly if the clause is included. In *Roberts v Toyota (GB)* [1980] EAT 614 it was held to be an implied term of the contract that a sales manager had to have a valid driving licence.

However, while the courts are cautious about adding terms to written contracts, they need have no such constraint when considering the personal services legislation. The rules for implied terms are thus likely to be taken as only the starting point for interpreting an IR35 hypothetical contract.

Extension of contract by other documents or practices

A contract can be extended by other documents or practices, such as Handbooks or Manuals, which set out how workers should behave. This may happen either expressly, or where it is indicated by the parties' conduct. In *Market Investigations* (see **5.3.3**) the 'Interviewers' Guide' was held to be incorporated into Mrs Irving's contract. The judge said:

> 'The instructions in the "Interviewers' Guide", after having been seen by the interviewer, are incorporated into the terms of any contract which the interviewer may thereafter make with the company to participate in a particular survey.'

This was of profound importance, because it was the level of control over Mrs Irving shown by the 'Interviewer's Guide' which determined her status as an employee.

However in *Grant v South-west Trains* [1998] IRLR 188, the court held that the company's equal opportunities policy was not incorporated into the worker's employment contract, and in any event, it could not override the express terms of the written contract. In the case of a hypothetical contract, there may be no such limitation. Secondary materials which are relevant to interpreting 'the arrangements under which the services are provided' may be taken into account (Sch 12, para 1(4) FA 2000).

Variation in a contract

Any variation in a contract should normally be agreed, either expressly or tacitly, by both parties. The court is generally reluctant to *imply* a variation to a contract:

> 'It is fairly difficult, in the ordinary way, to imply a variation of contract, and it is very necessary, if one is to do so, to have very solid facts which demonstrate that it was necessarily to give business efficacy to the contract.' *Horrigan v Lewisham London Borough Council* [1978] ICR 15 EAT

This protection from the imposition of implied terms will not apply to the hypothetical contract which is being considered by the personal services legislation. The court will construct the contract from the written documents and from the behaviour of the parties.

5.2.4 Where there is ambiguity, the contract normally decides status

If the status of the worker is ambiguous, a written agreement normally decides the matter. In *Massey v Crown Life Insurance Co* [1978] ICR 590, Lord Denning held that where the relationship of the parties:

> 'Is ambiguous and is capable of being one or the other, then the parties can remove that ambiguity, by the very agreement itself which they make with one another. The agreement itself then becomes the best material from which to gather the true legal relationship between them.'

Lawton J made a similar point in the same case (the author's italics):

> 'If in all the circumstances of the case, including the terms of the agreement, it is manifest that there was an intention to change status, then in my judgment there is no reason why the parties should not be allowed to make the change. In this case, there seems to have been a genuine intention to change the status, and I find that the status was changed . . .
>
> When I heard the facts of this case recounted by counsel on behalf of the appellant, I was . . . suspicious. It seemed nothing more than a device to deceive the Inland Revenue in order to get a tax advantage. The industrial tribunal went into the facts and in the end came to the conclusion...that there had been a genuine attempt to make an agreement changing the appellant's status, and they excluded illegality. If there was no illegality, and it was a genuine arrangement, there could be only one consequence under the terms of the contract: *the appellant changed his status.*'

This is often referred to as the 'tiebreaker' – if all other factors are neutral, or the employment status of the worker is ambiguous, the intentions of the parties decide the matter.

How this would be applied in the context of the personal services legislation is unclear. It is the contract between the client and the service company which contains the tiebreaker clause. There is only a hypothetical contract between the worker and the client.

A clause in the written contract stating that both sides are operating as independent third parties *might* be imported into the hypothetical contract, but this cannot be taken for granted. Since the written contract is between an intermediary, and either the client or an agency, it would be self-evident that there was no intention to create employment, but this would not necessarily be true of a hypothetical contract directly between the worker and the client.

If, having considered all the 'circumstances' in which the services were provided, it was unclear whether the worker would have been an employee of the client under the hypothetical contract, the court would of course have to decide the matter one way or another. In so doing, it may have regard to the fact that the parties did not want to create an employment. However, it might develop a different tiebreaker test, such as looking at the wider business arrangements of the worker, or the number of his clients.

If there was uncertainty about whether or not to use the existing 'tiebreaker' test, the principles of *Pepper v Hart* [1992] 65 TC 421 might be invoked. In the IR35 debate on the Welfare Reform and Pensions Act, Mr Timms confirmed for the government that 'the same criteria will be applied in the same way as they always have been in the past' (*Hansard* 3 November 1999, Col. 429). Thus it could be argued that Parliament intended 'the intention of the parties' to continue to be the tiebreaker.

Helpfully, the Revenue also consider that the intention of the parties remains relevant in the context of the hypothetical contract, see **7.4.10**.

Agreements between the client/agency or client/service company should of course continue to include a clause stating that the parties are contracting as independent third parties, see **9.10**. However it should be recognised that the tie-breaker precedents set out in *Massey v Crown Life Insurance* and in later cases, such as *BSM (1257) Ltd v Secretary of State for Social Services* [1978] ICR 894, cannot necessarily be relied upon in the context of IR35.

5.2.5 Reality differs from written contract

In the *BSM* case, the judge held that even where there is a written contract, it can be overruled if:

> 'There are provisions inconsistent with that relationship, or that in practice the relationship was other than that stated in the contract.'

This will even more clearly be the case under the personal services legislation, where the wider 'circumstances' have to be considered when determining the content of the hypothetical contract.

Examples of cases where the courts have overruled the written contract include *Young and Woods Ltd v West* [1980] IRLR 201, where a sheet metal worker purported to change his contract to one of self-employment. The Court of Appeal held that there was no difference between his working arrangements and those of the remaining Schedule E staff, and thus held on the facts that he had remained an employee. Similarly in *Withers v Flackwell Heath Football Supporters' Club* [1981] IRLR 307 the Employment Appeals Tribunal held:

> 'That both parties put the label "self-employed" on their relationship is far from conclusive and is to be disregarded when the reality is that the label, and the fiscal consequences that flow from its use, are adopted simply for fiscal reasons.'

5.2.6 No formal contract

Where there is no formal contract, but other documents exist, the House of Lords held recently that:

'It was open to the industrial tribunal to find, as a fact, that the parties did not intend the letters to be the sole record of their agreement but intended that it should be contained partly in the letters, partly in oral exchanges at the interviews or elsewhere and partly left to evolve by conduct as time went on.' (*Carmichael and Another v National Power* [1999] 4 AER 897)

Thus, where there is no formal contract, the court may look to a number of sources for the true nature of the contractual arrangement. In the case of the IR35 hypothetical contract the legislation indicates that sources other than the written contract will be considered as a matter of course.

However in the same case it was confirmed that where both parties agree on the terms of the engagement, this will normally determine the matter:

'The evidence of a party as to what terms he understood to have been agreed is some evidence tending to show that those terms, in an objective sense, were agreed. Of course the tribunal may reject such evidence and conclude that the party misunderstood the effect of what was being said and done. But when both parties are agreed about what they understood their mutual obligations (or lack of them) to be, it is a strong thing to exclude their evidence from consideration.' (Ibid)

It is thought that the same would be true of a hypothetical contract – what the worker and the client both understand to be the substance of the arrangements between them will be very significant in determining its nature.

5.2.7 Summary

When a court considers employment status, it starts by looking at the contract between the individual and his engager. It may occasionally imply or extend the terms of the contract, or ask whether it has been subject to variation. In general, it relies on the written agreement rather than on the subsequent behaviour of the parties, unless a clear contradiction exists between the contract terms and the reality of the relationship.

When considering the IR35 hypothetical contract, less reliance is likely to be placed on the written agreements. These form only part of the 'circumstances' under which the services are delivered to the client. The courts may be more willing to imply terms, consider variations, and import external documents when constructing the hypothetical contract than when deciding a status question for an individual.

Workers within IR35 must thus have regard to the wider context in which they are delivering their services, and be aware that other elements, in addition to the written agreements, could be used to determine the hypothetical contract. Nevertheless, written contracts remain the starting point, and while they may not be determinative, remain of great significance. Chapter 9 looks at ways of amending both the written contracts and the delivery of services to clients, so that the hypothetical contract will be less likely to fall within IR35.

Having explored the methodology of the personal services legislation, the next step is to consider the nature of the hypothetical contract. For it to be a contract of employment, there must be mutuality of obligation.

5.3 Mutuality of obligation

5.3.1 Summary

Before there can be either a contract of service, or a contract for services, the parties have to accept they have obligations to each other. If they have not, there is no contract of any sort. In any dispute about employment or self-employment, the first step is to consider whether mutual obligations exist between the parties.

Mutuality of obligation can be explained by saying that in a contract of service there is a continuing obligation on the employee to work, and on the employer to provide work – or, if there is no work, at least to pay the employee. There is no such obligation in a contract for services. It has also recently been held that 'an obligation by the one party to accept and do work if offered, and an obligation on the other party to pay a retainer during such periods as work was *not* offered, would . . . be likely to suffice' *Clark v Oxfordshire Health Authority* [1997] EWCA 4792 (see **5.3.5**).

A simple example is an electrician who comes to repair a fault in a company's power supply. He does the job and leaves; there is no obligation on the company to provide continuing work or on the electrician to do it. However, an electrician who is employed by a utilities company has to turn up for work each day, and his company is obliged to pay him.

It can be the case that an individual works for a business for years without establishing mutuality of obligation. A journalist who writes a weekly column to a newspaper each week, which the editor can accept or reject, and who is only paid for what is accepted, will be working under a series of small contracts for services, as no mutuality of obligation has been established.

Most cases concerning mutuality of obligation have been employment law disputes. The point at issue has been whether the worker is employed, and so entitled to claim various employment rights. The courts have thus considered, as a first step, what constitutes sufficient mutuality of obligation for an employment to exist.

This is clearly of interest in the context of tax law in general, and personal services in particular. It is no less relevant to the hypothetical contract between the personal services worker and his client than it has been to the real contractual arrangements between workers and clients examined by the courts over the years. For the personal services worker to be within IR35, there must be a hypothetical contract of employment.

A review of past cases shows that, apart from a standard contract of employment, there are the following possibilities, each of which is discussed at **5.3** below.

(a) *No mutuality* between the engager and engaged. In this situation there can be no contract of service, so the worker cannot be an employee. They are generally viewed as self-employed, although on occasion their status has been left unclear, see **6.4.3**. The leading case here is *O'Kelly v Trusthouse Forte plc* [1983] 3 AER 456; or

(b) A *series of small contracts* between the worker and the engager, which occur whenever the worker agrees to undertake each engagement. These engagements could be contracts of employment or self-employment; or

(c) A *gradual change*, so that mutual obligations are created over time by the regular giving and taking of work. This was the court's decision in both *Airfix Footwear Ltd v Cope* [1978] ICR 1210 and *Nethermere (St Neots) Ltd v Gardiner* [1983] ICR 319; or

(d) A *global or 'umbrella' contract* of employment, under which work is given and accepted from time to time, see *Boyd Line Ltd v Pitts* [1986] ICR 244; *Hellyer Brothers Ltd v McLeod* [1986] ICR 122 and *Clark v Oxfordshire Health Authority* [1997] EWCA 4792.

The overall conclusion of these cases is that if, from one day to the next, or from one small project to the next, the worker can decide whether or not to work, and the client can decide whether or not to offer the work, there is no mutuality and the individual is not employed.

This was found to be the position in a number of the cases discussed below, despite the fact that the individuals involved had supplied services to a single client for long periods, often for years. In other cases, although a contract of employment was found to exist, it is doubtful whether the same conclusion would have been reached had the individual worker been a professional supplying services.

5.3.2 No mutuality and no employment

There is likely to be no mutuality of obligation where:

- A person is asked to perform a service but is free to decline; and

- The engager does not have to offer available work to the individual.

Where these obligations do not exist, there can be no employment contract. It 'founders on the rock of absence of mutuality', as Lord Irvine said in the recent case of *Carmichael and Another v National Power*. In *Nethermere* Stephenson L.J. summarised the position in an oft-quoted phrase: 'there must be an irreducible minimum of obligation on each side to create contract of service'. A number of status cases demonstrate this principle, including *O'Kelly v Trusthouse Forte plc* and *Specialeyes (Optical Services) Ltd.*

O'Kelly v Trusthouse Forte plc

In *O'Kelly v Trusthouse Forte plc* [1983] 3 AER 456 the court held that there was:

- No mutuality of obligation;

- No successive small contracts of employment;

- No overriding umbrella contract; and

- The workers were self-employed

The facts of the case were as follows. The Grosvenor House Hotel in London engaged casual workers on a function by function basis. However a large number of these casual staff were so-called 'regular casuals', i.e., they were engaged to such an extent that some had no other work. The question at issue was whether they were employees of the hotel.

It was found that the casuals had the following characteristics of employment:

(a) They provided their services in return for remuneration for work actually performed. They did not invest their own capital or stand to gain or lose from the commercial success of the functions organised by the banqueting department;

(b) They performed their work under the direction and control of the 'employers';

(c) When the casual workers attended at functions they were part of the 'employers'' organisation, and for the purpose of ensuring the smooth running of the business they were represented in the staff consultation process;

59

(d) When working they were carrying on the business of the 'employers';

(e) Clothing and equipment were provided by the 'employers';

(f) They were paid weekly in arrears and under deduction of income tax and social security contributions;

(g) Their work was organised on the basis of a weekly rota and they required permission to take time off from rostered duties;

(h) There was a disciplinary and grievance procedure;

(i) There was holiday pay or an incentive bonus calculated by reference to past service.

In addition to the above, a number of factors were considered by the Tribunal to be 'not inconsistent' with employment status:

(j) They were paid for work actually performed and did not receive a regular wage or retainer. It was however held that the method of calculating entitlement to remuneration is not an essential aspect of the employment relationship;

(k) Casual workers were not remunerated on the same basis as permanent employees. They did not receive sick pay, were not included in the employers' staff pension scheme and did not receive the fringe benefits accorded to established employees. It was held that employers can, however, adopt different terms and conditions for different categories of employee;

(l) There were no regular or assured working hours. It is however not a requirement of employment that there should be 'normal working hours';

(m) Casual workers were not provided with written particulars of employment. There is a statutory obligation to furnish written particulars of employment to employees.

Of greater interest were the following, which were held to be *inconsistent* with a contract of employment:

(n) The engagement was terminable without notice on either side;

(o) The casuals had the right to decide whether or not to accept work, although whether or not it would be in their interest to exercise the right to refuse work is another matter;

(p) The 'employers' had no obligation to provide any work;

(q) It was the parties' view that the casual workers were independent contractors engaged under successive contracts for services;

(r) It was the recognised custom and practice of the industry that casual workers were engaged under a contract for services.

The Industrial Tribunal decided that, despite the fact that the engagements had many of the characteristics of employment, the absence of mutuality of obligation indicated by points (o) and (p) meant that there could not be a contract of service. As a result, the workers were self-employed. They were:

'In no different position than any independent contractor who offers his services for a particular purpose or event (e.g., a jobbing gardener or a day labourer) and it was by their choice that they made their services available to a single customer.'

The Tribunal did not think that the absence of the risk element which was usually present in self-employment was a concern:

'Where the commodity offered is the simple supply of semi-skilled labour for a specific occasion, or series of occasions, it is not to be expected that there would be a financial investment or participation in the profits or losses of the business.'

The Revenue's Schedule E Manual is dismissive of this case, saying that:

'It is clear that the Court of Appeal (and Industrial Tribunal) did not find that there were no separate contracts of employment because of any lack of mutuality of obligation but, rather, because the individuals were in business on their own account.' (SE 667)

However, this does not appear to be the case, but rather the reverse – it was the lack of mutuality which made the Tribunal decide that the individuals could not be employees, and therefore must be self-employed. At page 446 of the judgement, the decision of the Tribunal is as follows:

'It is freely recognised that the relationship of the (casuals) to the employers had many of the characteristics of a contract of service. In our view the one important ingredient which was missing was mutuality of obligation.

We are, of course, aware that lack of mutuality of obligation is not, in itself, a decisive factor and that outworkers can, in appropriate circumstances, be employees working under a contract of employment, even though there is no obligation to provide work or perform it: see *Airfix Footwear Ltd v Cope* [1978] ICR 1210 and *Nethermere (St Neots) Ltd v Gardiner* [1983] ICR 319. Nevertheless, this was a factor on which we placed very considerable weight in making our assessment.'

In the new Employment Status Manual the Revenue's position appears to have changed. They accept that 'in considering whether there was a continuous

61

contract, it was found that there was no mutuality of obligation and hence no umbrella contract' (ESM 1074). However they then seek to distinguish between the overall umbrella contract (see **5.3.5**) and the individual contracts which existed when the waiters worked for the hotel. In so doing they surprisingly seek to follow the decision of the EAT, which held that they were contracts of service, rather than that of the Court of Appeal, which overruled the EAT and concluded that they were in business on their own account in respect of the individual engagements as well as for the overall 'global' contract.

In a later case, *Four Seasons (Inn on the Park) Ltd v Hamarat* [1985] EAT 369, a 'regular casual' waiter was held to be employed. The case was distinguished from *O'Kelly*, because there was mutuality of obligation. Waite J. said in his summing up:

> 'The company treated themselves as being obliged to engage Mr Hamarat as a wine waiter whenever there was work for him to do, and Mr Hamarat treated himself as obliged to attend whenever he was asked to do so.'

These cases are important because the existence of an employment contract turned on whether there was mutuality between the parties. In *O'Kelly*, even though there was a regular supply of work between engager and engaged, and numerous factors pointing towards employment, there was still no mutuality of obligation and the workers were held to be self-employed.

The same decision must be possible under the hypothetical contract postulated by IR35. This turns on whether the worker would have been an employee had there been no intermediary. In *O'Kelly* there was no intermediary, and the lack of mutuality was decisive in the court's finding that there was no employment. Mutuality must therefore be a factor in establishing employment status under IR35 as it is in normal status disputes.

Specialeyes (Optical Services) Ltd

The case of *Specialeyes* (unreported, see *Taxation* 4 July 1991) also centres on mutuality. In 1989 the government introduced charges for eye tests, and in response to this change, Specialeyes engaged opticians to carry out sight-testing in its branches. As well as these 'locums', the company also employed its own opticians. Specialeyes treated the locum opticians as self-employed, and the Revenue challenged this.

The Special Commissioners found as follows:

(a) Specialeyes was not obliged to offer any of the opticians work, and the opticians were free to refuse engagements offered without penalty. They could also stipulate their own hours of availability, even though, in practice, many worked up to six days a week. There was thus no mutuality of obligation;

(b) The locum opticians took out their own insurance cover against malpractice claims, whereas Specialeyes paid for the insurance of its employee opticians;

(c) The opticians were paid by a fixed fee for each test performed, and submitted a monthly invoice, whereas the employee opticians received a salary, sick and holiday pay, medical insurance and a company car;

(d) Although Specialeyes provided all major items of non-portable equipment, the opticians supplied their own retinoscopes and ophthalmoscopes;

(e) The company had very little control over the opticians' professional work;

(f) The opticians attended the branches only to perform sight tests and carried out no other duties;

(g) Although the company could not function without the opticians, this did not mean that the opticians were 'part and parcel' of Specialeyes' organisation;

(h) Some of the opticians had their own practices elsewhere.

The Commissioners held that:

- There was there no mutuality of obligation;
- There was no overriding contract of employment;
- There was not a succession of small Schedule E contracts;
- Instead there was a series of separate contracts for services with the locum opticians, who were thus self-employed.

5.3.3 Series of small contracts of employment

In *O'Kelly* and *Specialeyes* the court considered whether the workers were employed, either under a series of small contracts, or under one general umbrella contract, and decided that they were employed under neither. However, in *Market Investigations Ltd v The Minister of Social Security* [1968] 2 QB 173 the decision went the other way.

This case concerned a part-time interviewer for a market research company. The court held that despite there being no overall mutuality of obligation, a series of separate employment contracts were created when the interviewer, Mrs Irving, accepted the engagements. This was despite the fact that:

(a) She undertook a number of short engagements over a period of time;

(b) She was free to accept or reject the work offered;

(c) She could work as and when she chose and did not necessarily have to complete seven hours' work during one day, although the work had to be completed by a specified date;

(d) There was no sick pay, holidays or overtime;

(e) She was free to work as an interviewer for other companies, although she didn't in fact do so.

The reasons given for the court's decision were that:

(f) She was subject to substantial control as to the manner and content of her work, although the court did hold that she did 'within the limits of her Instructions, deploy a skill and personality';

(g) She could not send a substitute without the prior permission of the company;

(h) She was paid on a daily basis plus a meal allowance, but could neither increase this amount by her own efforts, nor make a loss;

(i) She did not provide her own tools or equipment.

The decisive factor was the high level of detailed control to which she was subject once she agreed to do the work, so that the court held that she was not in business on her own account, and must be an employee.

In the case of a personal service worker who is engaged from time to time by a client to carry out intermittent work, it might be possible to argue:

• As in *O'Kelly* and *Specialeyes*, that there was no mutuality of obligation; and

• His position could be distinguished from *Market Investigations* because he has more control.

5.3.4 Gradual change to the relationship to create mutuality

There is case law to suggest that that a lack of mutuality can evolve over time into a contract of service as a result of a continuing relationship between the parties. The two leading cases are *Nethermere (St Neots) Ltd v Gardiner* [1983] ICR 319 and *Airfix Footwear Ltd v Cope* [1978] ICR 1210.

Airfix Footwear Ltd v Cope

In *Airfix Footwear Ltd v Cope* [1978] ICR 1210 Mrs Cope, an outworker, was provided with shoes to assemble at home. There was no obligation on Airfix to provide the work, nor on the worker to do it. The court however held that over time the relationship between the parties had hardened into one where mutual obligations existed. The judgement reads:

> 'Having considered all the facts, including the fact that for seven years, gener-ally five days a week, this company had delivered 12 dozen pairs of heels each day to the applicant for her to work on, except when lesser quantities were available, they found that there had by conduct been established a continu-ing relationship, a continuing contract of employment.'

The decision that this continuing relationship was a contract of service, rather than one for services, was however finely balanced. The Tribunal held that:

> 'The terms of the relationship . . . were as consistent with that of master and servant as with employer and independent contractor.'

Furthermore the decision might have gone the other way if Mrs Cope had been a skilled professional (the author's italics):

> 'If she was not an employee she must have been an independent contractor . . . In any event, *unlike a highly skilled and pre-qualified technical person* she had no skill to offer in the open market. Such skill as she learned was derived entirely from her experience of working with the appellants. In short, she was not a person in business on her own account.'

Nethermere (St Neots) Ltd v Gardiner

In the case of *Nethermere (St Neots) Ltd v Gardiner* [1983] ICR 319 the Appeal Tribunal found, by a 2:1 majority, that they had sufficient evidence to suggest that the *Nethermere* position was similar to *Airfix*. In other words, the original lack of mutuality had given rise to a continuing contract of service, and that:

> 'There was no reason why well-founded expectations of continuing home-work should not be hardened or refined into enforceable contracts by regular giving and taking of work over periods of a year or more.'

However, this decision was reached with some difficulty. One judge dissented, holding that the lack of mutuality meant that there was no binding contract. Stephenson L.J. found that 'on the evidence there was just enough material to make a contract of service a reasonably possible inference in favour of the applicants', while Dillon L.J. concluded, with considerable ambivalence:

> 'If it is permissible on the evidence to find that . . . a contract had been estab-lished between each applicant and the company, I see no necessity to con-clude that that contract must have been a contract for services and not a contract of service.'

Summary

Thus, where there is no initial mutuality, regular working for one engager can 'harden' into an employment relationship. However:

(a) *Airfix Footwear* draws a distinction between labourers and skilled workers, and suggested that the same implied contract of employment might not apply to the latter;

(b) *Nethermere* was borderline, and cannot be regarded as a strong authority;

(c) In the subsequent case of *Hellyer Bros v McLeod* (see **5.3.5**) it was submitted, and appears to have been accepted by the judge, that:

> 'The process of inferential enquiry approved in *Airfix* . . . and the *Nethermere* case – by an examination in the course of dealing for the purposes of deducing whether there was a contractual relationship between the two sides and (if so) what its terms were – is necessarily precluded in a case like the present where the parties have stated in meticulous detail in a series of contracts precisely what the terms of their relationships are.'

In other words, even if there is a course of dealing over time which might be interpreted as giving rise to an employment, this can normally be contradicted by a specific provision in the agreement between the parties.

In the case of a hypothetical contract envisaged by Schedule 12, FA 2000, however, the protection from 'inferential enquiry' given by such specific clauses is less certain. While it must be helpful to describe 'in meticulous detail' the relationship between the parties, and these details may be implied into the hypothetical contract, they may not be determinative, see **5.2** above.

Nevertheless, it would be difficult to use *Airfix* or *Nethermere* as a basis for saying that a contractor who works regularly for one engager has thereby created an employment relationship by 'the regular giving and taking of work'. The inclusion of specific terms in client contracts may also help protect the position.

5.3.5 Overriding umbrella contract

It is also possible that there can be an overriding or 'global' contract of employment. The leading cases on this issue do not consider whether an employment contract exists when the individual *actually* works for the client, but look at whether there is an umbrella contract of employment under which work can be given and accepted, which subsists even when the individual is not working. These cases are thus of less direct relevance to IR35, but as they tend to be referred to by the Revenue when mutuality is discussed, they are included here for completeness.

The two leading cases on global contracts were heard almost simultaneously, *Boyd Line Ltd v Pitts* [1986] ICR 244 and *Hellyer Brothers Ltd v McLeod* [1986] ICR 122, and they were followed by the more recent case of *Clark v Oxfordshire Health Authority* [1997] EWCA 4792.

In *Boyd Line* a trawlerman was engaged on a voyage-by-voyage basis; between voyages he was not paid by his employers and drew unemployment benefit. However it was held that there was 'a global contract covering the whole period of (his) employment' including the periods for which he was not in work.

In *Hellyer*, a very similar case heard a few days earlier, the court found the opposite: there was no overall global contract between the trawlermen and the employers. Once the voyage was over the men were free to go, and 'the employers ... were never under the least obligation in law to provide work for anybody.'

The difference between the two cases is very fine: indeed the judge summing up the later *Boyd Line* case said, with reference to the decision of the lower court:

> 'We feel it probable ... that we would have decided the matter differently from the Industrial Tribunal ... (but) there was in our judgement evidence on which they *could* have found as they did, that there was a global or umbrella contract.'

In short, of the two leading cases on the umbrella concept, one decided that there was no such contract, while the judges in the other suggested that they would have come to a similar decision (i.e., there was no global contract) had they been considering the issue as the court of first instance. But because of the rules governing appeals, see **7.8.3**, there were insufficient grounds to reverse the earlier decision of the Industrial Tribunal.

In the more recent case of *Clark v Oxfordshire Health Authority* [1997] EWCA 4792, the court looked in detail at whether a global contract existed. Mrs Clark was a 'bank nurse' and worked for the Health Authority from time to time, under a contract which provided many elements which suggested a continuing contract of employment. These included:

- Grievance and disciplinary procedures;

- Membership of the NHS superannuation scheme;

- A rate of pay which was described as 'on the scale of £10,700 and rising by annual increments to £12,390'; and

- The Conditions of Service for nurses known as the 'Whitney Council Conditions.'

Nevertheless the Court of Appeal held that there was no global contract of employment and made the following points:

(a) The Authority was at no relevant time under any obligation to offer the applicant work, nor was she under any obligation to accept it;

(b) The mutual obligations required to found a global contract of employment need not necessarily and in every case consist of obligations to provide and perform work;

(c) An obligation by the one party to accept and do work if offered, and an obligation on the other party to pay a retainer during such periods as work was *not* offered, would . . . be likely to suffice;

(d) However . . . *some* mutuality of obligation is required to found a global contract of employment. in the present case (the judge could) find no such mutuality subsisting during the periods when the applicant was not occupied in a 'single engagement'.

The question of whether Mrs Clark was an employee when she was actually carrying out nursing services for the Health Authority was remitted back to the Industrial Tribunal for consideration, and the results of that case are unreported.

Thus, from a personal services perspective, the individual engagement with the client *may* be a separate contract of service, along the liens of *Market Investigations*, see **5.3.3** above, but for there to be a 'global' contract, there needs to be clear evidence that mutuality of obligation exists in the gaps between the specific engagements.

5.3.6 Case law conclusion

The above review of case law leads to the following conclusions:

(a) A number cases, such as *O'Kelly* and *Hamarat,* demonstrate that mutuality of obligation has to exist before there can be a contract of service;

(b) Where a pattern of casual or sporadic work exists over a period, there may be a contract of service if there is also extensive control, as in *Market*

Investigations. But this level of control would be unusual where the worker was a professional;

(c) Although the concept that an absence of mutuality can 'harden' into an employment contract was accepted in *Airfix,* the court indicated they would have held that the workers to be self-employed had they been skilled professionals;

(d) Although *Nethermere* similarly came to the view that mutuality of obligation could develop over time, the Court of Appeal did not sound very convinced;

(e) Although the concept of a 'global contract' was narrowly accepted in *Boyd Line,* it was rejected in *Hellyer* and *Clark.*

Clearly there are occasions when, despite an initial lack of mutuality, a contract of employment can exist, but a detailed review of the cases suggests that this is actually more unusual, and harder to achieve, than might be thought from the Revenue Manual.

5.3.7 Revenue view of mutuality

The discussion of mutuality in the Revenue Manual begins as follows:

> 'The concept of "mutuality of obligation" is rarely of practical use when considering status for Income Tax purposes and it can easily confuse the issue. Do not consider it unless the engager or worker raises the subject.' (SE 663, retained in expanded form at ESM 0514)

The Revenue's view is summarised as follows:

> 'We ... follow *Airfix* and *Nethermere* which clearly demonstrate that short-term engagements can be under separate contracts of employment or separate contracts for services. As an alternative an umbrella contract of employment may exist. It all depends on the particular facts.'

In fact, *Airfix* and *Nethermere* did not find that there were a series of separate contracts – Dillon L.J. in the latter case said expressly:

> 'I find it wholly unrealistic to suppose that the van driver made a daily contract on behalf of the company with an outworker each time he agreed with the outworker the number of garments he was going to leave.'

Essentially, however, the Revenue are stating that lack of mutuality does not usually prevent an employment coming into existence, as there will normally either be a series of separate contracts or one overall umbrella contract.

However, case law suggests that a person may work regularly for another in engagements which have many of the characteristics of a contract of service, but that lack of mutuality can prevent the relationship being an employment.

5.3.8 Application to personal services workers

The key question for the personal service worker is whether, under the hypothetical contract with his client, the client has an obligation to offer him work, and he is obliged to accept the work if offered.

In seeking to answer this question it must be recognised that this is new ground. There is no case law on hypothetical contracts of employment, and the view of the courts can only be surmised. But the nature of contract work suggests that the hypothetical contract may sometimes lack 'the necessary elements of continuity and care' which have been held to be characteristic of the mutuality in a contract of service (*Wickens v Champion Employment* [1984] ICR 365).

Clearly, there can be mutuality of obligation between client and contract worker. For example, if a service company contracts to supply an individual for a three year period to install a computer system, mutuality probably does exist. But it is not always a foregone conclusion. Consider the following:

*   Where a PSC worker is supplied via an agency to carry out a short-term assignment for the client, is there any mutuality of obligation between the worker and the client? Would he not be closer to *O'Kelly* than to *Hamarat*?

*   Even where a worker does regular work for the client, as in *Nethermere* or *Airfix*, would the hypothetical contract be one of employment if the intermediary did not exist? In the case of a professional supplying services, it has at least to be doubtful;

*   Where he works regularly, but intermittently, for one engager, can he distinguish himself from Mrs Irving in *Market Investigations* on the basis of control?

*   Where the written contracts state that there is no mutuality between the parties, this is not determinative as it might be in a normal status case, see *Hellyer* **5.3.5** above. But it may be persuasive.

Where there is insufficient mutuality for a contract of employment to exist, the worker cannot be within the personal services rules. In other words, if he crosses the hurdle of mutuality, the other status tests do not have to be considered.

However, trying to escape IR35 by arguing a lack of mutuality will be strongly contested by the Revenue. Those seeking to stay outside IR35 are recommended to consider also the status tests. If they rely solely on mutuality, they can expect to defend their position in the courts.

5.4 Contracts with clients

Where a service company contracts directly with the client, the key question is the nature of the hypothetical contract between the worker and the client. Establishing whether this hypothetical contract is of service, or for services, and thus whether it falls inside or outside IR35 involves:

- Looking at all the 'circumstances', including but not limited to the written contract terms, see **5.1.1** above. In particular, the court may import other materials and patterns of behaviour in order to construct the hypothetical contract;

- Considering whether there is mutuality of obligation between the worker and the client, see **5.3** above; and if so,

- Reviewing the status tests, see Chapter 6.

Case law examples of workers who have succeeded in being classified as Schedule D because they have established a lack of mutuality of obligation are given in Chapter 8, along with other borderline cases.

5.5 Contracts with agencies

5.5.1 Both contracts are included

Many service companies use agencies. Commonly the service company contracts with the agency, and the agency contracts with the end-user. When constructing the hypothetical contract between client and worker, legislation requires that 'the terms of the *contracts* forming part of the arrangements' be considered. This suggests that the contracts between the service company and the agency, and that between the agency and the client, should both be taken into account in order to decide whether the engagement is caught by IR35.

5.5.2 Different terms in agency/client and service company/agency contracts

If the two contracts contain different terms, it will be more difficult to construct the hypothetical contract on which the personal services legislation depends. A judge could be expected to try and discover what had actually occurred, and would be likely to ignore written clauses which were unsupported by behaviour. The Revenue have confirmed that they will ask to see both contracts, see FAQ General 30.

It is thus inadvisable for a service company to enter into a contract with an agency if the contract with the end-user is on different terms. For example, if the clause between the agency and the service company allows the use of a substitute, while that between the client and the agency does not, the court would seek to discover whether this clause would have been contained within the hypothetical contract with the client. If the client had no knowledge of the clause, it would be difficult to see how it could be a term of the contract.

5.6 Agency as client?

There is one further point of interpretation which is of interest when an agency is interposed between the intermediary and the end-user. In order to come within the personal services rules the worker must:

> 'Personally perform, or (be) under an obligation personally to perform, services for the purposes of a business carried on by another person ('the client') . . . and the circumstances are such that, if the services were provided under a contract directly between the client and the worker, the worker would be regarded for income tax purposes as an employee of the client.' (Sch 12, para 1 FA 2000; SI 2000 No 727 Reg 6)

The question is whether the agency could be 'the client' in this paragraph? The individual is certainly providing services for purposes of the agency's business, since the latter derives its profits from supplying contractor companies' services to third parties.

If the worker *is* providing services for the agency's business, would he be an employee of the agency if the intermediary did not exist? In general, this is unlikely because:

(a) In most cases there will be insufficient mutuality of obligation for the worker to be an employee of the agency, see *Wickens v Champion Employment* [1984] ICR 365; *Ironmonger v Movefield Ltd* [1988] IRLR 461 and *Construction Industry Training Board v Labour Force Ltd* [1970] 3 AER 220;

(b) Although in *McMeechan v Secretary of State for Employment* [1997] IRLR 353, the Court of Appeal held that a worker was employed by the agency while he carried out an engagement for one of the agency's clients, this decision was based on specific contractual terms. They included a clause which said: 'you are under no obligation to accept any offer . . . but if you do so you are required to fulfil the normal common law duties which an employee would owe to an employer as far as they are applicable'. In contrast, *Knights v Anglian Industrial Services* [1996] EAT 640 held that an individual was not an employee of the agency even though he had worked exclusively for one client over a three year period; and

(c) The worker is not deemed to be an employee of the agency under s134 ICTA 1988, see **21.2.1**.

Thus it is possible that the agency could be 'the client' in the legislation, and if this were the case, the hypothetical contract between agency and worker is unlikely to be one of employment. Thus, the personal services legislation would not apply to the services provided by the worker to the agency.

However, it is doubtful whether this makes any real difference to the application of the legislation. Even if the worker is supplying services for the business of the agency, this does not preclude him also from supplying services to the client. In other words, the two are not alternatives. The essence of IR35 involves constructing the hypothetical contract under which a worker supplies services for the business of another. If he supplies services for the business of the agency *and* for the business of the client, both have to be considered. The fact that the hypothetical agency/worker contract is outside IR35 does not immunise the individual from IR35 in respect of the client/worker contract.

If the relationship between the agency and the worker *was*, exceptionally, within IR35, so that the worker had a hypothetical contract of employment with the agency, it could be argued that he could not have two hypothetical contracts of employment in respect of the same engagement, and thus could not have an IR35 contract with the client.

But, even if this were to be the case (which has to be uncertain, given that the legislation requires us to consider hypothetical contracts, not real contracts) it is again difficult to see that this would make a difference in practice. If the worker would have been an employee of the agency if the intermediary did not exist, the engagement which the agency required him to carry out would be within the personal services legislation in exactly the same way as if he had a hypothetical contract of employment with the client.

5.7 Summary

There is no case law on how a court will deal with the IR35 hypothetical contract. It is clear that the 'circumstances' under which services are supplied must be taken into account, and that these include the contractual agreements between the service company/client, or between the service company/ agency/ client.

Existing case law would also suggest that a court would consider whether there is sufficient mutuality of obligation between worker and client for the hypothetical contract to be one of employment, but exactly how this will be applied to a contract worker remains to be seen. What is certain is that interpreting IR35 will keep the courts busy for some time.

6 Employed or self-employed?

6.1 Introduction

The aim of the personal services legislation is to discover whether the individual would be regarded as an employee if he were working as an individual rather than via an intermediary. If the answer is yes, he will be within the scope of IR35.

In order to decide whether someone is within the personal services rules, it is necessary to establish the nature of the hypothetical contract between the parties, and whether any mutuality of obligation exists between them. If there is no mutuality, there can be no employment. This is discussed in Chapter 5.

This chapter examines the detailed status tests, and Chapter 8 looks at how the status tests work in practice, in the context of cases which are similar to the position of the IR35 worker. Chapter 7 reviews the Revenue guidance on status and considers how a Revenue determination might be challenged in the courts. Chapter 9 suggests whether and to what extent changes could be made to working practices so that individuals may more easily meet the status tests.

As a final point, it should be noted that some workers are deemed to be employed for National Insurance purposes, and this deeming provision has priority over the status tests for NICs, but not for tax. How this interacts with the personal services legislation is discussed at **12.7.2**.

6.2 Development and scope of legislation

It was initially proposed that a worker should fall within the personal services legislation if he was operating under the control of the client, see **2.3.2**. However, the government subsequently moved away from this crude measure, and adopted instead the existing tests, see *IRPR*, 23 September 1999:

> 'The rules will rely on the *existing* tests which are currently used to determine the boundary between employment and self-employment for tax and National Insurance Contributions purposes, instead of the alternative test put forward originally. Using these more familiar tests will help understanding of the new rules and ensure they are targeted on the right people.'

Mr Timms, speaking for the government, made the same point in the House of Commons on 3 November 1999:

> 'The conventional distinction will be used to decide whether the new rules apply to service company workers. That means that the same criteria will be applied in the same way as they always have been in the past.' (*Hansard* 3 November 1999, Col. 429)

The personal service legislation does not refer to the status tests as such, but they are implied. The rules apply where:

> 'The circumstances are such that, if the services were provided under a contract directly between the client and the worker, the worker would be regarded for income tax purposes as an employee of the client.' (Sch 12, para 1(1)(c) FA 2000)

As discussed at **5.1.1**, the 'circumstances' include, but are not limited to, consideration of the terms in the contracts between the service company and the client, or those between the service company/agency and agency/client. Because the legislation looks at the wider circumstances and not only at the written contracts, elements other than the written terms must also be taken into account.

These can be assumed to include factors such as whether the worker has a business organisation and the number and variety of his other contracts. In other words, the personal services legislation will look at the wider status tests and not simply at either the contractual terms, or the conditions of a single engagement.

6.3 Status tests and checklists

6.3.1 General

When faced by several hundred tax, National Insurance and employment law cases, together with others involving compensation and damages, the idea of using a checklist to determine whether or not IR35 applies looks like a tempting short-cut. But it may lead to the wrong decision: Cooke J. said in *Market Investigations Ltd v Minister of Social Security* [1968] 3 All ER 732 that:

> 'No exhaustive list has been compiled and perhaps no exhaustive list can be compiled of considerations which are relevant in determining that question, nor can strict rules be laid down as to the relative weight which the various considerations should carry in particular cases.'

More recently, in *Hall v Lorimer*, Mummery J. commented:

'In order to decide whether a person carries on business on his own account, it is necessary to consider many different aspects of that person's work activity. This is not a mechanical exercise of running through items on a check list to see whether they are present in, or absent from, a given situation. The object of the exercise is to paint a picture from the accumulation of detail.

The overall effect can only be appreciated by standing back from the detailed picture which has been painted, by viewing it from a distance and by making an informed, considered, qualitative appreciation of the whole. It is a matter of evaluation of the overall effect of the detail, which is not necessarily the same as the sum total of the individual details. Not all details are of equal weight or importance in any given situation. The details may also vary in importance from one situation to another.'

While accepting that checklists are inappropriate, nevertheless the Courts have, over the years, explained which details may be of greater relevance, and which are less important. This has led to the development of 'status tests' – measures against which an individual's employment or self-employment can be judged.

The status tests are not found in legislation, but have been developed over time as cases have been argued in the courts. They are not fixed, but change as society develops. As a result IR35 could be viewed as uniquely flexible, responding to change as commercial realities alter. Alternatively it could be seen as inherently uncertain, and inappropriate to self-assessment.

Like it or not, liability to tax under the new legislation depends largely on these status tests. It is therefore essential to understand how they work, as part of the process of deciding whether an individual is within or outside IR35.

6.3.2 Hierarchy of status tests

There are over a dozen status tests, but they are not of equal importance. For the purposes of this chapter they have been divided as follows:

- The 'in business on your own account' test. This is an umbrella test, in the sense that if a worker can show that he is running his own business, he will be self-employed. However, in order to demonstrate that he *is* running a business he will need to satisfy other specific status tests;

- Status tests which are so fundamental that if a single one of them is present, the worker will not be an employee, see **6.5.1**;

- Important status tests, which give strong support to an argument that someone is self-employed, see **6.5.2**;

- Minor status tests, which are helpful and persuasive when taken in context, see **6.5.3**.

6.4 The 'in business on your own account' test

If a person is in business on his own account, he will be self-employed and outside IR35. However, the opposite is not necessarily true.

6.4.1 The self-employed business

The simplest way of deciding whether someone is employed or self-employed is to answer the question: is he in business on his own account? This was the conclusion reached by Cooke J. in *Market Investigations*, who said:

> '"Is the person who has engaged himself to perform these services performing them as a person in business on his own account?" If the answer to that question is "yes", then the contract is a contract for services (i.e. self-employment). If the answer is "no", then the contract is a contract of service (i.e. employment).'

The judge went on to say that the status issue can be decided 'by asking whether the party is carrying on the business, in the sense of carrying it on for himself or on his own behalf and not merely for a superior'. In other words, the business must be that of the personal services worker; it is not enough that he contributes his skills to the business of another.

It is this question – *is the individual in business on his own account* – which has been one of the key issues courts have attempted to answer as they weighed up the facts in each case. In so doing they have set out a number of detailed status tests which are discussed below.

6.4.2 Being in business is not a necessary condition for self-employment

It is however possible for a person to be neither an employee, nor in business on their own account. Cooke J. concluded his statement above with the following less well-known dicta:

> 'The application of the general test may be easier in a case where the person who engages himself to perform the services does so in the course of an already established business of his own; but *this factor is not decisive*, and a person who engages himself to perform services for another may well be an independent contractor *even though he has not entered into the contract in the course of an existing business carried on by him*.'

78

The workers in the agency case of *Wickens v Champion Employment* [1984] ICR 365 were found not to be employees. The case had been appealed by Mrs Wickens on the basis that it had been wrongly decided by the lower court because:

> 'There is no evidence that these temporary workers were self-employed, no evidence that they were carrying on any business of their own or were doing anything other than working as employees for the employers.'

Nolan J. said that this was true, but not significant:

> 'The test (of employment/self-employment) does not include as a necessary element the question of whether the individual carries on a separate business. If it did, then it would follow that a casual worker must always be employed under a contract of service unless he has his own business and *that, plainly, cannot be the law.'*

These comments are extremely significant in the context of the personal services legislation. While it is undoubtedly easier to prove that a worker is not an employee if he is clearly self-employed and in business on his own account, it may be possible to fall outside of IR35 simply by demonstrating one would not have been an employee of the client had there been no intermediary.

6.4.3 A third way

In the case of *Construction Industry Training Board v Labour Force Ltd* [1970] 3 AER 220 Cooke J. further developed his thinking on types of contract. Instead of the two alternatives given in *Market Investigations* above, he suggested that there could be a third type of contract, which was neither a contract of employment, nor a contract for services:

> 'I think there is much to be said for the view that, where A contracts with B to render services exclusively to C, the contract is not a contract for services, but a contract sui generis, a different type of contract from either of the familiar two.'

This approach was followed by the Employment Appeal Tribunal in *Ironmonger v Movefield Ltd* [1988] IRLR 461. They took 'the view that the contract in this case is one sui generis' and thus that the relationship between Mr Ironmonger and Movefield was neither one of employment nor of self-employment.

Both these cases involved three parties, the agency, the client and the individual. They are, however, likely to be less relevant to personal services workers because IR35 postulates a hypothetical contract directly between the worker and the client. This removes some of the difficulties caused to the courts by the tripartite worker/agency/client relationships. They are nevertheless of interest in providing further support for the view that it is not necessary for a worker to be in business in his own account in order not to be an employee.

6.4.4 The professional

Lord Nolan developed a similar point in the case of *Hall v Lorimer* [1993] 66 TC 349, see **8.2.1**. While acknowledging that if a person is in business on his own account, he will be self-employed, he said that this was not a particularly useful test if the worker is a professional, such as a surgeon or singer:

> 'The question, whether the individual is in business on his own account, though often helpful, may be of little assistance in the case of one carrying on a profession or vocation. A self-employed author working from home or an actor or a singer may earn his living without any of the normal trappings of a business.
>
> For my part, I would suggest there is much to be said in these cases for bearing in mind the traditional contrast between a servant and an independent contractor. The extent to which the individual is dependent upon, or independent of, a particular paymaster for the financial exploitation of his talents may well be significant.'

6.4.5 Conclusion

If a person is 'in business in their own account' they will be self-employed and outside IR35. However, although employment and self-employment tend to be regarded as two sides of the same coin, this is not necessarily the case. It may be that a person is not in business on his own account but also does not have a hypothetical contract of employment. And if this is the position he will not be within IR35.

6.5 Fundamental status tests

6.5.1 Introduction

In the hierarchy of status tests (**6.3.2** above) three are fundamental:

(a) Substitution;

(b) Significant financial risk; and

(c) The ability to hire others to do the work in question.

If any of these can be proved to exist, the worker will fall outside of IR35.

6.5.2 Right to send a substitute

If an individual does not have to do the job personally, but can send a substitute, he is not an employee. This is because personal service is an essential ingredient of employment. However, a substitution clause is not a magic wand – the right to send a replacement must be real.

In the recent employment law case of *Express and Echo Publications Ltd v Tanton* [1999] IRLR 367, which concerned a newspaper delivery driver, the judge held that:

> 'Where . . . a person who works for another is not required to perform his services personally, then as a matter of law the relationship between the worker and the person for whom he works is not that of employee and employer . . . The only judgment which (the Tribunal) could properly have reached was that this was a contract for services.'

This was despite the fact that Mr Tanton's job had other characteristics which would normally indicate employment. For example:

- He was controlled as to where he delivered the newspaper – the management of Express and Echo ('E&E') told him the route he had to drive;

- The van he drove was supplied by E&E;

- He wore a uniform supplied by E&E;

- His remuneration was on a per journey basis, and fixed by E&E, not negotiated by Mr Tanton;

- He could not increase his earnings by doing more work.

Precedents for the importance of substitution can be found in the words of McKenna J. in *Ready Mixed Concrete (South East) Ltd v Minister of Pensions and National Insurance* [1968] 1 All ER 433. He said it was one of the touchstones of self-employment:

> 'Freedom to do a job either by one's own hands or another's is inconsistent with a contract of service, though a limited or occasional power of delegation may not be.'

In *McMenamin v Diggles* [1991] 64 TC 286, Mr Diggles was a barrister's clerk, who had changed his contractual arrangements so that he was no longer an employee but self-employed, although he still ran the affairs of the chambers as is required of a barrister's clerk. One of the key factors that led the court to hold that he was self-employed was that his contract required:

'The provision of the services of a full-time Head Clerk of not less than 10 years experience in that capacity *being either Mr. Diggles or some other Clerk with that qualification.*'

The clause accepted

In all three cases mentioned above – *Express and Echo, McMenamin v Diggles* and *Ready Mixed Concrete* – there was no doubt that the worker had a right to send a substitute, and that the client accepted this right.

In *Diggles*, the barristers for whom the clerk worked included the substitution clause in the contract at the outset of the engagement, and the court was told that it had been one of the factors which encouraged Mr Diggles to move from employment to self-employment:

'Mr. Diggles was at first reluctant to make the change because he would lose the security of employment . . . But he realised that self-employed status would have some advantages . . . The right to put in a substitute as Head Clerk might also be useful if he were sick or, later on, if he should want to ease up as he approached retirement. On reflection he was content to accept the change.'

In *Express and Echo* the judge commented that:

'(The) right for Mr. Tanton to provide a substitute driver was utilized by him from time to time and exceptionally, throughout a period of six months whilst Mr. Tanton was ill, Mr. Tanton paying the substitute driver, though receiving remuneration from the appellant. Clause 3.3 (the substitution clause), as the chairman expressly found, is not a sham.'

The clause disregarded

However, a substitution clause was ignored in the case of *Global Plant Ltd v Secretary of State for Health & Social Security* [1971] 3 All ER 385. Mr Summers had previously been an employed driver with Global Plant Ltd, but in 1968 asked to change his status to a self-employed contractor, and the company agreed. The new arrangements included a right to send a substitute, although the court was sceptical. Lord Widgery appears to have decided that the right was not genuine, and concluded that Mr Summers was an employee, saying that:

'Although it is recorded that if he could not work himself it was open to him to send another substitute driver if he was qualified to do the work. . . . I have little doubt that the intention of the parties was that Mr. Summers should continue to work exactly as he had before even though in terms his new bargain did not require him to do so.'

The clause was also disregarded in the recent employment law case of *MacFarlane and Skivington v Glasgow City Council* [2000] EAT/1277. Here the Tribunal distinguished the case from *Tanton* because:

- The individuals could only send a substitute if they were unable to attend in person; they did not have an absolute right to send a replacement;

- They could not send anyone suitable, but had to choose their substitute from the Council's register;

- The Council itself sometimes organised the replacement;

- The Council paid the substitutes, whereas in *Tanton* they were paid by the worker.

The position on payment is discussed in more detail at **9.2.4**.

The clause is not implied

In *Hall v Lorimer* [1993] 66 TC 349 (see **8.2.1**), Mr Lorimer sent a substitute in six of the 580 engagements which he carried out during the period under review. Although the fact that he had sent a substitute on these six occasions indicated that those particular engagements were not employments, this did not mean that Mr Lorimer was necessarily self-employed in respect of the other contracts he undertook. Lord Nolan said that:

> 'Mr. Goldsmith (Counsel for the Revenue) added, and I would agree, that (this) had no significant bearing on the proper classification of the other 574 engagements.'

So the court did not infer that there was a right of substitution in the other contracts, simply because it had been demonstrably shown to exist in some engagements. In *Lorimer*, however, there were 'no formal written conditions of engagement' between the worker and his clients. Had there been, the court might have read across from the contracts where the right was exercised, to the other engagements when he had no need of a substitute. But this is to speculate, as the facts in *Lorimer* were otherwise.

Client's permission or approval

If the client's permission has to be obtained for a substitute, case law suggests that there is no *right* of substitution. In *Market Investigations* (see **5.3.3**) Mrs Irving, a market research interviewer, was held to be an employee. One of the terms of her contract was that 'the Company do not allow interviewers to send a substitute without prior permission of the Company'. Being able to send a substitute with the client's permission does not amount to a 'right'.

Saying that substitution is not a right if the client has to give permission is not, however, the same as saying that the worker should be able to send anyone at all. In *Ready Mixed Concrete* the worker 'was entitled to employ competent substitute drivers, but if the company were dissatisfied he was to provide another substitute'. In *Express and Echo* Mr Tanton's contract said that:

> 'In the event that the contractor provides a relief driver, the contractor must satisfy the company that such a relief driver is trained and is suitable to undertake the services.'

In both cases the individuals were found to be self-employed. It is thus acceptable for the client to have the right of veto, but not that his permission should be required before a substitute can be sent.

No right to send a substitute

If a worker does not have the right to send a substitute, this does not necessarily mean he is an employee. Other factors must be considered in order to decide his status. In *McManus v Griffiths* [1997] 70 TC 218, a case concerning a caterer in a golf club, Mrs McManus was held to be self-employed despite the fact that:

> 'The club was insisting on Mrs. McManus personally (and not by a substitute) providing the service save during suitable holiday periods.'

But in this case other pointers towards self-employment outweighed the lack of a substitution clause, notably the fact that she could hire her own staff and was capable of profiting from the management of the business.

Summary

The case law on substitution can thus be summarised as follows:

- If a substitution clause is genuine, the worker is self-employed;

- The court will test whether the clause is genuine, and if it is not, it will be ineffective;

- Where a substitution clause is present in some contracts but not others, it will not become an implied term of the remaining contracts (see **5.2.3**), so explicit inclusion is recommended. This remains the case under IR35, where the terms of the contracts will be taken into account in deciding the 'circumstances', see **5.1**;

- The clause is ineffective if the client's permission has to be obtained, but this does not prevent the client from vetoing an unacceptable substitute;

- Lack of a substitution clause does not necessarily mean that the worker is an employee.

The Revenue view of substitution can be found at **7.4.1**, while possible changes to a worker's contractual arrangements so as to include such a clause are discussed at **9.3**.

6.5.3 Significant financial risk and opportunity to profit from sound management

Although frequently considered separately when status tests are analysed, the tests of taking on significant financial risk and the opportunity to profit from sound management are two sides of the same coin. For the test to be fundamental and conclusive, both must exist, and the degree of risk must be significant.

The identification of financial risk as a fundamental test of self-employment goes back to *Montreal Locomotive Works v Montreal and A.-G for Canada* [1947] 1 DLR 161. Lord Wright said that the simple control test was in need of replacement:

'It has been suggested that a fourfold test would in some cases be more appropriate, a complex involving (i) control; (ii) ownership of the tools; (iii) chance of profit; (iv) risk of loss.'

It was reiterated in *Market Investigations* and again in *Global Plant* where Lord Widgery held that:

'If a man agrees to perform an operation for a fixed sum and thus stands to lose if the work is delayed, and to profit if it is done quickly, that is the man who on the face of it appears to be an independent contractor working under a contract for services.'

In *Diggles*, one of the factors taken into account by the court in deciding that he was self-employed was that:

'Mr. Diggles submits a monthly account of clerking fees, plus VAT, to each member of chambers and this should be paid within 7 days. For one reason or another, however, he may be owed at any one time something between £3,000 and £6,000 by a member of chambers. Since he has to meet all the expenses of employing staff out of his fees, as well as meeting some chambers' expenses for which he is entitled to be reimbursed, he may run into cash flow problems which he did not experience before October 1985. He estimates that he needs to hold about £15,000 of his own money available to fund his financial obligations under the agreement.'

85

Lower levels of risk

Where the level of risk is lower, but still present, the case is less conclusive. The risk factor will need to be considered along with others in order to decide the matter. This was the case in *Lorimer*, where financial risk was only part of the picture. The Special Commissioner held that Mr Lorimer:

> 'Bears his own financial risk which is greater than that of one who is an employee, accepting the risk of bad debts and outstanding invoices and of no or an insufficient number of engagements. He has the opportunity of profiting from being good at being a vision mixer. According to his reputation, so there will be a demand for his services for which he will be able to charge accordingly. The more efficient he is at running the business of providing his services, the greater is his prospect of profit.'

However, the risk of not finding work is insufficient to bring the worker into Schedule D. In the Privy Council case of *Lee Ting Sang v Chung Chi-Keung* [1990] 2 AC 374 (see **8.3.1**),Lord Griffiths said:

> 'The picture emerges of a skilled artisan earning his living by working for more than one employer as an employee and not as a small businessman venturing into business on his own account as an independent contractor with all its attendant risks. The applicant ran no risk whatever save that of being unable to find employment which is, of course, a risk faced by casual employees who move from one job to another. . . .'

No risk

A complete absence of financial risk was however held to be compatible with self-employment in *O'Kelly* (see **5.3.2**), where other points supported a contract for services. The court held that:

> 'Where the commodity offered is the simple supply of semi-skilled labour for a specific occasion, or series of occasions, it is not to be expected that there would be a financial investment or participation in the profits or losses of the business.'

Summary

The case law can be summarised as follows:

- If a worker bears significant financial risk, he will be self-employed;

- If the risk is lower, but still greater than that borne by an employee, it is an indicator of self-employment, but not conclusive in itself;

- If the worker can increase his earnings, but not make a loss, he may be self-employed, but other factors will need to be considered;

- The risk of not finding work is not an indicator of self-employment;

- It is possible to be self-employed even if there is no financial risk.

The Revenue view of financial risk can be found at **7.4.2**; possible changes to a worker's contractual arrangements are discussed at **9.4** and **9.7**.

6.5.4 Hiring of staff

One of the key elements of an employment contract is the requirement that the worker provides personal service, see **6.5.1**. An individual will be self-employed if, having agreed to perform a task, he is free to hire someone else to help him to carry it out.

In the Privy Council case of *Australian Mutual Provident Society v Chaplin and Another* [1978] 18 Australian Law Reports 385, Lord Fraser said that:

> 'Power of unlimited delegation is almost conclusive against the contract being a contract of service.'

One of the decisive points in Mr Diggle's favour was that his contract required him to provide:

> 'A Junior Clerk or Junior Clerks and other ancillary staff . . . whose services may be reasonably necessary to enable the Head Clerk to render efficiently the Full Clerking Services.'

and he could show in court that:

> 'As from the same date and in accordance with the agreement Mr. Diggles engaged Miss Magnall and Miss Barnes as Junior Clerks and he also engaged an assistant Mr. Liam Mooney and occasional casual helpers. Miss Magnall (Mrs. Garlick) left in June 1989 to have a child and was paid statutory maternity pay by Mr. Diggles who engaged a new Junior Clerk Miss Helen Berkley with effect from 29 March 1989.' (*McMenamin v Diggles* [1991] 64 TC 286)

A contrasting case is *Andrews v King* [1991] 64 TC 332, where Andrews was engaged by a firm called Stanberrys as a gangmaster to select and transport men to pick and grade potatoes. At the end of each week, Stanberrys gave Andrews a cash sum, and he paid the workers.

The Revenue argued that Andrews was in business on his own account, and thus it was his responsibility to deduct any necessary PAYE from the sums paid to the workers. The courts disagreed, holding that there was a distinction between mere selection and hiring:

'As to the question whether or not he hired his own helpers, he certainly selected them but he did not himself pay them any wages. He did not engage men, pay them and then provide a gang en bloc to Stanberrys in return for a fixed charge. Having selected his gang, they all went together to the place of work selected by Stanberrys and the total sum paid for the work by Stanberrys was a sum which all the members of the gang had agreed, not Mr. Andrews by himself. The net proceeds, after deduction of petrol money were divided equally between them. In my judgment, it is impossible to call that "hiring helpers".'

Being unable to hire staff is an indicator of employment. In the case of *Lee Ting Sang v Chung Chi-Keung*, see **8.3.1**, the worker was regarded as an employee partly on the grounds that:

'He did not hire his own helpers; this emerged with clarity in his evidence when he explained that he gave priority to [Chung Chi-Keung's] work and if asked by [Chung Chi-Keung] to do an urgent job he would tell those he was working for that they would have to employ someone else . . . if he was an independent contractor in business on his own account, one would expect that he would attempt to keep both contracts by hiring others to fulfill the contract he had to leave.'

However, as with substitution, the inability to hire staff does not *necessarily* mean that an individual is an employee – Lorimer was in this position, see **6.6.2**, but was still held to be self-employed.

Conclusion

If the worker has a genuine right to hire helpers in order to carry out the contract with the client, he will be self-employed. Hiring helpers means taking responsibility for them, a point well made by the Revenue, see **7.4.4**. Possible changes to a worker's contractual arrangements to include such a clause are discussed at **9.5**.

6.6 Important status tests

6.6.1 General

In the hierarchy of status tests (see **6.3.2** above), some are fundamental (see **6.5.1**) and others merely supportive (see **6.7.1**). In the middle are a number of important tests, which give weight to an argument that an individual is self-employed. These are:

(a) Provision of significant equipment;

(b) Control; and

(c) The length and number of engagements: factors personal to the worker.

Of these, the third is of vital importance to the professional with his own service company, see **6.6.4** below.

6.6.2 Provision of equipment

Significant equipment

Where a worker provides significant equipment which is essential to carry out the task, he is probably self-employed. In the case of *Humberstone v Northern Timber Mills* [1949] 79 CLR the owner-driver of a truck was held to be self employed on the basis that:

> 'The contract . . . was to provide not merely his own labour but the use of heavy mechanised transport, driven by power, which he maintained and fuelled for the purpose. The most important part of the work to be performed by his own labour consisted in the operation of his own motor truck and the essential part of the service . . . was to be done by his own property in his own possession and control.'

Small tools

Providing significant equipment can be distinguished from supplying 'small tools', following a US case concerning the status of men who unloaded coal from railway wagons into bins which was quoted with approval by McKenna J. in *Ready Mixed Concrete*:

> 'We cannot agree that the unloaders . . . were independent contractors. They provided only picks and shovels. They had no opportunity to gain or lose except from the work of their hands and these simple tools.' (*US v Silk* [1946] 331 US)

No tools

In the *Lorimer* case the Revenue argued that he was an employee because:

> 'The studio company owns or procures the supply of the equipment. The production companies do not own such equipment, still less does Mr. Lorimer. The equipment is an integral part of the studio complex.'

However Lord Nolan disagreed with the Revenue interpretation:

> 'It is said that Mr. Lorimer provides no equipment (i.e. he has no tools), he provides no "work place" or "workshop" where the contract is to be performed, he provides no capital for the production, he hires no staff for it. No, he does not. But that is not his business.'

This was an important development. It means that where an individual is a professional the fact that he has no equipment is not relevant and should not be taken into account one way or the other. See also **8.2.2** and **7.4.5**.

Summary

In conclusion, where the equipment is major, the engagement is likely to be self-employment; where it is minor, it is more likely to be employment. But where the individual is providing skilled services, the absence of equipment provided by the worker is irrelevant, and other factors such as the length of the engagement (see **6.6.4**) and financial risk (see **6.5.3**) need to be considered. The Revenue view of the provision of equipment can be found at **7.4.5**; a discussion of the issue in the context of a worker's contractual arrangements is at **9.8**.

6.6.3 Control

The level and type of control exercised by the engager over the worker has historically been a key factor in deciding whether the contract is one of employment. Rights of control were divided into control as to *how, when, where* or *what* is done. In *Ready Mixed Concrete*, McKenna J. held that:

> 'Control includes the power of deciding the thing to be done, the way in which it shall be done, the means to be employed in doing it, the time when, and the place where it shall be done. All these aspects of control must be considered in deciding whether the right exists in a sufficient degree to make one party the master and the other his servant. The right need not be unrestricted.'

However, more recently the courts have dealt increasingly with skilled workers and professional people, over whom control is necessarily more limited. As a result the control test has declined in importance, although it still remains a factor for consideration. In a 1995 case, Mr Justice Lightman summed up the current position by saying that:

> 'The lack of "control" . . . does not have the significance today that it once may have had as the litmus test for a contract of employment. It is certainly

not a universal litmus test, and its importance (and indeed relevance) must depend in particular on the role to be played by the "employee" in the "employer's" business.' (*Horner v Hasted* [1995] 67 TC 439)

Control as to when and where the engagement is carried out

If the engager can control *when* and *where* the worker does his work, the worker is more likely to be an employee. But there are exceptions either way: In *Lorimer* (see **8.2.1**) the client could 'dictate the hours to be worked, where he shall work, the date he shall work. He has no discretion in these matters.' But Lorimer was nevertheless held to be self-employed.

In *Market Investigations* (see **5.3.3**), Mrs Irving could work 'as and when she chose and did not necessarily have to complete seven hours work during one day' and the engager had 'no right to alter the place or area within which (she) has agreed to work.' However, she was still held to be employed.

Control as to what is to be done during the engagement

If the engager can control *what* is to be done, this can indicate employment. In the old case of *Stagecraft Ltd v Minister of National Insurance* [1952] SC 288, the two comedians involved were 'controlled' by their producer as to what part they played, and were held to be employed earners for National Insurance purposes. Lord Thomson said:

'What I find of more significance is the fifth condition, where the "artiste agrees to play the part (or parts) assigned to him (or her) during the whole run of the production . . . this points to a definite contract of employment to serve the management by making his gifts available to the management in ways which the management can dictate over a period of time.'

Control as to how the work is to be carried out

In the case of *Collins v Hertfordshire County Council* [1947] 1 AER 633 it was suggested that the distinguishing feature of a contract of service is that the master can not only order or require *what* is to be done but also *how* it shall be done. This test has gradually become more complex and sophisticated. The current position is summarised below.

If the engager can control how the worker is to do the work, there will generally be an employment, unless other significant factors point to self-employment

It remains the case that if the engager can tell the worker how to do the work, he is probably an employee. In *Market Investigations* (*see* **5.3.3**), the company had the right to exercise 'very extensive [control] indeed' over the interviewer largely via the publication called the 'Interviewer's Guide'. This formed part of the contractual terms of engagement. Cooke J. said that 'the control was so extensive as to be entirely consistent with Mrs Irving's being employed under a contract of service'.

In the Privy Council case of *Narich Pty Ltd v Commissioner of Payroll Tax* [1984] ICR 286, the lecturers who conducted weight watchers classes were 'tied hand and foot' by the contract with regard to the manner of performing the work under it and were thus employees, despite having been engaged on a franchise basis as independent contractors.

If, however, other factors outweigh the engager's control over *how* the work is carried out, the contract may nevertheless be one of self-employment. In the Australian case of *Queensland Stations Pty v Federal Comr of Taxation* [1945] 70 CLR 539, a drover was engaged under a written contract to drive cattle to a destination. The contract provided that he should:

> 'Obey and carry out all lawful instructions and use the whole of his time, energy and ability in the careful driving of the stock, that he should provide at his own expense all men, plant, horses and rations required for the oper-ation, and that he should be paid at a rate per head for each of the cattle safely delivered at the destination.'

He was held to be an independent contractor in a judgement which was quoted with approval in *Ready Mixed Concrete*:

> 'In considering the facts it is a mistake to treat as decisive a reservation of control over the manner in which the droving is performed and the cattle are handled. For instance, in the present case the circumstance that the drover agrees to obey and carry out all lawful instructions cannot outweigh the countervailing considerations which are found in the employment by him of servants of his own, the provision of horses, equipment, plant, rations, and a remuneration at a rate per head delivered.'

Where the engager cannot control the work, the worker may be self-employed, but is not necessarily so.

However, it is not necessarily the case that a worker will be self-employed simply because he can decide for himself how to do the work. In *Cassidy v Ministry of Health* [1951] 1 AER 574, the judge pointed out that the owners of a ship may have no power to tell a certified ship's master how to navigate, but they may still have employed him under what is clearly a contract of service.

A more recent example is the case of *Lee Ting Sang v Chung Chi-Keung* [1990] 2 AC 374 (see **8.3.1**), where a craftsman was held to be an employee despite the fact that he was not controlled as to how to do his work. The Privy Council said that:

> 'It is true that he was not supervised in his work, but this is not surprising, he was a skilled man and had been told the beams upon which he was to work and the depth to which they were to be cut and his work was measured to see that he achieved that result . . . He was simply told what to do and left to get on with it as, for example, would a skilled turner on a lathe who was required to cut a piece of metal to certain dimensions.'

Control over how the work is done may be an unhelpful test where skilled professionals are concerned.

In *Morren v Swinton & Pendlebury Borough Council* [1965] 2 All ER 349, Lord Parker introduced a new element when he commented that:

> 'When one is dealing with a professional man, or a man of some particular skill and experience, there can be no question of an employer telling him how to do the work; therefore the absence of control and direction in that sense can be of little, if any, use as a test.'

This was further developed in *Hall v Lorimer,* see **8.2.1**, when the Special Commissioner said (the author's italics):

> 'The Crown's representative suggests that the production company has extensive control over Mr. Lorimer. It dictates the hours to be worked, where he shall work, the date he shall work. He has no discretion in these matters. The Crown's representative accepts that the production company has no control over Mr. Lorimer's skill in performing his functions and that Mr. Lorimer must use his judgement, but the scripts of scripted programmes indicate control is exercised through what I might call stage directions. The Crown's representative contrasts this with an independent contractor who supposedly would have a choice of views and exercise control himself over all other aspects of a vision mixer's function.
>
> *I cannot see that control of the kind adumbrated helps very much towards solving the problem.* If you accept an engagement for your services as a vision mixer, you must be provided with details of date, time and place, and of the period of time you are likely to be required. If you are part of a team to produce a show, it is inevitable that someone must organise it. You must attend rehearsals if they are necessary. If you play in an orchestra, you must pay attention to the conductor. In the production of a play, you must pay attention to the stage directions or to the producer's directions. That applies to the leading actor and actress, but they do not for that reason become

> "employees". *The independent contractor posited by the Crown's representative could hardly exist in the context of the production of a programme in conjunction with other people.'*

This suggests that if one is deciding whether a professional person is self-employed, the control test may be the wrong one to use.

No control

Absence of control means that the worker is not an employee, following McKenna J. in *Ready Mixed Concrete:*

> 'An obligation to do work subject to the other party's control is a necessary, though not always a sufficient, condition of a contract of service.'

Mr Diggles' barrister made the same point:

> 'Mr. Oliver, applying the control test which, although no longer regarded as decisive, remains relevant factor, says that Mr. Diggles was not under the control necessary for an employment. He had wide discretion as to the way in which he provided clerking services, with no fixed hours of work and no obligation to obey orders. He had to avoid breaches of the Bar code of conduct because he was supplying services to barristers who were bound by that code but that does not mean that he was controlled in the sense required for a contract of service.' (*McMenamin v Diggles* [1991] 64 TC 286)

Summary

One could thus summarise the case law position by saying that:

- If there is no right of control there will be no contract of employment;
- If a worker is controlled as to how, what, where, and when to do the work, he will almost certainly be an employee;
- If one or more of these elements is absent, he may be either an employee or self-employed, depending on other factors;
- If he is a professional, the control test may be useless as a determinant of status.

The Revenue view of control can be found at **7.4.6**; possible changes to a worker's contractual arrangements are discussed at **9.6**.

6.6.4 Length and number of engagements: factors personal to the worker

Professional workers

When Lord Nolan rejected the control test in the case of *Lorimer*, see **6.6.3** above, he turned instead to the question of 'the extent to which the individual is dependent upon, or independent of, a particular paymaster for the financial exploitation of his talents'. This has been summarised as 'factors personal to the worker' because it involves looking beyond each individual contract towards considering the pattern of the worker's engagements.

In the period under review, Mr Lorimer had about 580 engagements, most of one or two days' duration. The Revenue argued that:

'Each and every one of Mr. Lorimer's engagements must of necessity be a contract of employment. He is an employee of company A on a Monday, company L on Tuesday; he is out of work on Wednesday and Thursday; he is an employee of company C on Friday.'

This was rejected, even ridiculed, by the court. The fact that 'Mr. Lorimer customarily worked for 20 or more production companies and that the vast majority of his assignments lasted only for a single day' was described by Lord Nolan in the Court of Appeal as 'the most outstanding feature' of the case, and was decisive in the judgement that he was self-employed.

A similar point was made in *McMenamin v Diggles* [1991] 64 TC 286 where the barrister for Mr. Diggles pointed out that:

'A number of separate contracts indicates professional activity rather than employment: and . . . Mr. Diggles had a separate contract with each member of the Chambers, about 20 in all.'

This followed the much earlier decision in *Davies v Braithwaite* [1932] 18 TC 198 where Rowlatt J. held that:

'Where one finds a method of earning a livelihood which does not contemplate the obtaining of a post and staying in it, but essentially contemplates a series of engagements and moving from one to the other . . . in obtaining first one engagement and then another, and a whole series of them – then each of those engagements could not be considered an employment, but is a mere engagement in the course of exercising a profession.'

This may, however, be harder to apply in the case of the unskilled worker, see the case of *Lee Ting Sang v Chung Chi-Keung* [1990] 2 AC 374 discussed at **8.3.1**.

Application to personal services legislation

The personal services legislation appears at first sight to be drafted on the basis of single contracts rather than the whole picture of a worker's activity, because it requires that each '*engagement* to which this Schedule applies' be reviewed to see whether it should be classified as employment or self-employment (Sch 12, para 2(1) FA 2000).

However, the nature of the hypothetical contract between the worker and the client is determined by considering 'the circumstances' in which the services are provided, see **5.1** (Sch 12, para 1(4) FA 2000). Although the 'circumstances' include the terms of the contracts between the parties in respect of the individual engagement, other factors are also be taken into account. One would expect these to include the number and variety of the worker's engagements.

This interpretation would be consistent with early government assurances about the legislation. Mr Timms, speaking in the House of Commons on 3 November 1999 said:

> 'There is no intention of applying the rules in any different way. They are well established and well understood; they are flexible; *they take account of the whole pattern of a worker's engagement*, so that a skilled worker who works for many different clients can be treated as one who is self-employed.'

This has subsequently been developed in the Revenue's *Tax Bulletin 45* article as follows:

> 'In deciding a person's employment status it may sometimes be necessary to take into account factors which are personal to the worker and which have little to do with the terms of the particular engagement being considered. For example, if a skilled worker works for a number of clients throughout the year and has a business-like approach to obtaining his engagements (perhaps involving expenditure on office accommodation, office equipment, etc.) this will point towards self-employment.'

Conclusion

The position can be summarised as follows:

- Where there are many short term engagements, and the worker is a skilled professional, he is likely to be self employed;

- Where the worker is unskilled or semi-skilled, the case may be harder to prove, and other supporting status tests, such as taking significant risk or supplying equipment, may be necessary in addition.

6.7 Minor status tests

6.7.1 Summary

In addition to the fundamental status tests (see **6.5.1**) and those which are important (see **6.6.1**), there are others which are helpful in indicating whether an individual is an employee or in business on his own account. They include:

(a) Exclusivity;

(b) Terms of payment;

(c) Rights of dismissal;

(d) The intention of the parties;

(e) Business structure.

A sixth concept, whether the individual is 'part and parcel of the organisation' in which he works, is now regarded as of less use.

6.7.2 Exclusivity

Where a worker provides services to only one engager, and agrees not to provide his skills to anyone else, he is likely to be an employee.

However, this is not invariably so. In the recent employment law case of *Jowitt v London Symphony Orchestra Ltd* [1990] EAT 301, Mr Jowitt argued that he was an employee because he could not work for another orchestra. However, the Employment Appeals Tribunal held that there was no reason why a self-employed person should not say by agreement 'I will give my services to you (the employer or payer) for a given period of time'.

Conversely, if there is no exclusivity and the worker can provide services for others, this does not necessarily mean that he is self-employed, particularly where the work is not full time. The judge in *Market Investigations*, holding that the worker was employed, said:

> 'Nor is there anything inconsistent with the existence of a contract of service in the fact that Mrs. Irving was free to work for others during the relevant

period. It is by no means a necessary incident of a contract of service that the servant is prohibited from serving any other employer.'

Having said this, one would normally expect to find that a self-employed person was free to work for others, and that the freedom of an employee was more restricted. Possible changes to a worker's contractual arrangements so as to include an appropriate clause are discussed at **9.13**.

6.7.3 Payment terms

The way a worker is paid is an indicator of his employment status, but is not decisive. There are two elements to the question of payment terms, the way in which 'pay' is delivered, and whether there are any other 'benefits'. The Revenue view of payment terms can be found at **7.4.9**; the extent to which it may be possible to change a worker's contractual arrangements is discussed at **9.9**.

Pay

While being paid a fixed sum on a project basis is typical of self-employment, being paid by the hour doesn't mean the worker is an employee. Accountants and lawyers, who are clearly self-employed, measure their time and bill their clients on an hourly basis or even by the six-minute unit.

In *O'Kelly* (see **5.3.2**) the workers were paid for work actually performed, rather than receiving a fixed wage. The court held that 'the method of calculating entitlement to remuneration is not an essential aspect of the employment relationship'.

In *Lorimer* the judge said that charging method was less important than its underlying purpose:

> 'Many of the invoices, it is true, indicate the hours Mr. Lorimer attended for the shooting session, but the object appears to me to be to provide the reason for the particular charge out rate.'

Thus where a personal service worker can move to a project basis and be paid accordingly, it will strengthen his case for self-employment (see also **9.4**). However, if this is not possible or desirable, retaining an hourly rate does not necessarily mean he is employed.

Benefits

Generally, the receipt of benefits is indicative of employment. However:

(a) Where a worker receives no benefits he is not necessarily self-employed, see *Stagecraft Ltd v Minister of National Insurance* [1952] SC 288;

(b) Conversely, some workers have been held to be self-employed, even though they receive some 'employee type' benefits, because of the strength of other factors. In the *O'Kelly* case discussed at **5.3.2** above, the casual workers had a whole range of employee-type benefits but were held to be working under contracts for services.

Similarly, in the case of the actors McCowen and West, see **20.2.2**, they were held to be self-employed, despite the fact that their contracts had:

• Minimum rates of pay;

• Overtime, bank holiday and Sunday premiums;

• Agreed rates of touring and subsistence allowances;

• Holiday pay;

• Agreed disciplinary procedures.

6.7.4 Right of dismissal

Employees have a statutory right to a minimum period of notice, and their contracts will usually include a notice period, and perhaps a provision for payment in lieu of notice (PILON). The self-employed tend to be engaged until the task is finished, but can be dismissed if they breach their contract.

The fact that the workers in the *O'Kelly* case could be dismissed without notice was one of the key facts which led the court to decide they were self-employed (see **5.3.2**).

In *Morren v Swinton and Pendlebury Borough Council* [1965] 1 WLR 576 the judge compared the case of Mr Morren, who was held to be an employee, with that of another worker, Mr Kaufman, who was clearly self-employed:

> The respondents . . . *had the right to dismiss him,* he was paid such matters as subsistence allowance and for holidays, national insurance contributions were paid in regard to him, and, in addition, *there was provision for one month's* notice. Pausing there, it seems to me that, looked at on those facts, the only possible inference is that he was engaged under a contract of service. How different is the contract with Mr. Kaufman, who is not paid a subsistence allowance; nor is national insurance contribution provided in regard to him; and he is not entitled to holidays. Further, there is *no provision for termination of his services or service by notice.*

Where a worker has a notice period, but is claiming self-employment, some comfort can be taken from the words of the judge in *McManus v Griffiths* [1997] 70 TC 218:

> 'It is suggested on behalf of Mr. and Mrs. McManus that the three-month notice period is indicative of a contract for service rather than for services. I do not think that it is indicative of either. I regard the provision as neutral.'

Thus in conclusion, the lack of a notice period is indicative of self-employment, but its existence does not necessarily mean that the worker is employed. Possible changes to a worker's contractual arrangements so as to exclude such a clause are discussed at **9.14**.

6.7.5 Intention of the parties

The intention of the parties can be described as a 'tiebreaker.' If all other factors are evenly balanced, what the parties intend the worker's status to be will normally settle the matter. This was most clearly expressed in *Massey v Crown Life Insurance Co* [1978] ICR 590:

> 'It seems to me on the authorities that, when it is a situation which is in doubt or which is ambiguous, so that it can be brought under one relationship or the other, it is open to the parties by agreement to stipulate what the legal situation between them shall be.'

Similarly in *Global Plant* (see **6.5.2**) Lord Widgery held that:

> 'One must not overlook that the intention of the parties was that the relationship should be that of an independent contractor, and although the parties cannot by intention make a transaction into something which it is not, yet it is recognised that such intention is a factor for consideration in these cases.'

However, it is unclear whether this test will be effective in the context of the hypothetical contract between the worker and the client, see **5.2.4**. Nevertheless, it is recommended that it be included in contracts, see **9.3**. Even if it is effective, it is of course not possible to metamorphose an employment relationship into self-employment simply by a change of label, see **5.2.5**.

The Revenue view of this issue can be found at **7.4.10**; reassuringly they take the position that the tiebreaker still exists in an IR35 context.

6.7.6 Business structure

The existence of a 'business structure' is one of the factors which has been looked for when deciding whether someone is self-employed, see for example

Lorimer **8.2.1**. However Cooke J. held that a business structure was not essential, see **6.4.2** above.

His dicta was followed in the *Addison* case (see **20.5.2**) where the musicians playing for the orchestra were held to be self-employed although they had no demonstrable 'business structure'. They were 'pursuing his or her own profession as an instrumentalist, with an individual reputation' and this was enough.

However in a corporation tax case Vinelott J. interpreted 'business structure' widely, so as to bring within it the musicians, Mr Lorimer, and many contractors:

> 'The business structure or entity or organisation may assume any of an almost infinite variety of shapes . . . it may be represented by no more than the intangible elements constituting what is commonly called goodwill, that is, widespread or general reputation, habitual patronage by clients or customers and an organised method of serving their needs. At the other extreme it may consist in a great aggregate of buildings, machinery and plant all assembled and systematised as the material means by which an organised body of men produce and distribute commodities or perform services.' (*RTZ Oil & Gas Ltd v Elliss* [1987] 61 TC 132)

The Revenue view of business structure can be found at **7.4.11**; some practical recommendations are discussed at **9.12**.

6.7.7 Part and parcel of the organisation

The 'part and parcel of the organisation' concept was first put forward by Lord Denning in *Stevenson, Jordan & Harrison v MacDonald & Evans* [1952] RPC 10. Under this test, a worker will be an employee if he is integrated within the organisation where he works.

Cases where this concept was used with approval include *Cassidy v Minister of Health* [1951] 1 AER 574, where surgeons were held to be employees even though they were professionals providing a skill to the Health Service.

However the 'part and parcel' test has received short shrift from more recent judges. In *Ready Mixed Concrete* McKenna J. said that it:

> 'Raises more questions than I know how to answer. What is meant by being "part and parcel of an organisation"? Are all persons who answer this description servants? If only some are servants, what distinguishes them from the others if it is not their submission to orders?'

It was rejected in the Privy Council case of *Lee Ting Sang v Chung Chi-Keung* [1990] 2 AC 374 (see **8.3.1**), with the judge warning that:

> 'In the building and construction industry the test may lead to the error of only considering those on the permanent staff as employed under a contract of service.'

In *Lorimer* (see **8.2.1**), Lord Nolan felt that there was plenty of scope for people to become involved with an organisation without becoming part and parcel of it:

> 'Being one of a team to produce a programme does not, in my view, lead to the conclusion that, in Mr. Lorimer's case, he is "part an parcel" of the organisation . . . A violinist in an orchestra may be "part and parcel" of the orchestra for the performance being given but it does not follow that he is part and parcel of the organisation which runs or manages the orchestra.'

The Revenue appear to accept that the test is of limited use, saying in *Tax Bulletin 45* that:

> 'Establishing whether a person becomes "part and parcel" of a client's organisation can be a useful indicator in some situations. For example, someone taken on to manage a client's staff will normally be seen as part and parcel of the client's organisation and is likely to be an employee.'

Few contractors will be taken on 'to manage clients' staff' and even where they are, they may still, like Lorimer, be doing so as part of the delivery of a professional skill to the organisation with which they have contracted. In summary, this is not a test about which personal service workers should be too concerned.

6.8 Overall summary

Before considering the status tests, the existence of mutuality of obligation should be established, see Chapter 5. When the status tests are examined, they should not be seen as equally important. The courts have clearly shown that if a contract includes a genuine right to substitution or to hire workers, the worker is self-employed. If he takes significant financial risk, he will also be outside IR35.

Other factors are less clear cut. The extent of control over the worker should be considered, but is unlikely to be significant in the case of a professional; the equipment test is inconclusive on its own unless major items are supplied by the worker; and other minor factors have to be weighed in the balance.

The status tests should not be seen in isolation. It is the whole pattern of the worker's engagements that need to be considered, and this may have the effect of allowing someone to fall outside IR35 when the individual engagement, considered alone, would not.

The following chapters look at recent case law on status, at the Revenue's interpretation of these tests, and what can be done to improve a worker's position.

7 Revenue view of employment status

7.1 Introduction

This chapter reviews the guidance given by the Inland Revenue on status, notably in *Tax Bulletins 45* and *28*, in their booklets IR175 and IR56, and in the Revenue Manuals. It should be read against the background of:

- Chapter 5, which considers mutuality and the hypothetical contract which lies at the heart of the personal services legislation;
- Chapter 6, which reviews the status tests themselves; and
- Chapter 8, which looks at recent status cases.

If a worker wants to challenge the Revenue view, he is likely to need further advice, possibly from Counsel. The issue may eventually be decided by the Commissioners, and possibly the higher courts. Any such challenge will have repercussions for other workers, and could become a 'test case.' This chapter looks briefly at the ground rules which apply when a case goes to court, and how to get the best out of the appeal system.

7.2 General

Status tests have always been relevant for the self-employed, and those engaging workers directly have long been aware of the fine line that divides a contract of service from one for services. Booklet IR56: *Employed or Self-employed* has been available for many years, providing outline guidance on the status tests. In April 1997 the recategorisation of subcontractors prompted an article in *Tax Bulletin 28* as well as three useful worked examples, see **24.3**.

IR35 has now increased the numbers of those affected by categorisation, and the Revenue recognised the need for further and more focused guidance. Their *Tax Bulletin 45*, published in February 2000 and available on their website, looks at how the status tests affect personal service workers in general, and IT contractors in particular. A further three worked examples have been provided and are included at **24.2**.

In May 2000 a new booklet was published: IR175, *Supplying Services through a limited company or partnership*. There is, in addition, detailed guidance in the Revenue Manuals, available in every tax office, and soon to be accessible via the Revenue's website. Until recently the Schedule E Manual at paragraphs 535–710 provided the most complete summary of the Revenue's view of the employed/self-employed distinction.

However a new Status Manual is now in preparation, and the relevant parts of the Schedule E Manual are now to be found in the Employment Status Manual (ESM). At the time of writing, some parts, including that on service companies, were still incomplete. Where text has moved to the ESM from the earlier Schedule E Manual both references are given where possible.

In general Revenue guidance on status is clear and helpful. At times it bends over backwards to be fair to the taxpayer. However it is of necessity only an outline, and thus may be inappropriate when applied to borderline cases. In some of the guidance brevity means there are omissions, occasionally in areas which are particularly relevant to IR35 workers. Sometimes there is a certain colour to the guidance which means that it does not do full justice to the case law.

The following paragraphs look both at the Revenue's overall approach to the Schedule D/E divide, and at their published views on individual status tests.

7.3 Overall approach

7.3.1 General

The Revenue accept that a person's status can only be decided by looking 'at the picture as a whole' rather than 'by adding up the number of factors pointing towards employment and comparing that result with the number pointing to self-employment' (*Tax Bulletin 45*), see **6.3.1**. The Revenue also acknowledge that the 'in business on your own account' test has its limitations (see ESM 0507 and **6.4**).

7.3.2 Hierarchy of tests

Some factors are clearly more important than others, see **6.3.2**. Although the relative importance of each test can to some extent be inferred from the text of the Revenue commentaries, there is no overall guidance on which tests are decisive, and which merely supportive.

Booklet IR56 provides the most glaring example of this, and the same text has been borrowed for Booklet IR175. Under the heading: 'If you can answer "yes" to the following questions it will usually mean you are self-employed' the booklet correctly lists some of the key indicators of self-employment, including financial risk and the right to hire other workers to carry out the engagement. But it doesn't make it clear whether a worker has to answer 'yes' to all of these tests or just to some of them.

In reality if a worker met only *one* of the fundamental tests of self-employment (see **6.5.1**), such as the ability to hire workers to carry out the engagement, he would be self-employed. He could easily answer 'no' to the question:

> 'Do you provide the main items of equipment you need to do your job, not just the small tools many employees provide for themselves?'

and still be in business on his own account even if he provided no equipment at all, see **6.6.2** and **8.2.2**.

The *Tax Bulletin* article simply lists twelve status tests without trying to rank them, unless the order within the article is itself indicative of their relative importance. But if this is the implied intention, leaving 'Length of engagement' and 'Personal factors' to the end suggests that they are of minor importance, whereas they are likely to be central in a discussion of status for many IR35 workers.

7.3.3 Employment as the default position

While accepting that booklet IR56 contains a mere six pages on the status tests, and acknowledges its limitations in its introduction, it does treat employment as the default position. On page 3 of IR56 it says that 'if you can answer "yes" to the following questions you will probably be employed'; on page 6 that if you can't answer 'yes' to the self-employed questions 'you will normally be an employee'.

In reality it would be possible for a person to answer 'yes' to at least four out of five 'employment' questions and 'no' to a number of the 'self-employed' questions and still be in business on his own account, see **6.5.1**.

The *Tax Bulletin* professes independence, which is welcome. It says:

> 'The role of the Revenue is to provide advice and guidance about the employment status resulting from a given set of circumstances, not to impose any particular status.'

This is reinforced by the opening words of the Revenue's new status manual:

> 'The aim of employment status work is to ensure that the correct schedule of charge is applied and the correct class of NICs is paid. It is not to impose

any particular status. This is important because the Revenue is committed under 'Our Service Commitment to You' to

- treat all taxpayers and contributors with equal fairness; and

- help them get their affairs right, and

- a Revenue opinion on employment status will directly affect benefit entitlement.

In addition a status opinion might indirectly affect matters such as VAT.' (ESM 0005)

Taxpayers are likely to be sceptical, but may obtain some comfort from the number of IR35 contracts found to be outside IR35, see **7.7**.

7.3.4 Mutuality of obligation

Mutuality is conspicuous by its absence in either the *Tax Bulletin* or IR56. The comments in the Schedule E Manual, quoted at **5.3.7**, demonstrate that the Revenue consider that mutuality should be ignored on the basis that it is 'rarely of practical use' and 'can easily confuse the issue'(SE 663/ESM 0514).

However the courts have repeatedly held that it is fundamental to reviewing a worker's status. In *Nethermere (St Neots) Ltd v Gardiner* [1983] ICR 319, see **5.3.4**, Stephenson L.J. said that 'there must be an irreducible minimum of obligation on each side to create a contract of service'.

This has been followed in many subsequent court cases, such as *O'Kelly v Trusthouse Forte plc* [1983] 3 AER 456, see **5.3.2**, *Airfix Footwear Ltd v Cope* [1978] ICR 1210, see **5.3.4**, *Four Seasons (Inn on the Park) Ltd v Hamarat* [1985] EAT 369, see **5.3.2** as well as *Wickens v Champion Employment* [1984] ICR 365.

This issue is likely to be raised in the course of the next round of status cases which can be expected to follow the introduction of IR35.

7.4 Particular status tests

7.4.1 Substitution

Personal services is the essence of employment, and the right of substitution is thus a fundamental status test. If it is possible to send a substitute, there can be no employment. The case law on substitution is discussed at **6.5.2**, and the practical implications of including a substitution clause in a contract at **9.3**.

The Revenue accept that where a substitute is actually provided, there cannot be an employment. In *Lorimer*, the Revenue's barrister, Mr Goldsmith, conceded that:

'Tax could not be charged under Sch E in respect of the profits made by Mr. Lorimer on the six occasions when, with the consent of the production company concerned, he provided a substitute to carry out the work for which he had contracted. Mr. Goldsmith accepted that in those cases Mr. Lorimer could not be said to have earned his profit in the performance of a contract of service because in the result he was not paid for his own skill and labour.'

In *Tax Bulletin 45* the Revenue go further, saying that:

'Personal service is an essential element of a contract of employment. A person who has the freedom to choose whether to do the job himself or hire somebody else to do it for him, or who can hire someone else to provide substantial help is probably self-employed . . . However, this must be viewed in the context of the arrangements overall. For example, a worker may choose to pay a helper to take phone messages and deal with invoicing and general book keeping work for the intermediary. But this would not be directly relevant when considering an engagement where the worker is engaged to lay bricks for a client.'

While not completely conceding the point that the worker cannot be an employee if there is a *right* to send a substitute (note the word 'probably' in the text), nevertheless the *Tax Bulletin* article indicates that the Revenue accept the view that the right of substitution is incompatible with employment.

However, in the period following the publication of *Tax Bulletin 45*, the Revenue became concerned that the 'right' of substitution was being misunderstood. In April 2000 they added the following Frequently Asked Question to their website:

'*44. My contract specifies that I am allowed to hire a substitute. Will the Inland Revenue take this at face value? If not will I need to provide evidence to prove that this right is genuine?*

The Inland Revenue will want to ensure that the right to send a substitute is a genuine right before it can be taken into account in deciding employment status.

A right of substitution is only likely to exist where the client does not mind, from one day to the next for the duration of the contract, who carries out the work, provided that whoever does so is suitably qualified and experienced. We do not accept that such a right exists where the client's permission has to be obtained before sending a substitute.

Where the service company's contract is not with the client but with an agency, and there is a claimed right of substitution, the Inland Revenue would normally require a copy of the written contract between the agency and the client.

> If you are unable to get access to that contract then you should ask the agency to send a copy to the Inland Revenue direct. If this is not possible you may be asked to provide alternative evidence. This could take the form of a letter from the client which confirms that it has agreed to your service company providing a substitute and that it does not matter which worker is provided on a day to day basis over the course of the contract.'

The Revenue is clearly correct in stating that the right has to be genuine, and for this to be the case the client has to agree that a substitute can be provided. They also have case law support for the view that there is no right if the client's permission has to be obtained, see **6.5.2**.

However, for the right to be effective the client may not need to be indifferent as to 'which worker is provided on a day to day basis over the course of the contract'.

In *Diggles,* see **6.5.2**, the barristers had engaged their Senior Clerk to provide 'Full Clerking Services' and although a substitute could be provided, the barristers (if asked) could reasonably have been expected to express a preference for Mr Diggles. Similarly, Mr Tanton (see **6.5.2**) had been engaged as a driver, and although someone else stepped in when he was ill, this is not the same as saying the Express and Echo had no concern who did the job on a day-to-day basis. Thus the courts are unlikely to require that the client must be indifferent as to who actually does the work.

The Revenue accept that not being able to send a substitute does not mean that a worker is necessarily an employee:

> 'An obligation to provide personal services does not always prove there is an employment. An independent contractor may be required to do the work personally under the terms of the contract by which he is engaged. The fact that he is not allowed to hire others does not necessarily mean that the contract is a contract of employment.' (SE 603/ESM 1053)

7.4.2 Risk

If a worker takes significant financial risk he will not be an employee, see **6.5.3**. This position is generally accepted by the Revenue:

> 'An individual who risks his own money by, for example, buying assets needed for the job and bearing their running costs and paying for overheads and large quantities of materials, is almost certainly self-employed.' (*Tax Bulletin 45*)

The *Tax Bulletin* gives examples of what the Revenue would accept as evidence of financial risk, including:

- Quoting a fixed price for a job, with the consequent risk of bearing the additional costs if the job overruns;

- A skilled worker incurring significant amounts of expenditure on training to provide himself with a skill which he uses in subsequent engagements. This can be treated in the same way as investment in equipment to be used in a trade, as a pointer to self-employment, if there is a real risk that the investment would not be recovered from income from future engagements.

However in *Lorimer* (see **8.2.1**) the judge held that a relatively low level of risk was sufficient for the worker to be self-employed. Mr Lorimer:

> 'Bears his own financial risk which is greater than that of one who is an employee, accepting the risk of bad debts and outstanding invoices and of no or an insufficient number of engagements.'

The possibility that a lower level of risk might be acceptable in an 'exceptional case' is mentioned in the Manual (SE 622/ESM 1031) where they refer to the session musicians in *Addison and others v The London Philharmonic Orchestra Society Limited* [1981] ICR 261 and *Midland Sinfonia Concert Society Limited v The Secretary of State for Social Services* [1981] ICR 454, see **20.5.2**. In these cases the musicians were held to be self-employed even though they 'did not risk their own capital in orchestral performances'.

As discussed at **6.5.3**, there is a difference between significant financial risk, which is decisive in establishing that a worker is self-employed, and lesser levels of risk, which are merely indicative of Schedule D status. The distinction is not always evident in the Revenue guidance.

7.4.3 Profiting from sound management

If risk is one side of the coin, the opportunity to profit from sound management is the other, see **6.5.3**. The Revenue rather grudgingly say that:

> 'A person whose profit or loss depends on his capacity to reduce overheads and organise his work effectively *may well be* self-employed.' (*Tax Bulletin 45*, the author's italics)

They also say that this will apply to 'people who are paid by the job'. This is true. However in *Lorimer* Nolan J. said that the worker's exploitation of his own reputation was sufficient to allow him to profit from sound management, see **8.2.2**. A similar point was made in the *Addison* case referred to at **7.4.2** above.

7.4.4 Hiring staff

This is another fundamental status test, and if satisfied the worker will be self-employed, see **6.5.4**. The Revenue carefully explain its parameters:

(a) In IR56 they correctly distinguish between 'being free to hire people on terms of one's own choice to do the work which one has taken on, paying them out of one's own pocket,' which is characteristic of self-employment, and merely 'being authorised to delegate work or to engage others on behalf of one's employer';

(b) Similarly in *Tax Bulletin 45* they emphasise that the helper must be carrying out work which is intrinsic to the engagement, and not merely 'invoicing and general book keeping' see **7.4.1** above;

(c) In *Tax Bulletin 28* they warn that hiring others means that it is the worker's responsibility to decide on the employment status of those he has engaged:

> 'Are "gang masters" or "team leaders" employed or self-employed?
>
> The answer depends on the precise terms of the agreements entered into by the various parties. The gang master or team leader, and the individual gang or team members, may all be employees of the contractor . . . If, however, the gang master is responsible for engaging and paying the team members (out of his own all inclusive fee for delivering a particular task) he is almost certainly self-employed. The gang master or team leader would then have to decide if his men are employed by him, or self-employed.'

Thus the Revenue accept that the right to hire workers proves self-employment, but are keen to emphasise that it is a right that comes with responsibilities.

7.4.5 Provision of equipment

Where a worker provides significant equipment he will be self-employed, see **6.6.2**. The Revenue put this status test into the context of IT contractors as follows:

> 'Where an IT consultant is engaged to undertake a specific piece of work and must work exclusively at home using the worker's own computer equipment, that will be a strong pointer to self-employment. But where a worker is provided with office space and computer equipment that points to employment. The fact that a worker might occasionally choose to do some of the work at home using his or her own computer does not change that (many employees do just that).' (*Tax Bulletin 45*)

This suggests that not only is providing significant equipment a pointer to self-employment (which is correct) but also that not providing such equipment indicates employment. The same point is made in the Revenue Manual:

> 'In *Hall v Lorimer* a vision mixer was found to be self employed when the terms, conditions and facts surrounding his engagements were considered as a whole. This was despite the fact that the substantial and expensive equipment needed was provided by his engagers. Mummery J, in the High Court, considered that the provision of equipment by Lorimer's engagers undoubtedly pointed towards the existence of employment but this was not sufficient, by itself, to outweigh other pointers towards self employment that were present in that particular case.' (SE 605/ESM 1062)

In fact Lord Nolan in the Court of Appeal effectively overruled Mummery J.'s view that Lorimer's non-provision of equipment indicated employment. Lord Nolan ruled that it was *irrelevant* that Lorimer provided no equipment *because it was not his business to provide equipment*, see **6.6.2**.

Thus the Revenue conclusion that the provision of equipment by Lorimer's engagers 'undoubtedly pointed towards employment' and thus needed to be outweighed by other pointers towards self-employment is incorrect. It was not a factor either way, and thus did not need to be 'outweighed' by other factors pointing towards Schedule D.

The same could be said of an IT contractor providing specialist skills to a client with millions of pounds worth of computer equipment, or of an oil worker on a multi-million pound rig in the North Sea.

7.4.6 Control

The control test is complex and has developed over time, see **6.6.3**. The Inland Revenue's guidance is summarised in the *Tax Bulletin 45* article:

> 'A worker will not be an employee unless there is a right to exercise "control" over the worker. This may be a right to control "what" work is done, "where" or "when" it is done or "how" it is done. Actual control of this sort is not necessary – it is the right of control that is important.

> Where a client has the right to determine "how" the work is done this is a strong pointer to employment. But it is not an essential feature of employment – many "experts" who are employees are not necessarily subject to such control (for example, ship's captain, consultant brain surgeon, etc.).

> Equally, a right to determine "what" work is carried out is a strong pointer to employment. It will normally be a feature whenever a client needs a worker to undertake whatever tasks are required at any particular time or where the worker is required to work as part of a co-ordinated team.

A working relationship which involves no control at all is unlikely to be an employment.'

This is one of the more defensive sections of the *Tax Bulletin* article. It stresses the fact that an absence of control as to 'how' or 'what' does not necessarily mean that the worker is self-employed; it does not point out the obvious corollary that *absence* of control in these areas could indicate that the worker is Schedule D.

One key development is conspicuous by its absence – the court's view that control is not a very useful test in the case of professionals, see **6.6.3**. This point is, however, picked up in the more extensive Employment Status Manual at para 1024, but again the Revenue stress that this means a professional can be an employee even if he is not subject to much control, rather than pointing out the corollary: that the existence of control does not preclude the individual being self employed, as in Lorimer. The latter is very significant, particularly in the context of IR35.

On a point of relative detail, the suggestion that the worker will be an employee if he is 'required to work as part of a co-ordinated team' runs counter to Lord Nolan's comment in *Lorimer* that:

'If you are part of a team to produce a show, it is inevitable that someone must organise it . . . That applies to the leading actor and actress, but they do not for that reason become "employees".'

7.4.7 Number and variety of engagements

If one had to pinpoint a single reason why Mr Lorimer was held to be self-employed, it would be because of the number and variety of his engagements, see **6.6.4**. When mentioned by the Revenue it is usually in conjunction with the need to have a business organisation. For example, *Tax Bulletin 45* states:

'If a skilled worker works for a number of clients throughout the year, and has a business-like approach to obtaining his engagements (perhaps involving expenditure on office accommodation, office equipment etc.) this will point towards self-employment.'

In *Lorimer* there was no connection between the number of clients and any expenditure on office accommodation or equipment, see **7.4.11** below, and linking the two can therefore be resisted.

IR175 similarly mentions that having a large number of clients can be an indicator of self-employment, but the point highlighted in such a way as to suggest (perhaps unintentionally) a lack of Revenue enthusiasm for the concept:

'The number of clients you have **may** be relevant to the decision whether your work for each is as an employee, or as a self employed person. If you have many different clients this **may** indicate self employment, and be a factor that should be considered in addition to the actual details of each contract.'

However, more encouragingly, the number and variety of clients was the deciding factor in the Revenue's *Tax Bulletin* example Charlotte, see **24.2.4**, and in a similar situation one could thus expect the Revenue to agree that a worker was self-employed.

7.4.8 Regular or long engagements with the same client

Tax Bulletin 45 says that:

'Where this pattern of a number of different clients does not exist, but instead the worker is regularly engaged by the same client, this may indicate employment, see *Nethermere [St. Neots) Ltd v Gardiner* [1984] ICR 612.'

However the *Nethermere* case is not necessarily applicable to a professional working through a personal service company, see **5.3.4**. The Revenue may agree with this, because at the end of the article they qualify their earlier general comments by saying that (the author's italics):

'Long periods working for one engager may be typical of an employment *but are not conclusive*. It is still necessary to consider all the terms and conditions of each engagement.'

The most positive approach was until recently that of the Revenue Manual, which advised Inspectors to be patient and not jump to conclusions:

'Bear in mind though that someone commencing in business may in practice work for the same engager under a series of separate contracts because he or she is unable to obtain contracts elsewhere. For example, a professional worker may start in business, set up an office and endeavour to obtain engagements in a particular field on a self-employed basis with a variety of engagers. If he or she continues in that vein but only manages to obtain work for part of the time through short-term contracts from one engager *the fact that only one engager is involved would not necessarily mean those engagements are employments*.' (SE 690, the author's italics)

Sadly, this paragraph appears to have been omitted from the new Employment Status Manual, which may indicate an unwillingness to accept that, in the real world, it may take some time to establish a network of clients.

As a final point, *Tax Bulletin 45* includes a coded warning against splitting engagements into short periods in order to simulate a self-employed scenario:

> 'Where an engagement is covered by a series of short contracts, or an initial short contract subsequently extended for a longer period, *it is the length of the engagement* that is relevant, rather than the length of each contract.'

7.4.9 Payment terms

Pay

The guidance in the Manual here is to be preferred to that in the *Tax Bulletin*. In the latter the Revenue comment:

> 'Employees tend to be paid a fixed wage or salary by the week or month and often qualify for additional payments such as overtime, long service bonus or profit share. Independent contractors, on the other hand, tend to be paid a fixed sum for a particular job. Payment "by the piece" (where the worker is paid according to the amount of work actually done) or by commission can be a feature of both employment and self-employment.'

This contrasts the self-employed on a project basis with the employee, but doesn't point out that independent contractors are also frequently paid by the hour, see **6.7.3**. The Manual has the space to be more balanced:

> 'Care must be taken with this aspect as it is often inconclusive. There are many examples of employees who are paid by the piece or on the basis of commission and equally there many self employed individuals who charge by the hour or day.' (SE 631)

Benefits

The Manual and the *Tax Bulletin* make the same point:

> 'The absence of benefits such as sick pay, pension scheme membership, maternity rights, etc. in a short term engagement will almost certainly be because they are inappropriate in such circumstances. Their absence may therefore be of little relevance in this type of situation and certainly will not inevitably lead to the conclusion that an employment does not exist.' (SE 675/ESM 1075)

The opposite is also true, but passes without explicit comment – people can have benefits and yet still be self-employed, see **6.7.3**. The Revenue's new Employment Status Manual does, however, warn Inspectors not to put the cart before the horse:

'The important point to remember though is that the presence or absence of these rights does not necessarily determine whether a worker is employed or self-employed. On the contrary, it is the employment status (and the length of the contract) which determines whether the worker is entitled to many of these rights.' (ESM 1075)

7.4.10 Intention of the parties

There is doubt as to whether the intention of the parties is in fact conclusive in the context of the hypothetical personal services contract, see **5.2.4**. However, this doubt is not shared by the Revenue, who accept that:

'The intention can be decisive where the relationship is ambiguous and where the other factors are neutral.' (*Tax Bulletin 45*)

Helpfully, the Manual cites the unreported case of *WF and RK Swan (Hellenic) Ltd v The Secretary of State for Social Services* [1983] QBD, which found that tour couriers were independent contractors because this was the declared intention of the parties, and the other factors were equally balanced (SE 658/ESM 1101).

They also, correctly, warn against labeling a relationship as self-employed when the facts point in the opposite direction, see **5.2.5**.

7.4.11 Business organisation

In testing whether a worker should 'pass' the *Lorimer* business organisation test (see **7.4.1**), the Revenue ask whether he:

'Has a business-like approach to obtaining and organising his/her engagements and incurs expenditure in this area of a type not normally associated with employment (for example provision of office accommodation, office equipment, etc.).' (SE 685/ESM 1093)

This actually suggests rather more structure than was in place either for the session musicians, or for Lorimer. The personal service worker should thus satisfy the requirements if he simply has a business bank account; takes bookings; confirms them; and keeps appropriate records. Lorimer did no more than this.

7.5 Case studies

In *Tax Bulletin 28* the Revenue included three worked examples of subcontractors: a general labourer classified as Schedule E, a plasterer who was held to be in business on his own account, and a bricklayer who was borderline, but marginally Schedule E, see **24.3**.

In *Tax Bulletin 45* they followed the same model, with a further three case studies:

(a) Gordon, an IT consultant who works as part of the client's payroll team. Gordon would have been Schedule E had he worked directly for the client, and thus falls within the personal services rules, see **24.3.2**;

(b) Henry, a consultant engineer who would be classified as Schedule D, see **24.3.3**;

(c) Charlotte, who is borderline and just succeeds in falling outside IR35, see **24.3.4**.

These case studies can be found at Chapter 24, and demonstrate a practical and balanced approach to applying the status tests in the given situations.

7.6 Standard contracts

The Revenue have also commented on what they call 'standard contracts':

> 'The terms of contracts used by service company workers who obtain engagements through agencies tend to be of a standard form. Such contracts typically require the worker to work on the client's premises, use the client's equipment, work standard hours, be paid at an hourly rate and be subject to a high level of control. In such cases, the opinion of the Revenue about the engagement is likely to be that it would be employment.
>
> Where a worker is engaged on this type of contract for a period of one month or more, and cannot demonstrate a recent history of work including engagements which have the characteristics of self-employment . . . then we will say that the engagement would have been employment and therefore be covered by the new rules. Where the contract is for less than a month, then, although the engagement may still have been one of employment, the status position will be considered on a case by case basis.' (*Tax Bulletin 45*)

In publishing these comments the Revenue have sought to give clear guidance on those contractual arrangements which clearly fall on the employment side of the line, so that individuals who work in this way would know the result they would obtain if they sought a status review. In the opinion of the author, the Revenue are correct. A hypothetical contract derived from the standard client/agency/worker contracts would almost certainly be within the scope of IR35.

Included in the Revenue statement above are two important exceptions:

- Where the standard contract forms part of a wider picture which, taken together, suggests self-employment, they have accepted that in this situation the standard contract alone will not be decisive; and

- Where the engagement is *for a very short time* (as was the case in *Lorimer*) then the individual may be able to make a case for self-employment.

Both these points are discussed in more detail at **6.6.4**.

It should be noted that industries other than IT, also have standard contracts. In the acting world an Equity contract is accepted as Schedule D by the Revenue, see **20.2.2**. Oil industry contracts also tend to follow a similar form, and contain many elements which are suggestive of employment, see **20.6.2**. Chapter 9 discusses ways in which contractual arrangements could be changed so that they might in the future fall outside of IR35.

7.7 Status reviews

If individuals are in doubt about their status, they can ask the Revenue to give a ruling. However an opinion will only be given on signed contracts and not on draft agreements (*Tax Bulletin 45*). This may be because they are concerned that explaining the factor(s) which cause the contract to be classified as Schedule E will enable the arrangements to be amended so as to bring them outside IR35.

In order to obtain a Revenue ruling, the worker must send 'a copy of the relevant contract setting out the full terms and conditions of the engagement . . . together with details of any fact that he considers relevant to the status position.' (Ibid)

Once the contract has been received the Revenue may ask to see the contract with the client (see FAQ General 30) and they may also conduct interviews. This could be with the worker and/or with other parties such as the client or agency:

> 'The Inland Revenue will review the facts . . . In order to do this the Inland Revenue will review the contract or contracts which establish the relationship. They may also talk to you and others. If you do not agree with the Inland Revenue's opinion you can appeal against it.' (IR175)

As at June 2000, over 1,200 contracts had been submitted to the Revenue, and it was confirmed in the House of Commons that 53% were found to be within

IR35, and 47% outside it (Hansard, 6 June 2000). This suggests that the even-handed approach promised in the Status Manual and the Tax Bulletin (see **7.3.3**) may be more prevalent than may have been expected.

7.8 Challenging the Revenue view

7.8.1 General

If the Revenue believe a service company is within the personal service rules, but the worker disagrees, the issue will first be debated with the Inspector. This can be by letter or in a meeting. Professional advice at this early stage should ensure that:

- The strength of the worker's case is assessed;

- All available facts and arguments are mustered as soon as possible;

- No misleading facts or suggestions are made to the Inspector;

- The process is focused, so costs are kept to a minimum.

It is essential that the case law support for the worker's position be properly researched, and not by reference only to summaries and dicta. In the *Lee Ting Sang* case (see **8.3.1**) Lord Griffiths warned against such short cuts when he explained why the Privy Council was taking the unusual step of overruling the lower courts:

> 'Reliance upon these two dicta, culled from cases of a wholly dissimilar character, may have misled the courts below in their assessment of the facts of this case, and amount to an error of law justifying setting aside what are to be regarded as concurrent findings of fact.'

7.8.2 Questions of law and fact

The courts have debated for some time whether employment status was a question of law, a question of fact, or a mixed question of both law and fact. This is important because it is only possible to appeal to a higher court on a question of law, not a question of fact.

The current view is that it is a matter of law, but that it involves matters of degree and fact which should be decided at the first stage of the legal process (*O'Kelly v Trusthouse Forte plc* [1983] 3 WLR 605, see **5.3.2**). In a tax case this first stage is the General or Special Commissioners, in an employment law case it is the Employment Tribunal (formerly the Industrial Tribunal).

Exceptionally, where the case turns on the true construction of a legal document, this will be a question of law which can be referred to a higher court, see *McManus v Griffiths* [1997] 70 TC 218 and *Davies v Presbyterian Church of Wales* [1986] AC 508. This is unlikely to be the case with a status issue under the personal services legislation, because Schedule 12, para 1(4) specifically provides that the written terms are only part of the 'circumstances' to be considered, see **5.1**.

The facts which are decided at the Commissioners cannot be interfered with by a higher court. Lord Griffiths in *Lee Ting Sang* (see **8.3.1**) said that this was a pragmatic approach because of:

> 'The difficulty of devising a conclusive test to resolve the question, and the threat of the appellate courts being crushed by the weight of appeals if the many borderline cases were considered to be questions of law.'

7.8.3 Importance of agreeing the facts

Given the general proposition that determination of status involves matters of degree and fact which are decided by the court of first instance, it is vital that all relevant facts are put to the Commissioners. A higher court can only change the decision of the Commissioners if it can show that either:

- No reasonable Commissioner could have come to that decision on those facts; or

- The Commissioner made an error in the legal interpretation of those facts (*Edwards v Bairstow* [1956] AC 14 as applied by the Court of Appeal in *Nethermere (St Neots) Ltd v Gardner* [1984] IRLR 240, see **5.3.4**, and *McLeod v Hellyer Brothers Ltd* [1987] IRLR 232, see **5.3.5**).

In the *Lorimer* case, see **8.2.1**, the decision of the Special Commissioner that Lorimer was self-employed was upheld in the High Court and Court of Appeal. In the High Court Mummery J. said, commenting on the process:

> 'The Appellate Court will not interfere with the conclusion of the fact-finding tribunal where the decision as to the true nature of the taxpayer's arrangements comes within what has been described as the "band of possible reasonable decisions". The Appellate Court recognises that there are borderline or grey areas in which tribunals, properly instructed on the law and facts, can legitimately and reasonably arrive at different conclusions.'

This was put even more strongly by Lord Donaldson in the *O'Kelly* case, see **5.3.2**:

'The appellate court . . . may well have a shrewd suspicion, or gut reaction, that it would have reached a different decision, but it must never forget that this may be because it thinks that it would have found or weighed the facts differently. Unpalatable though it may be on occasion, it must loyally accept the conclusions of fact with which it is presented and, accepting those conclusions, it must be satisfied that there *must* have been a misdirection on a question of law before it can intervene.'

This serves to emphasise the vital importance of the first stage in the legal process, and the critical importance of the facts and arguments presented to the Commissioners. In the *Express and Echo* case discussed at **6.5.1** above, the judge said that further facts brought up on appeal should be ignored, despite the fact that Mr Tanton:

'Did not appreciate that there was such emphasis by the appellant on personal service by him as a requirement of a contract of employment, otherwise he would have given (further) evidence to the chairman at the Industrial Tribunal hearing. But no such evidence was given to the chairman, and . . . accordingly, that (further evidence) cannot help Mr Tanton.'

7.8.4 The legal process

It is beyond the scope of this book to explain either how best to argue a case before the courts, or the legal process which has to be followed as it progresses from the lower courts through the High Court and Court of Appeal to the House of Lords. However, before beginning a lengthy and expensive legal process, it is worth bearing in mind the words of Lord Griffiths in *Lee Ting Sang* **8.3.1** that:

'There will be many borderline cases in which similarly instructed minds will come to different conclusions.'

In other words, the result in a difficult status case may go either way. One comfort to taxpayers is that the Revenue are in the same uncertain position. This is despite the confident words in their *Decision Maker's Guide to Working Families Tax Credits* at paragraph 22005 that:

'The decision maker decides whether a person is an employed or a self-employed earner. The decision maker should rarely have difficulty in deciding which category will apply.'

8 Status cases and IR35

8.1 Introduction

This chapter looks at a number of recent court decisions on status in the context of the IR35 legislation, and gives some guidance on how they apply to personal service workers.

While some workers will clearly be self-employed, and others equally clearly employees, a third group occupies the grey area in the middle. In the immortal words of Mr Justice Rowlatt, it is necessary 'to formulate some line of cleavage', so that those in the grey area are divided into Schedule D and Schedule E. This is no easy process, as Mummery J. commented:

> 'How narrow the line often is between, on the one hand, carrying on a business on one's own account with a succession of regular or casual clients and, on the other hand, being in a state of discontinuous employment with a succession of different employers. It is particularly difficult to draw the line in those cases where a person claims that his business consists of providing only his personal services and skill to another, valuable though those skills may be.' (*Hall v Lorimer* [1993] 66 TC 349, see **8.2.1**)

It may not always be the same line, since, although there are agreed status tests, their relative importance varies. In *Walls v Sinnett* [1986] 60 TC 150, Vinelott J. said:

> 'It is in my judgement, quite impossible in a field where a very large number of factors have to be weighed, to gain any real assistance by looking at the facts of another case and comparing them one by one to see what facts are common, what are different and what particular weight is given by another tribunal to the common facts. The facts as a whole must be looked at, and what may be compelling in one case in the light of all the facts may not be compelling in the context of another case.'

Thus, although it is possible and necessary to consider the status tests one by one, as was done in Chapter 6, it is also important to see them in context. This is because reviewing status tests is like any other analytic process. Dissecting five hundred football matches demonstrates what leads to glorious victory and what to ignominious defeat. Combing *Macbeth* for character, imagery, and concepts of celestial harmony explains why it is a dramatic success. But for real understanding, matches have to be played and plays watched. It is the same with case law: to appreciate how the different status tests work they must be seen in the context of an individual's situation.

This chapter reviews three recent court decisions and applies them specifically to personal services. In each case it seeks to 'paint a picture' of each worker to show why the court came to its decision. The first concerns a professional, the second a manual labourer, and both provide useful lessons for personal service workers. The third involves a semi-skilled technician, and demonstrates the care which is necessary when using previous status cases as precedents. The chapter then looks at a number of other cases, and tries to identify some of the key factors which are relevant for personal service workers on the line between employment and self-employment.

8.2 Recent court decisions I: the professional

8.2.1 Hall v Lorimer

Hall v Lorimer [1993] 66 TC 349 was a milestone in the evolution of the status test. Ian Lorimer was a freelance professional in the TV industry, with no equipment and little business risk, who was held by the Courts to be self-employed. Some personal service workers may be able to use the same arguments, and so fall outside the scope of Schedule 12, FA 2000.

The reason the case is important for personal service workers is because Mr Lorimer passed few of the traditional status tests. The Revenue argued that he was an employee because he:

(a) Provided no equipment;

(b) Hired no staff to assist him in his work;

(c) Ran no financial risk apart from the risk of bad debts and of being unable to find work;

(d) Had no responsibility for investment in or management of the programmes on which he was working;

(e) Had no control over the time, place or duration of each programme on which he worked; this was entirely in the hands of the production company.

Although Lorimer was able to rebut some of these points to some degree – for instance, the court held that he ran greater financial risk than an employee – nevertheless they are in substance correct. He was however held to be self-employed, and the Revenue lost the case, despite having argued strongly that:

> 'All he is doing is contracting from time to time to put his work skills at the disposal of another for reward, that is not a business at all: it is the very essence of employment under a contract of service.'

Thus if the personal service worker's situation is substantially the same as that of Ian Lorimer, he too can make a case for self-employment. To succeed, he must show that he is selling a skill to a number of different clients, preferably for short periods; and that he has some rudimentary booking, invoicing and recording procedures.

8.2.2 Key factors leading to the decision

Skill is necessary, but not sufficient

Lorimer was a vision mixer, and the court devoted some time to hearing what this involved:

> 'A vision mixer's function is skilled. A programme may be televised "live" or it may be rehearsed, recorded and shown as if it were live. A mixer has to have a sense of timing, a feeling for mood, anticipation, a feeling for music and dexterity in operating equipment. He is a type of editor. In a live show he has only one chance to get it right.'

However, merely being skilled is not enough to prevent classification as an employee, see *Cassidy v Ministry of Health* [1951] 1 AER 574 (see **6.6.3**) where a surgeon was held to be employed by the health authority despite clearly being a highly specialist worker.

This principle that the skill alone is not enough was accepted in the *Lorimer* case. Lord Nolan said that:

> 'Mr. Goldsmith (for the Revenue) submitted that the degree of skill involved in the work cannot alone be decisive. Again I agree. A brain surgeon may very well be an employee.'

Number and variety of clients

Mr Lorimer had numerous very short engagements with 22 active clients. Although in his first year 48 per cent of his engagements were with five companies, this percentage fell over the next three years as his business expanded and he developed a wider client base. Each engagement usually lasted one or two days, with the longest being for eight. The fact that he was 'independent of a particular paymaster for the financial exploitation of his talents' was found to be one of the main reasons why he was classified as Schedule D.

125

This confirms that when deciding whether a worker is employed or self-employed it is not simply a question of looking at a single contract, but the 'whole pattern' of his engagements. This is also true when deciding the nature of the hypothetical contract between worker and client which lies at the heart of the personal services legislation, see **5.1.1**.

Mutuality of obligation

The issue of mutuality of obligation was discussed at length at **5.3** above. Although mutuality was not a focus of the *Lorimer* case, it was agreed that:

> 'There (is no) question of an "umbrella" contract. Mr. Lorimer can accept engagements or not as he wishes; similarly production companies are free to engage Mr. Lorimer's services or not as they choose.'

The Revenue tried to argue for a succession of small employment contracts, see **5.3.3**, but this was rejected by the judge. Thus it is reasonable to conclude that the court considered there was insufficient mutuality of obligation between Mr Lorimer and his various clients for there to be a contract of employment.

Business structure

Lorimer's business structure was rudimentary. In addition to having a business bank account:

> 'Bookings were usually made by telephone to his home, where he had an office, and were confirmed by letter which often stated the date, rate of pay, place of work and time. No formal written conditions were made. VAT was charged, Lorimer having registered for VAT from 1 February 1985.'

This was held to be a reasonable business structure for certain types of self-employment. Lord Nolan said that 'a self-employed author working from home or an actor or a singer may earn his living without any of the normal trappings of a business'.

Financial risk

The Revenue tried to argue that Lorimer's financial risk was inadequate, and thus indicative of employment. Their barrister said that:

> 'The risk he runs in not working for one production company under a long-term contract is that run by any employee who chooses to work on a casual basis. He runs the risk of being unable to find employment, of being unemployed and unpaid.'

However the court held that in fact he ran more risk than an employee. For example:

• He could and did lose money when a client becomes insolvent;

• Some clients were bad payers and made him wait up to three months before paying him;

However Mummery J., in the High Court, held that even this level of risk was not a necessary precondition for someone to be self-employed. Quoting *O'Kelly v Trusthouse Forte plc* [1983] 3 AER 456 (see **5.3.2**), he said that (the author's italics):

'The importance of that case is that the Court of Appeal held that it was quite possible for a fact-finding tribunal, properly instructed on the facts and the law, to conclude that a person was in business on his own account and not a party to a succession of contracts of employment *when all that he supplied was his own services, without providing any equipment or having any risk of loss of prospective profit.*'

Equipment

It was accepted by both sides in the case that:

'All of Mr. Lorimer's work as a vision mixer is done at the studios owned or hired by the production company on equipment owned or supplied by the studio company ... Mr. Lorimer does not provide or pay for any of the equipment which he uses in his work ... That equipment is complex and expensive and is provided by the studio company to the production company.'

The Revenue argued that the fact that he provided no equipment was one of the reasons why he was an employee, but Lord Nolan gave this short shrift:

'It is said that Mr. Lorimer provides no equipment (i.e. he has no tools), he provides no "work place" or "workshop" where the contract is to be performed, he provides no capital for the production, he hires no staff for it. No, he does not. But *that is not his business.*'

The judge was therefore saying that the provision of equipment or otherwise was irrelevant in deducing whether Lorimer was employed or self-employed. It was his business to sell his skill – the fact that he had no equipment was immaterial. This is a very significant development for professionals, who commonly work on expensive equipment provided by their engagers.

127

Opportunity of profit

Not only could Lorimer suffer greater losses than an employee, he could also make profits. The judge held that:

> 'He has the opportunity of profiting from being good at being a vision mixer. According to his reputation, so there will be a demand for his services for which he will be able to charge accordingly. The more efficient he is at running the business of providing his services, the greater is his prospect of profit.'

Expenses

Lord Nolan considered that the expenses Lorimer incurred were 'quite different in nature and scale from those likely to be incurred by an employee', giving as an example the fact that:

> 'In the period from 1 February 1985 to 30 April 1986, his expenses, including the cost of running his car or otherwise travelling in the course of his work and of running his office from home, amounted to £9,250 against fees received of £32,875, though it may be that the figure for fees included some reimbursement of expenses.'

Personal service workers might like to remember this when they review the expenses they can no longer deduct under the Schedule E rules – the very fact of having incurred the expense may itself be a small pointer towards self-employment! This point is in fact explicitly accepted in the Revenue's new Employment Status Manual, see para 1093.

8.2.3 Conclusions

The key facts in the Lorimer decision are that:

(a) He was a skilled professional;

(b) He earned his living by working for a large number of different clients;

(c) There was no mutuality of obligation between himself and his clients;

(d) His financial risk was slight, but more than that of an employee;

(e) He had a rudimentary business structure.

8.2.4 Application of the case to personal service workers

Clearly, if the hypothetical contract between the worker and the client can mirror these five points, IR35 should not apply. Looking at each in turn:

(a) Most professionals working through personal service companies will have no difficulty in proving, like Lorimer, that they are skilled workers;

(b) Some professionals will, like Lorimer, have a succession of small engagements;

(c) Mutuality of obligation is discussed in detail at **5.3**. The courts have held that it is easier for a professional not to establish mutual obligations than it would be for a manual worker. Whether mutuality of obligations exists in a particular case depends upon the individual facts;

(d) Most personal service workers are in a similar position to Lorimer as far as financial risk is concerned, whether they obtain work directly from clients or from a number of agencies. If only one agency is involved, there may be less risk, assuming the agency takes responsibility for paying the worker and is not simply a conduit for the client.

8.3 Recent court decisions II: the manual worker

8.3.1 Lee Ting Sang v Chung Chi-Keung

The 1990 Privy Council case of *Lee Ting Sang v Chung Chi-Keung* [1990] 2 AC 374 considered whether Mr Lee, a mason injured while chipping concrete on a building site, was an employee. Factors in favour of his self-employment were that he was a skilled artisan, his work was largely unsupervised and he worked for a number of different engagers.

However the Privy Council held he was employed because he:

(a) Provided no equipment, but used tools supplied by his engager;

(b) Hired no helpers;

(c) Had no responsibility for investment in, or management of, the work on the construction site;

(d) Did not price the job, which is normally a feature of a subcontractor with his own business;

(e) Was paid either a piece-work rate or a daily rate according to the nature of the work he was doing;

(f) Did not 'exercise any skill or judgement' but was 'simply told what to do and left to get on with it';

(g) Ran no financial risk, other than that of not finding work.

This sounds compelling, until one realises that Lorimer also provided no equipment, hired no helpers and had no investment in the projects on which he worked, and that, like Lorimer, Mr Lee worked for a succession of engagers. The differences between the two cases are set out below.

Opportunity of profit

Lorimer could set his own rates and profit from his reputation, see **8.2.2**; Mr Lee, in contrast, was paid a rate set by the building contractor or sub-contractor for whom he worked.

Risk of loss

Although the Revenue argued that Lorimer's risk of loss was insignificant, the court disagreed, see **8.2.2**. However Mr Lee fell the other side of the line. Lord Griffiths said that:

> 'The applicant ran no risk whatsoever save that of being unable to find employment, which is, of course, a risk faced by casual employees who move from one job to another.'

Skill and judgment

Although Mr Lee was described by the judge as 'a skilled artisan' his level of skill, in the context of the status tests, was apparently inadequate. The court held that:

> 'There was no question of his being called upon to exercise any skill or judgment as to which beams required chipping or as to the depths that they were to be cut. He was simply told what to do and left to get on with it as, for example, would a skilled turner on a lathe who was required to cut a piece of metal to certain dimensions.'

In *Lorimer*, Mr Goldsmith, the Revenue's barrister specifically distinguished the level and quality of skill exercised by the vision mixer with that of Mr Lee, saying that 'the work of Mr Lorimer, unlike that of Mr Lee Ting Sang, depended upon his own rare skill and judgement.'

Conclusion

On balance, the court in *Lee Ting Sang* found that:

> 'The picture emerges of a skilled artisan earning his living by working for more than one employer as an employee and not as a small businessman

venturing into business on his own account as an independent contractor with all its attendant risks.'

This contrasts with the *Lorimer* case where the Special Commissioner said:

'I find that the activities of Mr. Lorimer . . . bear the hallmarks of a man who is in business on his own account and they outweigh substantially such factors as may be thought to militate against my conclusion that Mr. Lorimer was in business on his own account.'

8.3.2 Relevance for personal service workers

The differences should be noted, because they were sufficient to make Mr Lee an employee and Mr Lorimer self-employed, despite the fact that they both worked on a number of short term engagements for different clients:

(a) Mr Lorimer was a skilled professional, Mr Lee an artisan, and although described as 'skilled', worked at chipping concrete and sharpening chisels. The level of skill is clearly an important factor in the dividing line between Schedule D and Schedule E;

(b) Although Lorimer's financial risk was slight, it was greater than the simple risk of being unemployed. He could suffer bad debts as well as cash flow problems;

(c) Similarly, his opportunity for profit was greater than that of Mr Lee as he could set his rate to match his reputation, and could save money by working efficiently; Mr Lee's rate was set by his engager;

(d) Mr Lorimer had a rudimentary business structure which Mr Lee lacked.

8.3.3 Conclusion

These two cases highlight the fact that the line between Schedule D and Schedule E is very fine. This point is further developed, using a further two tax cases, at **8.5** below.

The comparison also demonstrates that a professional, such as an IT contractor or a journalist, may find it easier to cross the line and reach the safe haven of Schedule D than would a labour-only subcontractor with his own service company. The same point is made in *Tax Bulletin 45*, when the Revenue say that the number of engagements is a factor which:

'Will usually carry less weight in the case of an unskilled worker, where other factors such as the high level of control exercised by the contractor are likely to be conclusive of employment.'

To be classified as Schedule D the unskilled worker is more likely to have to demonstrate other evidence of self-employment, such as greater risk, substitution, or the provision of significant equipment. The skilled worker has an inherently easier task.

8.4 Recent court decisions III: the special case

8.4.1 Barnett v Brabyn

Barnett v Brabyn [1996] 69 TC 133 contains elements which make it an attractive case to those seeking support in their arguments for self-employed status. However its facts are peculiar and those with personal services companies are advised not to rely upon it as a precedent.

Outline

Mr Barnett was a video technician working as an independent contractor with his father, who was one of two partners in a business called LTV. He filed tax returns on the basis that he was self-employed, and this was accepted by his Inspector.

However the Revenue subsequently discovered that Mr Barnett had not declared some of the money paid to him by LTV, and raised further assessments. Barnett argued that he was really an employee, and the tax liability was therefore not his, because PAYE and NIC should have been deducted by LTV. The court was made aware that he had fallen out with his father, and set up a business in competition with him.

The factors in favour of employment were that he:

(a) Was paid at an hourly rate, and had no realistic chance of making a loss;

(b) Continued to be paid when he was off sick and on holiday;

(c) Worked for no other business;

(d) Could not hire any workers without the consent of the partners;

(e) Operated entirely on the premises of the partnership and supplied no equipment;

(f) Provided no capital;

(g) Had no business bank account; and

(h) Did not submit invoices.

The factors in favour of self-employment were that:

(i) He chose his own hours of work;

(j) Both he and his father intended that he would be self-employed;

(k) Previous tax assessments had been made and accepted on a self-employed basis.

The judge held that he was self-employed, despite the number of factors which appeared to point to employment. The judge said that these 'might in an ordinary case carry some weight indicative of his status as an employee.' But he stressed the unusual facts in this case:

- Mr Barnett declined to give evidence in person, which meant that 'the findings of fact by the Commissioners are somewhat limited, and their decision had to be made on the basis of those limited findings';

- The significance of a number of the Schedule E factors 'must be very much affected by the family relationship between Mr. Barnett and LTV'.

Whether the court was also affected by Mr Barnett's clear intention to avoid his own tax liability and transfer responsibility to his father, is not mentioned in the case report.

However, the judge clearly said that there were special facts in *Barnett v Brabyn*, and effectively warned against taking it as a precedent. It would thus be unwise for other taxpayers to do so.

Importance of Barnett v Brabyn to personal service workers

This case is important for two reasons. Firstly, it shows clearly that the facts and circumstances surrounding individual status tests are taken into account by the court, even to the extent of arriving at a decision which appears at odds with previous precedents.

Secondly, it reinforces the importance of looking at case law in context. Extracting status tests from individual cases is useful only up to a point, and beyond that point can be dangerously misleading.

8.5 Other useful cases

8.5.1 Comparison of cases

Other status cases which are particularly useful for personal service workers are discussed in detail elsewhere in this book. They include:

- *Specialeyes*, see **5.3.2**;

- *Market Investigations*, see **5.3.3**;

- *O'Kelly*, see **5.3.2**.

The four cases, *Lorimer*, *Specialeyes*, *Lee Ting Sang* and *Market Investigations* all lie close to the Schedule E/Schedule D line. While bearing in mind the warning of Vinelott J. quoted at **8.1** above, it is nevertheless interesting to identify the factors which these four borderline cases have in common, and what differentiates Lorimer and the Specialeyes opticians who were judged to be self-employed, from Mrs Irving and Lee Ting Sang, who were classified as employees. The table below summarises the key status tests and their application to each case:

	Lorimer	Specialeyes	Lee Ting Sang	Market Investigations
Mutuality of obligation	No	No	Yes	On an engagement by engagement basis, see **5.3.3**
Provision of equipment	No	Some	No	No
Hire own staff	No except substitutes	No	No	No
Financial risk	Some	Negligible	No	No
Provision of capital	No	No	No	No
Control over where	No	No	No	No
Control over when	No	Unclear	No	Yes
Control over how	Yes	Yes	No?	No
Other engagers?	Yes	Not in most cases	Yes, in series	Allowed but not taken up
Send a substitute		Sometimes?	No	No

What this table shows is that:

- There was no mutuality of obligation (see **5.3**) in either Lorimer or Specialeyes;

- Both Lorimer and the opticians had control over 'how' they carried out their work (see **6.6.3**), and Mrs Irving and Mr Lee did not;

- In addition Lorimer had greater financial risk than an employee, the occasional right to send a substitute, and numerous engagers. These are not points which were necessarily shared by the opticians, although some did have other clients.

8.5.2 Summary

In summary, if there is no mutuality of obligation and the worker is a professional with control over *how* the work is done, he stands a reasonable chance of being classified as self-employed. This would also fit with the comments of the Tribunal in *Airfix*, see **5.3.4**, which suggests the homeworkers classed as employees in that case might have been regarded as self-employed had they been skilled professionals.

However, the differences between the decided cases are very slight. Arguments based on absence of mutuality, in particular, are likely to draw the Revenue's fire. It is therefore helpful if the worker can produce additional arguments to support his position. Remember that Lorimer had substitution, some financial risk, and numerous engagers, but still had to argue his case all the way to the Court of Appeal.

9 Changing the contractual relationship

9.1 Introduction

Contractual arrangements in the context of personal services are discussed in Chapter 5, along with a review of mutuality of obligation. Chapter 6 analyses the status tests which distinguish employees from the self-employed, and Chapter 7 comments on the Revenue view of status. This chapter considers the changes that could be made to individuals' contracts and working arrangements, so that they are more indicative of self-employment than employment. It concludes with a brief review of pre-packaged IR35 solutions.

9.2 General

Chapter 5 discusses the concept of the 'hypothetical contract' between the worker and the client, which lies at the heart of IR35. In order to see if this hypothetical contract is one of employment, the 'circumstances' of the arrangements between the parties must be considered. It is not simply a question of considering the written contracts between worker and client, or worker and agency, but looking at other elements in his arrangements.

If a worker makes a fundamental change to his working practices and contractual arrangements, such as taking on significant risk or incorporating the right to send a substitute, he will be 'self-employed' and fall outside IR35, see **6.5.1**.

Workers who are on the borderline between Schedule E and Schedule D may be able to make less fundamental adjustments to their working practices which, when considered together with their existing arrangements, may make Schedule D classification more likely.

Before making any changes to contracts, it is important to remember that alterations made for tax reasons may have other consequences. Those entering into, or contemplating changes to, contractual arrangements as a result of IR35 are thus advised to take legal advice on the wider effects of any amendments, and also to consider their commercial implications. In addition, personal service workers should discuss any proposed changes with their agencies and clients. The client's acceptance is particularly important, see **5.5.2**.

The following paragraphs suggest some amendments which could be made. They are examples only, and each worker's contractual arrangements are likely to need individual review. It is emphasised that it is not enough simply to change the written agreements; working practices must support the same interpretation. This is true to some extent in all status cases, but even more so in IR35, which emphasises the 'circumstances' of the hypothetical worker/client contract, see 5.1.1.

In the sample clauses, 'the Company' is the service company, and the other party is generally the client. Similar clauses could be drafted in which one of the contracting parties was an agency.

9.3 Substitution clause

9.3.1 Introduction

If a contract contains a genuine substitution clause, the engagement cannot be an employment, see 6.5.2. It thus falls outside the personal services rules. However, the Revenue have already warned against ineffective or sham clauses, see 7.4.1. It is thus likely that they would be unsympathetic if such a clause were later uncovered in a review of the worker's position.

A worker contemplating a substitution clause should consider the following:

9.3.2 Clause accepted by the client

To be genuine, a substitution clause must be accepted by the client. In practice many clients are resistant to such clauses, because the process of selecting a contractor can be lengthy, and involve both interviews and aptitude tests. Clients are often reluctant to surrender control over this selection process to the contractor himself. However, the client can reserve the right to reject a substitute, see 6.5.2, and this may be helpful.

Where a clause exists, it may be challenged by the Revenue, see 7.4.1. The worker should thus ensure that the client and any substitute would be prepared to support its authenticity, if necessary in court.

9.3.3 Appointment, permission and veto

It is the worker, not the agency or the client, who must have the right to appoint the substitute, see for example the recent case of *MacFarlane and Skivington* v *Glasgow City Council* [2000] EAT/1277 (see 6.5.2). There will be no right of substitution if the client goes back to the agency and asks for another worker because their normal contractor is sick.

The clause should not make provision of a substitute dependent on the client's permission, see **6.5.2**. This doesn't, however, preclude the client vetoing a particular substitute if he cannot satisfactorily deliver according to the terms of the contract. The clause contained in the *Express and Echo* case, see **6.5.1**, which was accepted as valid by the court, read as follows:

> 'In the event that the contractor provides a substitute, the contractor must satisfy the company that such a substitute is trained and is suitable to undertake the services.'

In this context the substitution clause could include a warranty that the substitute will be able to meet the requirements of the engagement.

9.3.4 Responsibility for work and for payment

If a contract has a substitution clause, responsibility for delivering the work remains with the contractor. The substitute effectively 'stands in the shoes' of the worker, and the latter can thus be held liable by the client for any breach of contract caused by his replacement. If the substitute does the work badly, the contractor is liable; if he breaches the client's procedures, the contractor can be sued.

A substitution clause means that if the worker is sick, the client can require him to send a competent replacement. If no appropriate person can be found, the client may claim damages against the service company.

It is also the contractor, not the client or agency, who has to pay the substitute. In *Express and Echo*, Mr Tanton was regarded by the Revenue as an employee and thus had PAYE and NIC deducted from his earnings, but nevertheless still paid his substitute. In *Ready Mixed Concrete* see **6.5.2**, Mr Latimer, with other owner drivers, employed and paid a relief driver with the company's consent.

If the substitute is an individual, and not another service company, responsibility for deciding his tax status rests with the intermediary who signed the contract with the client.

9.3.5 Identifying the substitute

Although case law talks about the *right* to send a substitute, it is helpful if a replacement has actually been sent in practice, as this is demonstrable evidence that the right exists. Lorimer (see **8.2.1**) and Tanton (see **6.5.2**) clearly had real live substitutes who stood in for them when required. The existence of an identifiable person who would take the place of the contractor has persuasive force, if only to convince the court that the right was not a sham.

9.3.6 The client contract

Where the service company contracts with an agency, and the agency with the client, the Revenue warn that they will ask to see both contracts (FAQ General 30). This would be necessary in any event to determine the 'circumstances' of the hypothetical contract between the worker and the client, see **5.1.1**.

If the first has a substitution clause, but the second does not, the Revenue are likely to argue the clause is a sham. At the very least, there will be uncertainty about the terms of the hypothetical contract, see **5.5.2**. In a court of law, this would make for a messy case.

9.3.7 Use of alternates

A Schedule attached to the contract giving the names of a number of workers, all of whom could equally well deliver the contract, amounts to substitution. An appropriate clause might read as follows:

> 'The Client acknowledges that the engagement will be undertaken by one or more individuals provided by the Company and nominated in the Schedule attached to this Contract. The Company reserves the right to change or replace such individuals, provided the Client is satisfied that the proposed replacement possesses the necessary skills and expertise to carry out the engagement.'

However, the Schedule could be challenged as a sham if all but one of the named individuals were either unable or unwilling to carry out the contract on the terms agreed.

9.3.8 Conclusion

If a worker has a genuine right to send a substitute and the client accepts that right, the worker will not be within IR35. But there are commercial risks involved in engaging a replacement, including that of being sued because the work had been done badly, and the costs of remunerating the substitute out of his own pocket.

9.4 Project-based work

9.4.1 General

As discussed at **6.5.3**, if a worker runs the risk of making a loss as well as a profit, he is almost certainly self-employed. A personal service worker who moves from an hourly basis to a project basis will have taken on significant risk. The Revenue accepts this, saying that:

> 'Financial risk could also take the form of quoting a fixed price for a job, with the consequent risk of bearing the additional costs if the job overruns.' (*Tax Bulletin 45*)

In *Global Plant Ltd v Secretary of State for Health & Social Security* [1971] 3 All ER 385 Lord Widgery held that:

> 'If a man agrees to perform an operation for a fixed sum and thus stands to lose if the work is delayed, and to profit if it is done quickly, that is the man who on the face of it appears to be an independent contractor working under a contract for services.'

Points to note in moving from an hourly basis to a project basis are discussed below.

9.4.2 Clause has to be genuine

The change has to be genuine, so that a worker who operates as part of a client team, for instance on an IT helpdesk, is unlikely to be able to change his contract in this way. But a designer of websites, a cameraman, or a journalist, may all be able to estimate the time it will take them to complete a piece of work and quote on that basis.

A typical clause will identify the task to be completed and the agreed fee, including the timing of any installment payments. Will there be a bonus if the project is completed earlier than scheduled, or a penalty if it is late?

9.4.3 There has to be real risk

The downside is that there is real risk. If the worker under-estimates, he will either have to finish the work in his own time or renegotiate the contract with the client; if he over-estimates, his profit will increase – and the client has to accept that. There may be cashflow issues, or unsatisfactory work which needs to be reperformed at no extra cost to the client. If an agency is involved, it will need to review the extent of its responsibility in a situation where the service company fails to meet its obligations.

9.4.4 Contract variations

Allowing changes to the content, timing or cost of the project gives flexibility, and permits further negotiation if the work proves more complex than expected. It is, however, recommended that any changes should be agreed in writing by both parties. This helps prevent the contract from imperceptibly slipping back to an hourly basis. An appropriate clause might be:

> 'Either party may request in writing changes to the type and scope of the services or to any other aspect of the Contract. Any such request must be sufficiently detailed to enable the other party to assess the effect of the proposed change on the cost, delivery dates or any other aspect of the Contract. Both parties agree to discuss and, if appropriate, agree such changes. Until a change is agreed in writing and signed by both parties, each party will continue to act in accordance with the latest agreed written version of the Contract.'

9.4.5 Other characteristics

Other parts of the contract should be consistent with the fact that the work is on a project basis. For example, it should:

- Include appropriate commercial warranties between the contractor and the client, and vice versa;

- Clarify ownership where intellectual property has been created during the project;

- Specify any requirements as to confidentiality;

- Include insurance cover, see **11.10** and **9.7**;

- Provide for termination of the contract only if there has been a breach of its terms by either party, see **9.14**.

9.5 Hiring staff

If a worker can hire staff to carry out part of the work he has undertaken to do for the client, this is a strong indicator of self-employment, see **6.5.4**. This is because the essence of employment lies in the provision of personal services. To be effective, the worker must be able to delegate part of the job to be carried out for the client: it is not enough to employ someone to carry out the book-keeping or accounting in respect of an engagement.

Many of the same practical points here apply as in substitution, see **9.3** above:

- The client must know and consent to this term of the contract;

- The right to hire the helper must rest with the worker, not the agency;

- While what matters is the right to hire someone else to do the job, it is helpful, if challenged, to be able to identify a 'helper';

- If the client has to give 'permission' for the worker to hire a helper, a right is unlikely to exist, see **6.5.2**;

- The worker is responsible for paying the helper.

An appropriate clause might be:

> 'The Company has the right to engage sub-contractors and other third parties to support it in fulfilling its obligations under this Contract. Any reference in this Contract to the Company's staff also includes reference to such sub-contractors or third parties. The Company is responsible for any third parties so engaged and remains liable to the Client in respect of any services provided by such third parties, subject to the other provisions of this Contract.'

9.6 Control

9.6.1 General

Every worker should review the control test, which is discussed in detail at **6.6.1**, and consider how it applies to them. It may be possible to argue, like Mr Lorimer, that it is irrelevant, see **6.6.3** and **6.6.4**. But not everyone will be in this position, and it would be naïve to think that simply because the judge said that the control test was peripheral in that case, that it can always be ignored.

9.6.2 Control over the specialist

Clauses which make contractors sound like Victorian housemaids are unhelpful:

> 'The Consultant shall at all times faithfully and diligently perform all duties in connection with the provision of the services.'

A far better reflection of the service supplied by a specialist contractor would be:

> 'The Company warrants that it undertakes this engagement as a specialist and that its staff will dedicate the time, skill and care which it requires, and will carry out this engagement in a professional manner at all times.'

9.6.3 Control as to when, where and what

Where it is possible for the worker to retain control over his hours, the place where he carries out the work, and the detail of what he delivers, this will be helpful in arguing for self-employment, see **6.6.3**. A contract might include a clause suggesting a minimal degree of control, such as:

> 'The Company agrees to comply with all statutory obligations and codes of practice, and any rules or obligations in force at the premises where services are performed under this Contract to the extent that they are reasonably applicable.'

9.7 Insurance

9.7.1 General

Even where the self-employed do not operate on a project basis (see **9.4**), they normally protect themselves from the risk of being sued by taking out Professional Indemnity and Public Liability insurance. No doctor, accountant or lawyer would work without this sort of cover. An appropriate clause might be:

> 'The Company shall ensure the provision of adequate professional indemnity insurance, public liability insurance, and employers' liability insurance, and shall make a copy of the policies available on request.'

Or, more specifically:

> 'The Company warrants that it will maintain the following levels of insurance cover for the duration of the Contract and for six months thereafter: Employers liability, £x; public liability £x; product liability £x and professional indemnity £x.'

However insurance is a real cost, not a cosmetic adjustment to a contract, and it may be expensive. For the Schedule E treatment of such insurance if the worker fails the status tests, see 11.10; for a general discussion of risk, see **6.5.3**.

9.7.2 Remedying defective work

In addition to PI and other insurance cover, the contractor can increase the level of risk by agreeing to take responsibility for defective work. A clause reflecting this obligation might read:

> 'The Company agrees to rectify any work notified to it by the Client as unsatisfactory, provided that such notification is received within 15 days following the progress report which relates to the unsatisfactory work.'

As with many of the other contractual changes discussed in this chapter, this clause has real financial consequences:

- The individual could be required to provide services without further pay in order to remedy work previously carried out;

- If an agency is a party to the contractual arrangements, it may become involved in any disagreement between the client and the service company concerning the extent or nature of any defects;

- If the company defaults on its contract and moves to take up an engagement elsewhere, the agency may be required, under its contract with the client, to supply a replacement worker without further cost. Although the agency would clearly have a cause of action against the service company, it may not be cost-effective to pursue the claim.

9.8 Providing own equipment

Lorimer established (see **8.2.1**) that providing equipment it is not an essential ingredient of self-employment. However, supplying retinoscopes and ophthalmoscopes was helpful in the *Specialeyes* case (see **5.3.2**), and the musicians in the *Addison* and *Midland Sinfonia* cases (see **20.5.2**) owned their own instruments. It is also clear from the Revenue example *Henry*, see **24.2.3**, that Henry's extensive use of his own computer for his engineering consulting project was taken into account when deciding his Schedule D status.

Thus while not a necessary condition, the provision of equipment may be helpful. A clause might refer to this obliquely:

> 'The Company shall, when utilising any of its own equipment or intellectual property in carrying out the engagement, ensure that any security requirements reasonably required by the Client are complied with.'

If the worker is classified as Schedule E notwithstanding, there might be no tax relief on this capital expenditure, see **11.11**. A discussion of the provision of equipment in the context of the status tests is at **6.6.2**.

9.9 Pay and benefits

9.9.1 Holiday pay and benefits

Some contractors receive employee-type remuneration, such as paid holidays. This 'benefit' may even be imposed by the client – in some companies it is an internal audit requirement that all workers, including contractors, take a break from their job to minimise the risk of fraud.

Paid holidays are, however, characteristic of employment, and it would be preferable if the worker's contractual arrangements simply provided for a maximum continuous period of work. The 'holiday' would then follow automatically.

A number of companies have also recently offered share options (normally an employee-type benefit) to third parties such as distributors or contractors, in order to forge closer links between the workers and the company.

If share options, holiday pay, or other benefits are provided, there is a presumption of employment. This can be rebutted if, for example, there is no mutuality of obligation, as in the *O'Kelly* case, see **5.3.2**, or there are other indicators of self-employment, as in *McManus v Griffiths* [1997] 70 TC 218. See **6.7.3** for a general discussion of benefits in the context of status issues.

9.9.2 Hourly rates

Although payment on a project basis indicates self-employment, an hourly or daily rate doesn't necessarily mean that the worker is employed, see **6.7.3**. Where work is charged on a time basis it should be properly invoiced by the service company, either to the agent or directly to the client, on headed paper, and appropriate records kept, see **9.12**.

The contractual clauses might be as follows:

> '*Fees and expenses* – The Company's fee has been set to reflect the time spent on the provision of the services, together with other factors such as the complexity and urgency of the work, the level of risk inherent in the engagement, and the utilisation of techniques, expertise and know-how previously developed by the Company.
>
> Unless otherwise agreed, fees will be calculated on the basis of 8 working hours each day from Monday to Friday, excluding public holidays. Time worked in excess of 8 hours or on public holidays or at weekends will be charged on a pro-rata basis plus 15 per cent. In addition to the fees, the Client agrees to pay all travel, accommodation and subsistence costs and other reasonable expenses incurred by the Company in connection with the provision of the services.'

9.10 Intention of the parties

The intention of the parties is normally a tiebreaker clause, so that if all other factors are evenly balanced, what the parties intend the worker's status to be determines the issue. However, in the context of the personal services legislation it is uncertain whether the tiebreaker will be effective, see **5.2.4**. However, its inclusion can do no harm, and may be useful.

A clause stating that the company and client intend to contract as independent third parties should therefore be included, as follows:

> 'The relationship between the Company and the Client is one of independent suppliers, and nothing in this Contract shall be interpreted as constituting any joint venture, partnership or relationship of employer and employee, as between the parties.'

The contract should also more generally reflect the fact that it is between independent third parties, and thus should set out the obligations of the client to the company as well as those from the company to the client. Possible clauses include:

- 'The Client shall ensure that the Company is accorded sufficient access to any of the Client's premises, information, data or personnel, as is required for the Company to carry out the services to be supplied under the Contract;

- The Client will ensure that its staff, including senior management, are available to give such assistance as the Company reasonably requires in order to carry out the services under the Contract;

- The Client warrants that its staff have the necessary skills and experience to provide the Company with the support needed for the Company properly to fulfil its obligations under the Contract;

- The Client shall ensure that it has appropriate back up, security and virus checking procedures in place for any computer facilities it provides;

- The Client agrees at its own expense to provide to the Company all information that the Company reasonably requires for the proper performance of the Contract and in accordance with any timetable or other target for progress or completion agreed in writing between the parties;

- The Client shall, at its own expense, retain duplicate copies of all information provided to the Company and the Company shall have no liability for any loss or damage to the information provided by the Client, howsoever caused;

- The Client warrants that all information provided to the Company is accurate and not misleading in any material respect.'

9.11 Tax clauses

Existing contracts may contain clauses which make the service company responsible for PAYE and NIC, such as:

'The Company shall be responsible for making appropriate PAYE deductions for tax and NIC from the remuneration it pays to its staff and the Company agrees to indemnify the Client in respect of any claims or demands which may be made by the relevant authorities against the Company in respect of income or other tax relating to the provision of the services by the Company.'

It would be surprising to find this clause in a normal contract for services. An accountant's engagement letter does not say he will pay his own tax: his clients take this for granted. Such a clause would thus fall into the 'officious bystander' category of implied terms which do not need to be spelled out, see **5.2.3.** Putting a tax clause into the contract thus suggests that the parties are unclear about the worker's status.

Not only does it provide a marker for the Revenue, it is also unnecessary unless either:

- The contract is with an individual rather than with a service company or partnership. This is because the PAYE or NIC responsibility then legally rests with the client. In this case IR35 will not be in point, see **4.7**; or

- The service company is overseas, in which case the client may have some liability under the provisions of s203C ICTA 1988 and the corresponding NIC rules, see **19.4.1** and **21.3.2.**

9.12 Business structure

Although an absence of business structure is not fatal to a claim to be self-employed, see **6.7.6**, it is nevertheless recommended that a contractor should have at least a rudimentary business structure, as did Ian Lorimer, see **8.2.1.** Office equipment such as a fax, internet line, answering machine and mobile phone is helpful. Business stationery, including invoices with appropriate letterheads and business cards are also recommended.

If the services available are advertised, this too supports the argument that the service company is carrying on a business. The self-employed may advertise in trade journals, Yellow Pages or on the internet. However, the absence of advertising should not jeopardise Schedule D status: many self-employed people obtain all their work through agencies or by word of mouth.

9.13 Exclusivity

Where a worker provides services only to one engager, and agrees he will not provide his skills to anyone else, he is likely to be an employee. Conversely, the freedom to work concurrently for a number of engagers is helpful in arguing for self-employment, see **6.7.2**.

Contracts should thus include a clause giving the worker the right to provide services to others during the period of the engagement. It may be done obliquely, as:

'The Company confirms that other engagements undertaken during the period of this Contract will not give rise to a conflict of interest between the Company and its Client.'

Or more directly:

'This Contract will not restrict the Company from providing services to other Clients, providing only that the services to be provided under this Contract are not thereby restricted or impaired in any way.'

9.14 Termination and notice

The issue of termination is discussed at **6.7.4**. It is relatively common for personal service contracts to include a notice period, and sometimes a provision for a payment in lieu of notice (PILON). The latter is particularly unhelpful if the worker is trying to claim Schedule D status, as a PILON is clearly indicative of employment.

If it is possible to change the terms of the engagement so that the contract ends at the end of a pre-agreed period, or on breach of the contract, rather than on notice, the worker's Schedule D position would be strengthened. A possible clause would read:

'This contract commences on (date) and shall continue until the date agreed between the parties following completion of the engagement, when it shall expire automatically. Notwithstanding this, the Contract will terminate without notice if the Company has committed any serious or persistent breach of any of its obligations under this Contract.'

In reviewing the issue of termination, the requirements of the client should also be considered. A notice period is often as much to protect the client and give time for him to find a replacement worker as it is to protect the worker from sudden termination of the agreement. Where a notice period is retained, reference can be made to the words of the judge in *McManus v Griffiths* [1997] 70 TC 218 quoted at **6.7.4**, which suggest that a notice period could be regarded as a neutral factor in determining questions of status.

9.15 Off-the-peg solutions

As an alternative to the painstaking and commercially risky task of contractual amendments, some contractors have been tempted by various 'off-the-peg' solutions, from employee benefit trusts to pre-packaged Schedule D contracts. Most of these are one or more of the following:

- Unduly simplistic, such as a Schedule D contract sold at a premium on the basis that it will take the worker out of IR35, which it will – but only if he works to the terms of the contract, which may be impossible;

- Over-complex, as is the case with various offshore employee benefit trust structures which are expensive to set up, costly to manage, and may be the next target of the Revenue's anti-avoidance teams;

- Administratively burdensome, so that the costs of running the structure come close to eliminating any benefit, and also run the risk of compliance failure;

- Commercially risky, because they give power over the worker's earnings to unknown individuals, and then make the worker responsible for meeting the costs of any problems which may later arise;

- Illegal. A number of schemes are based on a combination of non-disclosure and offshore company/agency structures. If the arrangement is fraudulent, the full panoply of Revenue powers may be brought to bear on both the company and the worker, see **16.5**;

- Technically faulty, so that they assume a pretence will bypass the rules. An example of this is a type of composite (see **21.4**) which has a large number of workers, each of whom carries out relevant engagements. The money earned is distributed to the workers by 'independent directors' without there being any apparent link between the distribution and the amount brought into the company by each worker;

This 'solution' is likely to fall within the widely drafted provision which catches workers if they receive 'a payment or benefit . . . which can reasonably be taken to be remuneration' (Sch 12, para 3(1)(b)(ii) FA 2000). It will be difficult to argue that the money paid to the workers in one form or another from the 'independent directors' is not in fact the income received from the client, simply rebadged.

If, on the other hand, the distribution of monies is genuinely independent, workers may not actually receive their fair share – a result which might be more costly than paying higher tax and NICs!

These schemes are the modern equivalent of the philosopher's stone – a magic solution to turn service companies back into gold mines. But alchemy does not exist, and belief is no substitute for tax analysis. Even if an off-the-peg scheme did bypass the legislation, it would be flashed around the world within minutes, and the Revenue would act swiftly to close the loophole.

The best solution to IR35 is a robust, thorough approach to case law, combined (where necessary) with changes to the worker's operating methods, see above and in Chapters 6 and 8.

10 Income and benefits from relevant engagements

10.1 Introduction

A deemed Schedule E calculation has to be carried out for all workers with relevant engagements, as does a National Insurance attributable earnings calculation (Sch 12, para 7 FA 2000; SI 2000 No 757 Reg 7).

The deemed Schedule E and attributable earnings calculations are generally identical, but interactions with overseas tax and the NICs deeming provisions mean that it is sometimes possible to have a deemed Schedule E calculation but not an attributable earnings calculation, or vice versa, see **12.7.2**. For simplicity, the calculation is referred to throughout this book as 'deemed Schedule E', unless specific identification of one or the other is required.

The calculation is in nine steps, of which this chapter covers the first two. These establish the income received by the intermediary from relevant engagements, and payments and benefits received by the worker from the client or other third party. The chapter concludes by looking in detail at the benefits which might be included at Step Two, and how they should be taxed.

Chapter 11 looks at Steps Three and Four, and the last five steps are discussed in Chapter 12.

10.2 Receipts basis

The normal rule is that earnings paid to employees or directors are taxable on the earliest of the following occasions (s202B ICTA 1988):

(a) When *payment is made* of or on account of the emoluments;

(b) When a person becomes *entitled* to payment of, or on account of, the emoluments;

And if the worker is a director:

(c) When sums on account of emoluments are *credited to the director's current or loan account* by the company;

(d) If the amount of the emoluments for a period is determined before the period ends, the time *when the period ends*;

(e) If the amount of the emoluments for a period is not known until the amount is determined after the period has ended, the time *when the amount is determined*.

If these rules had been applied to employees and directors within IR35, they would have been subject to PAYE and NICs on amounts invoiced to the client but not yet received. In order to prevent this onerous result, the deemed Schedule E calculation is on a received basis for both tax and NIC.

The corollary also applies: if a prepayment is received in one fiscal year for work to be done in the next, it is included in the earlier year's deemed Schedule E calculation, although the related services have not yet been carried out (Sch 12, para 10(5)(a) FA 2000).

The intermediary thus needs to keep records on both a received and an accruals basis, so that the deemed Schedule E calculation as well as the corporation or partnership tax returns can be completed correctly.

For the first year of the new rules there is an exception to the receipts basis. To prevent intermediaries accelerating receipts into 1999/00 for work to be done in 2000/01, the legislation says that 'payments or other benefits in respect of (services performed after 5 April 2000) shall be treated as if received in the tax year 2000/01' (Sch 12, para 22(2) FA 2000).

Where a benefit rather than cash has been provided, the date for it to be brought into the deemed Schedule E calculation is the date on which 'it is used or enjoyed' (Sch 12, para 10(5)(b) FA 2000).

10.3 Apportionments of income

The intermediary may have to apportion income received from clients, either because more than one individual in the company has worked on the relevant engagement, and/or because the income relates both to relevant and other engagements. The legislation requires that this be done on a 'just and reasonable basis' (Sch 12, para 9 FA 2000). Revenue booklet IR175 – *Supplying services through a limited company or partnership* warns that:

> 'The Revenue will re-apportion any payment if it appears the company's or partnership's basis of apportionment is unreasonable. The company can appeal against the decision of the Inland Revenue.'

Appropriate management of the invoicing process can simplify this apportionment. Separate bills could be submitted for different types of work, or the invoice could split relevant engagement income from other work, and identify the person who performed the relevant engagement.

10.4 A single employment

The legislation says that the deemed Schedule E calculation should be carried out as if:

• The worker were employed by the intermediary; and

• The relevant engagements were undertaken in the course of performing the duties of that employment (Sch 12, para 11(2) FA 2000).

Thus, although there may be many engagements with different clients, all the contracts are considered together, as derived from a single employment with the intermediary, when carrying out the deemed Schedule E calculation.

However, the calculation itself assumes that the 'worker is employed by the client' (Sch 12, para 7 Steps Two to Four, FA 2000). The two concepts appear contradictory. Is the worker to be regarded as employed by the client, or by the intermediary? In particular, where a client provides a benefit to a personal service worker, is he:

• Acting as third party, because the worker is employed by the service company; or

• Acting as employer, because the worker is regarded as his employee?

The answer makes a difference in a number of areas, such as entertaining, travel, gifts and vouchers.

Paragraph 7 calculates the deemed Schedule E payment, and paragraph 11 deals with applying the Income Tax Acts in a wider sense. The author's view is that where paragraph 11 conflicts with paragraph 7, the former takes precedence. This also seems to be the approach taken by the Revenue, see **11.6.3**. However the position is not beyond doubt, and where it makes a difference this has been noted in the text.

10.5 Steps One and Two of the deemed Schedule E calculation

10.5.1 General

Step One brings together all payments and benefits, not otherwise taxable under Schedule E, which have been received by the *intermediary* in respect of relevant engagements. This is then reduced by 5 per cent, which represents a round sum expense allowance, see **11.2**.

Step One thus includes both cash paid by the client to the intermediary in settlement of invoices, and also 'benefits' received, such as reimbursed travel and subsistence expenses.

Step Two then adds into the calculation any payments and benefits received *by the worker* otherwise than from the intermediary, i.e., from a client or other third party. Not included in Step Two are:

(a) Payments/benefits received by the worker from the *intermediary*, see **10.5.2**;

(b) Payments/benefits received by the worker otherwise than from the intermediary which would not be *chargeable* if the worker were an employee of the client, see **10.5.3**;

(c) Payments/benefits received by the worker otherwise than from the intermediary which are *already taxable* under Schedule E, see **10.5.4**.

If the worker is an employee or director, payments or benefits received from a client are almost invariably already taxable under existing rules, because they will have been provided by reason of the worker's employment with the intermediary (s154(1) ICTA 1988).

Partners, however, do not have an employment, and thus benefits provided by the client cannot be by reason of the employment. Step Two is most commonly used to bring into tax payments or benefits received by a partner from a client. It will not normally be used in the more common situation where the payment or benefit is provided by the client to a service company director or worker.

Where a benefit is included in Step Two, it must be valued at its 'cash equivalent' (Sch 12, para 10(3)(b)FA 2000). This is in line with the rules for employees. Specific requirements for the calculation of cash equivalents exist for some benefits, such as company cars, vans, accommodation and loans.

10.5.2 Payments/benefits received by the worker from the intermediary

A payment or benefit provided to the worker by the intermediary is not included in Step Two, because it is assumed to have been paid out of income received in Step One. To include it again would be double counting.

10.5.3 Payments/benefits which are not taxable

Clearly it would be unfair to include payments or benefits in the deemed Schedule E calculation which would not be taxed if the worker were employed directly by the client.

Payments and benefits which escape tax do so either under a specific legislative provision, or by way of an Extra Statutory Concession (ESC). The Revenue have confirmed that they will use their care and management powers to extend the benefit of ESCs to workers within the personal service rules.

Payments and benefits excluded from tax either by legislation or concession include:

- Small loans, exempted from tax under s161 ICTA 1988;

- Personal incidental expenses, which are not 'regarded as emoluments of the office or employment for any purpose of Schedule E' providing they do not exceed £5 a night or £10 if overseas, see **11.7**;

- Training provided by the client, which are not included in 'emoluments of the employee from the office or employment', see **11.8**;

- Meals in the staff restaurant, which are not taxable by virtue of ESC A74, see **10.6.6(d)** below.

These and other rules for allowable expenses are discussed further in Chapter 11.

10.5.4 Payments/benefits from a third party already within Schedule E

Payments or benefits which are received:

- From the client or other third party,

- By the director or employee of a service company, or the employee of a partnership,

are usually provided by reason of the worker's employment with the intermediary. They are thus already taxable under Schedule E and are therefore not included within the deemed Schedule E calculation. They are also subject to NICs, see Table 10.1 below.

Not only are the benefits already taxable, but the reporting responsibility almost invariably attaches to the service company. This is because where a payment or benefit has been provided by a third party 'by arrangement with' the employer, it is the employer who has the P11D reporting obligations, not the client. (SI 1993 No 744 Reg 46 and *SAT3(1995): Self Assessment – What it will mean for employers,* para 2.10.)

In a one-man company it is usually difficult (if not impossible) to argue that benefits provided to the worker by the client have not been arranged by the employer, because of the substantial identity between the 'employer' and the 'worker'.

The tax and NICs situation of the worker, the client and the intermediary in a range of different situations is examined at Table 10.1 below. The position differs depending on whether the payment is cash or a benefit, and whether it has been arranged or facilitated by the employer (i.e., the service company).

Table 10.1 Tax and NICs on payments/benefits provided by client to an employee/director of an intermediary

Item	By arrangement with worker?	Worker's tax position	Service company's tax position	Payer's tax position	NICs position
Business expenses	Yes	On P11D, claim under s198 ICTA	Include on P11D	No requirement	No requirement, see Note 7
Other cash, e.g., round sum allowance	Yes	Include on SA return, see Note 2	No requirement	Deduct PAYE, see Note 1	Service company's liability, see Note 3
Benefit e.g., use of car	Yes	On P11D	Include on P11D	No requirement, see Note 4	Service company's liability
Benefit	No	Include on SA return	No requirement	Provide details to worker, see Note 5	See Note 6
Hospitality e.g., gift or entertaining	No	See **10.6.6.**	See **10.6.6.**	See **10.6.6.**	See **10.6.6.**

Notes

1. Where a cash payment, such as a round sum allowance, is paid as a reward in connection with the employee's duties, the paying company has to deduct PAYE. This is because s203 ICTA 1988 states that:

    > 'On the making of any payment of, or on account of, any income assessable to income tax under Schedule E, income tax shall, subject to and in accordance with regulations made by the Board under this section, be deducted or repaid by *the person making the payment*.'

    In addition, under SI 1993 No 744 Reg 2, an 'employer' is defined as 'any person paying emoluments'. In the context of a relevant engagement, the client will thus have to deduct and pay over PAYE. This is confirmed by FAQ (Computation) 17:

    > 'If a client makes payments to a worker in connection with duties being performed, either for direct reward, as a round sum expense allowance, or a specific reimbursement of travel which was not business travel, and the worker is an employee of another, the payments are assessable on the worker and the client should deduct tax through PAYE from payments to the worker.'

2. If the client does apply PAYE, it will normally be on BR basis (SI 1993 No 744 Reg 28). The worker may thus need to pay further tax following completion of his self-assessment return. Third parties tend to inform the Revenue of such payments by letter, rather than formally completing a P60 and P35.

3. The client is however not liable for the NICs on these payments. The employer is always the secondary contributor, even when the payment is made by a third party. The service company therefore has to pay over the NICs in relation to any such receipts by the worker from the client (s7 SSCBA).

4. These benefits may have to be reported under s16 TMA, see 21.2.5; 21.3.1.

5. If, exceptionally, the rewards were not arranged by the employer, the third party must provide details of the benefit to the worker (SI 1993 No 744 Reg 46AB and *SAT3(1995): Self Assessment – What it will mean for employers* para 4.1). The value should be included on the individual's self-assessment return.

6. There is a Class 1A NICs liability on the intermediary for 2000/01 unless the third party volunteers to pay it; in subsequent years the liability is on the third party (SI 1979 No 591 Sch 1C para 10(a)).

7. There are no NICs as long as the payment is to meet a 'specific and distinct' expense (SI 1979 No 591 Reg 19(4)(b)). Costs cannot be apportioned for NICs.

All of the above payments are taxed under existing Schedule E or NICs provisions by virtue of the worker's employment with the intermediary. Thus, although they are all paid by the client, none are taxed as part of the deemed Schedule E payment.

10.5.5 Interaction between IR35 and PAYE/P11D rules

Benefits are of course not only provided by the client to an employee or director of an intermediary, they can also be provided:

• By the intermediary to the worker; or

• By the client to a partner;

• By the client to the intermediary.

In each case the interactions between the normal PAYE/P11D provisions and the personal service rules is different. The various options are described in (a) to (d) below, and summarised in Table 10.2. The Table also shows what happens if the benefit, having been provided, is either taxable under existing provisions, or escapes tax by virtue of some concession, exemption or relief. Benefits may be provided by:

(a) The intermediary, to the employee/director of a service company or to the employee of a partnership. These benefits are included on the individual's P11D and taxed under the normal rules. From 6 April 2000 they are also subject to Class 1A NICs, unless Class 1 already applies or there is some other exemption, see **12.3.3**. They are excluded from the deemed income calculation by Step Seven, because they are already taxable under normal rules, see **12.4**;

(b) The client, to the intermediary – such as a reimbursement of travel costs or phone bills. These amounts are included in Step One of the deemed income calculation, see **12.5.1**. They may then be excluded under Step Three, if they would have been deductible under the Schedule E rules, see **11.3**;

(c) The client, to the employee/director or a service company or to the employee of a partnership. These benefits will usually be included on the worker's P11D by the intermediary, because they will have been provided by arrangement with the employer, see **10.5.4** above. The worker may be able to claim tax relief under ss198ff ICTA, see **11.3.3**;

(d) The client, to a partner. These will be brought into the deemed Schedule E calculation under Step Two. Any relief for these costs is claimed in the partnership computation, not the deemed Schedule E computation, see **14.5.4; 15.3.4.**

Table 10.2 **Personal service legislation and benefits provided**

Text ref.	Provided by	Provided to	Include in deemed Sch E?	Remove from deemed Sch E if not taxable?	Tax relief otherwise available
(a)	Intermediary	Employee/director	No	Yes, Step 7	Yes, under s198 on SA return
(b)	Client	Intermediary	Step 1	Step 3	No tax because item removed under Step Three
(c)	Client	Employee/director	No	N/A	Yes,s198 on SA return
(d)	Client	Partner	Step 2	No	Yes, on partnership return

10.6 Common benefits

The nature of the contractual arrangements between most personal service workers and their clients means that benefits are not often provided. Risk areas include travel, subsistence, accommodation and phone costs. The temporary executive may receive a wider range of benefits, extending to private use of the company plane, a chauffeur and overseas trips.

An outline of the tax position for common benefits is given at **10.6.1–10.6.12** below. It concentrates on benefits provided by the client, either directly or by arrangement with the intermediary, rather than benefits provided by the intermediary.

10.6.1 Accommodation

There is no benefit charge if the accommodation satisfies the travel rules, see **11.6.** There is also an exemption for accommodation where the private use is 'not significant' (s155ZA ICTA 1988). In other situations its value must be ascertained in line with the rules set out in s145 to 146 ICTA 1988.

There are a number of exemptions from this charge, which apply if the accommodation is:

- Necessary because of a special threat to the employee's security;
- Customarily provided for the better performance of the duties; or
- Necessarily provided for the proper performance of the duties.

As with most exemptions from the Schedule E charge, few people qualify. Examples of workers who might satisfy the 'customary' requirement are locum veterinary surgeons, if they are required to be on call outside normal hours, are in fact frequently called out and the accommodation is provided so that the vet can quickly access the place where he performs his duties (SE 2254/SE 11352). Another example would be a supply teacher in a boarding school who had pastoral responsibilities.

Directors do not qualify for any of these exemptions other than the first. Since a director of a service company will usually be taxed under the normal rules for Schedule E rather than under the deeming provision of IR35, because the benefit has been provided 'by arrangement with' the service company, see **10.5.4**, he will thus not have access to most of these exemptions. However if a worker is a partner, or an employee of a service company or partnership, he would potentially be eligible for these reliefs.

If a personal services worker considers that one of these exemptions does apply to him, he should discover whether the client has previously come to an arrangement with the local Inland Revenue Inspector in relation to the tax position of previous users of the accommodation.

10.6.2 Assets

The private use of company assets, such as a boat or aircraft, is chargeable as a benefit under s156 ICTA 1988, see Example 10A.

Example 10A

John is a partner in a small firm of accountants. A local company asks him to take up a position for six months as temporary finance director, and signs a contract with the partnership for his services. It is agreed between John and the partnership that the earnings from this engagement will not be included in the partnership profit pool but paid directly to John. The engagement is thus within the scope of the personal services rules, see **14.2.2**. John is allowed the use of the company yacht at weekends. This is a benefit provided by the client and must be included in his deemed Schedule E calculation at Step Two.

> If John had been operating via a service company, the benefit would have been included on his P11D, because it would have been 'by arrangement with' his employer, the service company, see **10.5.4**.

The benefit is on the 'annual value' of the asset, unless specific provisions exist to tax it separately. The 'annual value' is 20 per cent of the asset's market value when it is first used privately.

Some particular points to note are:

- The cost of the asset includes VAT, whether or not this can be recovered either by the client or by the service company (SP A7);
- The 20 per cent charge is replaced by the actual cost of hiring the asset if this is greater (s156(7) ICTA 1988);
- If the asset is used by more than one employee, or it is used partly for business, an apportionment is required (s156(2) ICTA 1988; SE 3141/SE 21625). It is assumed that apportionment would also be applied where an asset was used by more than one worker under the personal services rules;
- The NIC legislation does not accept the concept of apportioning a benefit between business and private use. Thus unless the cost is 'specific and distinct' (SI 1979 No 591 Reg 19(4)(b)), or covered by an exemption, the full amount will be subject to Class 1A, see **11.4.2**. Where the item is included in the Step Two, as distinct from being on the P11D of a service company worker, then the tax rules rather than the NIC rules apply, see **12.3.3**. As a result apportionment may be permitted;
- If the asset is unavailable for part of the year, the benefit is reduced (s156(2) ICTA 1988);
- If ownership of an asset is transferred to the worker, there is only a benefit if the asset is transferred at less than its market value at the date of transfer. These rules are amended where there has been private use, see s156(4) ICTA 1988.

There are two useful exemptions from this charge:

(a) Computers provided by the client for the worker's private use. These are not taxable as long as the annual value is £500 or less (s156A ICTA 1988);

(b) Any assets where the private use is 'not significant' (s155ZA(3) ICTA 1988). This would cover the use of telephones, photocopiers and fax machines, as well as computers provided for work which do not fall within the s156A exemption. Unsurprisingly, this relief does not extend to the private use of aeroplanes, boats or cars, even if private use is not significant.

10.6.3 Cars

Where a personal service worker has been provided with a car by a client, he will be able to escape the scale charge if either:

- All travel in the car would have been allowable cost under the travel rules, see **11.6**; or

- The car is a pool car, see below.

Some problems which may arise when the worker is provided with a car by the client include:

Pool cars

Pool cars are not taxable, as long as the strict conditions in ss159 and 159AB ICTA 1988 are complied with. These are that:

(a) The car is available to, and actually used by, more than one employee (or worker within the personal services rules), and is not ordinarily used by any one of them to the exclusion of the others;

(b) The car is not normally kept overnight on or in the vicinity of the residence of any of the employees/workers except while it is being kept on premises occupied by the client. The Revenue have a rule of thumb that a car is not regarded as 'normally kept overnight' at employees' homes if the total number of nights on which it is taken home – for whatever reason – is less than 60 per cent of the total number of nights in the period under review (IR Booklet 480). However they also warn that: 'If a car or van is taken home often enough to approach the 60 per cent limit – though without breaking it – it is unlikely that all the home to work journeys will satisfy the "merely incidental" test' (SE 3492/SE 23803);

(c) Any private use of the car by any of the employees or workers is merely incidental to its business use, see Example 10B.

Example 10B

Stephen has his own personal service company specialising in computer game theory. He is working away from his home in Bath on a relevant engagement in Manchester, which is expected to exceed two years. He is provided with a car by the client so he can travel between different offices in the Manchester area. In the evenings he uses the car to drive to his favourite vegetarian restaurant in the centre of the city. This is merely incidental to the business use, and there is no benefit.

However one weekend he obtains the client's permission to use the car to visit his father in Devon. This is private use, and as a result the car is not a pool car and has to be included on his P11D, see SP2/96.

Cars provided in succession

Where a worker has been supplied with a number of cars in the course of a tax year, perhaps by different clients, he should treat them as if they had been sequentially provided by a single employer (Sch 12, para 11(2) FA 2000). This has the following consequences:

(a) If a car is available for only part of the fiscal year, the tax charge can be reduced. Thus if a contractor is provided with a car by one client for a month, and two weeks later another car by a different client for ten months, his benefit charge will be reduced to reflect the period when he had no car. The same would apply if a client made available two different cars on separate occasions;

(b) However, where the worker is given the use of the same car and there is a gap when it was not provided, there is no reduction in the benefit unless the car has been unavailable for at least 30 consecutive days. Unavailable means that the car itself cannot be accessed; it is not enough that the driver cannot drive for the period, for example because of illness or a driving ban (Sch 6, paras 6 and 9 ICTA 1988);

This could impact on contractors who are at a client for one week a month, and are always given the use of the same car. Because the gap would not be 30 days, there would be no reduction in the car benefit. It would thus be possible for a contractor to have several cars which were technically available for use, because they were each provided by different clients for part of a month. The benefit cost would then be unacceptably high;

(c) When the car is available for periods of less than a year, the normal reduction for business mileage in excess of either 2,500 or 18,000 miles a year is also pro-rated, so that a car used for six months will have a reduced benefit cost if the contractor drives 1,250 or 9,000 miles;

(d) The business mileage rules are also applied on a per car basis, and thus if the car is changed part way through the year, the mileage must be calculated for each car, see SE 3454/SE 23304 and *Henwood v Clarke* (1997) STC 789. This is likely to be an area of particular difficulty for personal service workers, see Example 10C.

Hire cars

A hire car provided by the client is still a 'company car' for tax purposes. The fact that it has not come from the client's own fleet is irrelevant.

Example 10C

Graeme is a newly qualified vet who works in partnership with his girlfriend. He takes up a relevant engagement working for the Head of Veterinary Science at the local zoo. The contract begins on 1 June 2000 and lasts for three months. He is supplied with a Ford Fiesta with a list price of £15,000.

He subsequently takes up a second relevant engagement in a government department replacing a vet who is on maternity leave. He is given the use of a Mercedes E Class, previously driven by a senior executive. The car's list price is £40,000. He begins the contract on 1 January 2001 and continues until 30 June. He drives 1000 business miles in the Fiesta, and 200 miles a month in the Mercedes.

The taxable benefit to be included in Step Two of his deemed Schedule E calculation for the fiscal year 2000/01 is:

Fiesta – 15,000 x 92/365 x 25% = £945

Mercedes – 40,000 x 95/365 x 35% = £3,643

The tax charge for both cars is reduced because they were each only available for three months during the tax year 2000/01. Although Graeme has driven more than 1,250 business miles in the 6 months, he only obtains the 25 per cent reduced charge in respect of the first car, because the percentage is calculated on a per car basis.

10.6.4 Chauffeur

Interim executives working through a personal service company may be supplied with a chauffeur. Where the chauffeur is only used for business journeys, or to and from a 'temporary workplace' under the travel rules, see **11.6**, there will be no benefit.

Where there is 'private use', provision of a chauffeur is taxable. The benefit charge is based on the relevant proportion of the chauffeur's wages, including waiting time, overtime, pension contributions, and NIC costs. The tax exposure is thus significant, but can be reduced if the chauffeur does other jobs for the client, see Example 10D.

> **Example 10D**
>
> Maeve has her own personal service company and is acting Chairperson of a major plc. She is given the use of a chauffeur, who picks her up from her home in Wolverhampton every morning and drives her to the client's offices in Birmingham. She has been in this role for three years.
>
> Her journeys from home to work are private mileage because a three year assignment is outside the travel rules. Provision of the chauffeur is thus taxable. His costs total £30,000 per year, but it is estimated that only 20 per cent of this relates to the Chairperson. The benefit to be included on Maeve's P11D is thus £6,000.

When a temporary executive has the use of chauffeur it may be possible to argue that it should not be taxable, based on the 'merely incidental' part of the pool car test, see **10.6.3** above. SP2/96 discusses the situation where:

- The car is also used by others;

- It is not kept at the individual's home overnight; and

- A chauffeur is needed because the individual needs to work on his confidential papers in the car.

10.6.5 Conferences

A personal services worker may attend a conference, such as an overseas sales convention, organised by the client. This may be work-related training provided by the client, and thus not taxable, see **11.8.2**. Otherwise it is likely to be a benefit unless wholly, exclusively and necessarily in the performance of the duties.

The Revenue may not accept that a conference was necessary if the individual himself decided to go *(Owen v Burden* [1971] 47 TC 476*)*. Workers should therefore ensure that they are 'instructed' to attend, and do not simply self-authorise their own attendance. There is likely to be an extra cost if the individual's spouse or partner accompanies the worker, subject to the exemptions provided by ESC A4.

Most clients with such events will have already discussed the tax treatment of attendees with their local district, and the worker should seek to discover what has been agreed.

10.6.6 Entertaining

This is an area when the liability to tax depends on whether paragraph 7 or paragraph 11 of Schedule 12 has priority, see **10.4**.

If paragraph 7 has priority, the worker will be taxed as if he were an employee of the client. Entertaining provided by an individual's employer is a benefit and included either in Step Two, if the worker is a partner, or otherwise on the worker's P11D.

However, if paragraph 11 has priority, which is more likely, the entertaining will have been provided by a third party. The following text has been written on the assumption that paragraph 11 has priority, but it should be noted that the position is unclear.

There is an exemption for employees provided with entertainment by third parties, where:

(a) The person providing the benefit is neither his employer nor a person connected with his employer;

(b) Neither his employer nor a person connected with his employer has directly or indirectly procured its provision; and

(c) It is not provided either in recognition of particular services which have been performed by the employee in the course of his employment or in anticipation of particular services which are to be so performed by him (s555(7) ICTA 1988).

However, personal services workers are unlikely to satisfy the above exemption, because the entertaining either:

• Normally falls outside (b) because the provision has been procured by the intermediary as part of the working arrangements; or

• Falls outside (c) because it has been provided by the client 'in recognition of particular services'; or

• Has been provided 'by arrangement with' the employer and thus is included on the employee/director's P11D on first principles, see **10.5.4**.

However, where the hospitality does meet the above tests, it will not be taxed.

The client will normally disallow these amounts as entertaining (or mistakenly include personal services workers in the firm's PSA, see **10.7** below). However, the amounts will generally be taxed again in the hands of the personal services worker. This was the case before IR35, as most entertaining provided by clients for personal service workers already falls outside the exemption in s555(7). While this double taxation is unwelcome, it is not a problem created by the new legislation.

The worker is likely to have practical problems establishing the value of the benefit to include on the P11D or in Step Two of the deemed income calculation. If the amounts are taxable, he should obtain details from the client in time to complete his calculation. He should also have regard to the defences listed below.

Defences

(a) The Revenue have accepted that some entertaining may be 'trivial' – for instance where a personal services worker joins a meal out with employees. They have indicated that this practice of ignoring trivial benefits would not however be appropriate if the functions were regular in nature or likely to involve significant costs per head, or were entered into chiefly for the personal services workers. They have suggested that this issue can only be resolved on a case by case basis, and recommended that any worker who is unsure about his position should consult his Inspector;

(b) An argument can be mounted that some meetings over a meal are necessarily incurred – the Revenue Manual (ECM 13209) suggests that this may be the case where, for example, the extension of a service contract is being discussed, or workers are detained beyond their normal hours for a briefing from head office;

(c) Where the personal services worker is entitled to tax-free subsistence under the travel rules, see **11.6.5**, the cost of the entertaining can be reduced by the amount of subsistence, or eliminated altogether, see NAG 5.130;

(d) There is an exemption for annual 'staff functions' under ESC A70 for amounts up to £75 per head. A contractor who moves from client to client may attend a number of such functions, each of which may be tax-free for the employees. However, as the worker is deemed to be employed by his service company (Sch 12, para 11(2) FA 2000) he is limited to £75 worth of staff parties per year. The Concession warns that:

> 'Where the cost of the entertainment is more than £75 per head, tax will be payable on the full amount assessable under the relevant charging provision. Where there is more than one annual function and their total cost per head exceeds £75, the functions that total £75 or less will not be taxed. Any other functions will be taxed in full.'

(e) Relief is also available under ESC A74 for free or subsidised meals provided for employees on the business premises, or in any canteen where meals are provided for the staff generally, or on the use of any ticket or token to obtain such meals, if:

- The meals are provided on a reasonable scale; and

- Either all employees may obtain free or subsidised meals on a reasonable scale, whether on the employer's premises or elsewhere, or the employer provides free or subsidised meal vouchers for staff for whom meals are not provided.

It is understood that the Revenue will apply this concession to personal service workers in the same way as it is applies to the client's staff.

10.6.7 Fuel

Where fuel has been provided by the client for private use in a company car for any part of the tax year the full scale charge is applicable, unless the car itself was not provided for part of the year, see **10.6.3** above. There is no reduction in the benefit charge because only a small amount of private fuel has been provided.

Home to work travel is however not 'private mileage' if it falls within the travel rules, see **11.6**. If the engagement is not covered by the travel rules, however, care is needed. A small error, such as occasional reimbursements of fuel when a worker is called to the office out of hours, can give rise to a considerable tax bill.

10.6.8 Gifts

A gift provided by a client may escape tax if:

- It is either provided on personal grounds (for example, a wedding present) or as a mark of personal esteem (SE 1182/SE 01460); or

- It falls within ESC A70. This exempts small gifts in kind provided by third parties of up to £150 per annum. However this concession is not available if the gift is 'made either in recognition of the performance of particular services in the course of the employment or in anticipation of particular services which are to be performed'. This may apply to some gifts provided by a client to PSC workers.

10.6.9 Loans

Loans are an unlikely benefit, though it is possible that long term contractors might be given a season ticket advance on the same terms as employees. Temporary executives may succeed in obtaining more substantial loans.

If the client does lend money to the worker, and there is either no interest or the rate is below the Revenue's official rate, a benefit will arise unless:

- The loan is no more than £5,000 at any point in the tax year (s161 ICTA 1988); or

- It is a 'qualifying loan', such as to invest in a partnership (s160(1C) ICTA 1988); or

- The client's business is the lending of money, and the loan is on the same terms as is available to members of the public (s161(1A) ICTA 1988).

If the loan is written off, the amount becomes taxable on the worker, even if the contract has already terminated, see s160(3) ICTA 1988.

10.6.10 Relocations

Some personal service workers may have their relocation costs reimbursed by the client. This will not be a benefit as long as:

- Only 'eligible' relocation expenses are paid; and

- The total cost is not more than £8,000 (Sch 11A, ICTA 1988).

10.6.11 Telephones

If the mobile phone is *provided by the client* it will not be taxable, even if it is used for private calls. However, with the exception of evidenced business calls, the following are a benefit:

- Reimbursement of the worker's home telephone bills; or

- Mobile phone charges relating to the worker's own phone; or

- Phone vouchers provided by the employer.

Line rental is generally a benefit unless the line meets the wholly, exclusively and necessarily requirement, see *Lucas v Cattell* [1972] 48 TC 353. This test will be met, for example, if workers can show that it is genuinely part of their duties to deal with emergencies, such as an IT worker on call to deal with computer crashes. In such cases the Revenue allows the same proportion of the rental charge as the business use of the telephone is to the overall use (ECM 13044).

10.6.12 Travel and subsistence

Travel and subsistence costs are dealt with at 11.6.

10.7 PAYE Settlement Agreements and Taxed Award Schemes

The client may use a PAYE Settlement Agreement (PSA) to meet the cost of some employee benefits. For instance, if the staff go on a day trip to Paris, the employer may calculate the tax and NIC and pay this over to the Revenue on a grossed up basis (s206A ICTA 1988).

However a PSA is not yet available where the benefit is provided for a third party, although this may however be possible in the future, see the Revenue's consultation document, *Simplifying National Insurance Contributions for Employers*, issued on 7 June 2000.

However, third parties have long been able to use the Taxed Award Scheme (TAS) for tax. Since April 2000, the TAS can also be used to cover the NICs liability in relation to benefits and non-cash vouchers provided to third parties.

A client with a large number of personal services workers could thus use a TAS to pay the tax and NICs on benefits provided. However, appropriate communication is needed, particularly if the client has a fluctuating contractor workforce. The PSC workers might otherwise be unaware of the TAS and include the benefit in their own deemed income calculation or on their P11Ds.

11 Expenses included in deemed payment

11.1 Introduction

IR35 aims to tax the worker broadly as if his relevant engagements were an employment. As a result, the Schedule E reliefs for both expenses and capital allowances are applicable, rather than the more generous Schedule D legislation.

Step Three of the calculation gives relief on a Schedule E basis for expenses borne by the intermediary. Step Four deducts capital allowances on assets owned by the intermediary.

Under Step One of the calculation, the worker can also claim an additional expense allowance equal to 5 per cent of income received from relevant engagements.

11.2 The 5 per cent allowance

11.2.1 General

When carrying out the deemed Schedule E calculation, income received from relevant engagements is first reduced by 5 per cent (Sch 12, para 7 Step One FA 2000). Points to note include:

- It is immaterial whether the individual has been paid his earnings during the year as salary, or whether they are subject to a deemed Schedule E calculation: the 5 per cent deduction is identical because it is based on the relevant income received by the intermediary;

- The deduction is available only against income received by the *intermediary*. There is no 5 per cent deduction available against amounts paid directly to the worker by the client. It is thus more tax efficient for expenses to be reimbursed to the intermediary rather than being paid directly to the worker. For example, it is better for travel costs to be reimbursed to the service company than for the worker to be provided with the use of a car.

11.2.2 What does the 5 per cent deduction cover?

The Revenue's first FAQ on expenses explains that:

'Service companies will be able to claim a flat rate deduction of 5% of the gross fees receivable for any relevant engagements. This 5% deduction is not available to employees but will be allowed for service companies to enable them to meet the additional costs of providing their services in this particular way.'

Because the tax relief for expenses under the Schedule E legislation is somewhat limited, a number of unavoidable expenses will be suffered by the intermediary for which no explicit deduction is available in the deemed Schedule E calculation. The 5 per cent allowance gives relief for some or all of these costs, which include:

• Secretarial support;

• Accountancy and tax advice fees;

• The costs of seeking contracts;

• Computer equipment if not eligible for capital allowances, see **11.11** below;

• Postage and stationery;

• Training costs, see **11.8** below;

• Employer's and public liability insurance, see **11.10** below;

• Use of home as office in most cases, see **11.3.6(4)** below;

• Bank and overdraft interest;

• Hire purchase payments, except in relation to vehicles used on business, see **11.6.8** below.

11.2.3 Interaction with corporation tax

Although in general an intermediary's actual expenses are likely to exceed the available tax reliefs, the opposite may also occur. The Revenue have confirmed that 'There will be no requirement to demonstrate expenditure: the 5 per cent deduction will be allowed in all cases'. (FAQ Expenses 3)

If the actual expenses are less than the 5 per cent allowed in the deemed Schedule E computation, some profits could remain within the charge to corporation tax, see Example 11A.

Example 11A

Jill, whose personal service company specialises in nursing services, has £70,000 of relevant income. A friend does her books and tax computation for £400 a year. She has no other expenses. Her year end is 5 April.

Her tax position is as follows:

Deemed Schedule E calculation

	Notes	£
Relevant income		70,000
5% deduction		(3,500)
		66,500
NICs	1	(6,754)
Deemed Schedule E payment		59,746

Corporation tax	£
Income	70,000
Expenses	(400)
Deemed salary	(59,746)
Employer's NIC	(6,754)
CT profits	3,100
CT payable at 10%	310

Notes

NIC calculated as $(66,500 - 4,385) \times (12.2/112.2) = £6,754$, see **12.5.2**.

If the 5 per cent allowance has not been fully utilised by actual expenditure, a salary could be paid to a family member who has insufficient taxable income to utilise his personal allowance, in exchange for administrative help. This will both ensure that no residual profit is taxed in the company, and the relative will receive the money free of tax and NICs. However, the Revenue may challenge the payment, see **3.4**.

11.3 Expenses in the deemed Schedule E calculation

11.3.1 Step Three

Step Three allows relief for:

> 'The amount of any expenses met in that year by the intermediary, that would have been deductible from the emoluments of the employment if the worker had been employed by the client and the expenses had been met by the worker out of those emoluments.' (Sch 12, para 7 Step 3 FA 2000)

The expenses which are allowable under the Schedule E rules for employees are discussed at **11.4** below.

11.3.2 Cash basis

The expense is deductible when the cost is borne by the intermediary, not when the liability arises. As with income in Step One, see **10.2**, the deduction for expenses is thus on a cash rather than an accruals basis. This is clearly explained in FAQ (Computation) 14:

> '*How do I apportion the expenses when working out the deemed payment where a contract straddles the end of the tax year?*
>
> When working out the deemed payment, relief should be given for all allowable expenses met by the intermediary in the tax year, in respect of relevant engagements, as set out at Step 3. Relief for the expense should be given by reference to the date when the intermediary meets the liability. This is the date when the bill is paid. There should therefore be no need to apportion any expenses.
>
> For example, an intermediary has a relevant engagement that runs from 1 January to 30 June 2001, during which the worker is required to work at a temporary workplace. In the course of this engagement the worker stays in bed and breakfast accommodation. The bill is settled on a monthly basis in arrears, with 14 days to pay. At the end of March a bill for £400 is issued which the intermediary pays on 12 April. The liability was met in the tax year 2001/02. Therefore, relief for the expense will be given when working out the deemed payment payable.'

11.3.3 Costs incurred by the employee/director rather than the intermediary

Since the deduction in Step Three is for expenses met by the intermediary, costs incurred directly by the worker do not come into the deemed Schedule E calculation. If these are allowable under the Schedule E rules, they can be claimed directly by the individual director or employee in his self-assessment form under ss198ff ICTA 1988. For partners, see **11.3.4** below.

This puts workers in the same position as employees who incur allowable costs in the course of their employment (Sch 12, para 11(4)(b) FA 2000).

However, it is not efficient for the worker to bear the costs. This is because, although he can claim tax relief on the expense, he will not obtain NICs relief. If, instead, the amounts are borne by the intermediary, they are taken out of the calculation at Step Three and so reduce the deemed payment. This saves both employer's and employee's NICs. Costs should therefore be borne by the intermediary, rather than by the worker.

Where a worker bears the expenses initially, the practical solution is for him to reclaim the amounts from the intermediary as business costs. They will then be deductible under Step Three.

11.3.4 Partners

Employees and directors have always been within the Schedule E rules, and thus should be more familiar with their requirements. Partnerships are now brought within the rules for the first time, and may have a steeper learning curve.

Where partners initially bear costs relating to a relevant engagement themselves, they should ensure that these amounts are reimbursed by the partnership for the same reason as employees and directors – it will reduce the NIC on the deemed payment.

If this is does not happen, the partner should ensure that the amounts are claimed in the partnership computation. This is because there is no equivalent to s198 ICTA for partners, so tax relief cannot be claimed on the individual's own self-assessment return, see **15.3.4**. However, it should be noted that relief is only available in the partnership computation for expenses borne personally if the cost would have been allowable under the rules for Schedule E, see **11.3.6** below (Sch 12, para 18(3) FA 2000).

11.3.5 Apportioned costs

Although IR35 has a specific provision concerning apportionment of income, see **10.3**, there is no equivalent for costs. The legislation (Sch 12, para 9 FA 2000) requires that income be apportioned on a 'just and reasonable basis', and a similar approach can be taken for costs.

A cost may be apportioned because:

(a) It is partly for the purposes of the business and partly private. This is normally agreed with the Inspector on the facts of the case;

(b) It relates partly to relevant engagements and partly to other work. If a deduction is to be allowed for an apportioned cost in the Schedule E calculation, then 'a definite part or proportion' of the expense must meet the tests set out in s198ff ICTA 1988 (IM 601e).

Although the NICs regulations do not recognise the concept of an apportioned expense, the tax rules take priority here, see **11.4.2**.

11.3.6 Expense disallowances

A practical question is the extent to which expenses disallowed in the deemed Schedule E calculation can be claimed in the corporation tax or partnership computation.

Partnership computation

A partnership can only deduct expenses relating to relevant income if they either meet the Schedule E tests or are within the 5 per cent allowance. It is thus not possible to offset 'surplus' expenses against other Schedule D income. (Sch 12, para 18(3) FA 2000.) A separate rule also prevents the Schedule E deemed payment from creating a loss (Sch 12, para 18(2) FA 2000), see **14.6.3**.

Corporation tax computation

No such explicit provision operates in the case of the corporation tax computation, so normal rules are followed. In some cases it is clear that an amount disallowed for Schedule E will be allowed for corporation tax. Examples include:

- Costs of accountancy and tax advice to calculate the deemed Schedule E amount, because the obligation to make the deemed payment is on the intermediary, not the individual;

- Filing costs relating to the company;

- Expenses of seeking contracts;

- Genuine costs of administrative assistance.

In other cases, even though there is no specific legal requirement to disallow excess costs as there is with partnerships, the deemed income calculation may focus attention on expenses which have previously been accepted as allowable by the Revenue.

For example, where part of the running costs of the home have been claimed as allowable for corporation tax, and the company's business is now seen to consist entirely of relevant engagements, the Inspector may question whether the deduction is justified – what work is actually being done at home and how much time does it take? Such questions could even lead into an enquiry into previous computations.

Care should thus be taken when completing the corporation tax computation – the 'wholly and exclusively' test, while less stringent than that for employees, is still real.

11.4 Schedule E expenses

11.4.1 Tax

The general Schedule E expenses rule is set out in s198(1) ICTA 1988. It allows deductions for expenses which have been 'wholly, exclusively and necessarily incurred in the performance of the duties of the employment'. The reliefs for travel and subsistence are more generous, only requiring that costs be 'necessarily incurred in the performance of the duties'(s198(1A) and Sch 12A ICTA 1988), see **11.6**.

Specific deductions are also available for:

- Personal incidental expenses, see **11.7**;

- Work-related training provided by clients or agents, see **11.8**;

- Expenditure on professional fees and subscriptions, see **11.9**;

- Indemnity insurance payments, see **11.10**; and

- Agents' fees paid by entertainers, see **20.2.4**.

11.4.2 National Insurance

Allowable expenses are deductible in the attributable earnings calculation. Although the NIC rules for allowable expenses are not identical to those for tax, where they differ, it is the tax rules which are used (SI 2000 No 727 Reg 7). If this were not the case, the calculation would have to be performed twice – once for NICs and once for tax. Fortunately, this complexity has been avoided.

11.5 The general rule: s198(1)

Meeting the 'wholly, exclusively and necessarily in the performance of the duties test' is extremely difficult. These words have been described as:

> 'Notoriously rigid, narrow and restricted in their operation. An expenditure may be "necessary" for the holder of an office without being necessary to him in the performance of the duties of that office; it may be necessary in the performance of those duties without being exclusively referable to those duties;

179

it may perhaps be both necessarily and exclusively, but still not wholly so referable. The words are indeed stringent and exacting; compliance with each and every one of them is obligatory if the benefit of the Rule is to be claimed successfully. They are, to my mind, deceptive words in the sense that when examined they are found to come to nearly nothing at all.' (*Lomax v Newton* [1953] 34 TC 558)

The s198 test refers to 'the holder' of the job, and it is thus based on the requirements of the duties rather than those of the specific individual carrying out the engagement. To satisfy the rule the expenditure must be necessary to each and every person who might perform those duties. See for example the words of Donovan L.J.:

'The test is not whether the employer imposes the expense but whether the duties do, in the sense that, irrespective of what the employer may prescribe, the duties cannot be performed without incurring the particular outlay.' (*Brown v Bullock* [1961] 40 TC 1)

However this does not mean that 'every holder of the job would have to incur the same amount of expense. If business travel is necessary, the cost of business journeys is deductible whether the employee travels by car, train or air' (SE 4031/SE 31645).

The expense must be incurred in actually performing the duties. The Revenue have summarised this as follows:

'It is not sufficient that an expense is simply relevant to or incurred in connection with the duties of the job. Nor will an expense be allowable which merely puts an employee in a position to start work or keeps him qualified to do it.' (SE 4034/SE 31650)

The cost must also be 'wholly and exclusively' incurred, although apportionment is possible 'if, on the facts, a definite part or proportion of an expense can be properly attributed to the performance of the duties' (SE 4038/SE 31661). This principle was established by the cases *Hillyer v Leeke* 51 TC 90 and *Woodcock v CIR* [1977] 51 TC 698, even though these judgements went against the taxpayers. If, for example, an aircraft is used partly for business and partly privately, its costs can be split between those which are allowable for Schedule E and those relating to the private use.

However, where the expenditure serves two or more purposes at the same time, one of which is not to do with the performance of the duties, nothing can be claimed. An example is the cost of ordinary clothing. In *Ward v Dunn* [1979] 52 TC 517 a surveyor had his arguments rejected:

'When Mr. Dunn purchases a suit he purchases it, maybe partly with a view to going round the sites but, at any rate, partly with a view to wearing it in the ordinary course as one wears clothing for comfort and for covering one's nakedness. Similarly, when he has clothing cleaned it is cleaned, doubtless partly as a result of what happens on the construction sites, but also so that he may wear clean clothing and not dirty clothing. Similarly, when it is repaired as a result of damage which it has sustained when he has visited sites, it is repaired so that he may wear clothes which hang together, not clothes which are in rags. . . . The mere fact that that clothing is his ordinary clothing makes it, in my view, completely impossible for it to be said that the money which he is now claiming is money which is "wholly" expended by him in the performance of his duties.'

Section 198 is thus much less generous than the comparable section for expenses incurred by a company or a partnership under Schedule D, which merely requires costs to be 'wholly and exclusively for the purposes of the business' (s74(1)(a) ICTA 1988). As a result, many costs for which tax relief was available before IR35 was introduced will no longer obtain relief – at least not in the deemed Schedule E calculation. Relief will still be due in the corporation tax computation, but this may simply create a loss, see 13.7.

Examples of expenses allowable under s198 include:

(a) Protective clothing worn as a matter of physical necessity because of the nature of the job, such as oil workers' overalls;

(b) Clothing which is recognisably a uniform. The Revenue do not accept that an item of clothing is 'uniform' if it can be worn away from the workplace without its identity as uniform being obvious. The inclusion of a prominent and permanently fixed company logo on the clothing is usually required;

(c) Books which have to be purchased by the worker in order to carry out the job, such as computer manuals necessary to operate the equipment for an IT consultant. But this is a difficult test to meet, see SE 4105/SE 32435.

11.6 Travel and subsistence expenses

11.6.1 General

The legislation for travel expenses (s198(1A) and Sch 12A ICTA 1988) is less stringent than the general rule. Instead of a requirement that costs be 'wholly, exclusively and necessarily incurred in the performance of the duties', travel expenses only have to be 'necessarily incurred in the performance of the duties'. Thus if a worker has to travel to Perpignan for a business meeting, the fact that he spends a few days beforehand cycling in the Pyrenees will not make his return trip to France inadmissible.

'Travel' includes any associated subsistence and other incidental costs such as car parking. Since many personal service workers have contracts which entitle them to travel and subsistence on top of a daily rate, it is important that these amounts fall as far as possible within the reliefs offered by the legislation.

The rules are complex, and explored at length in Inland Revenue booklet 490 (IR 490). The following summarises the key points relevant to those within the personal service rules.

11.6.2 Legislation

Section 198(1A) ICTA 1988 defines allowable travel expenses as follows:

(a) 'Amounts necessarily expended on travelling in the performance of the duties of the office or employment.' This covers journeys where the travelling itself is part of the duties, such as where the worker is a long distance lorry driver, and also trips between one place of business and another, such as between two offices of the same employer; and

(b) Other expenses of travelling which 'are attributable to the necessary attendance at any place . . . in the performance of the duties of the office or employment, which are not expenses of ordinary commuting or private travel.'

This gives relief for journeys to carry out necessary duties of the relevant engagement, such as travelling from home to meet a customer of the client. However, there is no tax relief when the journey is 'ordinary commuting' or 'private travel'.

11.6.3 Ordinary commuting

A journey counts as 'ordinary commuting' if it is travel between home and a permanent workplace (Sch 12A, para 2 ICTA 1988). However, travel to and from a *temporary* workplace is tax free. So too is any associated subsistence and accommodation. Thus for the personal service worker to gain relief for his travel and subsistence, he has to show that the client's office is a temporary workplace.

For a workplace to be 'temporary' either of the following tests must be satisfied:

(a) The duties of the employment are not performed to a significant extent at that place. 'A significant extent' is generally interpreted by the Revenue to mean more than 40 per cent (IR 490 para 3.12);

(b) The engagement is expected to, and actually does, last for two years or less.

This second relief – the two-year rule – does not apply if the engagement comprises 'all or almost all of the period for which the employee is likely to hold the employment' (Sch 12A, para 5 ICTA 1988).

Initially this gave rise to fears that contractors would be unable to claim for travel to clients' sites, because if they were deemed to be employees of the client for tax purposes, each engagement would be 'all or almost all of the period for which the employee is likely to hold the employment'.

However the personal services legislation treats the worker as an employee of the intermediary (Sch 12, para 11(2) FA 2000). Thus his 'employment' is with his own company, and travel to clients will not therefore comprise 'all or almost all' of his employment.

This interpretation has been confirmed by the Revenue in FAQ Expenses 6:

> 'A computer contractor provides services through a limited company; has a series of contracts with different clients around the country; and regularly travels from home to work at the premises of the company's clients.
>
> Provided the contractor does not expect to spend more than 40% of his or her working time at any one site, he or she is entitled to a deduction for all journeys from home to the client's premises. If he or she does spend more than 40% of his time at a single site, but the engagement is both expected to, and actually does, last for no more than 2 years, a deduction for travel costs will also be available.'

Subsequently, similar confirmation was given by Dawn Primarolo in the House of Commons debate on the Finance Bill, see *Hansard* 6 June 2000.

Two-year test

If at some point during the two year period it becomes likely that the engagement will be extended beyond the two-year point, travel and subsistence becomes taxable from that date. Great care is therefore needed when negotiating and communicating extensions to engagements.

The two-year test is applied from the start date of the contract. An engagement which began on 6 July 1999 will fail the two-year test if it is expected to run on until after 5 July 2001. The 6 April 2000 date, which marks the start of the new personal services regime, does not affect this in any way. This is true whether or not the relevant engagement is being carried out by a worker in a company (who will already be within the travel rules) or by a partner, coming into the rules for the first time. The important factor is the start date of the contract.

The following Examples 11B to 11J, adapted from IR 490, illustrate the various scenarios. The particularly harsh treatment in Example 11D should be noted, along with the fact that a period of work can remain continuous even where there is a break in attendance, see Example 11F (IR 490: 3.14).

Example 11B

Doris has set up her own personal service company based at her home in Warrington supplying secretarial services. Warrington is thus her permanent workplace. She is obtains a relevant engagement at an office in Wigan for 18 months. Relief is available for the full cost of Doris's travel between home and the temporary workplace in Wigan.

Example 11C

Duncan obtains a relevant engagement working full-time at a factory for 28 months. There is no relief for the cost of travel to and from the workplace, because his attendance there is known from the outset to be for more than 24 months, so the workplace is a permanent workplace. His home to work travel is therefore ordinary commuting for which no relief is available.

Example 11D

Dymphna's relevant engagement requires her full-time attendance at a workplace for 28 months but the posting is unexpectedly ended after 18 months. No relief is available for the cost of travel between her home and the workplace, because her attendance was expected to exceed 24 months (though in fact it does not). The workplace is therefore a permanent workplace and the journey is ordinary commuting.

Example 11E

Earl has a relevant full-time engagement at a workplace for 18 months. After 10 months the posting is extended to 28 months. Relief is available for the full cost of travel to and from the workplace during the first 10 months (while his attendance was expected to be for less than 24 months) but not after that (once his attendance was expected to exceed 24 months).

> *Example 11F*
>
> Ernest is a subcontractor with his own service company. He obtains a relevant engagement to work full-time on a construction project which is expected to last for six years. Each time Ernest gets close to having worked on the site for nearly two years his employer moves him to another workplace for a week before returning him to the long-term project site.
>
> Despite these moves, Ernest is spending a significant amount of his working time (more than 40 per cent) at one site and the period during which he is doing so is greater than 24 months. So Ernest is not entitled to relief for his travel from home to the site.

40 per cent test

The two-year test is in the legislation (Sch 12A, para 5(1)(a) ICTA 1988), whereas the 40 per cent test is Revenue practice. Examples 11G and 11H show how it will be applied:

> *Example 11G*
>
> Emily is a partner in a veterinary practice on the south coast. She obtains a relevant engagement under which she is required to supervise a seal sanctuary in Morecambe for one day each month. She has done this for five years. Although Emily goes to Morecambe for more than 24 months she does not spend more than 40 per cent of her working time there and she retains a permanent workplace on the south coast. So she is entitled to relief for her travel from home to Morecambe.

> *Example 11H*
>
> Ferdinand is a computer expert who provides his services via a personal service company. He is the company's only employee. Each year the company has around 15 contracts with different clients around the country to supply Ferdinand's services. He regularly travels from home to work at the premises of the company's clients. Provided he does not expect to spend more than 40 per cent of his working time for more than 24 months at any one site he is entitled to relief for all his journeys from home to the clients' premises.

Substantial effect test

Where a change in location 'does not have . . . any substantial effect on the employee's journey, or expenses of travelling, to and from the place where the duties fall to be performed' then the two year period will be measured from the beginning of the earlier contract (Sch 12A, para 5(3) ICTA 1988).

This means that if a worker has an engagement with a client for eighteen months, and then moves to a second contract in the next street, there is no 'substantial effect' on either the journey or the expenses of travelling. If the total time expected to be spent at both engagements taken together is more than two years, no tax relief will be available from the date on which the worker agrees to take up the second contract. Considerable care is thus needed when selecting engagements.

The substantial effect test can be difficult to apply. However the Revenue have confirmed that:

> 'Where a change in location has a significant effect on the journey an employee has to make to get to work and, in particular, the cost of the journey to work, the new location is a new workplace even if it is close to the old workplace.' (IR 490 5.8)

Example 11J demonstrates how the Revenue will interpret the rule:

Example 11J

Justin is a subcontractor with his own service company and obtains a relevant engagement working on a major bridge construction project. To begin with he works on the north shore but he is then transferred to work on the south shore. Crossing the river is inconvenient (which is why a new bridge is needed), and it takes Justin longer to travel to the south shore and costs much more than it did to travel to the north shore. The north and south shores could be described as a single construction site and, as the crow flies, they are not far apart. However, Justin's move from the north to the south shore has had a significant effect on his journey to work (and, in particular, the cost of that journey) so his workplace has changed for tax purposes.

Cessation of business

As explained above, the travel reliefs operate if the engagement does not comprise 'all or almost all' of the period for which the worker was employed. Since the worker is regarded as employed by his service company, this restriction will only become an issue if the employment is terminated following a single long engagement, or following an engagement which took up almost all of the period for which the worker operated via the intermediary, see Example 11K.

Example 11K

Chris was employed as a teacher trainer by a language school in London, but was made redundant in order to reduce headcount. However, the school quickly found they could not meet their commitments to students, and suggested he form his own service company. Chris worked for the language school for two years, and claimed over £1,000 a year in travel costs. In June 2000 he decided to close down the company to concentrate on writing novels. As he had only one engagement which comprised 'all or almost all' of the period for which he held the engagement, his travel costs could be disallowed.

Some workers may be able to take advantage of the practice set out in Revenue booklet 490 at paragraph 3.18:

> 'The Inland Revenue will not normally use this rule to deny relief for travel to a workplace which is the final posting for someone whose contract of employment has lasted for at least 5 years.'

11.6.4 Private travel

This is travel between either:

- The employee's home and a place that is not his workplace; or

- Between two places neither of which is his workplace.

The legislation here is stating the obvious – there is no tax relief for a private journey, such as between home and the football ground, or between the football ground and the pub.

11.6.5 Accommodation and subsistence

If business travel is allowable, so too is any associated accommodation or subsistence, see Example 11L.

Example 11L

Michael is required to spend three months working at the site of one of his clients. He travels to the site every Monday morning, stays in a hotel close to the temporary workplace and travels home late every Friday evening, eating dinner on the way. During the week he takes some of his meals in the hotel and others at a nearby restaurant. The cost of the accommodation and all the meals are part of the cost of his business travel.

However some expenditure which may be incurred during a business journey is not attributable to that travel. Private telephone calls, newspapers and laundry, for example, are 'essentially personal in nature and do not, therefore, qualify for relief as integral parts of the cost of business travel' (IR 490 5.8). Where the worker stays overnight, some limited relief is available, see **11.7** below.

11.6.6 Working rule agreements

Working rule agreements (WRAs) are collective agreements drawn up between representatives of employers and trade unions. They generally cover travel, accommodation and subsistence and are normally payable to specific groups of employees within the construction and allied industries.

The Inland Revenue and the Contributions Agency are not a party to these agreements but have accepted that certain WRA allowances paid for daily travel and lodging should not be taxed or subjected to NIC. This is broadly on the basis that the workers would otherwise be able to claim a deduction for the expenses under s198(1A) ICTA 1988, although the Revenue have indicated that:

> 'It now seems likely that many such expenses payments might not be deductible under the general expenses rule, with the result that the tax treat-ment of WRAs is, at least in part, concessionary.' *(Employee Travel and Sub-sistence Consultative Document,* May 1996, para 5.3.1)

The modified tax procedures are negotiated nationally and apply only where the client adopts the terms and conditions of the relevant WRA. However the client does not have to be a member of the relevant employers' federation, nor do workers have to belong to the union negotiating the allowances, for these procedures to operate (*IRPR* 13 February 1981).

It is understood that WRA amounts received by workers who are within the personal service rules should be treated in the same way as those received by ordinary employees. Thus, where (as is normal) the WRA is paid to the worker, it will not be brought into the deemed Schedule E payment under Step Two, because it is not chargeable to tax. However, if it were paid to the inter-mediary, it would be brought into the calculation under Step One. Only the actual costs borne by the intermediary would then be deductible under Step Three, and this may be less advantageous.

11.6.7 Planning for travel costs

Workers can maximise their tax reliefs for travel and subsistence as follows:

(a) Costs should be borne by the intermediary rather than being paid directly to the worker by the client, see **11.3.3** above;

(b) If the worker undertakes a series of short engagements, each of which satisfy the travel rules, he can claim home to work travel in each case, irrespective of whether the cost is reimbursed by the client. So a worker whose home is in Brighton, but who has an 18 month contract in London, can have his home to work travel costs reimbursed by his service company;

(c) Engagements at a single location which require both more than 40 per cent of the worker's time and are expected to last for more than two years, should either be avoided, or priced accordingly;

(d) Extreme care should be taken when negotiating an extension to a contract beyond the two year point, because the costs become taxable from the point when it is *expected* to exceed two years;

(e) It is possible to have a contract at a single location, for more than two years, if it does not take up more than 40 per cent of the worker's time;

(f) Where a worker has an engagement with a client which requires him to work at a number of different sites, it is the *sites* which must be considered for the purposes of the travel rules, not the contract. So a single contract can extend for more than two years if the worker's location changes during the period, and he is within the travel rules in respect of each location;

(g) A new engagement should be a reasonable distance from the last, so as not to fall within the 'substantial effect' rule discussed at **11.6.3** above.

Additional tax reliefs may be available if the engagement is abroad, see **17.10.2**, or if the worker is from overseas, see **17.12.4**.

11.6.8 Vehicle running costs and business mileage

A car, bike or cycle owned by the worker and used in the performance of the duties of the relevant engagement will qualify for capital allowances, see **11.11** below. In addition the worker can either:

- Claim mileage costs, based on the Revenue's authorised mileage rates; or

- Deduct the proportion of his total costs which relates to his business use. This is calculated as the appropriate proportion (based on mileage) of the actual running costs of the vehicle including road fund licence, insurance, servicing and maintenance, annual subscriptions to breakdown/recovery services and the consideration, if any, for hire of the car under a hire purchase agreement. It also includes the actual cost of fuel consumed for business mileage, but does not include depreciation (IM 710).

In practice business mileage is often reimbursed by the client. If the reimbursements are less than the amounts which the worker could claim under either the Revenue's authorised mileage rates, or the more detailed calculation method, the difference can be deducted under Step Three as an allowable travel cost (s198(1A) ICTA 1988).

However where *excess* amounts are reimbursed to the intermediary, they will be brought into the calculation at Step One and only the allowable amount will be deductible at Step Three.

NICs and travel costs

Where travel expenses are reimbursed using the authorised mileage rates, different rules apply for NICs, because the Revenue accept that the two-tier system of mileage rates required for tax is not practicable for NICs:

> 'In practice, as long as reimbursed traveling expenses do no more than cover the full cost of business travel there will be no liability for NICs. Only where travel payments are made over and above the full cost of business travel will there be a liability for NICs.' (IR 490 para 6.4)

However, this difference is irrelevant for the purposes of the deemed payment. This is because the attributable earning calculation uses the same expense rules as for tax, see **11.4.2** (SI 2000 No 727 , para 7).

11.7 Personal incidental expenses

Contractors often incur incidental expenses, such as laundry, personal phone calls and newspapers, when staying away from home. These do not form part of the individual's allowable subsistence costs, see **11.6.5**. Instead, there is limited relief for these expenses under s200A ICTA 1988.

This allows the worker to incur up to £5 per night (£10 outside the UK) if he is away on business overnight. This can be by reimbursement or claimed as an allowance. Particular note should be taken of the following:

- If the payment is more than £5, the whole amount is taxable and subject to NIC;

- If an employee stays away for several nights consecutively, the total allowance is £5 multiplied by the number of nights away. For example, where an employee stays away for four nights and claims £5 on the first night, £5 on the second, £6 on the third and £4 on the fourth, he is within the exemption because the total does not exceed £20. Where the number of nights is not consecutive, no averaging is allowed.

11.8 Training

11.8.1 Training paid for by the worker

Normally no deduction will be given under s198(1) ICTA 1988 for training paid for by a worker within the personal service rules no matter how closely related it is to his job. This is because the expense is not incurred 'in performance of' the duties, see *Blackwell v Mills* [1945] 26 TC 468; *Humbles v Brooks* [1962] 40 TC 500 and *Parikh v Sleeman* [1990] 63 TC 75.

11.8.2 Training paid for by the client or agency

Training provided by the client

Relief for employees' training paid for by the client is available under s200B ICTA 1988. This covers 'work-related' training, defined as 'any training course or other activity which is designed to impart, instil, improve or reinforce any knowledge, skills, or personal qualities' which:

- Are, or are likely to prove, useful to the worker when performing his duties in relation to the client or the agency which provided the training; or

- Will qualify (or better qualify) the worker to undertake the relevant engagement, or to participate in charitable or voluntary activities arising through the engagement.

There is no restriction on the way the training is delivered. Self-tuition packages, computer based training, distance learning, work experience, work placement or informal teach-ins are all acceptable, along with more formal classroom based methods. It does not matter whether training is delivered internally or externally, or on a part-time or full-time basis, see SE 1172/SE 01220.

However training provided for recreational reasons or to reward the worker is excluded from relief under s200C ICTA 1988.

Training provided by the agency

The legislation states that:

> 'This section applies for the purposes of Schedule E where any person ("the employer") incurs expenditure on providing work-related training for a person ("the employee") who holds an office or employment under him.' (s200B ICTA 1988)

Where training has been provided by the employer, a deduction is thus clearly available under Step Three because the expense 'would have been deductible ... if the worker had been employed by the client.'

However, the Revenue appear to have extended the relief to cover training provided by the agency. In FAQ Expenses 8 they say that 'Any training provided by clients or agencies will not count as a taxable benefit, and no tax charge will arise.' The basis for this concession is unclear, but is nevertheless welcome.

11.8.3 Limits of relief

During the consultation on IR35, it was proposed that relief should be available in the deemed Schedule E computation for training carried out by the service company, as well for as that paid for by the client or agency. These representations were rejected by Dawn Primarolo on 2 December 1999. She said that:

> 'There have been suggestions, especially from IT and engineering consultants, that expenses for "work related training" should be an allowable deduction in the calculation of the minimum amount of tax and National Insurance Contributions that workers with service companies should pay, if their engagements meet the accepted definition of employment. Our intention is that workers in service companies should be in the same position as employees with regard to what help they can get with training they pay for themselves ... No deduction for training is therefore appropriate for service companies in calculating the minimum salary for tax and NIC purposes.
>
> I announced, on 23 September, that a 5% flat rate deduction for expenses would be allowed on top of all the other expenses ... It is for the service company to decide how best to use the 5% deduction and that choice could be to provide for the worker's training needs.'

The Revenue have subsequently confirmed that:

> 'The deductions allowable ... are based on those available to employees. Employees cannot generally get tax relief for money they spend on their own training, either while they are employed or in between jobs, and no deduction will be allowed for service companies in calculating the minimum salary for tax and NIC purposes. However, the 5% allowance for general expenses is available to cover such expenses as training costs.' (FAQ Expenses 8)

11.8.4 Individual learning accounts

The Budget which announced IR35 also launched individual learning accounts (ILAs):

'Contributions made by employers into ILAs held by their employees will qualify for a deduction from taxable profits and will be tax and national insurance contributions free in the hands of their employees, provided employers contribute to the ILAs of their lowest paid workers on similar terms. ILAs will provide a 20% discount for everyone, on eligible training costs of up to £500 a year.'

The legislation implementing the ILA was subsequently incorporated as new ss200E to 200H ICTA 1988. Thus an employer can make a contribution into an employee's ILA without the employee suffering any tax or NICs. The employer also receives a deduction for the contribution against his corporation tax charge.

The benefits of the ILA were mentioned by Dawn Primarolo when she rejected service company workers' plea for a more generous training deduction. She said that:

'ILAs will introduce a range of discounts and grants for eligible learning. Anyone, including a service company worker, will be able to open an ILA.'

It is of course true that a personal services company worker can open an ILA, but the Revenue have confirmed that if a contribution is made into an ILA by the service company, this contribution will not be an allowable deduction in the deemed Schedule E calculation. However, if the client or agency makes a contribution to the service company worker's ILA, it will not be taxable.

It is a rare client who will pay for a contractor's training, but rare indeed is the client who would be willing to fund a contractor's ILA. However, if he does, the Revenue have confirmed that the cost will be deductible in the client's corporation tax computation.

If the service company makes a payment into the worker's ILA, the contribution will be deductible for corporation tax – but if all the company's income is from relevant engagements, it may have no profits out of which to make the payment.

11.8.5 Indicator of self-employment

Some small compensation was provided for service company workers who spend their own money (or that of the service company) on training. The Revenue's February *Tax Bulletin*, analysing the status tests, said:

'Another example of a financial risk is where a skilled worker incurs significant amounts of expenditure on training to provide himself with a skill which he uses in subsequent engagements. This can be treated in the same way as investment in equipment to be used in a trade, as a pointer to self-employment, if there is a real risk that the investment would not be recovered from income from future engagements.'

Thus, where an intermediary pays for the worker's training, it may help him to fall outside IR35. For a discussion of financial risk, see also **6.5.3** and **7.4.2**.

11.9 Professional subscriptions

Employees can obtain tax relief for fees and subscriptions paid to professional bodies such as the Institute of Chartered Accountants and the Chartered Institute of Taxation. A list of approved organisations is available from the Revenue.

Subscriptions are commonly paid directly by employees and deducted on their self-assessment returns. In the case of a personal service worker it is more tax efficient for them to be paid by the service company or partnership on the worker's behalf, as this will reduce the relevant income subject to NICs, see **11.3.3** above,

11.10 Insurance

Tax relief is available for professional indemnity insurance (PII) under s201AA ICTA 1988. PII protects the worker from being sued for negligence by clients. Amounts paid by the service company in settlement of such claims are also allowable. PII also does not reduce the individual's net relevant earnings for pension purposes (s646(2) ICTA 1988).

However there is no similar tax relief for either:

(a) Public liability insurance, which protects the worker against legal liability if he accidentally causes damage or loss to someone else's property, such as a computer owned by a client. It also covers accidental injury caused by the worker to another person on the client's premises; or

(b) Employers' liability insurance, which protects employers against claims for injury or illness brought by employees. It is a statutory requirement – the Employers' Liability (Compulsory Insurance) Act 1998 requires employers to maintain a minimum cover of £5m. Many personal service workers don't take out this type of policy because they are the company's only employee. It is nevertheless a legal requirement, because there is both an employer (the company) and an employee (the worker).

Employer's and public liability insurance costs can therefore only be relieved as part of the 5 per cent allowance, see **11.2**.

11.11 Capital allowances

11.11.1 Step Four

Step Four gives relief for capital allowances:

> 'In respect of expenditure incurred by the intermediary that could have been claimed by the worker under section 27 of the Capital Allowances Act 1990 if the worker had been employed by the client and had incurred the expenditure.'

Points to note include the following

(a) To be deductible at Step Four the expenditure has to be incurred by the intermediary, not the worker;

(b) If assets are *actually* purchased by the individual, allowances must be claimed on the individual's self-assessment return, or the partnership return (see **15.3.4**). They cannot be deducted at Step Four;

(c) It is preferable for assets to be owned by the intermediary, because the allowances deducted in Step Four reduce the deemed Schedule E amount and thus the NICs payable. If the assets are owned directly, there is tax relief but no NICs relief;

(d) The assets have to satisfy the narrower Schedule E rules for claiming capital allowances, discussed at **11.11.2** below, as follows:

- Assets which have been 'necessarily provided for use in the performance of the duties' (s27(2)(a) CAA 1990); or

- Cars, motor bikes, and cycles used in the performance of the duties (s27(2A) CAA 1990);

(e) Where an asset is accepted as within s27, the allowances will be subject to apportionment if the equipment is also used for private purposes (s79 CAA 1990);

(f) Step Four is a computational provision to allow the correct calculation of the deemed Schedule E income. It does not move title to the allowances from the company to the worker, or prevent the personal service company or partnership from claiming capital allowances under the normal rules for corporation tax or Schedule D.

11.11.2 Assets generally

Capital allowances deductions in the Schedule E computation are likely to be a major bone of contention between service company workers and their Inspectors. The Revenue view is as follows:

'A deduction will only be given for capital allowances in working out the deemed payment where the plant or machinery is necessarily provided for use in the performance of the duties of the relevant engagement. This is a strict test and means that relief will only be given where the duties of the engagement meant that the (service) company had to provide the equipment in question. If the company purchases the equipment out of choice then no deduction will be given.

For example, where an IT contractor is required to use the client's computer equipment then no relief will be due for expenditure on computers owned by the service company. Neither will any relief be due where the client makes all the equipment necessary to do a job available but the worker uses his or her own computers, out of choice.' (FAQ Expenses 10)

In general, the Revenue are dismissive of claims by employees that their home computers are 'necessary'. They say that:

'Most employees are unlikely to be successful in satisfying the statutory test for capital allowances in Section 27(1) CAA 1990 in relation to the purchase of computers, word processors and their peripherals. Even if they can show that such equipment is essential for their duties, it will normally be the case that the employer will supply what is needed. It is insufficient for the taxpayer to claim that what the employer provides or will provide is inadequate.' (SE 4850/SE 36730)

A gleam of hope appears in the Schedule E Manual, where Inspectors are advised as follows:

'If the expense is substantial, it would normally be expected that the contract of employment would make specific reference to the requirement to incur it. If there is nothing explicit in the contract, find out whether the employee has approached the employer to provide the item, or to reimburse its cost, and, if so, with what response.' (SE 4806/SE 36560)

It might be thought from the above that if the contract between the service company and the client requires the service company to supply certain computer hardware, then the allowances can be claimed. However, this may not be enough, as the capital allowance test is an objective one: what the job requires, not what the client and worker agree should be provided. The Revenue may also check with clients whether the expenditure was in fact 'necessary':

'You may also need to investigate whether other workers with similar duties have also incurred the same sort of expense and if not, how they manage to perform their duties.'(SE 4806/SE 36560)

However, if the service company genuinely requires the assets in order to carry out its relevant engagements, allowances will be available. In addition, the Revenue Manual instructs Inspectors to agree capital allowances claimed for computers where:

• An employee has a job which is paid entirely or largely by results; and

• Although the object, such as selling life insurance, is clear, the method by which the employee is to achieve results is not stereotyped; and

• He is required to bear the cost of any equipment performing functions or activities intended to achieve that objective (that is, the employer will not provide or pay for such equipment) (SE 4850/SE36730).

These paragraphs may allow some personal service company workers to have their capital allowance claims accepted.

11.11.3 Cars, motor bikes and bicycles

The necessary test is disapplied in the case of 'mechanically propelled road vehicle or a bicycle' (s27(2A) CAA 1990). Allowances are due providing the asset is used 'in the performance of the duties'. This is not a difficult test to meet, although if there is private use only part of the cost is allowed.

As an alternative to a capital allowances claim, the intermediary can use the Revenue's authorised mileage rates, see **11.6.8** above. This is likely to be more simple, particularly where there is a private use adjustment.

If the vehicle was purchased by a loan, a deduction is allowed for the interest (s359 ICTA 1988). This is in addition to any amounts claimed under the capital allowances regime or the authorised mileage rates. If the car has been hired, a proportion of the hire charge is allowed (s35(2) CAA 1990).

12 Completing the deemed Schedule E calculation

12.1 Introduction

The deemed Schedule E calculation begins with the income received by the intermediary in the fiscal year (Steps One and Two, see Chapter 10). Any allowable expenses and capital allowances are then deducted (Steps Three and Four, see Chapter 11). This chapter deals with the remaining five steps necessary to arrive at the result in Step Nine. These are deductions for:

- Pension contributions paid by the employer;

- NIC paid on salary and benefits;

- Amounts taxed under Schedule E other than via this calculation; and

- NIC due on the deemed Schedule E payment.

The chapter also looks at what happens where a worker has attributable earnings for NIC, but no deemed Schedule E, or vice versa. It concludes with a worked example showing the effect of IR35 on the take-home pay of a personal service worker and her spouse.

12.2 Step Five

12.2.1 General

Step Five gives relief for pension contributions made by the employer in the fiscal year. The various pension options open to a personal service company are discussed at 3.6. Two particularly important issues within the context of the deemed income calculation are:

- The availability of NIC relief on the pension contribution, see 12.2.1 below; and

- The calculation of net relevant earnings, see 12.2.4.

12.2.2 NIC relief

It is recommended that pension contributions be made by the company rather than by the individual in order to obtain relief from employer's NIC.

Contributions made by the individual will reduce only the tax due, and not the NIC.

However, using pension contributions to reduce the NIC cost is not possible for partners. Step Five of the deemed Schedule E calculation gives a deduction for 'any contributions made in that year for the benefit of the worker by the intermediary' if they:

(a) Are made to a scheme approved under Chapter 1 (retirement benefit schemes) or Chapter IV (personal pensions) of Part XIV of the Taxes Act 1988; and

(b) Would not have been chargeable to income tax if they had been made 'by an employer for the benefit of an employee' (Sch 12, para 7 FA 2000).

Although it would appear at first sight as if this allowed partnerships to pay contributions into the personal pension schemes of their partners, there is no mechanism for this to happen under the relevant sections of Chapter IV – see for example s643 ICTA 1988. This is also the Revenue view, see note (3) to Example 14A.

Where partners fall within the deemed Schedule E calculation, they cannot reduce the deemed Schedule E amount by having their pension contribution paid by the intermediary. The NIC they suffer will therefore be higher than that of workers in a PSC who otherwise have the same income and expenses.

12.2.3 Timing of payments

Pension contributions are deductible under Step Five if they have been paid in the fiscal year to which the deemed payment relates. So a contribution paid *in* 2000/01 will be allowed in that year's earnings calculation, but a payment *based on* the deemed Schedule E amount and made after the year end will be deductible only against the following year's deemed payment.

Although individuals can use the carry-back rules to pay pension contributions based on the previous year's net relevant earnings (s641 and s641A ICTA 1988), this option is not open to employers. Any employer contribution must be made, and the cheque cleared, by 5 April.

12.2.4 Net relevant earnings

The deemed Schedule E payment counts as net relevant earnings ('NRE'), see 3.6.3, for the purposes of making pension contributions (Sch 12, para 11(7) FA 2000).

Certain expenses which are allowable at Step Three of the deemed Schedule E calculation do not reduce the individual's NRE for pension purposes, see s646(2) ICTA 1988. These include:

(a) Training provided by the client, see **11.8** (s200B ICTA 1988);

(b) Indemnity insurance, see **11.10** (s200AA ICTA 1988);

(c) Personal incidental expenses, see **11.7** (s200A ICTA 1988);

(d) Agency fees for actors, see **20.2.4** (s201A ICTA 1988).

Where these expenses have been deducted under Step Three, they should be added back in working out the maximum NRE.

12.2.5 Calculating the maximum contribution

Where the pension contribution depends on NRE, the calculation can be complex:

• Since the deemed payment will in practice be calculated after the end of the fiscal year, advance planning is needed if the pension contribution is to be deductible in the same fiscal year as the earnings are deemed to be paid;

• The pension contribution is deducted in arriving at the deemed Schedule E payment, but it is also a percentage of the payment. Since grossing up is also required for the employer's NIC, an algebraic formula is required if the maximum contribution is to be paid, see Example 12A.

Example 12A

Emma's PSC provides services to the video and TV industry. In the year to 5 April 2001 she has £20,000 of relevant earnings after deducting the 5 per cent allowance and her Schedule E expenses. She is 40 years old and so can make a pension contribution of 20 per cent. She is also employed part-time with the BBC, and her salary was £10,000 after tax and NIC.

To calculate her maximum pension contribution on the deemed Schedule E payment, the algebra is as follows:

$x = (N - ax) \times (100/[100+y])$

Where:

'x' is the deemed Schedule E amount;
'N' is the result of all Steps except Five, Eight and Nine;
'a' is the maximum contribution payable under the Net Relevant Earnings rules; and
'y' is the Employer's NIC rate for the year.

In this case the calculation is: $x = (20,000 - 0.2x) \times (100/112.2)$
This gives the following result:

	£
Earnings	20,000
Pension contribution	(3,025)
Employer's NIC	(1,846)
Deemed Schedule E payment	15,129

Had Emma had no other Schedule E earnings, the calculation would also have needed to take the employer's NIC threshold of £4,385 into account. The algebra is as follows:

$x = (N + by) / (1 + a + y)$, where 'b' is the employer's earnings threshold and the other values are as given above.

For the numbers in Example 12A the calculation would be as follows:

$x = [20,000 + (4385 \times 0.122)] / (1 + 0.2 + 0.122)$

This gives the following result:

	£
Earnings	20,000
Pension contribution	(3,107)
Employer's NIC	(1,360)
Deemed Schedule E payment	15,533

Once stakeholder pensions come into being, the link between the pension payment and net relevant earnings will be broken for contributions of no more than £3,600 gross, see **3.6.4**. Contributions of more than £3,600 must be supported by net relevant earnings. However this higher amount can continue to be paid for five years without any need for further NRE calculations (s646 ICTA 1988 inserted by Sch 13, para 22(1) FA 2000). Use of this higher amount may enable the pension contribution calculation to be simplified, although it could of course remain desirable to base the pension payment on the actual NRE if this is higher.

In practice many of those who are making serious provision for their retirement are using a SSAS or an EPP, see **3.6.5**. Since these types of pension do not depend on NRE, the problem caused by the deemed payment is reduced.

12.2.6 Over-contributions

There is no relief for contributions made, and later refunded (Sch 12, para 7 Step Five FA 2000). Thus if the calculation is incorrect, and the deemed Schedule E earnings are lower than estimated before the end of the year, excess contributions will have been paid.

These will have to be refunded to the employer by the pension fund, because they are unsupported by net relevant earnings. The deemed Schedule E payment will thus be have to be recalculated because of the refunded amount, which in turn may mean that the NRE for the year reduces further, so creating a circular effect.

12.3 Step Six

12.3.1 General

Step Six gives a deduction for any employer's NIC already paid for that tax year in respect of the worker. This covers both Class 1 NIC on salary paid to the worker in the year, and Class 1A on benefits provided, see **12.3.2** and **12.3.3** below.

Step Six refers to NIC paid 'for' the year, not 'in' the year. Class 1A NICs relating to a tax year which are paid on 19 July following the end of the tax year are therefore still deductible in the deemed income calculation.

12.3.2 Class 1 NICs

Class 1 NICs is payable on salary and some benefits, including:

- Loans written off by the employer;

- Many vouchers;

- Tax paid by the employer to cover the employee's liability;

- Tradable assets;

- Payment of the employee's personal costs, such as household bills;

- Private use of a company credit card, which will be brought into Class 1 NIC during the tax year 2000/01.

Both employees and employers pay Class 1 NICs, but employees only pay to the extent that their earnings fall between the Employee's Earnings Threshold and the Upper Earnings Limit (UEL). The maximum employee NICs payable in 2000/01 is £2,387. Employer's Class 1 NICs are payable from the Employer's Earnings Threshold, and have no upper limit. Only employer's NICs are deductible in the deemed Schedule E calculation.

Class 1 NICs are due on the 19th of the month following receipt by the worker of the payment or benefit, and the total for the year must be included on Forms P14 and P35, see **16.2.3**.

12.3.3 Class 1A NICs

From 6 April 2000, Class 1A NICs are due on all benefits unless *either* Class 1 already applies, *or* the benefit is:

- Covered by a dispensation;

- Included in a PAYE settlement agreement;

- Provided to employees (other than directors) earning less than £8,500. A deemed Schedule E payment is included in calculating whether the earnings meet the £8,500 threshold (Sch 12, para 11(3)(b) FA 2000);

- A reimbursed expense which is wholly for business; or

- Shares or options. In some cases these will already be subject to a Class 1 NIC charge.

Class 1A is due both on benefits provided by the service company and those provided by the client. See **10.5.4** and **12.4.3** for the responsibilities of the client and the service company.

Class 1A has to be paid over by 19 July following the end of the tax year, two weeks after the submission deadline for the P11D form on which the Class 1A is based. However, if the deemed payment is delayed until this deadline, there will be interest on the overdue PAYE and NIC, see **16.4.2**. If interest is to be avoided, the service company will need to work out the Class 1A NICs by 19 April rather than by 19 July.

12.4 Step Seven

12.4.1 General

Step Seven gives relief for:

> 'Any payments or other benefits received in that year by the worker from the intermediary, in respect of which the worker is chargeable to income tax under Schedule E.'

This covers both salary paid and benefits provided to the worker in the same tax year. These are discussed in more detail at **12.4.2** and **12.4.3** below. Salary and benefits cannot be provided to partners, so this step is redundant if the worker is a partner.

The Step Seven deduction is granted on the basis that the intermediary may have used the income from relevant engagements to provide either salary or benefits to the worker. Since both will be taxed in any event under the normal rules for PAYE and P11Ds, they are excluded from the deemed income calculation to prevent double taxation.

There is no attempt to link salary or benefits paid to the worker with relevant income received, so that if salary was paid in, say, June, but relevant income was not received until September, the salary would still be deductible in Step Seven.

If, following Step Seven, the answer to the calculation is nil or negative, the legislation says that 'there is no deemed Schedule E payment'. If the answer is positive, the calculation continues with Step Eight.

12.4.2 Salary

A deduction is only available for salary *paid* in the tax year. The amount of salary on a worker's P60 may therefore not be the same as that to be deducted under Step Seven. This is because, under the normal rules for PAYE, salary is taxable on the earliest of a number of events, including receipt, entitlement and crediting in the company's books (s202B ICTA 1988), see **10.2**.

12.4.3 Benefits

The worker can receive a benefit by four routes, of which only those in (a) below are deducted in Step Seven. A benefit can be provided:

(a) By the intermediary;

(b) By the client by reason of the worker's employment with the intermediary, and arranged or facilitated by the intermediary;

(c) By the client by reason of the worker's employment, not arranged or facilitated by the intermediary;

(d) By the client or third party, not by reason of the employment.

These are discussed in turn below.

Benefits provided by the intermediary

Benefits provided to the worker by the intermediary are deducted in Step Seven. They are included on the individual's P11D for the tax year and reported on his self-assessment form.

Benefits provided by reason of employment, facilitated by intermediary

Benefits provided:

- By the client or other third party;

- By reason of the employment;

- Which have been arranged or facilitated by the service company;

are taxed under the normal rules for Schedule E, see **10.5.4**. They are thus not brought into the deemed Schedule E calculation either:

(a) in Step One, because they have not been received by the intermediary, but by the worker; or

(b) in Step Two, because they are otherwise chargeable to income tax under Schedule E.

Since they have not been included in the calculation in the first place, they are not excluded at Step Seven. They will, however, be included on the P11D, since the intermediary must report benefits which it has facilitated. They will then be taxed via self-assessment or a coding adjustment.

Benefits provided by the client by reason of the employment, which have not been facilitated by the intermediary

As discussed at **10.5.4**, most benefits provided by the client to the worker will have been facilitated by the service company, because of the substantial identity between employer and worker. Where, exceptionally, the benefit has not been facilitated by the employer, the client or other third party is responsible for passing details of the benefit directly to the worker, see **10.5.4**. The details should then be included on his self assessment form, see **15.3.4**.

Benefits provided by third party, not by reason of the employment

Benefits provided other than by reason of the employment are brought into the calculation at Step Two. Partners who fall within the personal services legislation are the most likely to be in this situation – they do not have an employment. The legislation does not deem them to be employees, but merely requires them to complete the deemed Schedule E calculation, see **10.5.3**.

Since partners are not taxed under the normal rules for Schedule E, there can be no deduction at Step Seven.

12.4.4 P11Ds

The P11D includes:

* Benefits which need to be removed from the calculation at Step Seven, because they are provided by the intermediary; and

* Benefits which are not removed from the calculation at Step Seven, because they are provided by the client but facilitated by the intermediary.

It is thus important that the P11D is not blindly followed when identifying amounts to be removed from the deemed Schedule E calculation.

The deadline for completion of P11Ds is 6 July following the end of the tax year. If personal service companies take advantage of this two month period, they will be unable to finalise their deemed Schedule E calculation until after that date, so incurring an interest charge, see **16.4.2**.

12.4.5 Interaction with Step Three

Step Three gives relief for:

> 'The amount of expenses met in that year by the intermediary, which would have been deductible from the emoluments of the employment if the worker had been employed by the client and the expenses had been met by the employer out of those emoluments.'

Step Three thus allows amounts which are deductible from an employee's emoluments to be removed from the deemed Schedule E calculation. Such amounts include allowable travel and subsistence, PII cover, and other costs which meet the 'wholly, exclusively and necessarily' test, see **11.4**.

However, most of these amounts are technically 'chargeable' on the worker – the legislation simply allows them to escape assessment if an appropriate claim is made. They would thus also be deductible under Step Seven, which gives relief for all amounts 'in respect of which the worker is chargeable to income tax under Schedule E'. To prevent a double deduction, the legislation prevents any amounts which were deducted in Step Three from being relieved again under Step Seven (Sch 12, para 7 Step 7(b) FA 2000).

The Step Three deduction is broader than that in Step Seven, which would not allow relief if an amount was not 'chargeable'. This would include Personal Incidental Expenses, which are not 'regarded as emoluments of the office or employment for any purpose of Schedule E' (s200AA ICTA 1988) and amounts included within a dispensation, which are ignored for all tax purposes (s166 ICTA 1988).

12.5 Step Eight

12.5.1 Class 1 charge

The deemed Schedule E payment is itself subject to Class 1 NICs. Although both income and benefits may be included within the calculation, there is mercifully no attempt to separate the NIC into Class 1 and Class 1A (SI 2000 No 727 Reg 8(1)).

The service company is, of course, subject to Class 1A in respect of any benefits provided to the worker by the intermediary, but these benefits will have been deducted at Step Seven, and the NICs at Step Six, in arriving at the amount of attributable earnings, see **12.3** and **12.4** above.

12.5.2 Calculation of NIC due

Step Eight deducts the employer's NIC on the deemed payment. This is of course itself dependant on the deemed payment, and is thus calculated by a formula, see Example 12B.

Example 12B

David has a personal service company supplying tax services. Most of his work falls outside Schedule 12, FA 2000. However in July 2000 he takes up a relevant engagement for three days a week assisting the Inland Revenue. His company charges out his services at £2,000 a month, and David pays himself a salary of £1,000 a month. He has allowable travel expenses of £537 reimbursed by the service company.

	Notes	£
Step One: Income received		18,000
5% allowance		(900)
Step Three: Allowable expenses		(537)
Step Six: Employer's NIC on salary paid	1	(563)
Step Seven: Salary paid		(9,000)
Income after expenses, salary and NIC on salary		7,000
Step Eight: NIC on deemed payment	2	(762)
Deemed Schedule E payment		6,238

Notes
1. $9,000 - 4,385 = 4,615 \times 12.2\% = 563$
2. $7,000 \times (12.2/112.2] = 762$

However this formula only works where the individual has other earnings which utilise the Class 1 NIC-free band (£4,385 in 2000/01). However, this is not invariably the case, and never applies to partners, who receive no actual salary, only deemed salary. In these situations the NIC-free band must be taken into account in Step Eight, see Example 12C:

> **Example 12C**
>
> In 2001/02 David doesn't pay himself a salary, but uses his other income to pay himself in dividends. After deducting expenses his relevant income is £15,000 before deducting employer's NICs.
>
> | | £ |
> |---|---:|
> | Income after expenses | 15,000 |
> | NIC: $(15,000 - 4,385) \times (12.2/112.2)$ | (1,154) |
> | Deemed Schedule E payment | 13,846 |

For the further complexities in the calculation where the worker wants to calculate his pensions contribution, see **12.2.6**; for interaction with Class 2 and Class 4 NICs on partnership income, see **14.7.1**.

12.6 Step Nine

Step Nine states simply that 'the result is the amount of the deemed Schedule E payment'.

12.7 Attributable earnings but no deemed Schedule E, or vice versa

In general a worker will either be within IR35, and thus liable for both Schedule E and NIC, or outside, and liable for neither. However, this is not always the case.

12.7.1 Overseas interactions

Where a personal services worker carries out a relevant engagement overseas, he may be non-resident for tax, and thus have no deemed Schedule E calculation. However he may remain within the UK NIC regime, and so have an attributable earnings calculation.

The opposite is also possible: an overseas worker can be UK resident for tax, but not an employed earner for NICs. These situations are discussed in more detail in Chapter 18.

12.7.2 National Insurance deeming rules

There are also a number of specialised occupations which are deemed to be employments for NICs, but not for tax. Although a worker may be self-employed under the status tests at Chapter 6, this status may be overridden for National Insurance by various deeming provisions. The Social Security and Benefits Act 1992 says at s2(b) that:

> 'Regulations may provide . . . for a person in employment of any prescribed description to be treated, for the purposes of this Act, as falling within one or other of the categories of earner defined . . . above, notwithstanding that he would not fall within that category apart from the regulations.'

The personal services legislation applies, for National Insurance purposes, if:

> 'The circumstances are such that, had the arrangements taken the form of a contract between the worker and the client, the worker would be regarded for the purposes of Parts I to V of the Contributions and Benefits Act as employed in employed earner's employment by the client.' (SI 2000 No 727 Reg 6(1)(c))

If the NIC provisions would have deemed a worker to be an employed earner had he been operating as an individual, then he will also be an employed earner under IR35. So an actor who is self-employed under the status tests can nevertheless be deemed an employed earner for NICs. If he was operating via a service company he would have an attributable earnings calculation but no Schedule E payment. In other words, he works through Steps One to Nine (Chapters 10 to 12), and pays NICs on the result, but not PAYE.

Examples of workers who are deemed to be employed earners for NICs include:

(a) Teachers and lecturers, see **20.9.2**;

(b) Actors and entertainers, see **20.2.2**;

(c) Office cleaners and cleaners of telephone apparatus;

(d) Employment of a person by his or her spouse for the purposes of the latter's employment or self-employment. This is unlikely to have any effect on service company workers as any payments to the worker's spouse will be made by the company. The spouse will thus be an employee of the service company and already subject to NICs.

A deeming provision also exists under which examiners are treated as self-employed for NICs, even though they are employed for tax, if the whole of the work is performed under a contract of less than twelve months (SI 1978 No 1689 Sch I and II). They are therefore liable to pay Class 2 NICs but, if taxable under Schedule E, there will be no Class 4 NICs liability, see ESM 4150. The Revenue have said that if an examiner disputes his employed status for tax, they are prepared to take the case to the Commissioners (ESM 4152).

Directors

Directors will always be within IR35 for NICs, but will only be within the tax legislation if there is a hypothetical contract of employment between them and their client in addition to the hypothetical contract in respect of the directorship. This is discussed more fully at **20.3.2**.

12.8 Worked example

The purpose of this example is to illustrate the extra tax costs which might be incurred under the personal services regime as compared to the position before IR35. The facts are the same as those in Chapter 3, Examples 3D and 3E. In Example 3D the couple paid themselves a small salary, taking the balance in dividends. In Example 3E all remuneration was paid as salary. In this example the couple are within the personal services regime.

The example demonstrates that:

- The combined tax and NIC rate on the company's income increases by 15 per cent, from the **24.5** per cent in Example 3D, to 39.5 per cent under the personal service rules;

- Because Cherie suffers a deemed payment she can only extract the money via a dividend, see **13.6**;

- The tax bill could be reduced if pension payments were made, see **3.6** and **12.2.1**;

- The actual tax and NICs rate in any given case will be affected by a number of variables, such as disallowable costs, the tax position of the spouse and marginal tax bands.

Example 12D

Tony and Cherie have a personal service company, through which Cherie provides legal advice. Tony is an employee of the company, writing up the books and making appointments. He works 26 hours a week for the company, and Cherie an average of 50, for 45 weeks a year. Cherie owns 65 shares in the company and Tony 35. In the year to 5 April 2001 the company's turnover is £100,000, ignoring VAT. They pay themselves a salary which meets the minimum wage requirements and utilises their personal allowances. They are within the personal service regime. Cherie uses dividends to access the deemed Schedule E payment. The tax due is as follows:

Calculation of deemed Schedule E income

	Notes	£
Step One: Income received	1	100,000
less: 5%		(5,000)
Step Three: Allowable expenses	2	
Travel & subsistence	3	(500)
PII cover		(1,000)
Step Six: Employer's NIC on salary paid		(481)
Step Seven: Salaries actually paid		
Tony	4	0
Cherie		(8,325)
Step Eight: Employer's NIC on deemed salary		(9,209)
Step Nine: Deemed Schedule E income		75,485

1. The income received is, for simplicity, assumed to be the same as the amount included in the accounts on an accruals basis, see **13.2.1**.

2. Other expenses included accountancy and training costs, which are not deductible under the PSC rules.

3. Travel and subsistence is reduced to £500 because abortive travel to interviews which failed to produce contracts is not allowable for Schedule E.

4. Since all the company's income is from relevant engagements, Tony's salary is not deductible against the income received. However, because of the minimum wage rules, it continues to be paid, see **22.2.2**.

Tax on deemed Schedule E payment

	Notes	Income £	Tax £
Balance of basic rate band 22.0%	1	24,460	5,381
40.0%		51,025	20,041
Tax on deemed Sch E payment		75,485	25,422

Notes

1. Cherie has already used up £2,420 of her basic rate band for her small salary payment, see Example 3D. The balance is taken against the first slice of her deemed Schedule E amount.

Corporation tax computation

			£
Turnover			100,000
Salaries			
Tony			(4,329)
Cherie			(8,325)

	Notes	Income £	Tax £
Employer's NIC			
Tony			0
Cherie			(481)
Deemed Schedule E payment			(75,485)
NIC on deemed Schedule E payment			(9,209)
Other expenses			
Capital allowances			(750)
Travel & subsistence			(600)
PII cover			(1,000)
Other			(970)
Profits (loss) subject to CT			(1,149)

Company Profit and Loss Account

	Notes	£
Turnover		100,000
Less:		
Salaries paid to Tony		(4,329)
Salary paid to Cherie		(8,325)
Employer's NIC on Cherie's salary		(481)
Employer's NIC on deemed Schedule E payment		(9,209)
PAYE on deemed Schedule E	1	(25,422)
Employee NIC on deemed Schedule E	1,2	(1,950)
Other expenses	3	(3,320)
Net profit before tax		46,964
Corporation tax (as above)		–
Profit available for dividend		46,964

Notes

1. The PAYE and Employee NIC are paid by the company, and are deductible in the accounts. They are not deductible for corporation tax, see 13.3.

2. Employee NIC of £437 already paid on salary, see Example 3D. Because employee NIC is capped at £2,387, the balance payable is £1,950.

3. For simplicity, depreciation is assumed to be equal to the capital allowances claimed in the tax computation.

Take home cash

	Notes	Tony £	Cherie £	Total £
Salary		4,329	8,325	12,654
Tax		–	(687)	(687)
Employee NIC		(38)	(437)	(475)
Dividend	1	16,437	30,527	46,964
		20,728	37,728	58,456

Total tax & NIC paid

		£	£	£
Employer's NIC			9,690	9,690
Employee NIC		38	2,387	2,425
Income tax			26,107	26,107
Corporation tax				0
				38,222

Effective rate of tax on turnover				38.2%
Effective rate of tax on profit (£100,000 less expenses of £3,320)				39.5%

Notes

1. The only way that Cherie can access the deemed Schedule E payment is to pay it as a dividend, see **13.6**. This is not subject to further tax because it is covered by the deemed Schedule E payment. However it is split between Tony and Cherie according to their shareholdings.

13 Corporation tax, dividends and VAT

13.1 Introduction

A personal service company which has a deemed salary calculation is not thereby absolved from the requirement to carry out a corporation tax computation. It is and remains a company, and thus within the scope of corporation tax. Similarly, the fact that the income is deemed to be the salary of the worker does not take supplies made by the company outside the scope of VAT.

There are however significant differences between the corporation tax rules and those for Schedule E. Different provisions govern expenses, the timing of receipts, and capital allowances. The taxation of personal services brings both sets of rules together. This chapter looks at some of the resulting complexities. One key issue is the timing of relief for the deemed payment, which can only be deducted in the accounting period when it is 'treated as made'. If the company has an accounting year end other than 5 April, excess tax can arise which may not be relieved, see 13.3 below.

When seeking to understand the interaction between the two taxes, it may be helpful to remember that IR35 is anti-avoidance legislation. It aims to encourage those within the personal services rules to pay themselves their relevant income as salary through the year. If they do, they will have no deemed Schedule E payment. However, there are likely to be no profits available for distribution, and may even be a loss for corporation tax purposes, see 13.7.

Where sufficient salary is not paid during the year, the Schedule E calculation deems an amount of income to be subject to PAYE and NIC. However, once the tax and National Insurance have been paid to the Revenue, the balance cannot simply be paid tax free to the individual. In other words, the tax and NIC does not frank a subsequent salary payment. If the net Schedule E amount is paid to the worker, he will be regarded as having received further salary which will itself be subject to tax and NIC, see 13.5.2 below.

If the worker wants to extract the taxed money from the company without suffering further tax, he can only do so as a dividend, see 13.6. This is because relieving provisions prevent double taxation if the money is withdrawn in this way.

13.2 Recognition of income

13.2.1 Corporation tax basis

Corporation tax computations are based on the accounts, and income is thus taxed on an accruals basis. This is required by both legislation and case law:

- Section 42(2) FA 1998 requires that computations be calculated on 'an accounting basis which gives a true and fair view, subject to any adjustment required or authorised by law in computing profits for those purposes'. This 'true and fair view' applies to both self-employed individuals and companies, since corporation tax follows income tax principles (s9 ICTA 1988);

- Case law similarly requires that computations follow recognised accounting principles, see for example *Herbert Smith v Honour* [1999] STC 173; *Gallagher v Jones* [1993] 66 TC 77; *Revenue Press Release* 137/99, issued 20 July 1999.

For corporation tax purposes, income is therefore included if it has been earned in the period, even if it has not been received, subject to any relief for bad debts.

13.2.2 Deemed Schedule E basis

In contrast, the deemed Schedule E amount is based on income *received* in the fiscal year, see **10.2** (Sch 12, para 7 FA 2000). It is therefore important that the company's records are capable of analysis on both a received and accrued basis so that both the CT computation and the deemed Schedule E payment can be correctly calculated.

13.3 Accounting year end other than 5 April

The deemed payment is only deductible for the accounting period in which it is treated as made (Sch 12, para 17(2) FA 2000). As a result, year ends other than 5 April can cause double taxation which may never be relieved. Accounting periods ending on 31 March give the worst result. This problem, and some possible solutions, are explored below, using a series of worked examples.

Example 13A

Sarah has her own personal service company supplying advice to government ministers. The company's accounting period ends on 31 March. It receives £50,000 in the year to 2000/01 in relation to a relevant engagement for the Chancellor of the Exchequer. Corporation tax allowable expenses are £8,000. None of these are deductible for Schedule E. Income received in the fiscal year equals that accrued in the accounting period to 31 March. She pays herself no salary or dividends.

In 2001/02 the facts are identical; for simplicity NIC thresholds and rates are assumed to be the same as in 2000/01.

Year ended 31 March 2001: Corporation tax position

	Notes	£	£
Income			50,000
Expenses	1		(8,000)
Net profit			42,000
Tax at 10%		1,000	
Tax at 22.5%	2	7,200	
Tax due			(8,200)
Net profits			33,800

5 April 2001: Deemed Schedule E payment

	Notes	£
Step One: – relevant income		50,000
– Less 5%		(2,500)
		47,500
Step Eight: – NICs	3	(4,688)
Step Nine: – the deemed payment		42,812

Notes

1. No relief is received for the deemed payment relating to this period as it has not been paid by 31 March.

2. The marginal tax on profits between £10,000 and £50,000 is calculated at 22.5 per cent, see **3.2.2**

3. NICs on the deemed payment calculated as $(47,500 - 4,385) \times (12.2/112.2)$, see **12.5.2**.

In the tax year 2000/01, Sarah pays tax on £42,812, and her company pays tax on £42,000 making £82,812. However the total income received is only £50,000, and this reduces to £42,000 on a CT basis once expenses are deducted, and to £47,500 on a PSC basis.

The problem is not solved in 2001/02, when the deemed Schedule E amount is the same, and therefore Sarah pays further income tax on £42,812, and the company carries back a loss of £5,500.

Year ended 31 March 2002: Corporation tax

	£
Income	50,000
Deemed Schedule E payment	(42,812)
Employer's NICs paid	(4,688)
Expenses	(8,000)
Net loss c/back against previous year	(5,500)

Year ended 31 March 2001: Corporation tax (revised)

	£	£
Income		50,000
Expenses		(8,000)
Net profit		42,000
Loss carried back		(5,500)
		36,500
Tax at 10%	1,000	
Tax at 22.5%	5,963	
Tax due		(6,963)
Net profits		29,537

After the loss carried back, Sarah pays tax on £79,312 in the tax year 2000/01. This means that an excess of £36,500 has been subject to tax when compared to the amount required to be taxed under the deemed Schedule E calculation.

This results from the fact that the deemed payment is deductible only in the period of account in which it is paid, rather than the one to which it relates.

13.4 Possible solutions to accounting year end date problem

13.4.1 Summary

Possible solutions to the problem examined in **13.3** above include:

(a) Treating 31 March and 5 April as identical. However this is not permitted by the Revenue, see **13.4.2**;

(b) Allowing a corporation tax deduction for the deemed Schedule E payment in the same way as a deduction is allowed for an actual salary payment. This has been rejected by the Revenue, see **13.4.3**;

(c) Providing for actual salary equal to the deemed Schedule E amount, see **13.4.4**. This improves the corporation tax position, but forces the payment of further salary, which is subject to tax and NICs;

(d) Making a terminal loss claim, see **13.4.5**;

(e) Changing the accounting year end to 5 April, see **13.4.6**;

(f) Paying the relevant income (net of allowable deductions) as salary before 5 April, so that the deemed Schedule E payment is de minimis, see **13.5**.

Of these, (e) and (f) are both realistic options, with (d) as a 'backstop' for companies who were initially unaware of how the rules worked.

13.4.2 31 March deemed to be 5 April?

For personal tax, the Revenue operate a concession whereby 5 April and 31 March are treated as interchangeable. This means that self-employed individuals who make up accounts to either date are treated as if they were on the fiscal year basis, see for example the article on self-assessment in *Tax Bulletin 10*, February 1994 and paragraph 1.98 *SAT1 (1995)*.

However, this concession does not apply for corporation tax purposes. If it were to be applied to personal service companies, the accounting date problem would disappear, at least for 31 March year ends. It would nevertheless remain to a greater or lesser extent for other accounting periods. However, the Revenue have not agreed to extend the concession to those affected by the deemed payment regime.

13.4.3 Provision for deemed payment?

One solution would be to provide for the deemed payment in the accounts, and allow this to be deducted for corporation tax purposes. This was raised with the Revenue, but the idea was rejected, see FAQ Computation 9:

> 'The deemed payment is a balancing item, to make up any shortfall in salary paid during the tax year. It will not therefore be possible to attribute any part of that amount to amounts provided for in a particular period. Service companies will still be able to make provision for actual salary payments made within nine months of the end of the accounting period. But the deemed payment can only be treated as a deduction in the corporation tax computation for the accounting period in which it is deemed to be paid.'

219

Such a provision might in any event not be allowable in the accounts, as it does not sit easily with the requirements of Financial Reporting Standard 12.

13.4.4 Provision for actual payment?

An apparent solution to the accounting date problem is for an amount equal to the deemed Schedule E payment to be provided, not as a deemed salary, but as actual salary. This ensures that relief is available in the appropriate accounting period, and so avoids the large overpayment of tax which may otherwise arise in year one (see Example 13A).

However, a provision causes other problems:

- It has no effect on the deemed Schedule E amount for that year, as a deduction is only available in the Schedule E calculation for salary actually paid (Sch 12, para 7, Step Seven, FA 2000);

- It is only deductible for corporation tax if it is paid out as actual salary within nine months of the year end (s43 FA 1989). Further tax and NIC will be due on this actual salary, in addition to the tax paid on the deemed Schedule E amount, see **13.5.2**.

Thus while the provision is effective in reducing the large corporation tax overpayment in year one, it causes PAYE and NICs to be paid twice on what is effectively the same income. It therefore does not remove the problem, but simply transfers it from corporation tax to income tax.

13.4.5 Making a terminal loss claim

On cessation of a business, trading losses can be carried back against the profits of the last three years of trading, under s393A ICTA 1988. The benefits of this can be seen by extending the worked example, Sarah, at Example 13A.

Example 13B

Sarah decides to take up permanent employment with the Cabinet Office. She therefore resigns from her company on 31 March 2003. Her resignation causes the deemed payment to be accelerated, so it occurs on 31 March, see **16.3.1**, and the company ceases to trade.

Her income and expenses for the year to 31 March 2003 are the same as in the previous two years, and for simplicity the employer's NIC rate is assumed to remain at 12.2 per cent for all years.

Corporation tax position 2002/03	
	£
Income	50,000
Deemed Schedule E payment for 2001/02	(42,812)
Employer's NICs paid for 2001/02	(4,688)
Deemed Schedule E payment for 2002/03	(42,812)
Employer's NICs paid for 2002/03	(4,688)
Expenses for 2002/03	(8,000)
Net loss available	(53,000)
Carried back to 2000/01	(36,500)
Loss unrelieved	(16,500)

The loss unrelieved is made up of the difference between the expenses allowable for corporation tax (£8,000) and those deductible in the deemed Schedule E calculation (£2,500), making £5,500 a year, or £16,500 over the three-year period.

Example 3B shows that Sarah can carry back the loss on termination against the profits arising in 2000/01 (s393A(2A) ICTA 1988). However, had she continued with her company for longer than three years, she would have been unable to make use of this carry back provision and would have suffered excessive taxation.

Making a terminal loss claim has thus succeeded in capturing the tax relief on the earlier deemed payment. However, it is far from ideal in cashflow terms and should thus be regarded as a 'rescue' alternative for companies who did not appreciate how the personal services rules interacted with those for corporation tax.

13.4.6 Change of accounting date to 5 April

A better solution is to change the accounting date to 5 April. This allows relief in the year for the deemed payment, and protects the intermediary from the overpayment scenario shown in 13.3 above. Even where efforts are made to ensure that the relevant income is paid out as salary, so that the deemed payment is small or negligible, see 13.5.3 below, a 5 April accounting date is a useful backstop against underpayments. Example 13C shows how it would work.

Example 13C

If Sarah had changed her accounting date to 5 April, the results would be as follows, if all other facts were the same:

Year ended 5 April 2001: Corporation tax position

	£
Income	50,000
Deemed Schedule E payment	(42,812)
Employer's NICs paid	(4,688)
Expenses	(8,000)
Net loss c/forward	(5,500)

The same loss will arise each year, as it is the difference between the allowable expenses for corporation tax and those deductible in the Schedule E deemed calculation. For a discussion of corporation tax losses, see **13.7** below.

Other consequences of changing the accounting date

Changing the accounting date has other effects:

(a) Shortening the accounting period may defer corporation tax on other (non PSC) profits which occur after the new date;

(b) Similarly the extension of an accounting period may accelerate relief for losses. However, many PSCs will struggle to find a use for the losses created, see **13.7.2** below;

(c) A company must to notify the Registrar of Companies, using form 225(1) or 225(2), if it proposes to alter the accounting date (s225 Companies Act 1985);

(d) There are restrictions on the number of times a company may extend its accounting period;

(e) Following a change in date, care is needed with respect to the timing of claims and elections.

13.5 Withdrawal of funds

13.5.1 Options available

Most people need to withdraw money from their service companies to fund normal living costs. For a company within the personal services legislation, there are three possibilities, of which the first is inadvisable:

(a) Calculate the deemed Schedule E amount at the end of the fiscal year, pay over the tax and NICs, and then withdraw the net amount. This will cause further PAYE and NICs to arise, see **13.5.2** below;

(b) Pay sufficient salary during the year so that there is no deemed Schedule E amount at the year end, see **13.5.3** below;

(c) Pay out the profits of the company as a dividend. The legislation prevents double taxation of dividends covered by the deemed Schedule E payment, see **13.6**.

Of these three options, the first is clearly to be avoided. If there are no other factors, the tax cost of options (b) and (c) are the same, see Example 13H. However there may be other issues, both practical and legal, which cause one route to be preferred over the other.

13.5.2 Withdrawal of funds following deemed Schedule E calculation

Where funds have been subject to PAYE and NIC under the PSC rules, they will be taxed again if they are subsequently withdrawn as salary. This is because there is no 'franking' of an actual salary payment by the deemed Schedule E amount – tax has to be paid on all salary received by the individual.

Particular care should be taken over credits to the director's current account, which count as payment of salary under s202B(1)(c) ICTA 1988. If the deemed Schedule E amount is calculated, PAYE and NIC paid over, and the net amount transferred to the director's current account, it will be taxable as earnings received by the director, see Example 13D.

> *Example 13D*
>
> Olivia is a model with her own personal service company. In the year to 31 March 2000 she had taxable income of £30,000, and CT allowable expenses of £2,803. She paid herself a salary of £500 per month.
>
> In the year to 31 March 2001 her income remained at £30,000 and her other (non-salary) expenses decreased to £2,603. She continued to pay herself £500 a month.
>
> In 2000/01 one of her engagements was within the scope of the personal services regime, and she received £12,428 of relevant income. On 19 April 2001 she calculated that she had a deemed Schedule E amount of £5,000 in respect of this relevant engagement, and paid over the tax and NIC by the due date. After PAYE and employee NIC, the net deemed Schedule E amount was £3,600, and this was transferred to her director's current account.

Corporation tax computation 31 March 2001

	Notes	£	£
Income			30,000
Expenses:			
General		2,803	
Salary (12 x 500)		6,000	
Employer's NIC paid	1	197	
Expenses	2		(9,000)
Net profit			21,000
Tax at 10% on £10,000		1,000	
Tax at 22.5% on balance	3	2,475	
Total tax paid			3,475
Profits remaining			17,525

Notes

1. NIC due on salary of £6,000 is $(6,000-4,385) \times 12.2\% = 197$

2. There is no relief against the profits of the year for the deemed Schedule E calculation, as it is not paid within the accounting period, see **13.3** above.

3. The marginal tax on profits between £10,000 and £50,000 is calculated at 22.5 per cent, see **3.2.2.**

Deemed Schedule E calculation 5 April 2001

	£
Step One: Relevant income	12,428
5% allowance	(621)
Step Six: NIC on salary paid	(197)
Step Seven: Salary paid	(6,000)
Step Eight: Employer's NIC on deemed payment	(610)
Step Nine: Deemed Schedule E amount	5,000

Corporation tax computation 31 March 2002

	Notes	£	£
Income			30,000
Deemed Schedule E payment 2000/01		(5,000)	
Employer's NIC on deemed payment		(610)	
Salary paid at £500 a month		(6,000)	
Employer's NIC on salary paid	1	(192)	
Transfer to current account	2	(5,000)	
Employer's NIC on salary paid		(595)	
Other expenses		(2,603)	
Total expenses			(20,000)

Net profit	10,000
Tax at 10% on £10,000	(1,000)
Profits remaining	9,000

Notes

1. Assuming a NIC free amount of £4,385 as for 2000/01, the employer's NICs are $(6,000 - 4,385) \times 11.9\% = 192$. For simplicity the NIC free amount has been deducted from her monthly salary, rather partly from this and partly from the current account transfer.

2. The transfer of the balance remaining after tax and NIC to her current account amounts to a further salary payment, see **13.5.2**. The gross salary is the £5,000 on which employer's NICs of £595 are due at the 2001/02 rate of 11.9%.

The key point here is that 'making' a deemed payment simply establishes the amount of tax and NIC to be paid by the company to the Revenue. It does not 'frank' any subsequent salary payment. If the net amount is paid as salary, further tax and NIC will be due. In Example 13D tax has thus been paid twice on what are essentially the same funds.

Relief for the extra tax will be obtained in the following year's deemed Schedule E computation, when the taxed salary will be deducted from that year's income, see Example 13E below.

Example 13E

The background is the same as in Example 13D above. In the year to 5 April 2002, Olivia receives a further £12,428 of relevant income. Her deemed Schedule E computation is as follows:

Deemed Schedule E calculation 5 April 2002

	Notes	£
Step One: relevant income		12,428
5% allowance		(621)
Step Six: NIC on salary paid (192 + 595)		(787)
Step Seven: Salary paid (6,000 + 5,000)		(11,000)
Step Eight: Employer's NIC on deemed payment		(2)
Step Nine: Deemed Schedule E amount	1	18

Notes

1. The difference of £18 has been caused by the change in the NIC rates.

Example 13E shows that relief is obtained in the following year for the extra salary paid, so almost eliminating the deemed payment. However, if the relevant income in the second year is inadequate to cover the full salary paid, excess tax will be suffered, see Example 13F. This problem is explored further in Example 13G.

Example 13F

The background is again the same as in Example 13D above. However, in the year to 5 April 2002 Olivia received only £7,000 of relevant income. Her deemed Schedule E computation is as follows:

Deemed Schedule E calculation 5 April 2002

	£
Step One: relevant income	7,000
5% allowance	(350)
Step Six: NIC on salary paid (192 + 595)	(787)
Step Seven: Salary paid (6,000 + 5,000)	(11,000)
Excess	(5,137)

No deemed Schedule E payment

Thus, although the payment of the net amount as salary is deductible in the following year's deemed income calculation, this is only effective if the individual continues to have sufficient relevant income to absorb the deduction. It can be seen from Example 13F that by taking the net deemed payment as additional salary, Olivia has paid tax on £5,137 more than was required under the personal service rules.

13.5.3 Salary during the fiscal year

Paying the relevant income as salary over the course of the fiscal year has many advantages:

(a) The deemed Schedule E amount will be nil or negligible, and the corporation tax and income tax problems discussed in **13.3** and **13.5.2** above thus disappear;

(b) Paying salary is likely to be simpler than the dividend route, see **13.6** below;

(c) The lower the deemed Schedule E amount, the lower the risk of a large interest charge arising because of a delay in paying over the tax and NICs resulting from the deemed Schedule E calculation, see **16.4.2**;

It is sometimes thought that paying a salary reduces the income which forms the basis of the 5 per cent deduction. This is not the case: the deduction is 5 per cent of the gross amount received by the intermediary in respect of relevant engagements. It is thus immaterial, as far as the 5 per cent deduction is concerned, whether salary is paid during the year or whether there is a deemed Schedule E amount at the end of the year.

Problems with salary payments

(a) If the company's actual costs exceed the allowable Schedule E expenses, it may be unable to pay sufficient salary to reduce the deemed Schedule E amount to nil without risking insolvency, see **13.7.4** below. The balance would then be subject to PAYE and NIC, even though it could not be paid out. However, a similar situation would arise under the dividend alternative, as the excess costs reduce the dividend payable, see **13.6.3** below. If the company has adequate reserves brought forward this problem will not arise;

(b) The tax and NIC is due on 19 April following the deemed payment, rather than on 19 April following the month end, as is the position when salary is paid during the year. The deemed payment thus gives the company a slight cashflow advantage;

(c) If more salary is paid in the year than is required under the personal services rules, the excess cannot be carried forward or back into other years. Unfortunate timing of salary payments can thus cause an increased tax liability, see Example 13G. In comparison, dividends may be more flexible, see **13.6** below.

Example 13G

Wendy has her own service company which provides gardening and horticultural services. In 2000/01 she receives £10,000 from a relevant engagement with the local Council, plus £20,000 of other earnings. Expenses relating to the relevant engagement are £500 and those relating to other work are £4,000. She pays herself a salary of £1,500 a month.

In 2001/02 the Council increases her hours and responsibility, so she receives £30,000 from the relevant engagement and £16,000 from other work. The service company's expenses are £1,000 for the relevant engagement (deductible under s198 ICTA 1988) and £3,000 for the other work. She continues to pay herself a salary of £1,500 per month. The Employer's NIC threshold is assumed to be £4,385 as in 2000/01.

Her deemed Schedule E income calculation is as follows:

---

5 April 2000/01

	£
Step One: Relevant income received	10,000
5% allowance	(500)
Step Three: Expenses	(500)
Step Four: Employer's NIC on salary paid	
$(18,000 - 4,385) \times 12.2\%$	(1,661)
Step Six: Salary paid $(12 \times 1,500)$	(18,000)
Excess	(10,661)

No deemed payment

Fiscal year 2001/02

	£
Step One: Relevant income received	30,000
5% allowance	(1,500)
Step Three: Expenses	(1,000)
Step Six: Employer's NIC on salary paid	
$(18,000 - 4,385) \times 11.9\%$	(1,620)
	25,880
Step Seven: Salary paid	(18,000)
	7,880
Step Eight: NIC on deemed Schedule E payment	(856)
Step Nine: Deemed Schedule E payment	7,023

No relief is available for the excess salary paid in the earlier year. As a result, more income is taxed than is strictly necessary under the PSC rules, see below:

	£
Total relevant income over the two year period:	
$(10,000 + 30,000)$	40,000
Total salary/deemed salary subject to PAYE and NICs	
$(18,000 + 18,000 + 7023)$	43,023
Salary taxed in excess of relevant income	3,023

13.6 Dividends

13.6.1 Using dividends to extract profits

Where a deemed Schedule E payment has already occurred, a dividend is the only way to extract the money without suffering further tax. This is because Sch 12, para 13 FA 2000 operates to prevent a double charge to tax when there is both a dividend and a deemed payment, and the net dividend is no greater than the net deemed payment.

A simple example is the easiest way of understanding how the two interact. In order to demonstrate comparability between the salary route and the dividend route, all other factors have been simplified.

Example 13H

Caroline is a supply teacher of Russian and Polish, with her own personal service company. All her engagements fall within the scope of Schedule 12, FA 2000. She is trying to decide whether to pay herself via a salary or dividends. In the year to 5 April 2001 she has income from relevant engagements of £60,000. Her expenses are £3,000, exactly equal to 5 per cent of her income.

Option 1: Pay salary equal to deemed schedule E amount

Under this option Caroline works out what the deemed Schedule E amount would be, and then ensures it is paid as salary on or before 5 April 2001.

Deemed Schedule E calculation

	£
Step One : Relevant income	60,000
5% allowance	(3,000)
	57,000
Step Eight: NICs	(5,721)
Step Nine: Deemed Schedule E amount	51,279

This amount is paid as salary on or before 5 April 2001.

Income tax

	£ Income	£ Tax
Personal allowance	4,385	
Tax at 10%	1,520	152
Tax at 22%	26,880	5,830
Tax at 40%	18,494	7,398
	51,279	
Class 1 employee NICs (maximum)		2,387
Total tax	(15,767)	15,767
Take home pay (51,279 – 15,767)	35,512	

Corporation tax

	£
Income	60,000
Expenses:	
General	(3,000)
Salary	(51,279)
Employer's NICs	(5,721)
CT profits	nil

Option 2: Using dividends to extract profits

Caroline calculates the deemed Schedule E amount as in Option 1 above, but does not pay it as salary. Instead, she pays over the PAYE and NIC on the due date, and then uses dividends to extract the funds from the company.

Deemed Schedule E tax and employee NICs paid

	£
As per calculation in Option 1:	15,767

Corporation tax

	Notes	£
Income		60,000
Expenses:		
General		(3,000)
Deemed Schedule E amount		(51,279)
Employer's NICs		(5,721)
Corporation tax profits		nil

Accounting profits

	Notes	£
Turnover		60,000
Employer's NICs on deemed payment		(5,721)
PAYE/employee NICs on deemed payment	1	(15,767)
Expenses		(3,000)
Profits distributed as a dividend	2	35,512

Notes

1. Although PAYE and employee NIC liabilities normally attach to the individual, in this case it is a liability of the service company and should be deducted in the accounts. It is of course not deductible in the corporation tax computation.

2. All the profits are distributed as a dividend. £35,512 equals the net after-tax deemed Schedule E amount, and so no further tax is due on the dividend.

Example 13H demonstrates that the salary and dividend routes are neutral in terms of tax suffered, if all other factors are held constant. In both cases Caroline will receive £35,512 in cash. However in practice a number of factors may influence a person to take one route or the other, see **13.5.3** above and **13.6.2** below.

If there had been no relief under Sch 12, para 13 FA 2000, further tax would be payable of £1,951 as follows:

Example 13J

Income tax (with no relief for deemed Schedule E payment)

	£ Income	£ Tax
Dividend income (grossed up by 10%)	39,458	
Covered by tax credits and personal allowances	(32,785)	
Higher rate tax due on balance @ 32.5%	6,673	2,168
Less: tax credits		(217)
Higher rate tax		1,951

This would be in addition to the £15,767 already paid via the deemed Schedule E calculation.

13.6.2 Claiming relief for double taxation

In order to obtain the tax relief, there must be both a dividend and a deemed Schedule E amount. In addition, there must actually be double taxation. A claim is necessary to obtain the relief.

There must be both a dividend and a deemed Schedule E amount

(a) The company must have paid a dividend after 5 April 2000 and also made a deemed Schedule E payment (Sch 12, para 13(1) FA 2000);

(b) The dividend can be paid before the deemed payment, see Sch 12, para 13(1)(c)FA 2000. Dividends paid during the first year of the personal services legislation will therefore fall out of tax if they are subsequently followed by a deemed payment;

(c) Where part of the dividend is paid out of relevant income, and part out of other Schedule D income, the taxpayer does not have to identify the source of the dividends;

(d) In applying the relief, distributions made in earlier tax years (but after the commencement of the legislation) are taken before those made in later years. Where more than one distribution is made in a tax year, the earliest is taken first (Sch 12, para 13(5)(a) and (c) FA 2000).

There must be double taxation

(a) There must have been a double charge to tax as a result of the dividend and deemed payment (Sch 12, para 13(3) FA 2000);

(b) The relief operates to reduce or eliminate the tax paid on the dividend; it does not change the tax due on the deemed Schedule E payment (Sch 12, para 13(4) FA 2000);

(c) Where the dividend is received by a basic rate taxpayer, there will be no further taxation, and thus no need to claim tax relief;

(d) The relief is available to any recipient of the dividend; it is not restricted to dividends received by the worker who carried out the relevant engagements. Other shareholders may therefore receive an unexpected windfall, if appropriate care has not been taken to obtain effective waivers in advance of the declaration of the dividend;

(e) Where both the worker and another person have received the dividends, the tax relief is given first to the worker (Sch 12, para 13(5)(b) FA 2000).

Method of giving the relief

(a) The relief must be claimed by the intermediary in writing (Sch 12 para 13(4) FA 2000). Where the recipient of the dividend is not the controlling shareholder, and wishes to claim the tax relief, he is thus dependant on the intermediary making a claim and passing on the information about the result of the claim;

(b) The draft legislation gave a time limit for the claim, stating that it had to be made before 31 January following the tax year in which the distribution is made. This has however been removed in the final legislation, and so it is assumed the normal self-assessment time limits will apply, see 15.2;

(c) The legislation reads as follows:

> 'If, on a claim being made, the Inland Revenue are satisfied that relief should be given in order to avoid a double charge to tax, they shall give such relief by way of amending any assessment, by discharge or repayment of tax, or otherwise, as appears to them appropriate.'

Considerable discretion thus rests with the Revenue as to their operation of the relief. In particular, it suggests that the computations of both the service company and the worker will be subject to review in order to work out the amount of any relief and the manner in which it should be given.

However in practice this may not be necessary. If the net dividend is less than the net deemed Schedule E amount, it should be clear that the dividend is covered by the Schedule E amount, and that it should not be taxed;

(d) Where the amount of the dividend is reduced by a claim under this section, the tax credit is (as one would expect) proportionally reduced as well (Sch 12, para 13(6) FA 2000).

13.6.3 Restriction on dividends payable

Paying dividends which are unsupported by distributable profits is illegal, see 3.10.3. Therefore, it will not always be possible to withdraw the full Schedule E amount from the company as a dividend if:

• Some expenses are disallowed in the Schedule E computation; and

• All the income is 'relevant'.

This is because the net profits in the company will be lower than the deemed Schedule E amount. Consequently, some part of the deemed payment will not be able to be withdrawn as a dividend.

This apparently unfair consequence arises because the legislation is attempting parity, so far as possible, with the tax position of employees. If the company's funds have been used to pay expenses which would not be allowed under Schedule E, then the operation of the legislation will ensure that part of the worker's taxed income is effectively used to cover these costs, so leaving a smaller amount to be withdrawn as a dividend. See also 13.5.3 for the similar situation under the salary route.

13.7 Corporation tax losses

13.7.1 Expenses exceed 5 per cent of income

If a personal service company's only income is from relevant engagements, and its corporation tax allowable expenses exceed 5 per cent of the income, there will be a corporation tax loss in the service company, see Example 13K.

Example 13K

Nick works in the music industry via his own personal service company. The company's accounting period ends on 5 April. In the fiscal year 2000/01, Nick takes up a relevant engagement with a London radio station, which produces relevant income of £100,000 in the fiscal year. The company has the following costs:

	Notes	£
Expenses		
Travel to London from Bristol each week		2,500
Accommodation in London		9,000
Training course		2,000
IT support provided by his brother Richard		2,000
Accountancy and tax advice costs		2,500
Public liability insurance		500
Total expenses		18,500

Capital costs		
Purchase of electronic keyboard		3,000
Purchase of computer		2,500
Deemed Schedule E payment		
Step One: Relevant income		100,000
5% allowance		(5,000)
Step Three : Schedule E expenses	1	(11,500)
		83,500
Step Eight: Employer's NIC	2	(8,602)
Step Nine: Deemed Schedule E amount		74,898

Notes

1. Allowable expenses are accommodation and travel only, see Chapter 11.

2. Calculated as $(83,500 - 4,385) \times (12.2/112.2)$ – see 12.5.2.

Corporation tax calculation	
	£
Income	100,000
Deductible expenses:	(18,500)
Capital allowances – computer 100%	(2,500)
keyboard 40%	(1,200)
Deemed Schedule E amount	(74,898)
Employer's NICs	(8,602)
Loss	(5,700)

A loss is likely to occur where a company has one or more of the following:

- Outstanding commitments, such as hire purchase costs or lease payments, which are not deductible under the Schedule E rules;

- Capital assets, for which allowances are not due under the rules for Schedule E, see **11.11**;

- Other Schedule E disallowable expenses which outweigh the 5 per cent allowance. Examples might include wages for administrative assistance; training costs borne by the company and not the client (see **11.68**); accountancy and tax advice fees, or insurance obligations (see **11.10**).

There is a risk that expenses previously accepted as allowable by the Revenue may now be challenged, see **11.3.6**. If the costs were disallowed, the corporation tax loss would of course evaporate.

13.7.2 Using corporation tax losses

The legislation allows relief for corporation tax losses as follows:

(a) Against other trading profits of the company arising in the same accounting period (s393A(1) ICTA 1988). The claim must be made within two years of the end of the accounting period;

(b) If losses still remain, the company can make a further claim against profits of the previous accounting period (s393A(1) ICTA 1988);

(c) Losses can also be surrendered against the profits of another group company. Companies are 'members of a group of companies' if one is the 75 per cent subsidiary of the other or both are 75 per cent subsidiaries of a third company (s413(3)(a) ICTA 1988). The company owning the shares in the subsidiary must also be beneficially entitled to at least 75 per cent of profits available for distribution and to 75 per cent of assets available in a winding-up (s413(7) ICTA 1988). The rules for groups are subject to substantial anti-avoidance legislation, see Sch 18, ICTA 1988;

(d) If no claim is made, any losses will be carried forwards against future profits of the same trade under s393(1) ICTA 1988;

(e) Loss relief is available under s393A(2A) ICTA 1988 on cessation of the trade, see Example 13B above.

13.7.3 Management of corporation tax losses

No immediate relief for the loss may be possible, because there are:

- No other trades against which the loss can be offset;
- No profits in earlier years against which the loss can be carried back; and
- No other group companies.

In this situation, attention should be paid to trying to manage the loss. Possibilities include:

(a) Undertaking some non-IR35 engagements which fall outside the personal services rules;

(b) Introducing other taxable income, such as bank interest, into the company, to offset against the trading loss. The capacity for such offsets is however limited by the decisions in *Bank Line Ltd v IRC* [1974] 49 TC 307 and *Nuclear Electric plc v Bradley* [1996] 68 TC 670, when the offsetting of losses against surplus funds was disallowed. In *Nuclear Electric*, Lord

Jauncey held that 'whether income from investments held by a business is trading income must ultimately depend upon the nature of the business and the purpose for which the fund is held';

(c) Developing other trades or businesses within the company, so as to offset the profits arising against the loss. Note that a loss *carried forward* can only be offset against profits of the same trade (s393 ICTA 1988);

(d) Forming a trading group, perhaps with a company belonging to another family member, and offsetting the losses against the other company's profits. There are, however, provisions to prevent group relief applying to profits arising before a company joins the group (s403A ICTA 1988). Forming a group will also have commercial consequences, which must be evaluated alongside any tax benefits.

13.7.4 Insolvency

If there is an accounting as well as a tax loss, there is a danger the company might become insolvent. The consequences of insolvency are beyond the scope of this book, but in the context of the personal service legislation it could occur where:

- It has received only relevant income;
- A salary equal to the deemed Schedule E amount has been paid;
- Costs and financial commitments exceed the sum of (a) the 5 per cent allowance and (b) deductible Schedule E expenses; and
- Insufficient existing reserves are held within the business to cover the loss.

Advance planning is thus needed to ensure that the legal and financial position, as well as the tax issues, are being correctly managed. It should also be noted that some contracts with clients become void if the service company becomes insolvent.

13.8 Cessation and liquidation

13.8.1 Options available

Following IR35, an individual may decide to:

- Retain his company;
- Close down his service company and become an employee in someone else's business;
- Freelance as a self-employed individual.

There is no single answer as to which course of action is appropriate; the decision must be made in the light of the facts in each individual case.

13.8.2 Retaining the company

Reasons for keeping the company include:

(a) A personal service company still has some tax advantages when compared to an employment, notably the 5 per cent allowance (see 11.2) and the more generous travel rules (see 11.6);

(b) If a loss arises in the first year of IR35, it can be carried back to the previous year. Tax paid in that year will be refunded, see 13.7.2;

(c) Some clients and agencies will only offer work to service companies. Continuing with the company may thus offer more extensive work opportunities;

(d) Rates of pay tend to be higher for contractors than for permanent staff, and this may outweigh the costs of IR35;

(e) Contracting is more flexible than employment;

(f) It may be possible to include some non-IR35 work within the company, and thus take advantage of the tax planning opportunities set out in Chapter 3;

(g) The company's shares will be business assets for taper relief purposes. However, for the shares to have any value the company must have real business assets, which could include goodwill.

13.8.3 Closing down the company

Reasons for closing down the company could include the following:

(a) The significant tax benefits, notably the NIC saving, have largely evaporated;

(b) The administration involved in managing IR35 is complex. The worker is likely to require additional professional support, which will tend to increase costs;

(c) The worker may be able to negotiate a salary package which would not be accessible if he continued to operate via a service company. For example, an employer might offer him a non-contributory final salary pension scheme or share options;

(d) If he is a subcontractor, the cashflow consequences of continuing with a company are prohibitive, see 20.8.5.

13.8.4 Freelance

If the individual decides he would be self-employed if he was operating without the company, he may decide to go freelance. His Schedule E/Schedule D status would then be judged by the same tests, but if he was wrong the costs would be likely to fall on his engager rather than on the service company, see **21.3.4**.

13.8.5 Travel costs

If, on cessation of the company, a worker has been engaged on a single contract which comprised 'all or almost all' of his employment with the intermediary, the travel expenses in respect of that engagement may not be allowable, see **11.6.3**

13.8.6 Timing

There are several stages to the process of cessation and liquidation:

(a) Cessation of the company's trade;

(b) Resignation of the director;

(c) Liquidation or dissolution of the company.

In the case of a one-man company within the personal services regime, the director should resign his directorship at the same time as he stops work. This is because:

• When the director stops work, the trade of the company ceases. If he resigns his directorship at the same time, he precipitates a relevant event under Sch 12, para 12(2), see **16.3.1**. As a result the deemed Schedule E payment is regarded as made immediately before his resignation. It will then be deductible against the corporation tax profits of the final accounting period, see Example 3B;

• If he stops work, but does not resign the directorship, the deemed payment is not accelerated. There is thus a risk that no deduction will be available for the payment against the profits of the final period of trading (s105 ICTA 1988);

• Normally one would recommend that a provision be made for the post-cessation expense, but in the case of the deemed payment, the provision is not allowable, see **13.4.3** above.

Thus where the company stops trading, the director should ensure that he also precipitates a relevant event to ensure that the final deemed payment is deductible for corporation tax purposes.

13.9 Planning points

The interaction between corporation tax and income tax is complex; and individual advice may be needed. The following is a general summary based on the points discussed in more detail elsewhere in this chapter.

(a) The company should decide whether to pay an amount approximately equal to the deemed Schedule E amount as salary during the year, or whether to pay the accounting profits as a dividend. Although here are advantages and disadvantages to both, see **13.5.3** and **13.6**, the salary route is simpler and easier to manage;

(b) If the company decides to use the dividend route, so that it will definitely have a deemed payment, it should change its accounting date to 5 April forthwith. This will allow corporation tax relief to be obtained in the same period and prevent the excessive taxation highlighted in **13.3**;

(c) If the company plans to use the salary route, the deemed payment will be nil or negligible. There is then less need to change the accounting date, though it may nevertheless represent a good insurance policy;

(d) A particular danger is paying the net deemed amount, i.e., after PAYE and NICs, to the director either directly as a bonus or by way of credit to his current account. This will constitute a further payment of salary on which further PAYE and NIC will be due, see **13.5.2**.

(e) A loss in the first year can be carried back against the company's profits for the previous year, see **13.7**;

(f) Injection of other income or another trade into a service company may help absorb other corporation tax losses; alternatively the company may be able to become part of a group and surrender its losses, see **13.7.2**;

(g) If the shares are held other than by the worker/director, the dividend route may be problematic, see **13.6.2**.

13.10 Value added tax

The fact that all or most of the income within a personal service company is taxed under Schedule E does not change the VAT position. The company is still providing the services of the worker to the client, and must therefore comply with VAT legislation and regulations, see FAQ (General) 29:

> 'The VAT position will be unaffected by the new legislation. Fees charged by a service company for the provision of personal services will remain subject to VAT, even when these services fall squarely within the proposed new rules.

This is because it is still the intermediary company that is contracting to provide services to its clients and as such the supply remains within the VAT regime. VAT would be chargeable as appropriate on any supplies and input tax recovery would be subject to the normal rules.'

Some particular points to note are:

(a) Income taken into Step 1 of the deemed Schedule E calculation is net of any VAT on the invoice from the sub-contractor to the client;

(b) Partially exempt clients, such as banks or other financial institutions, may consider that the extra fees charged by contractors to compensate for IR35, together with the largely irrecoverable VAT on this fee increase, make service companies too expensive. They may consider reverting to direct employment, or possibly to shared employment structures with agencies;

(c) Where companies are below the VAT registration threshold they may, as previously, wish to opt for voluntary registration, in order to recover the VAT suffered on purchases such as computer equipment.

14 Partnerships

14.1 General

Very few partnerships fall within the personal services legislation, but if they do, the effects are significant. The interaction of partnership taxation with Schedule E gives rise to considerable complexity, affecting expenses, income and the timing of tax payments.

The government has said that the aim of the personal services rules is not:

> 'To place unnecessary burdens on partnerships ... what they want to do is to distinguish between partnerships which can be used by a worker to control the form in which income from relevant engagements is passed on to him or her, and partnerships which are legitimate businesses but may occasionally second a partner to work for a client in circumstances which might otherwise be caught by our legislation.' (FAQ General 6)

It is easiest to look first at these exceptions and concessions, before reviewing the impact of the legislation on partnerships which are within IR35.

14.2 Exceptions

14.2.1 No relevant engagements

Partnerships are excluded from the personal services legislation provided:

- No partner supplies personal services for the business of another;

- In circumstances which would have been an employment if carried out as an individual without the 'wrapper' of the partnership (Sch 12, para 1 FA 2000).

This exclusion will cover many professional practices, such as veterinary surgeons, doctors, architects, accountants and lawyers. To the extent that these firms have small amounts of Schedule E income, they are likely to be covered by the concessions set out in **14.3** below.

14.2.2 The statutory exemptions

The legislation sets out a number of tests which have the effect of excluding most partnerships. They state that a partnership is outside the rules, even where personal services are provided, unless one or more of the following apply:

(a) The worker, alone or with one or more relatives, is entitled to 60 per cent or more of the profits of the partnership; or

(b) Most of the profits of the partnership derive from the provision of services under (relevant) engagements either:

    (i) to a single client; or

    (ii) to a single client together with associates of that client; or

(c) Under the profit sharing arrangements the income of any of the partners is based on the amount of income generated by that partner through the provision of services under (relevant) engagements (Sch 12, para 4 FA 2000).

These are discussed below.

The 60 per cent test

If a worker, alone or together with one or more relatives, is entitled to 60 per cent or more of the profits, then he will potentially be within IR35.

This catches most family partnerships. 'Relative' is interpreted as 'husband or wife, parent or remoter forebear, child or remoter issue, or brother or sister' (Sch 12, para 4(2) FA 2000). It should also be noted that 'a man and a woman living together as husband and wife are treated as if they are married to each other' (Sch 12, para 21(4) FA 2000).

This 60 per cent test was first outlined in the Revenue's Frequently Asked Questions, Series 4, where it referred to situations where 'an individual, or persons connected with him or her, is entitled to 60 per cent or more of the profits'. There have been two significant changes since this FAQ. The first is the narrowing down of the test so that the 60 per cent interest has to be held by the *worker* i.e., the person carrying out the relevant engagements. Secondly the phrase 'persons connected with him or her' has been restricted to the more limited phrase, 'relatives'. Thus a number of partnerships who believed they were caught by the rules when they reviewed the Revenue's website, now fall outside IR35.

A partnership which is caught by this rule could of course change its structure to take itself outside the legislation. Involving some more remote family members in the business, such as brothers-in-law and sisters-in-law, or uncles and aunts, so as to reduce the worker's interest to below 60 per cent, would be effective. However care should then be taken not to stream profits to the worker, and so fall within (c) above.

Single clients

Where most of the profits of a partnership are derived from services to a single client, or a single client plus associates, the partnership is caught. There is no definition of 'most'; it is understood that the Revenue have preferred to leave it open for 'common sense' negotiation.

Where the client is a company, its associates include any person connected with the company as set out in s839 ICTA 1988. This broad definition states that a company is connected with another company if:

- The same person has control of both; or

- A person has control of one and persons connected with him have control of the other; or

- A person has control of one and, together with persons connected with him, also has control of the other; or

- A group of two or more persons has control of each company, and the groups either consist of the same persons or could be regarded as consisting of the same persons by treating (in one or more cases) a member of either group as replaced by a person with whom he is connected.

In addition, a company is connected with another *person* if that person has control of it or if that person and persons connected with him together have control of it.

Where the client is an individual in business as a sole trader, the definition of associate is discussed in **4.5.2**; where the client is another partnership, the definition of associate is 'any associate of a member of the partnership' (Sch 12, para 19(c) FA 2000).

Interestingly, this test is based on the *profits* of the partnership which *derive from* the relevant income. The link between profit and income may not necessarily be straightforward. The partnership's relevant engagements may be less profitable than its other engagements, and if this is the case, it should be taken into account in applying the test. Whether the legislation is referring to accounting profits or taxable profits is not specified, but the latter may be assumed.

Profit sharing arrangements

This subparagraph is somewhat strangely worded. It states that 'under the profit sharing arrangements the income of *any of the partners* is based on the amount of income generated *by that partner* by the provision of services under (relevant) engagements'. It is understood that the intention here is that where there is a streaming of income received from relevant engagements through to the worker who undertook those engagements, then the individual is within the legislation.

However, where the partnership profits are pooled and shared between the partners according to some agreed formula, the receipt of income from relevant engagements will not be within the legislation unless it falls within one of the other tests listed above.

14.3 Concession and practice

14.3.1 Introduction

The Revenue have confirmed that both Extra-Statutory Concession A37 and the administrative practice set out in SE 1226/SE 03001-3 have been retained in the context of personal service companies. These are discussed below.

14.3.2 ESC A37: 'Tax treatment of directors' fees received by partnerships and other companies'

The text of the concession is as follows:

'Where fees are received in respect of directorships held by members of a professional partnership, they are in strictness assessable on the individual partners under Schedule E. It is however the practice of the Revenue to accede to a request from the partnership for the inclusion of the fees in the Schedule D assessment provided that–

(a) the directorship is a normal incident of the profession and of the particular practice concerned;

(b) the fees are only a small part of the profits; and

(c) under the partnership agreement the fees are pooled for division among the partners.

Partnerships seeking such treatment are expected to provide the Revenue with a written undertaking that directors' fees received in full will be included in the gross income or receipts of the basis period, whether or not the directorship is still held in the year of assessment and whether or not the partner concerned is still a partner.'

It should be noted that the concession is not automatically applicable, but requires action from the partnership – firstly to request that the concession be applied, and secondly to supply the written undertaking.

14.3.3 Revenue practice

The Revenue practice set out in SE 1226/SE 03001-3 extends the scope of the above concession to cover not only directors' fees but other Schedule E income received by partners. It is slightly narrower in its application – for instance, it requires that the fee be 'small' in relation to the income of the individual partner, while the concession looks at the fee in the context of the firm's profits. It says that:

'There would be particular practical difficulties if Schedule E were applied to the fees received by certain taxpayers ... For example, accountants acting as company auditors or secretaries and solicitors acting as company registrars or secretaries often hold numerous such offices concurrently as an integral part of their professional practice. Similar difficulties can arise where a partner holds an office or employment and the fees are to be included with partnership income and pooled amongst the partners (e.g. a Solicitor who is clerk to a body of commissioners or a GP with a part time NHS hospital appointment). The amount of tax payable under the rules of the different Schedules will often be similar in these types of situation.

In these circumstances it is permissible to allow such fees to be treated as ordinary professional receipts within Case II of Schedule D and to allow any expenses admissible under the rules of that Schedule. This treatment should however only be applied where all the following conditions are met:

- The duties of the office or employment (in terms of time taken) are small in relation to other practice work (of the individual or partner) which is clearly of a Schedule D nature;

- The office or employment is in a field related to the profession and particular practice concerned;

- In a case involving a partner, there is an agreement between the partners that the fees are included as income of the partnership and pooled for division amongst the partners – and that agreement is acted upon;

- The individual and any partners agree that the income be treated for tax purposes in this manner and agree to pay tax on the fees on that basis (where appropriate as part of the partnership profits) – written confirmation should be obtained from all concerned to this effect;

- The fees are not derived from the directorship of a company and are small in relation to the receipts of the practice generated by the individual or partner.'

One of the requirements for applying this practice is that the office or employment must be in a related field. In assessing this, the nature of the duties of the office or employment should be compared with those of the practice conducted by the partnership and the profession concerned. For example, a solicitor who takes up an appointment as Clerk to the Special Commissioners would be occupying an office in a related field but if he became the secretary of a cycling club he would not.

Where the partner is appointed to a public tribunal such as a Royal Commission, and income from the appointment is to be pooled amongst the partners, the Revenue accept that the appointment is in a related field, even where the partner is appointed because of general business acumen rather than to provide specific input in respect of his own profession.

Again it should be noted that application of this practice to a partnership is not automatic, and undertakings are required from all affected partners.

14.3.4 National Insurance

There is a similar, statutory, National Insurance relief for directors' fees received by partners where:

- Being a director of a company is a normal incident of membership of that profession;

- The director is required by the terms of his partnership to account to his firm for the payment; and

- The payment forms an insubstantial part of the gross returns of that firm (SI 1979 No 591 Reg 19B).

It should be noted that the NIC relief is only applicable to director's fees, and not to small amounts of other Schedule E earnings, and it is thus narrower in scope than the tax rules.

However, as long as the partner can satisfy both the 19B NIC requirements, and either SE 1226/SE 03001-3 or ESC A37, the engagement will not cause the partner to come within IR35 for either NIC or tax.

14.4 Workers within partnerships

As well as the partners themselves, the personal services legislation also includes employees in a partnership where:

- a payment or benefit, not chargeable to tax under Schedule E;
- is received or receivable by a worker;
- directly from the intermediary;
- which can reasonably be taken to represent remuneration for services provided by the worker to the client (Sch 12, para 4(3) FA 2000).

These rules, discussed at **4.6.1**, apply to catch a worker in any partnership, even those where the partners themselves are excluded because of the exceptions set out above.

This is largely a 'backstop' anti-avoidance provision to prevent partnership-type structures which might otherwise have replaced service companies.

14.5 The deemed income calculation

14.5.1 Introduction

If a partnership is within IR35, it broadly follows the same steps as regards the deemed income calculation as a corporate intermediary. These are set out at Chapters 10 to 12. However, there are a number of points where the detailed legislation and the consequences for partners are different from those which affect companies, and these are discussed below.

14.5.2 Step One

Step One requires the inclusion in the calculation of all 'payments and other benefits received by the intermediary in that (fiscal) year in respect of relevant engagements'.

Receipts basis

The deemed income calculation is on a received basis. There will thus be a difference between this, and the amounts brought into the partnership accounts on an accruals basis (s42(1) FA 1998). It will now be necessary to track receipts and expenditure both on a cash basis and an accruals basis in order to satisfy both sets of rules.

Fiscal year basis

The deemed Schedule E calculation is on a fiscal year basis. However, few partnerships have a 5 April year end, because only nine months and 25 days remain until the following 31 January, when the related tax return, accounts and computations have to be filed, and any balance of income tax and Class 4 NICs for the year paid. A 5 April year end does have the advantage of eliminating any overlap profit arising from the opening years and simplifies the tax filing, but these are commonly thought to be less valuable than the extra time for filing and payment.

However, partnerships affected by the personal services rules may now need to review their year end date, see **14.6.4** below.

The 5 per cent allowance

Once all the income received by the partnership in the fiscal year has been calculated, a round sum allowance equal to 5 per cent of total income is deducted. A summary of the expenses which it will have to cover is at **11.2** above, along with a discussion of the following points:

- Profits will remain taxable in the partnership if there are insufficient actual expenses to utilise the 5 per cent; and

- The allowance is available only against income or benefits received by the partnership. In particular, there is no 5 per cent reduction of amounts brought into the calculation at Step Two, because they have been received directly by the partners from the clients rather than being paid to the partnership. It is thus more tax efficient for amounts to be received by the intermediary rather than being paid or provided directly to the partner.

14.5.3 Step Two

Step Two adds into the calculation all payments and benefits received by the worker:

> 'Otherwise than from the intermediary, which are not chargeable to income tax under Schedule E, and which would have been chargeable if the worker were an employee of the client.'

This step is of particular relevance to partners. This is because, where an individual provides personal services via a company, any payments or benefits received directly from the client will commonly be by reason of his employment with the service company, and thus fall into tax apart from these rules under s154(1) ICTA 1988. Benefits from the client to a PSC director or worker rarely come within Step Two, see **10.5.4**.

However the same is not true of partners. Partners do not have an employment, and thus benefits provided by the client cannot be provided by reason of the employment. This Step is thus the mechanism by which payments and benefits which pass directly from the client to the individual partner are brought into the deemed Schedule E calculation. Examples of benefits which might be so provided, and comments on any applicable reliefs and exemptions are discussed at **10.6**.

14.5.4 Step Three

Step Three allows relief for:

> 'Any expenses met in that year by the intermediary that would have been deductible from the emoluments of the employment if the worker had been employed by the client and the expenses had been met by the worker out of those emoluments.'

The deduction is for expenses met by the partnership. Costs incurred directly by the partner do not come into the deemed Schedule E calculation.

Relief for directly incurred costs can be obtained in the Schedule D computation of the partnership, but only if the expenses would have been allowable 'if the worker had been employed by the client and the expenses had been incurred by the worker' (Sch 12, para 18(3) FA 2000). In other words, the expense must satisfy the Schedule E tests to be deductible in the partnership's Schedule D computation.

Expenses borne personally cannot be claimed by the individual partner in his self-assessment return, see **15.3.4**.

It is therefore essential that partners who incur expenses while carrying out their relevant engagements ensure that these costs are either met by the intermediary (either directly or by reimbursement) or included in the partnership's SA return. The same applies to capital allowances, see **14.5.5** below.

The general rules for Schedule E expenses are discussed at **11.4**, and the more generous travel and subsistence reliefs at **11.6**. Partnerships need to pay particular attention to both, because while service company workers have always fallen within s198ff ICTA 1988, the Schedule E rules are new to partners.

14.5.5 Step Four

Step Four gives relief for capital allowances in the deemed income calculation, but only if the stringent Schedule E tests are met. These require that the item be 'necessarily provided for use in the performance of the duties' (s27(2)(a) CAA 1990). A less demanding test, excluding the word 'necessarily', applies to cars, motor bikes and bicycles, for which allowances are due, providing the asset is used 'in the performance of the duties' (s27(2A) CAA 1990).

Step Four only gives a deduction where the capital asset has been purchased by the partnership. Capital allowances on assets owned by the partners personally, but used in the business, are not allowable in the deemed Schedule E computation. Instead, they may be deductible against partnership profits (s65(1) CAA 1990), but subject to restrictions where the asset is used for relevant engagements, see **14.6.3** below.

Again, as with expenses (**14.5.4** above), partners should ensure that assets used in relevant engagements should either be:

(a) Owned by the partnership; or

(b) Owned by the partner but with the allowance claimed by the partnership (para 5.17 SAT1 (1995)).

Of these (a) is preferable as the inclusion of the allowance in the deemed income calculation reduces the NIC on the deemed payment, see **11.11**.

Cars are the partnership asset on which capital allowances are most commonly claimed. They are generally used both for business and privately, and a private use proportion is usually agreed with the Revenue. The business proportion must now be further split into the amount relating to relevant engagements. The Revenue's answer to FAQ Computation 12 (Example 14A below) shows how this would operate in practice.

Example 14A

John and Mary are married, and work in partnership providing art and design services. They each carry out relevant engagements during the year. 50 per cent of the partnership income arises from such engagements and 50 per cent from other sources. Profits are split equally. Each is provided with a car, both of which are provided as partnership assets. The private use proportion of the motoring expenses is 30 per cent.

Partnership accounts show the following results:

Year ended 5 April 2001

	£
Income	80,000
Expenses (includes motoring expenses of £3,000)	17,000
Profit	63,000
Depreciation, private expenses etc.	(2,000)
Tax adjusted profit	65,000

Notes

1. Payments from relevant engagements: 80,000 × 50% = 40,000

2. Schedule E expenses allowed against deemed payment: 3,000 x 70% × 50% = 1,050

   This apportionment depends on the facts. In this case relief is available for 50 per cent of the business expenses reflecting the use of the cars in the relevant engagements. A further apportionment has to be made between the expenses relating to each partner. Where a car is concerned this is likely to be based upon mileage. The claim can be based upon the actual expenses incurred and capital allowances or, as an alternative, upon the Inland Revenue Authorised Mileage Rates, see **11.6.8**.

3. As a partnership, any pension contributions will be paid personally by the individual partners and relieved under the usual rules, see **14.5.6** below.

Calculation of deemed payment at 5 April 2001

	Mary £	John £
Step One: Payments from relevant engagements	25,000	15,000
5% allowance	(1,250)	(750)
Step Three: Schedule E expenses	(700)	(350)
Step Eight: Employer NIC on deemed payment	(2,031)	(1,036)
Step Nine: Deemed payment	21,019	12,864

Recalculation of partnership taxable profit

	£
Partnership profit	65,000
Plus disallowed expenses (Note 4, below)	4,450
Less deemed payments:	
John	(12,864)
Mary	(21,019)
Taxable profit	35,567

Recalculation of personal liability

	Mary £	John £
Partnership profit	17,783	17,784
Deemed payment	21,019	12,864
Total taxable income	38,803	30,648

Note 4

The expense restriction is calculated as follows:

	£
Total expenses	17,000
Disallowed under Sch D rules	(2,000)
	15,000
Relating to relevant engagements: 50%	7,500
Allowable: Car expenses	(1,050)
5% allowance	(2,000)
Expense restriction	4,450

14.5.6 Step Five

Step Five gives relief for pension contributions made by the employer. However, where the worker is a partner in a partnership, the contributions cannot be made by 'the employer' as there is no employment. It is thus not possible for the partners to use pension contributions to reduce the National Insurance charge on their deemed payment, as it is for workers and directors within service companies, see **12.2.2**. Where a worker is an employee of the partnership, however, contributions can be made and relief obtained.

14.5.7 Steps Six and Seven

Step Six deducts any employer NIC already paid for that tax year in respect of the worker, and Step Seven gives relief for 'any payments . . . in respect of which the worker is chargeable to income tax under Schedule E'.

Since a partner will not have had any Schedule E income or benefits, apart from under these provisions, these steps are redundant in the context of a partnership.

14.5.8 Steps Eight and Nine

Step Eight gives a deduction for the employer's NIC on the deemed payment. This is calculated by a formula, see **12.2.4**. For the interaction between the Class 1 NIC payable on this deemed payment, and any Class 2 and Class 4 liability, see **14.7.1** below.

Step Nine states simply that 'the result is the amount of the deemed Schedule E payment'.

14.6 Interaction of deemed payment and partnership tax position

14.6.1 Deemed payment a requirement

In the case of a company, salary can be paid to the worker before the end of the fiscal year in order to eliminate the deemed Schedule E amount. However, this option is not open to partnerships, see **12.4.1** above. Where there is a relevant engagement, partnerships are thus forced to make a deemed payment and pay over the tax and NICs.

14.6.2 Timing of deemed payment

The deemed payment is normally treated as made on the last day of the fiscal year, see Sch 12, para 2(2) FA 2000. However, this date is accelerated as follows if a 'relevant event' occurs:

- Where the worker leaves the partnership, the day before he ceases to be a partner or employee;

- The dissolution of the partnership or it ceasing to trade, the day before the dissolution or cessation of trading (Sch 12, para 12(3) FA 2000).

14.6.3 Deduction in partnership computation for deemed payment

Once the deemed payment has been calculated, both the payment and the associated employer NIC 'must be taken into account for the period of account in which the deemed Schedule E payment is treated as made' (Sch 12, para 17(2) FA 2000).

However, the legislation applies two restrictions to the deductibility of a partnership deemed payment which do not apply to companies. These place limits on both loss relief and expenses. The reason for these restrictions was explained by Dawn Primarolo in the debate on IR35:

> 'The legislation contains the special rules for partnerships because, if a worker uses a company as an intermediary, any loss arising in the company can be used only to reduce the profits of that company. If a partnership is used, any loss by that partnership can be used to reduce the partner's own tax liability and can be set against the tax due under Schedule E.' (*Hansard*, 6 June 2000)

Loss restriction

The amount of the deduction for the deemed payment is limited to the amount that reduces the profits of the partnership to nil (Sch 12, para 18(2)

FA 2000). This means that the deemed payment cannot create a loss, in contrast to the corporation tax position, see **13.7**.

Expense restrictions

Expenses relating to the relevant engagement can only be deducted from partnership profits if they are also deductible in the deemed Schedule E computation. In other words, there is no scope to deduct any excess expenses, which might otherwise be allowable under the more generous Schedule D rules, from partnership income, if these expenses relate to the relevant engagement (Sch 12, para 18(3) FA 2000). This restriction is demonstrated in Example 14A, Note 4.

As explained in **14.5.4** above, where an expense relating to a relevant engagement is borne by the partner personally, it can similarly be deducted in the partnership computation only if it satisfies the Schedule E rules for expenses.

Capital allowances are now treated as expenses rather than 'allowances' for partnership computation purposes (s140 CAA 1990). Thus where a capital asset is used for the relevant engagement and no allowance is due under s27(2)(a) or s(2A) CAA 1990, then there will also be no relief in the partnership computation.

14.6.4 Accounting dates

The deemed payment is regarded as paid on the last day of the tax year. In a continuing partnership, the rules for partnership basis periods mean that tax relief for the PAYE and NIC on the deemed payment would be considerably delayed – perhaps until the following fiscal year, see Example 14B.

Example 14B

Carol and Richard are a married couple who work in partnership providing theatrical support services. From June to December 2000 Richard has a relevant engagement with the local theatre, and calculates that he has a deemed Schedule E payment of £10,000. Profits are split equally between the partners.

The partnership has a 31 December accounting date. Their profits, unadjusted for the deemed Schedule E payment are:

• Year to 31 December 2000: £35,000,

• Year to 31 December 2001: £45,000.

The deemed payment is deducted from the profits in the period of account in which it is made, namely the year to 31 December 2001. The adjusted partnership profit for that year is as follows:

	£
Profits before adjustment:	45,000
less: deemed payment	(10,000)
NIC on deemed payment	(1,220)
	33,780

This period of account forms the basis period for tax year 2001/02, and the taxable income is split: Carol: £16,890; Richard £16,890.

The tax will be due for payment on 31 January 2002 (interim), 31 July 2002 (2nd interim) and 31 January 2003. In addition, Richard has a PAYE and NIC liability payable on 19 April 2001. Richard thus has tax to pay in the calendar year 2001 as follows:

31/1/01 – tax relating to profits of £17,500 (50% of 2000/01 partnership profits of £35,000)

19/4/01 – tax relating to deemed Schedule E payment on 5 April 2000 for 2000/01

31/7/01 – tax relating to profits of £17,500 (50% of 2000/01 partnership profits of £35,000)

Example 14B demonstrates that a partner in Richard's situation will have to pay Schedule D tax in full for the year in which he also has earned the deemed payment. It cannot be reduced by deducting the deemed Schedule E amount because the payment date falls into the following period of account.

He is also unable to reduce the interim payments in January and July 2001, because they are correctly based on the profits of the year ended 31 December 2000. However, in the following year his payments on account will be based on the profits to 31 December 2001. These will be much lower because of the deemed Schedule E amount, and he can thus apply to reduce the interim payments in January and July 2001 (s59A(3) TMA 1970). However, in the meantime he has suffered a severe cashflow disadvantage.

Change of accounting date to 5 April

To ameliorate the cashflow disadvantage, partnerships may want to change their accounting date to 5 April. If the business commenced within the last three years this can be done without having to meet any statutory requirements. Otherwise, the partnership must fall within the rules contained in s62 and s62A ICTA 1988, as follows:

(a) The new accounting period must not exceed 18 months;

(b) The Revenue must be notified of the change of date; and

(c) There must have been no change of date within the last five years, *or*, if there has been such a change, this further change must be made for genuine commercial reasons. It is specifically stated in the legislation that 'obtaining a tax advantage will not be accepted as a genuine commercial reason for a change of accounting date' (s62A(9) ICTA 1988).

The Revenue guidance on self-assessment commented on this as follows:

> '"Tax advantage" is not defined in the legislation. But since income tax is a personal liability "tax advantage" will include any cash flow advantage arising from the deferral of tax, as well as an absolute reduction in profits or an absolute increase in losses.' (SAT1 1995 1.54)

Avoiding the cashflow problem caused by the interaction of the Schedule D and IR35 rules thus appears to be a 'tax advantage'. Therefore, unless a partnership can fall within the five year rule in condition (c) above, or began trading within the last three years, it will be unable to change its accounting date under these normal rules.

If a partnership can satisfy the normal rules, then the change of date will crystallise some or all of the overlap relief (s63A ICTA 1988).

Election for discontinuance

The Revenue recognised that the new rules would create a difficult cashflow position for partnerships, and realised that some would be unable to change their accounting date because of the restriction in (c) above. As a result, the personal services legislation contains a specific provision allowing partnerships to elect for discontinuance at the end of the 1999/00 year, so that a new business will commence on 6 April 2000 (Sch 12, para 23 FA 2000).

This will allow the 'new' partnership to deduct the deemed Schedule E payment against the profits of the same period, and so achieve a better cashflow position. The deemed discontinuance and recommencement will not affect the ability of the partnership to carry losses forward from the old partnership to the new one (Sch 12, para 23(3) FA 2000).

This is a transitional relief, and applies only where:

(a) A partnership is carrying on business at the beginning of the fiscal year 2000/01; and

(b) Is treated as making one or more deemed Schedule E payments in that year.

It therefore does not apply when a partnership in a future tax year makes a deemed payment for the first time.

If the partnership does elect for discontinuance, it will have the effect of changing the accounting date to 5 April, see **14.5.2** above, and crystallising the full overlap relief.

A partnership which can choose between the discontinuance option and the normal change of accounting date rules should compare the results of both options before making the decision. One possibility for a partnership which can use the s62A ICTA rules is to change its accounting date to 30 April. This will not give a complete match with the fiscal year, but the difference should be manageable. A 30 April year end gives a much longer period for filing accounts and returns, see **14.5.2** above.

A further point to consider is that the discontinuance option will use the full overlap relief against the profits of the final period, while a change of accounting date may utilise only part of the relief.

14.6.5 Effects of deemed Schedule E payment on other partners

The effect of the deemed Schedule E calculation is to increase the tax charge on the partner who has carried out the relevant engagement. There are also consequences for the other partners:

- The deemed Schedule E payment, including the Class 1 NIC, is deducted from total partnership profits, although the tax liability on this amount is the personal liability of the individual partner, see Sch 12, para 11(5) FA 2000;

- The allowable expenses deducted from the partnership's taxable profits may be restricted, see **14.6.3** above and Example 14A.

If the partnership profit shares remain unchanged, and are based on the gross earnings of the partnership before tax, then the take-home pay of each partner will be significantly affected by the existence of the deemed payment.

In example 14B, the profits would normally be shared equally, giving Carol and Richard £22,500 each. Under the new provisions Carol only pays tax on

£16,890, but Richard pays tax on £26,890. Similarly, in Example 14A, Mary pays tax on £38,803, but John only pays tax on £30,648, even though profits were again shared equally. There are also NIC implications, see **14.7** below.

In situations where one or more partners have relevant engagements, the partners may thus wish to review their profit sharing arrangements.

14.7 National Insurance

14.7.1 Interaction with Classes 2 and 4

A partner who is within the personal service rules is 'treated as employed in employed earner's employment' by the partnership. He or she thus has 'attributable earnings' which are assessable under Class 1. This has the consequential benefit of allowing the partner to claim jobseeker's allowance, statutory sick pay and statutory maternity pay.

These earnings are 'treated as received by him in his personal capacity and not as income of the partnership' (SI 2000 No 727 Reg 8(3)).

Assuming that the individual also has Schedule D earnings from the partnership in the fiscal year, he will thus have paid Class 1, Class 2 and Class 4 contributions. In consequence he may have overpaid NIC in the year. If the total Class 1, Class 2 and Class 4 paid in 2000/01 is more than £2,432.70, the partner can apply for a refund. If he can anticipate the situation, he can apply for deferment of Class 2 (if total contributions are expected to be more than the value given above) and/or for Class 4 (if any Class 1 contributions at all are expected to be paid) with a 'catch-up' payment at a later date if total contributions prove inadequate.

In addition to the employee contributions, the partnership will have paid employer's NIC at 12.2 per cent on the deemed payment. This is deducted from the taxable profits of the partnership, see Examples 14A and 14B above.

14.7.2 Small earnings exception

If, after deducting the attributable earnings from the deemed Schedule E computation, the Schedule D earnings of the individual from the partnership are within the 'small earnings exception', he will escape Class 2 (s11(4) SSCBA 1992). The partner must apply for this exception; it is not granted automatically (s11(5) SSCBA 1992). For 2000/01 the limit is £3,825. The exception can take effect up to 13 weeks before the application date and continues for the rest of the fiscal year.

Where exception has not been applied for in time, but would have been available had an application been made within the time limit, a repayment of contributions maybe obtained, less any amount paid by way of contributory benefits which would not have been received but for the Class 2 contributions which are now being repaid (SI 1979 No 591 Reg 26A(4)–(6)).

A claim for repayment must:

- Be in writing to the Inland Revenue;

- Be supported by evidence of the earnings (i.e., profits) of the tax year in respect of which a repayment of Class 2 contributions is sought;

- Not be made before the beginning of the following tax year;

- Be made by 31 December in that following tax year (SI 1979 No 591 Reg 26A(1)(2)).

Thus partners who may be able to claim this relief should be aware of their overall NIC position before 31 December following the end of the fiscal year.

14.8 Payment of PAYE and NICs

The payment deadlines for the PAYE and Class 1 NIC on the deemed Schedule E amount are discussed in Chapter 16. There are a few points which particularly affect partners:

(a) The concession relating to penalties on late payment of the PAYE and NIC liability, discussed at **16.4.2**, is dependent upon the intermediary making a 'payment on 19 April of a lower amount on account of the tax and NICs due'. In the case of a company, payment of salary will often have been made at some point during the tax year. But where the worker is a partner, no salary can have been paid. Thus to obtain the benefit of the concession on PAYE penalties, *some* tax and National Insurance must be paid on or before 19 April – it is understood that 'payment of a lower amount' cannot be interpreted as a nil figure!

(b) The partnership has to submit Forms P14 and P35 in respect of the deemed Schedule E payment by the normal deadline of 19 May. This is because the intermediary is treated as the secondary contributor in respect of the worker's attributable personal service earnings (SI 2000 No 727 para 6(3)(b)). If the amount paid on 19 April is provisional, this should be indicated on the form, see **16.4.2**;

(c) A supplementary return including the correct final figure for the deemed payment should be sent in to the Revenue by 31 January following the end of the tax year.

15 Self-assessment and personal services

15.1 General

Individuals and companies are both within the UK self-assessment system. Under self-assessment it is each person's responsibility to consider whether there is tax to pay, and if so, to determine the amount of that liability. If a person's self-assessment is incorrect, he is likely to suffer interest and penalties.

Companies, partnerships and individuals within the personal services regime must self-assess their own liability based on whether or not they have relevant engagements. Although the Revenue have offered help in reviewing individual contracts, see 7.7, at the end of the day the onus to get it right is on the taxpayer. In practice, however, most policing of the personal services regime is likely to occur via reviews of the intermediary's PAYE compliance, see 16.9.

This chapter does not cover all aspects of the self-assessment system, but considers how the rules impact upon personal service workers and their intermediaries. The references given are to the boxes for the 1999/00 tax return, and may need amendment for subsequent years. It should also be noted that this chapter is being written well before the end of the 2000/01 fiscal year. There may be further amendments to the self-assessment forms before they are issued in early April 2001.

15.2 Outline of self-assessment for individuals and partners

Everyone within the UK is potentially within the self-assessment (SA) system, but only some eight million people receive a return. If an individual has a liability to tax which has not been collected directly (e.g., via PAYE or by deduction from bank interest), but does not receive a return, he must notify the Revenue by 5 October following the end of the fiscal year.

The basic individual return is eight pages long, and covers interest, dividends (including those from a personal service company), allowances and reliefs.

There are supplementary pages covering employment income (including any deemed Schedule E income, the provision of personal services), self-employment, partnership income, foreign income and other special areas. It is the individual's responsibility to ask for the pages he needs. In addition to the form and any supplementary pages, the Revenue send each person a calculation guide, which helps to work out the tax liability.

If the completed return is received by the Revenue by 30 September following the end of the tax year, the Revenue will calculate the individual's tax. If the return is sent after this date, the taxpayer must work out his own liability using the calculation guide, and send it to the Revenue. Any return not received by 31 January following the end of the tax year will incur an automatic £100 penalty unless the individual has a 'reasonable excuse' (see **16.7.3**), the tax due is less than the penalty, or the filing deadline was extended.

The Revenue will process the return, and, based on the self-assessment, tell the individual if he has any tax to pay or whether he is due a refund. Any tax outstanding must be settled by 31 January following the end of the fiscal year, whether or not the return has been submitted, or there may be interest and penalties, see **16.5** and **16.6**.

Assuming the return was submitted on time, the Revenue have until the following 31 January to raise questions on the return. These might be on a single issue (an 'aspect enquiry') or a more general review (a 'full enquiry'), see **15.5.4** below. If the return is received late, the Revenue's enquiry deadlines are extended.

If the filing deadline was met, and the Revenue do not give notice of an enquiry by the following 31 January, the tax return becomes final and conclusive, subject to the rules for 'error and mistake' and 'discovery', see **15.5.3** and **15.5.5**.

If the return is issued but not sent back to the Revenue, they can determine the tax liability. If the return is subsequently submitted, the Revenue's determination will be superseded by the self-assessment.

The individual taxpayer has an obligation to keep the records on which his self-assessment is based until 31 January following the filing date (or later, if the filing deadline was missed). Partnerships must keep records for five years from the same date. There is a maximum penalty of £3,000 for failing to comply (s12A TMA 1970).

15.3 Reporting personal services income via self-assessment

15.3.1 Notifying chargeability

An individual who has carried out relevant engagements within the UK is within the scope of UK tax and thus both the personal services regime and self-assessment. However, because the liability to tax on a deemed payment is dealt with via PAYE, there may be no further tax to pay. Where this is the case, and no return has been received, there is no requirement to request or complete a return.

15.3.2 Salary and deemed Schedule E income [1.8]

An individual within IR35 will have salary, deemed Schedule E income, or both. Deemed Schedule E income arises on the last day of the tax year, and should be included on the self-assessment return along with any actual salary received. This applies both to partners who have relevant engagements just as it does to employees and directors of service companies.

It is not expected that there will be a special box on the self-assessment form for the deemed income, though at the time of writing it is understood that the Revenue's guidance notes to the return form will provide some assistance.

As well as requiring the salary and deemed income to be included, the return also asks for the PAYE suffered on both the actual earnings and the deemed Schedule E payment. In practice it is expected that both will be combined on the worker's P60, and it should simply be a question of taking the number off the P60 and including it on the self-assessment return.

The fact that the worker has not actually received the deemed Schedule E income does not change his tax liability. The legislation deems it to be his income, PAYE has been deducted by the service company, and the deemed earnings and the related tax should be included on his self-assessment return.

15.3.3 Benefits [1.12–1.23]

Employees and directors

Where a benefit has been received from, or by arrangement with, a service company, its value should have been included on his P11D, and the individual should enter it on his tax return. This will include most benefits from clients, see 10.5.4.

If the benefit has been received from the third party otherwise than by arrangement with the intermediary, the third party has to provide details of the benefits to the individual by 6 July following the end of the tax year (SI 1993 No 744 Reg 46). This should also be included on the individual's tax return.

Partners

Any benefits received by a partner from a client in respect of a relevant engagement are included within the deemed Schedule E calculation (see **10.5.1**) and are not entered on the SA return.

15.3.4 Expenses and capital allowances [1.32–1.36]

Employee or director

An employee is allowed to deduct certain expenses from his taxable income under ss198ff ICTA 1988, see **11.3.3**. Where these costs have been borne directly by the individual they should be claimed on his tax return. Any capital allowances on assets purchased by the worker which satisfy the narrow tests in s27 CAA 1990 are also included here, see **11.11**.

However, as explained at **11.11.1(c)**, it is more efficient if:

- Assets on which capital allowances can be claimed are owned by the company rather than the worker;

- Allowable expenses are borne by the intermediary rather than the worker.

This gives both a cashflow advantage and a reduction in the Class 1 NIC on any deemed payment.

Partners

Partners who incur expenses carrying out their relevant engagements should ensure that these costs are met by the intermediary (either directly or by reimbursement) so they can be deducted in the deemed Schedule E calculation (see **14.5.4**). Alternatively, but less tax-efficiently, they should be included in the partnership's SA return. The same is true of capital expenditure. Otherwise they no relief will be obtained for these amounts because:

(a) Partners are not employees, and so cannot claim a deduction under ss198ff ICTA 1988. As a result they cannot offset expenses directly against their deemed Schedule E income;

(b) Equally they cannot make a capital allowances claim under s27 CAA 1990 to deduct allowances from their deemed Schedule E income;

(c) Where a partner has met the expense or owns the asset personally, he cannot deduct the expense or claim the allowance on his SA Schedule D partnership return; it must be included in the partnership return. This point is explained in the Inland Revenue's booklet *The new current basis of self assessment* at paragraph **5.17** (SAT1 (1995)).

'Any expenditure incurred by a partner on behalf of the partnership must be included in the partnership return. It will not be possible for individual partners to make supplementary claims, whether to expenses or capital allowances, in their own tax returns.

This is because revenue expenditure incurred by a partner only qualifies for relief if it is made 'wholly and exclusively' for the purposes of the partnership business. And the only legal basis for giving relief for any such expenditure is as a deduction in the calculation of the profits of the partnership business.

Similarly the only legal basis for giving relief for expenditure qualifying for capital allowances is as a deduction in the calculation of the profits of the partnership business.

However, this does not mean that expenditure incurred by a partner can only be relieved if it is included in the partnership accounts. The Inland Revenue will accept adjustments for such expenditure in the tax computations included in the partnership return providing the adjustments are made before apportionment of the net profit between the partners. But once the adjustments have been made the expenditure will be treated, for all practical purposes, as if it had been included in the partnership's accounts.'

15.3.5 Reliefs [1.3.8 and 14]

If a pension contribution has been made by the individual, a claim for tax relief should be made on the tax return. Where the intermediary is a company it is more efficient for the pension contributions to be paid by the employer rather than by the individual, as this reduces the NIC due as well as producing a minor cashflow benefit, see 12.2.2.

Where the intermediary is a partnership this is not possible, and relief for pension contributions must be claimed via the individual's SA tax return. This may result in a repayment of tax already deducted under PAYE on the partner's deemed Schedule E income.

There is also relief for:

- Interest on a qualifying loan to buy into the partnership or to buy shares in the service company;

- Foreign tax suffered. This can be deducted against taxable income by making a claim in box **1.3.8**. However, the most efficient way to claim relief for foreign tax is as a deduction against the Schedule E *tax* using the Foreign Pages, see **15.3.8** below, rather than against the *income*. Thus in most cases it is recommended that box **1.3.8** should be left blank. The Notes to the Foreign Pages explain the position in detail, see 'Foreign tax paid and tax credit relief.'

15.3.6 Dividends

Where a company has paid both a deemed Schedule E amount, and a dividend, the dividend may be outside the scope of tax, see **13.6.2**. Where this is the case, it is understood that it will not have to be included on the tax return. It may be advisable to include an explanatory note in the 'Additional Information' section of the tax return explaining why the dividend has not been brought into tax. However this point should be covered in the Notes to the 2000/01 tax return, which have not been published at the time of writing, and these may indicate that no such disclosure is necessary. For dividends from an overseas company, see **15.3.8** below.

15.3.7 Student loan repayments

At the time of writing, no student loans had been repaid via the SA return. The first returns requiring an entry for student loan repayments will be in 2000/01. The interaction of student loan repayment amounts with the personal services rules, in particular with dividends and partnership income, is discussed at **22.4**.

15.3.8 Overseas income and residence status

The definitions of residence, ordinary residence, and domicile are discussed in Chapter 17. An individual who is resident, but either not ordinarily resident or not domiciled, will receive a tax return on the same basis as the rest of the population. A non-resident may receive a return, since the Revenue approach is that 'Income from employment will normally be taxed through PAYE, with a final settling up with the non-resident through Self Assessment where necessary'(*Tax Bulletin 18*, August 1995).

Non-resident, not ordinarily resident and/or not domiciled

If an individual is claiming that he is non-resident, not ordinarily resident and/or not domiciled for all or part of the tax year, he must complete the non-residence supplementary pages of the tax return. This is discussed at 17.7.3 and 17.11.5. Use should be made of the additional information ('white space') if the individual considers that there are any particular facts concerning his residence status which he wishes to draw to the attention of the Inspector.

Overseas implications of personal services legislation

There are a number of possibilities here. If the individual:

- Is resident, ordinarily resident and domiciled in the UK, he is within the scope of the personal services regime even if his service company is non-resident (see 19.5.1), or he has worked on relevant engagements overseas (see 17.10.1);

- Is resident in the UK, but has suffered foreign tax on income earned overseas and wishes to claim double tax relief, this is deductible in the first instance against the corporation tax suffered by the company, see 17.10.2. However, where there is insufficient corporation tax for relief to be obtained, the foreign tax may be deductible against the individual's Schedule E income. This should be claimed using the supplementary foreign pages of the tax return [6.9].

- Is resident, but either not ordinarily resident and/or not domiciled, his overseas personal services income may be on the remittance basis. See 17.11.5 for his reporting obligations;

- Is non-resident but has carried out work here, he is within Schedule E for any earnings or deemed earnings on his relevant engagements, see 17.8. However, he may argue that the income is 'merely incidental' to his overseas work, see 17.8.2, or that under provisions of a double tax treaty no tax is due, see 17.8.3.

Dividends from an overseas company

Many service companies, even those registered abroad, are in fact resident in the UK because they are managed and controlled here, see 19.2.3.

If the company is not resident in the UK, any dividends will be Schedule D Case V income, and should be reported using the foreign pages of the SA return. However workers taxed on a remittance basis (see 17.13) are only subject to UK tax on an overseas dividend if it is brought into the UK.

As with UK dividends, there will be no tax if the service company has made a deemed Schedule E payment which effectively covers the dividend, see 13.6.2 above.

15.3.9 Self-employed individuals

An employee or a director of a personal service company has to decide whether he is inside or outside IR35. To do this he has to consider whether he would be Schedule E or Schedule D in respect of his relevant engagements if he was working directly for the client. If he would have been Schedule D, he escapes IR35.

However this Schedule E/Schedule D test merely establishes whether he should be within the personal service rules; *it does not mean he is self-employed*. He remains an employee or director of his company. He can thus ignore the self-employment pages unless he has a separate Schedule D business.

15.3.10 Partners

A partner who has deemed Schedule E income from relevant engagements is required to:

- Complete the employment income part of the SA return as if he were an employee, see **15.3.2** above;

- Ignore any benefits received from the intermediary or a third party, as they will have been included in the deemed Schedule E calculation, see **14.5.3**.

In addition, partners have to complete the supplementary partnership pages, even if all the partnership income derives from relevant engagements and is thus taxable under the employment income section of the return. A partnership return is also required.

Expenses allowable against the partnership's trading income may need to be restricted, as explained in **14.6.3**. There may also be a limitation on the partnership losses. These adjustments should be made in the partnership return, and the partners should then be informed of the correct amount to include in the partnership pages of their own SA return.

Where the worker is a partner in a foreign partnership, a special tax return, Partnership Foreign, must be completed.

15.4 Disclosure

15.4.1 General

Where the taxpayer has additional facts which are relevant to his tax liability, it is usually recommended that he disclose these on the additional information or 'white space' area of his tax return. Once he has made this disclosure, then, providing no enquiry is received, his return will be closed from 31 January following the filing deadline, and cannot be re-opened (s9(6)(a) TMA 1970). If the return was submitted late, the enquiry window remains open for longer.

Disclosure thus gives the individual finality about his tax position. If there had been no disclosure, the Revenue have six years (longer if there has been fraud) to make a later 'discovery', see 15.5.5, and to collect tax, interest and penalties. Thus the 'reward' for disclosure is that the assessment is closed after a relatively short time.

15.4.2 Personal services

The individual's tax liability under the personal services regime depends on whether he would have been self-employed in respect of his relevant engagements had he not have been operating via an intermediary. Because of the complexity of the status tests, this may not be an easy decision to make.

The taxpayer can ask the Revenue to rule on a contract-by-contract basis as to whether each engagement is inside or outside IR35, see 7.7. If he does this, and provides all relevant details to the Revenue, he should be able to rely on the ruling when completing his tax return.

If he does not seek a ruling, he has to decide whether to disclose the basis for considering that IR35 does not apply. However, it could be argued that disclosure via SA is not appropriate, because:

(a) Self-assessment is exactly that – the individual is supposed to work out whether he has a tax liability and if he has, to assess it. The rules for disclosure are not meant to cover issues where the tax payer has either given himself the benefit of the doubt, or is uncertain about the operation of the tax legislation. Whether an individual falls inside or outside IR35 could thus be said to be an inappropriate area for disclosure: the individual is either within the rules, in which case he should have a deemed payment, or he is not;

(b) Liability to pay the tax and NICs in respect of a relevant engagement rests in the first instance with the intermediary. Once the service company or partnership has decided whether the worker has a liability to PAYE and NICs under IR35, it is required to pay over the tax and National Insurance. Details of the gross Schedule E deemed payment and the PAYE and employee's NIC are then provided to the individual via his P60. If the intermediary considers that there is no liability, there will be no deemed payment on the P60.

If the intermediary is wrong, and the worker is within IR35, the Revenue will seek back PAYE and NICs, plus possibly interest and penalties, from the service company or partnership. This will be the normal route by which compliance with the personal services legislation is enforced, see **16.9**;

(c) The usual time limit for a PAYE investigation is six years. Disclosure on the individual's SA return of the reasons why an individual believes he falls outside IR35 will not protect the company or partnership from a PAYE audit. Thus, while there may be 'finality' under self-assessment by 31 January following the filing date, this has little meaning given that the company can continue to be pursued for six years under the PAYE rules. If the company cannot meet the liability, the Revenue may seek to collect the PAYE from the worker, see **16.8.2**.

As mentioned in (b) above, investigations into the operation of the personal service legislation are likely to be carried out by employer compliance, rather than by targeted sampling of self-assessment returns, see **16.9**. However, like other taxpayers, the personal service worker may be selected for enquiry (see **15.5.4**) either on a random basis or because of some other question about his tax return. As part of the enquiry process the Revenue may ask why the individual considers the personal services legislation does not apply. This may then lead to a PAYE audit of the intermediary, and the collection of interest and penalties by that route.

The individual thus has a vulnerability under the SA rules to interest and penalties if he has under-assessed his taxable employment income, although SA is not likely to be the normal route by which the Revenue will police the personal services legislation. Any back tax, penalties and interest are more likely to be collected from the service company under the PAYE regulations.

15.5 Changing the tax return

15.5.1 Methods of changing the return

Once the tax return has been submitted, it can be changed:

- By the taxpayer, using either the rules for 'amendment' or those for 'error or mistake', see **15.5.2** and **15.5.3**;

- By the Revenue, following an enquiry into the return, see **15.5.4**;

- By the Revenue, if they re-open the return under the 'discovery' provisions, see **15.5.5**.

If any of these changes causes the tax assessed to increase, there may be interest and/or penalties. Disclosure of the relevant facts on the return minimises the chances of 'discovery' and should prevent penalties.

15.5.2 Amendments

An individual may amend his return at any time within twelve months following the filing date, which is normally 31 January following the end of the fiscal year (s9A(4) TMA). A similar rule applies to partnerships (s12AB(2) TMA).

The taxpayer can thus change his mind about the tax position of his personal services income within this period. Clearly, an amendment to the SA return should not be considered in isolation from the PAYE/NIC position of the service company. If there is a change of view, so that IR35 is considered to have applied in that tax year, the individual should amend his self-assessment return, and the intermediary should make a late payment of PAYE and NICs. If the worker is a partner, the partnership return will also need amendment, and this will also affect the SA returns of the other partners.

An amendment may extend the period for which the Revenue can open an enquiry. Usually the extended period will relate only to the amended item, but 'there may be cases in which the amendment is so fundamental to the return that the whole return will be considered for enquiry.' (*SAT2* 1995 para 4.33). No amendment can be made after the Revenue have notified the taxpayer that they are enquiring into the return. An amendment does not protect the taxpayer from penalties if he originally acted fraudulently or negligently, see *Tax Bulletin* September 1998 p597.

15.5.3 Error or mistake

If the taxpayer has paid too much tax, so that for instance he and the intermediary have assumed that the IR35 provisions apply, but three years later he finds this is not the case, he can claim for the tax overpaid to be refunded. This 'error or mistake' claim can be made at any time during the five years after 31 January following the year of assessment (s33 TMA 1970). A similar claim can be made by partners, and this may also cause the assessment of the other partners to be adjusted (s33A TMA 1970).

A claim is not accepted, however, if the original SA return was made in accordance with the practice generally prevailing at the time – so if, for example, the law on status tests changed as a result of a House of Lords case, it would not be possible for taxpayers to go back six years and re-open their closed assessments (s33(2A) TMA 1970).

15.5.4 Enquiry

The Revenue have 12 months after 31 January following the filing date to open an enquiry (s9A TMA 1970). This deadline is extended if the return has been filed late. They do not have to give a reason for opening the enquiry and have said they will not do so.

The enquiry may be into one area of the return – an 'aspect' enquiry – or it may be more wide-ranging – a 'full enquiry'. A percentage of enquiries are random, generated by a computer programme, but most are not. The taxpayer will not be told if his is a random enquiry. In the Revenue's 1997 *Self-Assessment Tax Bulletin*, they said that:

> 'The vast majority of returns selected for enquiry will have been selected because of the potential risk that they are incorrect or incomplete. Selection for enquiry may be on the basis of a risk assessment of the information contained in the return, or on the basis of information from other sources, or a combination of both.
>
> About one return in every thousand will be selected for full enquiry at random . . . These cases are selected centrally and notified to local offices at the time of the bulk issue of returns in April each year. Selection of a small proportion of enquiries at random will mean that no one who is not complying with his or her obligations can feel safe from detection.
>
> The depth and scope of all enquiries will be tailored to the circumstances of the individual case and proportionate to the risk of error or omission. We will not pursue risks that are trivial or remote, or seek information that can be verified from our own records.'

They also comment elsewhere that 'the 12 month time limit before finality is achieved will allow information from third parties – employers, contractors, financial institutions – to be used in the enquiry selection process' (SAT2 1995 4:32).

If a return is selected for enquiry, the Revenue may ask for underlying records or other documents, and they may want to meet with the taxpayer. It is recommended that professional advice is sought if the Inspector enquires into the tax position of the individual's PSC income.

15.5.5 Discovery

The Revenue can re-open a tax return under the 'discovery' provisions if information subsequently becomes available which indicates that the self-assessment was too low, see SP8/91 and s29(3) TMA 1970. However, a discovery cannot be made unless either;

(a) The loss of tax is the result of fraudulent or negligent conduct by the taxpayer or any person acting on the taxpayer's behalf; or

(b) The Revenue could not have been reasonably expected to have identified the circumstances giving rise to the loss of tax, before the expiry of the normal enquiry period, or before the conclusion of any enquiry, using the information that had then been 'made available'.

Information will be treated as having been 'made available' if it is:

- Contained in the *SA return* for the relevant period (or the two preceding periods); or

- Contained in any *accounts, statements or documents supplied with the SA return*; or

- Contained in any *claim* made for the relevant period (or the two preceding periods), or in any of the accounts, statements or documents supplied with the claim; or

- Contained in any documents, accounts or particulars supplied in connection with an *enquiry* into a return or claim; or

- It is information which could *reasonably be expected to be inferred* from any of the above; or

- It is information that was *notified to the Revenue officer in writing* by the taxpayer (s29 TMA 1970).

The Revenue have confirmed that 'a change of opinion on information that has previously been made available to the Revenue will not be grounds for a discovery' (SAT2 1995 4:99). However they have pointed out that:

> 'There is clearly an onus on the taxpayer to draw attention to any important information relevant to a tax liability, particularly if there is some doubt as to the interpretation that can be placed on that information. It is not sufficient just to provide that information if it is hidden away or obscure' (SAT2 1995 4:100).

Thus if information has been clearly disclosed in the tax return,, there can be no discovery.

15.6 Interest and penalties

15.6.1 Alternatives

The Revenue have a range of penalty and interest legislation which can be used against the taxpayer if he submits late or incorrect SA returns. However, since the tax on the deemed Schedule E payment is primarily a PAYE liability, it is more likely that the penalty and interest provisions under that legislation will be used, see **16.9**, rather than those applicable to self-assessment. This is however their choice, and the SA provisions could be called upon if required.

15.6.2 Tax paid late

If tax is paid laid, interest runs from the due date to the date of payment. There is also a 5 per cent surcharge on any tax unpaid by 28 February following the year of assessment and a further 5 per cent surcharge on any tax unpaid by the following 31 July. If the surcharges are not paid within 30 days of the issue of the surcharge notice, interest begins to accrue on the surcharge itself.

If the taxpayer has a 'reasonable excuse' for paying the tax late, the interest will be waived or reduced. In the context of personal services, the complexity of the legislation, or not being able to work out the extent of liability before 31 January, may constitute a reasonable excuse in the period after the introduction of the regime, see **16.7.3**.

Where tax has been overpaid, interest runs from the due date (or date of payment if later) to the date of repayment. The rate of interest on tax overpaid is lower than that on overdue tax.

15.6.3 For late submission of returns

Penalties are also exacted where the return is not submitted by the due date, see **15.2**. These are:

- £100 if the return is not received by 31 January following the end of the fiscal year;

- A further £100 if it has still not been received by 31 July;

- In addition the Revenue can ask the Commissioners to impose a daily penalty of £60 a day;

- If the return is outstanding a year after the due date, a penalty equal to any tax due can be imposed (s93 TMA 1970).

If the amount of tax due is less than the fixed £100 penalties, the penalty will be reduced (s93(7) TMA 1970; EH 640).

Partners are subject to similar rules, but without the tax-geared penalty; they are also unable to reduce the £100 fixed penalties (s93A TMA 1970).

15.6.4 For fraud or negligence

There are also tax-geared penalties for fraud or negligence (s95 TMA 1990). The maximum penalty equals the tax unpaid. The general law concerning fraud and negligence is discussed at **16.6.3**.

In the context of the personal services legislation, negligence could include understating the tax due because the worker was considered (incorrectly) to fall outside the personal services legislation. However in the period following the introduction of the regime, the government have promised that the Revenue will apply a 'light touch', and give individuals the benefit of the doubt, see **16.7.2**.

However, this gentle approach will not apply:

> 'In the rare cases in which avoidance *(sic)* of tax and national insurance liability is deliberate and intended.' (Dawn Primarolo, House of Commons, *Hansard* 3 May 2000, Pt 24, Col. 26)

So if the worker knew he was within the new rules, but deliberately took steps to conceal his liability, for instance by using an offshore company to hide the profits, this could amount to fraud and the individual would be subject to the full rigours of the system.

15.7 Interim payments under self-assessment

If the tax due under self-assessment is more than a certain de minimis amount, it is collected by means of two interim payments of equal amounts, based normally on the liability for the previous year. These are due on 31 January in the year of assessment and the following 31 July, with a final balancing payment on the 31 January of the next year.

Interim payments are not collected if substantially all of a taxpayer's liability is covered by deduction of tax at source, including PAYE. Before IR35 a worker might have been within the interim payment regime because he received significant dividends from his service company or because he received his partnership income as Schedule D. If he is now within the personal services legislation, all or almost all of his income is likely to be taxed under PAYE.

He may therefore be able to apply to have his interim payments reduced or eliminated using Form SA 303. However, in some cases the interaction between interim payments and PAYE mean that there is still significant overlap. An example of the interim payment position in the context of a partner is at **14.6.4.**

15.8 Corporation tax self assessment

15.8.1 Outline of system

Corporation tax self assessment (CTSA) came into effect for accounting periods ending after 1 July 1999. As with individual self-assessment, responsibility for determining the tax due rests with the taxpayer, not the Inland Revenue. When returns are received they are processed without checking, unless an amendment is necessary for the return to be processed. Any enquiries are carried out later, see (g) below.

(a) A company which does not receive a tax return but has a corporation tax liability must notify the Revenue of this within 12 months following the end of the accounting period. Failure to notify chargeability may lead to penalties (Sch 18, para 2 FA 1998);

(b) The return must generally be filed within 12 months following the end of the accounting period, together with supporting accounts, computations and any other relevant information. The return must include a declaration that the return is correct and complete to the best of the knowledge of the person making it (Sch 18, paras 3 and 14 FA 1998);

(c) Claims, such as for group relief, should be made as part of a return. If they are made later, they are technically an amendment to the return (see **15.8.2**). Group relief claims may be particularly relevant to a PSC because it is likely to make losses, see **13.7**; the rules for group relief are given in Sch 18, paras 66-77 FA 1998;

(d) Tax should be paid within nine months and one day following the company's year end (s59D TMA 1970), unless the company is 'large' when quarterly payments are required. This is unlikely to apply to a PSC;

(e) Losses should be included in the return in the same way as profits, and can equally be the subject of amendment and enquiry;

(f) There are penalties for submitting a late return (Sch 2, paras 17-19 FA 1998), for failing to keep documents (Sch 18, para 23 FA 1998), and for fraud or negligence, see **16.6.3** (Sch 18, para 89 FA 1998). Interest may also be charged (s87A TMA 1970);

(g) Enquiries can be made by the Revenue within twelve months following the filing date, unless the return was sent in late, in which case the enquiry deadline is extended (Sch 18, para 24 FA 1998). If there has been no enquiry within the time limit, the return will become final, subject to the rules for discovery, see **15.5.5** and Sch 18, para 42ff FA 1998;

(h) The usual time limit for an assessment is six years following the end of the accounting period, extended to 21 years in the case of fraud or negligence (Sch 18, para 46 FA 1998).

15.8.2 Implications for personal services

Interactions between the personal services legislation and CTSA occur in a number of areas, including amendments to the return, error or mistake claims, loss reliefs, changes of accounting date and double tax reliefs. In addition, the return may be selected for enquiry.

Amendments to the return

The company may amend its return within twelve months of the filing date. There is no official form for an amendment, and it is usually done by correspondence.

If the amendment is made after the normal filing date, the Revenue time limit for making an enquiry is extended. The new deadline is the quarter day following the first anniversary of the making of the amendment. The Revenue have confirmed that, in this situation, enquiries will be limited to the area of the return that was amended, see *Guide to Corporation Tax Self Assessment* paragraph **6.6.11**.

A personal service company may need to amend its CTSA return if it realises that it should have taken account of IR35, but did not do so. This is because the deemed Schedule E payment is deducted for corporation tax purposes 'for the period of account in which (it) is treated as made' (Sch 12, para 17(2) FA 2000). If there was a unrecognised obligation to make a deemed payment in an earlier accounting period, which is later acknowledged, it is understood that the deduction attaches to the corporation tax period in which the payment should have been 'made'.

Error or mistake

If the assessment needs to be corrected outside the time limit for amendments, an error or mistake claim may be possible. Again, this may be necessary if a

PSC has to make a late payment of PAYE on a deemed Schedule E amount following an employer compliance review. A claim must be made within six years of the end of the accounting period to which the error or mistake relates. This relief is not available in the case of an incorrect claim or election or where the original assessment was made in accordance with the practice generally prevailing at the time (Sch 18, para 51 FA 1998).

Loss reliefs

The PSC legislation may cause corporation tax losses, because the deemed Schedule E amount, together with any actual salary paid and the existing expenses, are likely to exceed the company's taxable profits, see **13.7**.

A claim to use these losses must be made within the appropriate time limits, see **13.7.2**. From the point of view of CTSA, a loss claim is regarded as an amendment to the return.

Change of accounting date

A company may wish to align its accounting date with the 5 April deemed payment date in order to ensure that tax relief is obtained, see **13.4.6**. A change of date:

- Will move the CTSA filing date and thus the date on which corporation tax is payable;

- May change the profits against which a later loss relief claim is carried back;

- Alters the time limits for claims and elections, so care is needed.

Double tax relief

Where work is carried out overseas, the service company may suffer foreign tax on its profits. A foreign tax authority may also withhold tax in respect of payments made to the company. Relief for any such foreign tax credits is normally given against the company's UK tax liability.

However, the Revenue have confirmed that:

> 'Where the company does not have sufficient UK tax liability to give full effect any such credit, but the worker does, then the balance may be allowed against the tax liability on the deemed payment. Relief can only be given where it is possible to directly link the work in the overseas country and the deemed payment.' (FAQ General 35)

How this will work is discussed in more detail at **17.10.2**.

Enquiries

Although it is anticipated that the enforcement of the company's PAYE requirements by the Revenue's Employer Compliance Unit is likely to be the main method by which personal service companies are investigated, see **16.9**, nevertheless CTSA enquiries may also lead to a review of the company's compliance with IR35.

Under CTSA the Revenue have 12 months from the company's filing date to open an enquiry into the return, and this date can be extended if the return is amended, see above. They do not have to justify an enquiry either by stating dissatisfaction with the return or by identifying particular aspects which have given cause for concern, and will not in fact give reasons for opening the enquiry, although they may identify particular areas of focus (*Guide to Corporation Tax Self Assessment*, pararaphs 6.1.12ff).

The Revenue's *Code of Practice into Company Tax Returns* (COP 14) says that:

'We carry out a comprehensive programme of checks. We look at information in the company's return and compare it with information we hold. Following these checks, if we think there is a risk the company return may be incorrect, or if we think something requires fuller explanation, we start enquiries. We also enquire into some returns at random.'

The return may be subject to an 'aspect' enquiry or a 'full' enquiry. An aspect enquiry may range from requests for clarification of particular entries, to detailed consideration of whether those entries have been treated correctly for tax purposes. In COP 14 the Revenue explain the scope of a full enquiry as follows:

'We may decide to conduct an extensive examination which considers all aspects of the company's tax affairs. Enquiries of this type will typically involve an in-depth review of the records on which the company's tax return was based. As part of this review we may ask for information relating to third parties, for example, directors or shareholders.'

The CTSA enquiry may thus lead into a separate Revenue investigation of the directors or shareholders. Conversely an SA enquiry may lead to a CTSA investigation. COP 14 says:

'We may need to keep enquiries into the company's tax return open where other enquiries (for example, into the directors' or shareholders' personal tax returns or tax returns of other companies) suggest that the company's tax return may not be correct. Where we need to do this we will tell you why we are not able to close the enquiry into the company's tax return.'

The Revenue's Investigation Handbook takes this one stage further, recommending that the CTSA inspectors 'arrange joint visits to business premises with Employer Compliance staff to examine business records'(IH 2334). This would allow the CT return to be checked along with the company's compliance with its PAYE and NIC obligations.

This indicates a high degree of connectivity between different Revenue investigating units. Inappropriate categorisation of personal services relevant income, or erroneous calculation of the deemed Schedule E amount could thus be unearthed by:

- CTSA enquiries into the company's returns;

- SA enquiries into the personal returns of the directors or shareholders; or

- An Employer Compliance Unit review of the PAYE, P11D, SLR and NIC returns.

16 Tax payments, penalties and investigations

16.1 Introduction

This chapter discusses the timing of tax and NIC payments on the deemed Schedule E amount. It also reviews the case law and legislation on penalties and interest, and discusses how penalties might be reduced or eliminated. It looks at whether, and to what extent, the Revenue may be able to pursue directors or workers for uncollected PAYE and NIC, and briefly covers Revenue investigations into intermediaries' compliance with the personal services rules.

16.2 PAYE and P11D administration

16.2.1 PAYE and NIC deductions

The aim of the PAYE system is that the tax deducted during the year should be, as far as possible, equal to that due on the worker's Schedule E income. The system operates via coding notices, which take account of expected salary, benefits, reliefs and allowances.

However, where a deemed payment is treated as made to a worker who had no previous Schedule E income, he will have no coding notice. This scenario is most likely to arise with partners who are only within the Schedule E rules by virtue of the personal services legislation. In this situation, the employer is advised to operate code BR, see *Employer's Quick Guide to PAYE Card 5*. The BR code deducts basic rate tax from the worker's deemed payment, and any overpayment or underpayment of tax is collected via self-assessment.

If a worker is on a week one/month one basis, and receives a large deemed payment on 5 April, this may cause an over-deduction of tax. Although this will be recovered in due course, the cashflow effect may be significant.

For NICs, personal service workers are on an annual earnings period, whether or not they are directors. The implications of this are discussed in **4.8.2**.

16.2.2 P11Ds

Most personal services workers other than partners will receive a P11D even when they have a deemed Schedule E payment. This is because amounts are excluded from the deemed Schedule E if they are otherwise taxable, either as:

*   *A benefit provided by the employer.* Where the intermediary provides a benefit for the worker, this is removed from the deemed Schedule E calculation by Step Seven. It will then be included on the P11D in the normal way;

*   *A benefit provided by the client by arrangement with the employer.* In the case of a one-man company, most benefits received from the client are commonly 'by arrangement with the employer' and thus fall to be taxed under the normal Schedule E rules. These amounts are not included in the deemed Schedule E calculation in the first place, see **10.5.4**. Instead, they are reported on the P11D.

Timing issues

The P11D deadline is 6 July following the end of the fiscal year. However, the tax and NIC on the deemed Schedule E calculation is due on or before 19 April. In order to calculate the deemed payment, the intermediary needs to know what amounts to exclude under Step Seven, i.e., items included on the individual's P11D. Similarly, the amount of Class 1A NIC on the P11D benefits is needed for Step Six.

Thus, if service companies wait until 6 July to determine the amounts to include on the P11D, they will delay completion of their deemed payment calculation; **16.4.2** below discusses the consequences of delay.

16.2.3 End of year returns

Forms P14 and P35 must be submitted by 19 May following the end of the tax year. The P14 shows earnings and various Class 1 NIC liabilities for each 'employed earner'. The P35 gives the total earnings and Class 1 NIC liabilities of the workforce. The deemed Schedule E amount is included on this return. See **16.4.2** for details of the Revenue requirements if the deadline cannot be met.

16.3 Timing of deemed Schedule E payment

16.3.1 Relevant events

The deemed Schedule E payment is in normal circumstances 'treated as made at the end of the tax year' (Sch 12, para 2(2) FA 2000). However the date is brought forward in some circumstances, known as 'relevant events'. These occur in the following situations:

- If a worker leaves his personal service company, or ceases to be a director of the company, the deemed Schedule E payment is treated as made on the day before he departs or ceases to be a director;

- If the intermediary is a partnership, and the worker leaves the partnership, the deemed Schedule E payment is treated as made on the day before he ceases to be a partner or employee;

- If the intermediary is a partnership and it is either dissolved or ceases to trade, the deemed Schedule E payment is treated as made on the day before the dissolution or cessation of trading.

If there is more than one relevant event in a tax year, the deemed payment is made on the earliest of them.

This acceleration of the deemed payment date means that the due date for PAYE and NICs is brought forward, see Example 15A.

Example 15A

Mike is a partner in a partnership supplying actuarial services. He is entitled to 65 per cent of the profits, and works 4 days a week at the firm's major client. The partnership received relevant income of £50,000 in the six months to October 2001 relating to Mike's work. Mike leaves the partnership on 8 October and becomes an employee of his client.

His deemed schedule E payment is treated as made on 7 October 2000. The PAYE and Class 1 NIC relating to it must therefore be paid by 19 November 2000.

16.3.2 Receipt of income after relevant event

The acceleration of the deemed payment date does not allow amounts to escape the personal service rules, for example because they have been received after the deemed Schedule E amount has been calculated. The legislation says that:

> 'The fact that the deemed Schedule E payment is treated as made before the end of the tax year does not affect what receipts and other matters are taken into account in calculating its amount.' (Sch 12, para 12(2) FA 2000)

A late receipt may thus cause interest and penalties to arise, see **16.5**, **16.6** and Example 15B. However in this situation it should be possible to argue that there was a reasonable excuse, see **16.7.3**, and that no penalty should be levied. Interest would however be due from 19 April, see **16.5**.

Example 15B

Mike's deemed schedule E payment of £16,000 was treated as made on 7 October 2000, and the PAYE and NIC relating to it was paid on 19 November 2000. However in May 2001 a further amount of £2,000 was received. The deemed Schedule E calculation is thus incorrect, and PAYE and NIC is overdue on the £2,000. Interest runs from 19 April 2001.

16.4 Payment of PAYE and Class 1 NICs

16.4.1 19 April payment deadline

The PAYE and NICs legislation and regulations apply to the deemed Schedule E amount (Sch 12, para 11 FA 2000; SI 2000 No 727 Reg 8). As a result, the PAYE and NIC relating to the deemed payment must be paid over by 19 April following the end of the tax year. However in practice this is an impossible deadline for most personal service businesses and their accountants – it is at best ten working days, and two of these are commonly Easter bank holidays.

The Revenue were asked to extend the payment deadline, either to 6 July in line with P11Ds, or to a date following each intermediary's accounting year end. But both were rejected on the grounds that they gave an additional cash flow advantage to those who worked via intermediaries rather than directly as employees of the client.

16.4.2 Concession on penalties

The Revenue did concede, however, that a provisional payment could be made at some time on or before 19 April – either during the tax year or following it, and the balance paid later. Although interest will be charged, there will be no penalties on the shortfall. The original guidelines suggested that:

'If you are not able to calculate the amount of tax and NICs due on the deemed payment by 19 April, you should make a provisional calculation, pay the tax and NICs based on that, and tell the Collector that this is what you have done . . . Interest will run from 19 April, but no penalties will be charged under Section 98A TMA if these procedures are complied with and the provisional calculations are done in good faith.' (FAQ Computation 7)

However this was felt to be too prescriptive, as in many cases the service company or partnership would not be in a position to make a best estimate by 19 April and so could not submit returns 'in good faith'.

The guideline was therefore amended and expanded by the revised FAQ, as follows:

'Most of the information needed to calculate the deemed payment should be available before 5 April, and it should be possible to make a good estimate of the tax and NICs due at that point. It will be important to keep records of relevant income and expenditure so that you can do this.

If you are not able to calculate the amount of tax and NICs due on the deemed payment by 19 April, we will accept a payment that date of a lower amount on account of the tax and NICs due, as long as the Revenue is notified on the Employer's Annual Return that the amount is provisional. This should mean that the worker need not necessarily consult his accountant before making the payment on 19 April.

You should submit your Employer's Annual Return (Form P35) by 19 May. If you are able at that time to finalise the calculation, you should show the correct figure and pay the difference or request a repayment. Otherwise, you should make it clear that the figure is still provisional.

You should seek to finalise matters as soon as possible thereafter, and send in a supplementary return with a final payment, or request for repayment.

Interest will be charged, calculated from 19 April when the original payment was due, but no penalties will be sought for late filing if:

(a) an Employer's Annual Return is received by 19 May, showing remuneration paid during the year, plus an amount on account of the deemed payment, with tax and NICs correctly calculated on the aggregate figure; and,

(b) a supplementary return including the correct final figure for the deemed payment is sent in to the Revenue by 31 January following the end of the tax year.'

In practice accountants should warn their personal service company and partnership clients that an interest charge is likely on the shortfall. Clearly this can be minimised by paying roughly the correct amount of salary on a monthly basis, see 13.5.3.

16.5 Interest

Where payment of the tax or NIC on the deemed payment is late, interest runs from 19 April (SI 1993 No 744 Reg 51 and SI 1979 No 591 Reg 28A(1)). As explained at **16.4.2** above, the late filing concession granted for the deemed payment extends only to penalties and not to interest.

Where the deemed payment has been accelerated because of a relevant event, see **16.3.1** above, there is no interest on late payment of PAYE or NICs until the 19 April following the relevant event.

16.6 Penalties

16.6.1 General

A range of penalties can be exacted for non-compliance with PAYE or NIC liabilities, from fixed monthly amounts to imprisonment and confiscation of assets.

However a personal service intermediary will not be liable to penalties if it is within the concession discussed at **16.4.2** above. In addition the intermediary may be able take advantage of the 'benefit of the doubt' approach described by Dawn Primarolo (see **16.7.2** below) or claim reasonable excuse (see **16.7.3**). If penalties are nevertheless due, mitigation may be possible (see **16.7.4**).

16.6.2 Fixed penalties

If the end of year return is not filed on 19 May, the Revenue can levy a fine of £100 for each month or part month for which the return is not filed, up to a maximum of 12 months. The penalties are greater where there are more than 50 employees, but this will not normally be the case in a personal service company or partnership. The same legislation applies where the end of year NIC return has not been filed, but where (as is generally the case) the same return covers both, there is only one penalty (Sch 1, para 7(3) SSCBA 1992).

If the failure continues beyond 12 months, there is an additional penalty not exceeding the tax that was unpaid 14 days after the end of the year to which the return relates (s98A(2)(b) TMA 1970). Where both tax and NIC are overdue, the maximum penalty equals the sum of the total tax and NIC unpaid (Sch 1, para 7(5) SSCBA 1992). Similar provisions apply to the end of year return in relation to student loan repayments (SI 2000 No 944 Reg 42(5)).

16.6.3 Fraud and negligence – generally

Fraud

The classic definition of fraud was given by Lord Herschell when he said that 'fraud is proven when it is shown that a false representation has been made knowingly, or without belief in its truth, or recklessly, careless whether it be true or false'. *Derry v Peek* [1889] 14 AC 337.

In their Investigations Handbook at paragraph 5010 the Revenue say:

> 'Fraud (in relation to the Revenue) includes, in its various forms, falsification with an intention to deceive and this may be present even as a mere conscious understatement in, or omission from, a return or accounts. Thus, the active intention to deceive may, on the one hand, be so slight that the falsification differs little from that resulting from carelessness or negligence. On the other hand, falsification may be deliberately planned with the clear intention of deceiving and cheating the Revenue by, for example, the omission, manipulation or invention of figures, or other records. This may require consideration by Special Compliance Office and even, possibly, the institution of criminal proceedings.'

Negligence

Negligence has been defined as 'the omission to do something which a prudent and reasonable man would do '(*Blyth v Birmingham Waterworks Co* [1856] 11 Ex 781). In the Revenue's view a reasonable man would, among other things:

- Comply with the requirements of the law by, for example, notifying his chargeability (see 15.2);
- Make, promptly, a complete and correct return of his income and gains when required to do so under statutory authority;
- Keep such records as are necessary to enable him to make accurate returns or prepare accurate accounts;
- Read carefully the notes supplied with the return form, so far as they affect his own circumstances;
- Seek professional help with matters, such as the preparation of accounts, which he is unable to cope with satisfactorily himself (IH 5050).

Establishing fraud or negligence

The onus is on the Revenue to establish the evidence for fraud or negligence, and in the recent case of *Rochester (UK) Ltd and another v Pickin* [1998] SSCD 138 it was held that:

- The standard of proof was the balance of probabilities; and

- The cogency of the evidence required to meet the standard of proof depends on the seriousness of the allegations.

However once the evidence has been established, the onus is on the taxpayer to prove his innocence. The earlier case of *Brady v Group Lotus Car Companies plc and Another* [1987] 60 TC 359 held that:

> 'The burden of proof, as distinct from the evidential burden, was through-out on Lotus to show that the assessments were wrong.'

The Revenue explain this as follows (where 'you' is a Revenue officer):

> 'Although the onus is always on you to demonstrate that there has been fraud or negligence, you will normally show that there has been an error or omission and that there is no known acceptable explanation. The onus will then be on the taxpayer to establish that the error was entirely innocent and involved neither fraud nor negligence: this is not an easy task.' (IH 5065)

If the area is highly technical (and the application of the personal service legislation may fall into this category) and the taxpayer is unrepresented by a professional adviser, he may succeed in claiming ignorance of the legislation, and thus be able to argue he was not negligent, see IH 5000.

Where a return is submitted by a professional adviser, the taxpayer nevertheless remains responsible and it is very difficult to argue that there has been no negligence. In the case of *Pleasants v Atkinson* [1987] 60 TC 228 an accountant submitted an incorrect computation on behalf of an architect. The court held that the while the architect had not been personally guilty of negligence, his accountant had committed a negligent act on his behalf.

16.6.4 Penalties for fraud or negligence

If an incorrect return has been submitted fraudulently or negligently, the maximum penalty is the difference between the amount payable under the return and the amount which would have been payable had the return been correct (s98A(4) TMA 1970).

Where NIC is unpaid as well as tax, a single penalty may be exacted up to the total of any tax and contributions remaining unpaid. This is because s98A TMA 1970 applies to NIC as it does to tax, by virtue of Sch 1, para 7 SSCBA 1992.

Finally, if student loan repayments, see **22.4**, have not been correctly deducted, the same penalty and interest provisions apply as for PAYE and NICs (SI 2000

No. 944 Regs 41 and 42). The maximum penalty is £3,000 per employee per year. This applies where 'an employer fraudulently or negligently (a) makes incorrect deductions; or (b) makes or receives incorrect payments in a year of assessment' (SI 2000 No 944 Reg 51).

If the service company incorrectly took the view that there had been no relevant engagements, this might be seen as negligent, leading to an assessment on the company for:

(a) Unpaid PAYE and NIC;

(b) A penalty which could equal the unpaid PAYE and NIC;

(c) Interest for late payment, see **16.5**;

(d) A fixed penalty for late payment, see **16.6.2** above;

(e) Any student loan repayments, plus interest and penalties.

The company may be able to reduce or eliminate any penalties, particularly in the early years of the personal service regime, see **16.7** below.

16.6.5 Criminal penalties for fraud or negligence

In addition to the specific fraud and negligence provisions in the Taxes Acts and the Social Security legislation, the Revenue can also call on sanctions contained within the criminal law. These are however rarely used: Statement of Practice 2/88 explains that the Revenue will usually seek a financial settlement and not a criminal prosecution. If a case does go to court, the standard of proof in a criminal case is much higher than where charges are brought under the civil law. It was held in *Hornal v Neuberger Products Ltd* [1957] 1 QB 247 that:

> 'A civil court, when considering a charge of fraud, will naturally require for itself a higher degree of probability than that which it would require when asking if negligence is established.'

The criminal sanctions are:

• The new offence of 'fraudulently evading income tax' introduced into FA 2000 at Report stage. This applies both to the taxpayer and any other individual who is 'knowingly concerned' in the fraudulent evasion, and takes effect from 1 January 2000;

• Section 5 of the Perjury Act 1911, for 'knowingly and wilfully' making materially false statements or returns for tax purposes, see for example the accountant referred to in the case of *Tudor and Onions v Ducker* [1924] 8

TC 591 who perjured himself giving evidence that the accounts he had prepared for his clients were correct, and was prosecuted;

- The common law offence of cheat, used in the recent cases of *R v Cunningham, Charlton, Wheeler & Kitchen* [1996] STC 1418, and *R v Dimsey and
  Allen* [1999] STC 846, which centred on offshore companies;

- The Theft Act 1978, see *R v Hiscox* [1978] 52 TC 497, which concerned
  forged subcontractor certificates, and *R v Downes* [1983] CLR 819, also a
  subcontractor case;

- Conspiracy to defraud, which was discussed but not used in the *Dimsey*
  case, and rejected by the judge in *N Ltd v H M Inspector of Taxes* [1996]
  SSCD 346;

- Section 6, Forgery Act 1913 which was also used in the case of *R v Hiscox*
  above.

16.7 Reducing the penalties

16.7.1 Summary

The intermediary can seek to reduce or eliminate the penalties by one or more
of the following routes:

- Using the 'benefit of the doubt' concession explained by Dawn Primarolo;
- Claiming 'reasonable excuse';
- Asking for the penalties to be mitigated.

These are explained below

16.7.2 Benefit of the doubt

In the House of Commons debate on IR35, Dawn Primarolo said that:

> 'Officials are to give the benefit of the doubt where businesses make genuine
> mistakes when trying to comply with the rules. This is only fair, given the
> change during this period. It is a light-touch approach. Of course, in the rare
> cases in which avoidance (*sic*) of tax and National Insurance liability is delib-
> erate and intended, the same compliance regime and penalties will apply as
> exist in the tax system for trying to avoid paying tax and National Insurance.'
> (*Hansard* 3 May 2000, pt 24 Col. 216)

The Minister's assurances are welcome. She has acknowledged that those
struggling to come to terms with the complexity of the new regime need

assistance rather than punishment. It is comforting to know that the full force of the penalty regime will not be invoked against them.

It should be noted, however, that the Minster spoke of 'avoidance', not 'evasion'. Where the taxpayer has actively sought to avoid the new regime, and has not succeeded – perhaps because the scheme he entered into was technically faulty, or because his substitution clause was found to be a sham, then the normal penalty rules will apply.

16.7.3 Reasonable excuse

The reasonable excuse legislation is contained in s118(2) TMA 1970, a text which demonstrates the need for the Tax Law Rewrite:

> 'For the purposes of this Act, a person shall be deemed not to have failed to do anything required to be done within a limited time if he did it within such further time, if any, as the Board or the Commissioners or officer concerned may have allowed; and where a person had a reasonable excuse for not doing anything required to be done he shall be deemed not to have failed to do it unless the excuse ceased and, after the excuse ceased, he shall be deemed not to have failed to do it if he did it without unreasonable delay after the excuse had ceased.'

The Revenue consider that 'reasonable excuse' is not an absolute:

> 'There are no absolute standards by which the words 'reasonable excuse' can be defined. Generally, it can be said to be an excuse which sounds reasonable in the mouth of the person giving it, that is, the standard of reasonableness can vary according to the type, education, background etc. of the taxpayer concerned.' (IH 5062)

They accept that the following are reasonable excuses (*Tax Bulletin 34*, April 1998):

- Where a cheque is dishonoured solely through bank error (and payment is made immediately after the taxpayer learned of the bank's action);

- Where a cheque is lost in the post or by the Revenue (although evidence may be required to show that every effort was made to pay by the due date);

- Serious illness of the taxpayer or a close relative or domestic partner which began shortly before the due date; or

- The death of a close relative or domestic partner at or around the due date.

Excuses not considered reasonable by the Revenue include:

- Pressure of work;

- Failure by a tax agent (see *Nunn v Gray* [1997] SSCD 175);

- Not knowing how much to pay; or

- The absence of a reminder that the tax is due.

However, if the taxpayer disagrees with the Revenue's interpretation and considers he does have a reasonable excuse, he can go to the Commissioners. In the recent case of *Akarimsons Ltd v Chapman* [1997] SSCD 140 the court cancelled a penalty and agreed that the taxpayer had a reasonable excuse for the late submission of a return because:

(a) The director and company secretary were seriously ill;

(b) 'The company secretary was confused by [the form] and…regarded its contents as ambiguous'; and

(c) As the judge said, 'the Revenue cannot escape responsibility for some of the muddle which occurred'.

In *Steeden v Carver* [1999] SSCD 283, the Commissioners accepted that a taxpayer who relied on the Revenue's advice concerning a time limit had 'as reasonable an excuse as could be found'.

16.7.4 Mitigation of penalties

The Revenue have complete discretion to mitigate or eliminate any penalty (s102 TMA 1970). However, for fixed penalties their normal practice is not to use these powers: if the taxpayer does not have a 'reasonable excuse' which takes him out of the penalty altogether, they will not mitigate at all.

In the case of tax-based penalties where a maximum penalty of 100 per cent could be exacted, their normal procedures are to start with the figure of 100 per cent and then take the following factors into account:

(a) *Disclosure.* A reduction of up to 20 per cent (or 30 per cent where there has been full voluntary disclosure), depending on how much information was provided, how soon, and how that contributed to settling the investigation;

(b) *Co-operation.* A reduction of up to 40 per cent, depending upon a comparison of the extent of co-operation given in the investigation with the co-operation which the inspector believes would have been possible. The Revenue view of co-operation in the context of a PAYE audit is as follows:

'If you supply information quickly, produce records when asked, answer questions honestly and accurately, and give all the relevant facts, you will get the maximum reduction for co-operation. If you put off supplying information or producing your records, give untrue answers to questions, do nothing until formal action is taken against you and generally obstruct the progress of the review you will get no reduction at all. Between these extremes, there is a wide range of possible circumstances.' (Revenue booklet 109)

(b) *Gravity*. A reduction of up to 40 per cent, depending upon the nature of the offence, how long it continued and the amounts involved (Revenue pamphlet IR 73).

16.8 Assessment and collection

16.8.1 Time limits for collection

In most cases there is a six-year time limit for collecting unpaid PAYE and NIC (s34 TMA 1970; SI 1993 No 744 Reg 49(7)). However this can be extended in the case of fraud or negligence to 20 years from 31 January after the year of assessment in which the fraud or neglect occurred (s36 TMA).

It would, however, be unusual for an assessment to be made outside the six year time limit unless there was a serious and culpable action or omission by the taxpayer. To extend the time limit the Revenue have to prove, on the balance of probabilities, that there was fraud or negligence, see *Rochester (UK) Ltd and another v Pickin* [1998] SSCD 138 (see **16.6.3** above) for a recent case in which they did not succeed.

16.8.2 Collection of unpaid tax and/or NICs from the worker or director

PAYE

If the company does not pay the amount assessed, for instance because it is insolvent, the Revenue may be able to pursue the individual worker or director for the uncollected tax under Regulations 42(3) and 49(5) of the Income Tax (Employments) Regulations 1993. These regulations allow the Revenue to collect the under-deduction from the employee, instead of from the employer. However they can only do this if they consider the employee received the payment of remuneration knowing that the employer's failure to operate the PAYE correctly was wilful.

However, at the time of writing (May 2000) it appears these regulations will not operate to catch underpayments of PAYE on deemed Schedule E amounts. Regulation 42 reads:

> '[Where] the Board are of the opinion that an employee has received his emoluments knowing that the employer has wilfully failed to deduct the amount of tax which he was liable to deduct under these Regulations from those emoluments, they may direct that the amount which they consider to constitute the excess . . . shall be recovered from the employee.' (SI 1993 No 744 Reg 42(3))

The wording of Reg 49(5) is similar. However, in the case of a deemed Schedule E payment, the employee has not *received* any emoluments, and no tax could therefore have been deducted from the emoluments. To be effective, the regulations would need to be amended to cover the non-payment of tax on deemed payments.

Since the policing of the personal services legislation depends in part on having the full panoply of powers available under the PAYE Regulations, an amendment is likely.

National Insurance contributions

The Revenue have powers to collect unpaid NICs from individuals as follows:

> '(Where) the body corporate has failed to pay the contributions at or within the time prescribed for the purpose; and the failure appears to the Inland Revenue to be attributable to fraud or neglect on the part of one or more individuals who, at the time of the fraud or neglect, were officers of the body corporate ("culpable officers"), the Inland Revenue may issue and serve on any culpable officer a notice . . . specifying the amount of the contributions to which this section applies . . . requiring the officer to pay . . . a specified sum in respect of that amount; and specified interest on that sum.' (s121C SSAA 1992)

> 'Where an offence under this Act . . . which has been committed by a body corporate is proved to have been committed with the consent or connivance of, or to be attributable to any neglect on the part of, a director, manager, secretary or other similar officer of the body corporate, or any person who was purporting to act in any such capacity, he, as well as the body corporate, shall be guilty of that offence and be liable to be proceeded against accordingly.' (s115 SSAA 1992)

These sections operate differently from the PAYE regulations, in that:

- The liability can be transferred to individuals if they are responsible for an offence against the Act, and thus the legislation should be effective in a situation where a service company has failed to apply IR35;

- Under the PAYE regulations an individual worker who has received emoluments can be required to pay the tax. Under the NICs regulations the liability attaches to the directors or other managers of the company;

- The NIC regulations allow interest to be collected from the responsible individuals; this is not currently possible under the PAYE regulations.

Since the personal services legislation is largely aimed at avoidance of NICs, these powers are more important than the equivalent PAYE regulations, and it may matter less that the latter appear ineffective.

In addition a new criminal offence of fraudulently evading NICs was introduced by the Social Security Act 1998 (s114A SSAA 1992) and took effect from 6 April 1999. The section is aimed at large scale and repeated evasion, and at directors of 'phoenix' companies, but it is wide enough to cover other situations. Directors caught under these provisions are liable not only for the debt outstanding, interest and penalties, but can also lose their homes and personal assets.

16.9 Investigations

It is understood that most of the responsibility for policing the personal service legislation will rest with the Revenue's employer compliance unit, see FAQ (General) 9:

> *What will happen if someone fails to follow the new rules?*
>
> Where the Inland Revenue discover the new rules have not been followed, they will follow the normal approach to cases of PAYE/NICs failure set out in Inland Revenue leaflet IR 109 – "Employer compliance reviews and negotiations".

The Employer Compliance Unit is likely to target intermediaries that have not applied the personal service legislation, in order to establish whether they are genuinely outside IR35. An investigation might be triggered because:

- A review indicates that very little PAYE was paid on a relatively high turnover;

- The Revenue are aware from other information that the company is potentially within the personal services regime;

295

- Data gathered from clients and agencies under s16 TMA 1970 as to the identity of intermediaries and amounts paid to them has been cross-checked to PAYE returns;

- A self-assessment enquiry into the worker's tax affairs, or a CTSA enquiry into the company's return, has led to questions about the company's compliance with the personal services regime, see **16.9**;

- The company is being checked as part of a regular cycle of audit visits.

In the context of IR35, it should be noted that the Revenue have access to the following information sources:

- The individual's own self assessment return, see **15.2**;

- The company's corporation tax return, for which the period of enquiry is likely to be longer than that for the SA return, see **15.8**;

- Information under the s16 TMA from agencies and clients, see **21.2.5**. This is already required in some industries, such as film and TV, see **20.10.2**;

- Information under the Oil Taxation Act from North Sea oil and gas operators, see **20.6.5**;

- Data received from overseas tax authorities under the exchange of information provisions within double tax treaties;

- Miscellaneous gossip supplied by neighbours and former friends.

17 Overseas implications – tax

17.1 General

17.1.1 Introduction

In the House of Commons debate on IR35, Mr Trend asked:

> 'How do the government think British businesses are going to adapt to the
> e-commerce revolution when the consultants who put those systems in place
> have left the country?' (*Hansard* 3 November 1999, Col. 414)

In saying this he was merely reflecting an oft-repeated threat that the skilled
people caught by IR35 would go overseas to avoid its impact. However, as
Robert Maas has aptly remarked:

> 'Emigration is . . . the ultimate form of tax avoidance . . . As a form of tax
> planning it ought therefore to be looked on as a last resort.' (*Tolleys Tax Plan-
> ning 1999*)

Some of those affected by the personal services legislation will nevertheless
seek to work abroad, hoping to find a more benign regime. However, they
must be aware of, and comply with, UK tax rules on residence and non-residence.

Parliament has also highlighted the interaction between personal services and
tax residence for those coming to the UK from overseas. Richard Ottaway,
speaking in the House on 3 May 2000, said:

> 'Would Laetitia Caster, the model chosen to represent the symbol of the
> French Republic, La Marianne, have come to the United Kingdom if she had
> known about IR35? She almost certainly works through a personal service
> company . . . It comes as no surprise that when she arrived and saw what was
> going on, she quickly announced that she would not be resident in the UK
> for tax purposes.' (*Hansard* 3 May 2000, Col. 185–6)

17.1.2 Outline and scope

This chapter looks first at the position of service company workers coming
here from overseas, and then at the consequences for those leaving the UK to
work abroad. It concludes with a brief note on partners.

International tax is complex, and this chapter only outlines the main issues from a UK tax perspective; detailed guidance should be sought in individual circumstances.

Different residence rules apply for capital gains tax, and these are outside the scope of this book. Special rules apply to EU officials and Crown servants, entertainers (20.2.6), sportspeople (20.7.3), oil workers (20.6.3) and mariners, and these are not covered in this chapter. National Insurance is dealt with in Chapter 18.

17.2 Residence and personal services

If an individual is within the personal services rules, he is subject to Schedule E tax. However the rules for Schedule E differ depending on the individual's residence, ordinary residence and domicile. Thus it is necessary to understand these concepts to know to what extent an individual falls within the personal services legislation, and whether its impact can be avoided or reduced.

Schedule 12, para 11(3) FA 2000 makes this link with the Schedule E residence rules explicit. It specifically excludes individuals from the scope of the personal service legislation:

> 'If, or to the extent that, by reason of any combination of the following factors –
>
> (a) the worker being resident, ordinarily resident or domiciled outside the United Kingdom,
>
> (b) the client being resident or ordinarily resident outside the United Kingdom, or
>
> (c) the services in question being provided outside the United Kingdom,
>
> he would not be chargeable to tax under Schedule E if the client employed the worker, the worker performed the services in the course of that employment, and the deemed Schedule E payment were a payment by the client of emoluments from that employment.'

In other words, if the rules for residence and domicile would have allowed a worker to escape Schedule E tax had he been an employee of his client, then he will also escape from IR35. This has important implications for individuals who are non-resident or not ordinarily resident in the UK, or who have a foreign domicile.

17.3 Definitions

Despite the fact that residence, ordinary residence and domicile are fundamental to an individual's UK tax liability, they are not defined in statute. Indeed, over 70 years ago Viscount Sumner warned that:

> 'The words "resident in the United Kingdom", "ordinarily" or otherwise, and the words "leaving the United Kingdom for the purpose only of occasional residence abroad", simple as they look, guide the subject remarkably little as to the limits within which he must pay and beyond which he is free. This is the more likely to be a subject of grievance and to provoke a sense of injustice when, as is now the case, the facility of communications, the fluid and restless character of social habits, and the pressure of taxation have made these intricate and doubtful questions of residence important and urgent.' (*Levene v CIR* [1928] 13 TC 48)

As a result of this lack of definition, questions of residence and domicile are mostly decided using a mixture of case law and Revenue practice. On occasion, such as in the case of *Reed v Clark* [1986] 58 TC 528 (see **17.9.3**), the Revenue may seek tax even where an individual has relied on their published guidance. Workers seeking to avoid liability to IR35 by using an overseas residence or non-domiciliary route are thus advised to take great care and not to cut corners.

17.4 Outline of the rules

The legislative basis for the income tax treatment of residence, ordinary residence and domicile is found in s19(1) ICTA 1988. This divides Schedule E into three sub-categories, Case I, Case II and Case III.

If a worker is resident, ordinarily resident and domiciled in the UK, he will be taxed under Case I on all his earnings, whether the work was carried out in the UK or overseas. All his engagements are thus potentially within the personal services rules.

On the other hand, he will escape Schedule E, and therefore the personal services rules, either wholly or partly in the following situations. If he is:

- Non-resident in the UK, he is not taxed on earnings from work carried out overseas. He is taxable under Case II of Schedule E in respect of relevant engagements carried out in the UK, but may be able to escape tax by arguing that his UK work is 'merely incidental' to his overseas engagements, see **17.8.2** below. Alternatively, he may be excluded from UK tax by a double tax treaty, see **17.8.3**;

- Resident, but not ordinarily resident, he is not taxed on earnings from engagements carried out overseas, as long as the earnings are not remitted to the UK. He is taxable on earnings from any UK relevant engagements under Case II of Schedule E, and under Case III on any remitted monies from the overseas work;

- Resident and ordinarily resident here, but not domiciled, he is within an exception to Case I. He will escape the personal services rules for work carried out wholly overseas for an overseas client, as long as the money is not remitted here. Money earned for work carried out overseas by a non-domiciliary is known as 'foreign emoluments'(see **17.12.3**; s19(1) ICTA 1988; FAQ General 35).

17.5 Coming to the UK from overseas

17.5.1 Residence

Outline

If an individual is non-resident he will be able to shelter all overseas earnings from the deemed income calculation; he may also be able to protect UK earnings by arguing that they are 'merely incidental' or covered by a double tax treaty, see **17.8.2** below. It is thus important that a personal services worker retain non-resident status for as long as possible, and does not accidentally become resident here.

This is possible, because the residence position of an individual who has come to the UK from overseas depends not only on how long he spends in this country but also on what his plans are. Care is therefore needed, as it is possible to accelerate UK residence and ordinary residence by an expression of intention, or by certain actions, such as the purchase of a house.

A further issue is that some residence rules take retrospective effect from the beginning of a fiscal year, so a change of status may bring money already earned into the scope of IR35.

The tax position of non-residents is discussed in more detail at **17.8** below.

Residence rules

An individual will be tax resident in the UK for a fiscal year if:

- He spends more than 183 days here, when he will be tax resident from the beginning of that fiscal year. Inland Revenue booklet IR20 states sternly that 'there are no exceptions to this.' However, if an individual is tax resident in two countries, he may be in the UK for more than 183 days and still be regarded as resident in the other country by virtue of a 'tie-breaker' clause in a double tax treaty;

- He owns a property here, or takes a lease on a property which is for three years or more. He will then be tax resident and ordinarily resident from the beginning of the year in which he buys or leases the property. However, if accommodation is the only factor which causes him to be classified as resident and ordinarily resident, and he disposes of the property and leaves the UK within three years, the status ruling may be reversed (SP 3/81; IR20, para 3.12);

- He arrives in the UK to take up permanent residence or to spend at least two years here. He is then resident from the date of arrival to the date of departure, provided that:

  'Prior to his arrival he was . . . not ordinarily resident in the UK. The concession would not apply, for example, where an individual who had been ordinarily resident in the UK left for intended permanent residence abroad but returned to reside here before the end of the tax year following the tax year of departure.' (ESC A11)

- He is in the UK for 90 days a year, on average, over a four-year period. He will then be both resident and ordinarily resident from the beginning of the fifth fiscal year. If he decides, before the end of the four year period, that he will spend an average of 90 days a year here, he will be resident and ordinarily resident from the beginning of the fiscal year in which he formed that intention, providing he carries it out. (*Reid v CIR* [1926] 10 TC 673; *Levene v CIR* [1928] 13 TC 48; IM 40).

These possibilities are summarised in Table 17.1. It should be noted that where an individual has been classified as resident and/or ordinarily resident on the basis of his intentions, and these change, his residence status can be reversed.

17.5.2 Ordinary residence

Definition

In addition to residence, the legislation also contains a second concept: ordinary residence. This is also not defined in the Taxes Acts, but it suggests greater permanence than 'residence'. If an individual is resident year after year, he is ordinarily resident. In *Levene* Viscount Cave said that it 'connotes residence in a place with some degree of continuity and apart from accidental or temporary absences.' This was expanded by Lord Warrington in the same case, who held that:

'It is in my opinion impossible to restrict its connotation to it duration. A member of this House may well be said to be ordinarily resident in London during the Parliamentary session and in the country during the recess. If it has any definite meaning I should say it means according to the way in which a man's life is usually ordered.'

An individual may be resident but not ordinarily resident here in a fiscal year. The Revenue consider that the converse is possible, so a person may be ordinarily resident without being resident. This might be, for example, because he usually lives in the UK but is absent on an extended holiday throughout a tax year (IR20, para 1.3). However Viscount Cave in *Levene* expressed doubt about this, saying that 'I find it difficult to imagine a case in which a man while not resident here is yet ordinarily resident here.'

Table 17.1 **Residence in the UK**

Individual's position	Resident from	Other points
In UK for 183 days or more in a tax year.	Beginning of that tax year.	Double tax treaty may make him resident in another country under tie-breaker test.
Purchases a house or takes a lease for three years or more.	The beginning of the fiscal year in which the property was acquired.	Will also be ordinarily resident. Status may be reversed if disposes of the property and leaves UK within three years.
Plans to spend more than 90 days p.a. in UK over a four-year period.	From beginning of tax year when he made the decision.	Will also be ordinarily resident. Status can be reversed if doesn't stay in the UK as planned.
Spends more than 90 days p.a. in the UK over a four-year period.	From beginning of fifth tax year.	Will also be ordinarily resident.
Plans to live in the UK for at least two years.	From date of arrival to date of departure, subject to meeting ESC A11 conditions.	

Importance of ordinary residence

If a worker can establish that he is not ordinarily resident in the UK, any earnings from work carried out overseas is not within Schedule E, unless it is remitted here. In the context of the personal services regime, this means that earnings received by a service company for work carried out wholly overseas will not be included in the deemed income computation, provided it is not brought into the UK. For an explanation of the remittance basis, see **17.13** below. If the money is subsequently remitted, a deemed income calculation needs to be performed, see **17.13.5** below.

As with residence, it is possible to accelerate a determination of ordinary residence by behaviour (such as the acquisition of a property) or by declared intention, see below. A personal services worker with overseas engagements should endeavour to remain not ordinarily resident for as long as possible, in order to shelter his foreign income from IR35. Examples of residence and ordinary residence determinations are given at **17.5.3** below.

Determining ordinary residence

An individual will be regarded as ordinarily resident on the earliest of the following events:

- Buying a house here, or taking a lease of at least three years;

- Deciding to remain in the UK. The Revenue say that an individual remains in the UK if he is 'here on a continuing basis and any departures are for holidays or short business trips' (IR20 para 3.1);

- Making regular visits here averaging 90 days a year over a four-year period, or intending to make such visits.

This is set out in Table 17.2, which is based on SP 17/91 and IR20.

Table 17.2 **Ordinary residence**

Individual's position	*Ordinarily resident from*
Purchases a house or takes a lease for three years or more.	The beginning of the fiscal year in which the property was acquired. Residence status may be reversed if property is disposed of and the individual leaves within three years.
Decides to stay in the UK for at least three years, counting from date of arrival.	Beginning of the fiscal year in which the decision was made.
Stays in the UK for more than three years	Beginning of the fourth fiscal year.
Plans to spends more than 90 days here each fiscal year, on average over a four year period.	Beginning of fiscal year in which the decision was made.
Spends more than 90 days here each fiscal year, on average, over a four-year period.	Beginning of the fifth fiscal year.

17.5.3 Examples of residence and ordinary residence determinations

The following examples (based on IR20 paras 3.3, 3.5 and 3.10) show how these rules are applied:

> ### Example 17A
>
> (a) Mwangi first came to the UK during 1999-2000, and intended visiting regularly until at least 5 April 2003. His visits average at least 91 days a tax year. He is resident and ordinarily resident from 6 April 1999, assuming he carries out his intention;
>
> (b) Svetlana came to the UK with no definite intentions, but visited regularly during the tax years 1999–2000 to 2002-2003 and her visits average at least 91 days a tax year. She is resident and ordinarily resident from 6 April 2003;
>
> (c) Xiao Liu first came to the UK during 1999–2000 with no definite intentions; she came again in 2000–2001 and 2001–2002; during 2001-2002 she decides she will come regularly in future years, and her visits will average at least 91 days a tax year. She is resident and ordinarily resident from 6 April 2001, assuming that she carries out her intention;
>
> (d) Duke came to the UK to work on 14 July 1999 on a two-year contract, but in December 2001 his contract was extended until after July 2002. He is resident and ordinarily resident from 6 April 2001.

17.6 Counting the days

In deciding whether an individual is resident or ordinarily resident, the number of days spent in this country are significant. The normal rule is that days of arrival in and departure from the UK are ignored (IM 50; IR20 para 1.2). However:

- This is concessional: the legislation imposes a liability to tax if the individual is in the UK during the fiscal year, see *Mitchell v CIR* [1951] 33 TC 53 and *Neubergh v CIR* [1977] 52 TC 79;

- There is authority in case law for a stricter hourly basis (*Wilkie v CIR* [1951] 32 TC 495). It is thus prudent to ensure that the taxpayer is not dependent solely on carefully monitoring his days of arrival and departure to obtain non-resident or not ordinarily resident status;

- In the case of *R v Inspector of Taxes (ex p. Fulford-Dobson)* [1987] 60 TC 168 the taxpayer relied on the split year concession relating to capital gains tax (ESC D2), but was defeated. This was because his admitted intention was to go overseas to avoid CGT, and (as stated inside the front cover of Revenue pamphlet IR1, which lists the Extra Statutory Concessions in operation), a 'concession will not be given in any case where an attempt is made to use it for tax avoidance'.

- This rule about days of arrival and departure is not relevant to the concessionary split year treatment under ESC A11, see **17.5.1**; **17.9.2** and **17.9.4**;

- Any days spent in the UK for exceptional circumstances beyond the taxpayer's control, for example because of illness, are not normally counted for the purpose of establishing the number of days in the United Kingdom (SP2/91; IR20 para 2.2).

Useful worked examples demonstrating how to calculate the days in the UK are given in IR20 at paragraphs 2.10 and 3.6.

17.7 Procedure for establishing residence status

17.7.1 Introduction

It is no longer possible to obtain a formal Revenue ruling on a worker's residence status. The UK has a self-assessment system, and individuals must now self-assess their status. It is recommended that those arriving in the UK also complete Form P86 – the Arrival Questionnaire.

Great care must be taken when completing either P86 or the self-assessment form, as statements made about the worker's intentions may be difficult to rebut at a later stage.

17.7.2 Form P86 – arrival questionnaire

Form P86 settles the individual's residence status at a practical level: when it is received by the Inland Revenue, they use the information provided to produce an accurate PAYE code. This may prevent overpayments of PAYE during the tax year of arrival.

Where worker is within the personal services regime, obtaining a correct code may be particularly important, as the PAYE on the deemed Schedule E amount will be due in one lump sum. An incorrect coding may thus cause cashflow issues.

However the P86 process does not amount to a ruling. Inspectors are advised that 'the information given on form P86 should therefore be taken at face value without further enquiry wherever possible. Speculative enquiries should be avoided' (EPM 8089).

17.7.3 Self-assessment form

Individuals certify their residence status and domicile as part of their self-assessment (SA) return. If an individual wants to claim he is non-resident, not ordinarily resident or not domiciled, and this affects the tax he has to pay, he will need to complete the non-residence pages NR1 and NR2 and submit these as part of his SA tax return. Additionally, where double tax relief is sought, further forms are generated through the supplementary non-residence pages.

If, following receipt of a SA return submitted by a personal services worker, the Revenue open an enquiry into his residence status, it is recommended that he supplies the Revenue with a copy of his contract along with any other information from the client or agent which indicates the intended length of his UK assignment, or otherwise supports his position. See also 17.11.5 and 15.3.8.

17.8 Non-residents

17.8.1 Outline

An individual will be non-resident in the UK if he is here for less than 183 days in the tax year, and doesn't fall within any of the other tests for residence set out at **17.5.1** above.

The fact that an individual is treated as non-resident for tax purposes does not, however, necessarily mean that he has no liability to tax (s19(1) ICTA 1988). A non-resident can be taxed on work carried out in the UK, unless either:

- The work is 'merely incidental' to the work done abroad (s132 ICTA 1988), see **17.8.2** below; or

- It is covered by a double tax treaty, see **17.8.3**.

If the work carried out in the UK by the worker is neither merely incidental, nor covered by a tax treaty, he will be within the scope of the personal services legislation for his UK-based work, assuming that the contract was a 'relevant engagement'.

17.8.2 'Merely incidental'

The words 'merely incidental' are not defined in the Taxes Acts, but it has been said:

> 'The words "merely incidental" are . . . apt to denote an activity . . . which does not serve any independent purpose but is carried out in order to further some other purpose.'(*Robson v Dixon* [1972] 48 TC 527)

The Revenue view of 'merely incidental' is as follows (the author's italics):

'To determine whether work done in the United Kingdom is "merely incidental", you need to know the nature of both that work and the work done overseas. If the work done in the United Kingdom is subservient or ancillary to that done overseas, or if it is of a subordinate nature, it should be taken as being "merely incidental". If, on the other hand, the work done in the United Kingdom is of *the same kind* as that done overseas, or *if not the same it is of equal importance*, it will not be "merely incidental".' (SE 5052/SE 40203)

In the *Robson v Dixon* case quoted above, a pilot flew aircraft from Amsterdam to various parts of the world, rarely taking off or landing in the United Kingdom. He failed in his claim that his visits to the UK were merely incidental because they were so few in number. The case proved that the test is one of quality, not quantity: it is the nature of the duties performed in the UK, not the time spent on them, which matters.

Having said this, the Revenue do not accept that work done here can be merely incidental if 'the employee works in the United Kingdom for more than three months in a year' (IR20 para 6.7). They also give the following examples of whether work done by a non-resident will be regarded as 'merely incidental':

(a) An overseas representative of a United Kingdom employer, while on visits to the United Kingdom, which total less than three months in a year, does nothing more than report on trade conditions and results in his area, consult his employer on questions of policy, or receive instructions, or collect samples in preparation for his next tour. The duties he performs in the United Kingdom should be regarded as merely incidental;

(b) An overseas employee visits the United Kingdom for periods of training which do not exceed three months in the year. If he does no productive work while he is in the United Kingdom, the duties performed here are regarded as merely incidental;

(c) A company director, although usually working abroad, attends directors' meetings in the United Kingdom. That activity is basic to the joint duty of a board of directors to manage the company and therefore cannot be incidental to work done overseas;

(d) A courier visits many countries in the course of his work. Visits to the United Kingdom, however few and however short, are of the same importance to his job as visits to other countries and therefore cannot be incidental.

Where an individual operates through his own service company, the same tests should be applied in relation to the work done for an overseas client. A personal service worker who would meet the 'merely incidental' test if he were employed by his client, will thus fall outside the scope of UK tax and will not be within the PSC regime.

Using the Revenue examples, a non-resident individual who is contracted to work for an overseas company, and is sent by the client to report on trade conditions in the UK, would fall into the same category as the employee in (1) above; a contractor sent here by his client only for training would fall within (2) above.

Example (3) demonstrates that it is difficult to argue that work done by a director is 'merely incidental'. However, where a director of a service company is in the UK to carry out work for a client, and the work would have been 'merely incidental' if carried out by an employee of that client, he will be able to meet the test.

17.8.3 Double tax treaties

The UK has over 100 double tax treaties with different territories. They are not identical, and the relevant treaty must be reviewed in order to see which provisions apply in any particular case.

Having said this, standard OECD articles are found in most treaties. The article relating to 'dependent personal services' is of most relevance to the personal services worker. It states that where work is carried out in the UK by an individual from a treaty state (other than an entertainer or sportsman, see **20.2** and **20.7**) he escapes taxation in the UK if he fulfils all four of the following conditions:

(a) He is not tax resident in the UK; and

(b) He is present in the UK for not more than 183 days in any continuous period of twelve months; and

(c) His remuneration is paid by an employer who is not a resident of the UK; and

(d) His remuneration is not borne by a permanent establishment or fixed base which the employer has in the UK.

In the context of the personal services legislation, the worker needs to establish that he would meet the four tests above, if he were an employee of his client. Note that the 'presence in the UK' test in (b) refers to any 12-month period, not a calendar year or a fiscal year.

It should usually be easy enough to decide whether tests (a) to (c) are satisfied; (d) may sometimes be more problematic. The reason for this requirement was set out *Tax Bulletin 17*, June 1995 as applying where:

> 'A formal contract of employment remains with the overseas employer, but the employee works in the business of the United Kingdom company, which obtains the benefits and bears any risks in relation to the work undertaken by the employee. In economic terms this state of affairs is recognised by the overseas employer recharging the cost of the employee's remuneration to the United Kingdom and the UK company might be described as the "economic employer".'

The Revenue have confirmed that they do not allow the treaty relief to operate where an employee's true 'economic' employer is in this country. It is thus important that the worker discovers whether his costs are being recharged to the UK.

If his costs are recharged, he may still qualify for exemption from the PSC rules, as the Revenue have said that they will not apply the 'economic employer' test where:

* The employee is in the United Kingdom for less than 60 days in a tax year; and

* That period does not form part of a more substantial period of time for which the taxpayer is present in the United Kingdom (*Tax Bulletin* 25 October 1996).

17.8.4 Apportionment of income

Where a non-resident worker does not satisfy the merely incidental test, and cannot claim double tax relief, he will be taxable on earnings from his UK work. This means that he will fall partly within and partly outside the UK tax system.

Thus a non-resident personal services worker who takes up a contract with an overseas client involving some UK work may find that his service company is required to carry out a deemed income calculation in relation to that UK work. For the responsibility of the company in this respect, see Chapter 19.

When dividing earnings between those taxable here and those taxable abroad, the Revenue normally accept that this should be on a time-apportioned basis, see SP 5/84 and **17.13** below. This time-apportioned basis will, however, not be accepted if there are special facts, for instance where it is clear that more income relates to the UK work than to the work carried out overseas. Dual contracts are an alternative, see **17.8.5** below.

17.8.5 Dual contracts for non-residents

Dual contracts are an alternative to apportionment, and, as discussed at **17.12.4** below, also shelter overseas income when the apportionment option is not available. In the context of the personal services legislation, the existence of separate contracts for UK and overseas work may simplify the administration, and make it less likely that the amounts brought into the deemed Schedule E computation will be challenged, see **16.9**.

However it is important that the contracts are sound. For example:

(a) The UK contract and the overseas contract should be with separate clients, such as the UK subsidiary and the French parent company;

(b) Separate invoices should be submitted for each engagement;

(c) Records of expenses and capital expenditure related to each contract should be kept;

(d) The duties to be carried out for each client should be distinguishable;

(e) The amount charged for each engagement should be commercially sustainable. Attempts to 'load' the overseas contract are likely to be carefully examined.

17.8.6 Tax allowances for non-residents

If a worker is non-resident, he is nevertheless entitled to a full UK personal allowance if he is a Commonwealth or EU citizen, or comes into another approved category, see IR20 para 7.3. He can thus reduce the UK tax liability on his personal services income (and other UK source income) by offsetting it against the personal allowance.

Non-residents who are not domiciled in the UK, and who meet certain other requirements, can obtain tax relief for travel to the UK by family members, see **17.12.4** below.

17.8.7 Tax treatment of dividends received by non-resident personal services worker

If an individual is non-resident, he is not normally entitled to recover the tax credit on any dividend paid to him by a UK-based personal service company,

310

unless this is permitted under the terms of a double tax treaty. However, he is also not subject to UK tax on the dividend (s233 ICTA 1988). Thus there should be no need to invoke the double tax clause in the personal services legislation, see **13.6.2**. There may, however, be overseas tax implications: the overseas fiscal authorities may seek to tax the dividend even though the underlying income has already been included in the deemed Schedule E calculation. If this is the position, the worker should extract his money from the company by salary, not by a dividend, see Chapter 13.

17.9 Working overseas

17.9.1 Introduction

Contractors are a mobile workforce, and many already operate outside the UK. IR35 may now persuade others who have lived in the UK all their life to move abroad and seek overseas contracts in order to avoid the deemed Schedule E charge.

To be non-resident in the UK a personal services worker must:

(a) Work abroad for a fiscal year; or

(b) Not set foot in the UK for a fiscal year; or

(c) Take up permanent residence abroad.

These are discussed below.

17.9.2 Full time contract of service abroad

The Revenue practice is to accept that an individual has become non-resident if he goes abroad for full-time service under a contract of employment and:

• All the duties of his employment are performed abroad (or any he performs here are incidental to his duties abroad); and

• His absence from the UK in the employment is for a period which includes a complete tax year; and

• Interim visits to the UK do not amount to six months or more in any one tax year or three months or more on average.

The period of non-residence for income tax purposes begins the day following the date of his departure until the day preceding the date of his return, providing he was in the UK as a resident and not a short-term visitor (ESC A11; IR20, paras 1.6 and 2.2).

An individual who satisfies the 'full time service under a contract of employment' test can therefore achieve non-residence status if he is away for at least a complete tax year, and his return visits are kept within the specified limits.

Clearly personal service workers with their own companies can give themselves a contract of employment which requires them to be overseas for a fiscal year. However this is unlikely on its own to amount to 'full time service'. The Revenue gave guidance on what they see as 'full time' in *Revenue Interpretation (RI) 40*, as follows:

'There is no statutory definition of "full-time" in this context, nor any guidance from the courts. The phrase can only therefore be interpreted in accordance with its ordinary, non-technical meaning. Where an individual is working "full-time" in an employment will always depend upon the particular facts of the case.

In general terms, where a job involves a standard pattern of hours and an individual is putting in what a layman would clearly recognise as a full working week, [the Revenue] would accept it as full-time. There is no fixed minimum number of hours for this purpose, but 35–40 hours is obviously a typical UK working week.

Some jobs, however, do not have a straightforward structure. There may, for example, be a mixture of round-the-clock working followed by a rest period; or, in the case of sportsmen, days of playing and training interspersed. Some jobs may not have a formal structure with any fixed number of working days. In deciding whether such jobs are full-time employments, [the Revenue] would look at the nature of the job, and, where appropriate, would take account of local conditions and practices in that particular occupation. Someone who had several part-time jobs overseas concurrently might also be accepted as being in full-time employment. If, for example, they had several appointments with the same employer or group of companies, it might be reasonable to aggregate the total time spent on them for the purposes of the full-time test. This approach could also apply where an individual was simultaneously engaged in employment and self-employment abroad.

Where a person has a main employment abroad but also works in the UK in some unconnected occupation (for example, as director of a family company), [the Revenue] would need to consider whether the extent of the UK activities might cast any doubt on the full-time nature of the main employment outside the UK. Again, [the Revenue] would have to look at the facts of the particular case in reaching a decision.

In [the Revenue's] experience there is rarely in practice much difficulty in deciding whether an individual is working full-time. These notes indicate [their] general approach in the minority of cases at the margins where the position may be less clear.'

Thus if the personal service worker is carrying out a series of engagements overseas during a tax year, as the director/employee of his company, and these amount to working 'full time', then the criteria for non-UK residence will be satisfied. However, contractors should also be warned that:

'If there is a break in full-time employment, or some other change in your circumstances during the period you are overseas, [the Revenue] would have to review the position to decide whether you still meet the conditions in paragraph 2.2. If at the end of one employment you returned temporarily to the UK, planning to go abroad again after a very short stay in this country, [the Revenue] may review your residence status in the light of all the circumstances of your employment abroad and your return to the UK.' (IR20 para 2.3)

Thus a return to the UK between contracts could jeopardise non-residence status, and the personal services worker should take this into account when planning holidays back home.

Accompanying spouses

If an individual satisfies the criteria set out in ESC A11, see **17.9.2** above, his spouse will also be treated as not resident and not ordinarily resident on a split year basis, if:

- The purpose of the trip was to join, or to accompany, the husband or wife who was working overseas; and

- The spouse satisfies the other conditions of ESC A11, apart from the requirement to be in full time employment overseas (ESC A78).

17.9.3 Out of the UK for a whole tax year

The Revenue have accepted that 'an individual who is not in the United Kingdom *at any time* during a particular tax year is not normally regarded as resident for that year' (IM 36).

However in the case of *Reed v Clark* [1986] 58 TC 528 the Revenue argued that this did not apply – no doubt relying on the phrase 'normally'. Although the case was found in favour of the taxpayer, there remains some risk of attack where the individual cannot satisfy the 'full-time working abroad test'.

Having said this, the Revenue's internal guidance states that Inspectors are prepared to give a final non-residence decision where an individual has not been in the UK for a whole tax year, see **17.9.5** below, and this should give some further comfort.

17.9.4 Permanent residence abroad

Where an individual has been resident in the UK and leaves to live abroad permanently, or for a period of at least three years, he will qualify for the split year concession, providing he is not ordinarily resident in the UK on his departure. He will thus be taxed as resident only up to the day he leaves the UK (ESC A11).

The same split year basis will apply if he can show that he has 'gone abroad for a settled purpose', has actually been out of the UK for a whole tax year, and has not visited the UK for more than 183 days in a tax year or 90 days on average (IR20 para 2.9).

In order to show that the individual has taken up permanent residence abroad, the following steps are helpful:

(a) Limiting visits to the UK, especially during the year of departure and the following three fiscal years. Ideally, there should be no visit at all in the tax year following departure. Visits in subsequent years should be as few as possible. It is unwise to return for the full 90 days each tax year, as the Revenue (despite the guidance) may take the view that the individual has remained resident;

(b) When visits to the UK are made, a record should be kept of the reasons for these visits to the UK in order to demonstrate that they were not part of the individual's normal pattern of life. For example, a visit to the UK because of illness (either of the individual or another person) would be regarded as a temporary purpose;

(c) The Inland Revenue's internal guidance seeks to establish whether the individual has a home overseas, and whether their former home here has been either sold or let. In seeking to establish an overseas residence, it is thus important to rent or buy a property as soon as possible, and it is advisable to make the UK property inaccessible, either by selling it, or by letting it, preferably for four years. The Inspector is invited to ask the would-be émigré if he 'has a reason for having accommodation for use in the United Kingdom which is consistent with the aim of permanent residence abroad' (IM 41; IR20 para 2.8);

(d) If, for commercial reasons (such as the provisions of the Assured Tenancy legislation), a shorter let is recommended by the estate agency, there should be some evidence – perhaps a letter to the agency – setting out the intention to make the property available for at least a four year period.

17.9.5 Procedures for obtaining non-residence status

When an individual leaves the UK, it is recommended that he submit a form P85 to the Revenue together with details of the departure and his intentions. The Inspector will either accept the position, or ask for further details. Once it has been accepted, it should be possible to rely on this, as long as the individual's circumstances do not change for the next three years, although it is not a formal ruling.

The Revenue's own guidance states that the claim to be non-resident:

> 'May be admitted on a provisional basis at the outset, with effect as from the day following the date of departure, if the grounds on which it is based are adequately proved; but in no circumstances can a final decision be made until the individual's absence from the United Kingdom has extended over a period which includes a full tax year.
>
> If adequate proof is not immediately available, a decision on the claim is postponed for up to three years from the date of departure, and the position is determined by reference to what has actually happened since the date of departure. During this period of up to three years, except for any complete year of absence, any claim in respect of allowances and reliefs due to a resident is granted provisionally.' (IM 41)

In addition to the P85 procedure, individuals may have to complete a self assessment form The procedures for this are discussed in Chapter 15.

17.9.6 Residence status abroad

When an individual goes to work abroad, he does not disappear, but enters another tax system. It is important that he receives proper advice on his tax liabilities and how they interact with UK taxes. This advice should be sought before he leaves the UK, as he could otherwise either miss some important planning points, or subject himself to double taxation.

17.10 UK residents working abroad

17.10.1 Tax basis

If an individual is UK resident, ordinarily resident and domiciled, he will be within the UK tax system, and thus the deemed income calculation, in respect of all his earnings, whether the work was carried out in the UK or overseas. Where his overseas earnings have suffered foreign tax, he may be able to claim relief against the PAYE on his deemed income calculation, see **17.10.1**; a deduction may also be available for the costs of travel by family members, see **17.10.3**.

17.10.2 Relief for overseas tax suffered

Where a PSC worker is UK resident but works overseas, and the income received by his service company has suffered overseas tax, the normal rule is that this tax should be deducted from the UK corporation tax due on the service company's profits.

However, in many cases the PSC will have no corporation tax liability, since the personal services legislation will create losses, see **13.7**. The Revenue addressed this point as follows:

> 'Where work is carried out overseas then the company may suffer foreign tax on its profits. A foreign tax authority may also withhold tax in respect of payments made to the company. Relief for any such foreign tax credits is normally given against the company's UK tax liability.
>
> However, where the company does not have sufficient UK tax liability to give full effect to any such credit, but the worker does, then the balance may be allowed against the tax liability on the deemed payment. Relief can only be given where it is possible to directly link the work in the overseas country and the deemed payment. Relief cannot be given against the National Insurance liability.
>
> Where it is considered that relief should be given in this way a claim should be made to the tax office dealing with the worker's tax affairs.' (FAQ General 35)

This concession is welcome and will help minimise double taxation suffered by those who use personal services companies. It is an extension and development of the existing practice which applies to entertainers and sports people, see **20.2.6**.

According to the FAQ, tax relief is only available against the income tax on the deemed payment if it cannot be relieved against the company's corporation tax liability. This raises the following issues:

(a) It will be necessary to know what the company's tax position will be in respect of the accounting period in which the foreign tax could be claimed, before claiming a reduction in the individual's income tax;

(b) If a company pays a lower amount of PAYE because it believed it would be able to offset the overseas tax against the income tax arising on the deemed payment, but subsequently this proves not to be the case, an interest charge will arise, see **16.5**;

(c) If the overseas tax *can* be offset against the company's liability, the rate of tax suffered in the company may be lower than that borne on the foreign source income, resulting in irrecoverable overseas tax.

17.10.3 Travel expenses

Where an individual is resident and ordinarily resident in the UK, and works overseas for a continuous period of at least 60 days, he can claim a deduction for the cost of two outward and return journeys by his spouse and any children under the age of 18 (ss193-4 ICTA 1988). The requirement that the 60 days be continuous is strictly enforced (SE 4615/34060). The sections also allow relief for the individual's travel costs, but these will generally escape tax under s198 ICTA 1988 in any event, see **11.6**.

In order to be allowable, the cost must actually be borne by the intermediary, though reimbursement of the expenses by the service company is sufficient for this condition to be met. These travel costs will be deducted under Step Three of the deemed income calculation, see **11.3.1**.

Relief is not available if the earnings are foreign emoluments (see **17.12.3**), and unlike the normal Schedule E travel rules, see **11.6**, there is no relief for any associated accommodation and subsistence.

17.11 Domicile

17.11.1 Concept of domicile

Tax law also includes a third concept, domicile. A person's domicile is the place he considers to be 'home'. An individual may leave the UK and spend his working life overseas, yet intend to retire in Tiverton. He thus still considers the UK to be his home, and is domiciled here. Equally a Jamaican who has worked in Birmingham since he was 18, but who intends to go back to the West Indies once he retires, remains domiciled there.

17.11.2 Domicile of origin

Each person begins life with a domicile of origin, which is normally the country where his father was domiciled at the time of the child's birth. If a child is illegitimate, it acquires the domicile of its mother. Domicile of origin never changes, unless the child is adopted, when he obtains the domicile of his adoptive father.

This is important, because it means that a person born here may still have a foreign domicile if his father had not abandoned his domicile of origin, see Example 17B.

Example 17B

Divya, a tax adviser with her own personal services company based in North London, was born in Kenya to parents of Indian origin. She came to the UK when she was a child. Her father had Indian domicile when she was born, and he did not abandon that domicile. Divya will not be domiciled in the UK, despite having lived here most of her life, providing she does not make the UK a domicile of choice, see **17.11.4** below.

17.11.3 Married women

Women who were married before 1 January 1994 acquired their husband's domicile, and they will have retained this unless the position has changed by the acquisition of a further domicile, or a revival of a domicile of origin.

17.11.4 Domicile of choice

From the age of 16, or on marriage if earlier, an individual can change his domicile of origin and acquire a domicile of choice. In order to establish a change of domicile, the individual has to prove that he intends to reside permanently in the new country, see for example *Udny v Udny* [1869] LR 1 Sc and Div App 441, *Plummer v CIR* [1987] 60 TC 452 and the recent case of *Mrs F and S2 (Personal Representatives of F deceased) v CIR* [2000] SSCD 1.

A domicile of choice is not easily achieved – radical action, such as changing nationality, severing ties with the home country, and buying property in the new territory, including a grave plot, are all recommended if an individual is serious about changing his domicile. In *Henderson v Henderson* [1965] 1 All ER 179, Sir Jocelyn Simon said that:

> 'To displace the domicile of origin in favour of the domicile of choice, the standard of proof goes beyond a mere balance of probabilities.'

Domicile is not the same as nationality, as was reinforced in the recent case of *Anderson (Anderson's Executor) v CIR* [1998] SSCD 43. The Special Commissioners held that there was:

> 'An inherent improbability in a 65-year-old Scotsman, who has lived in Scotland all his life, abandoning his roots and intending to acquire a domicile of choice in England.'

In contrast to residence and ordinary residence, an individual can only be domiciled in one territory at a time.

17.11.5 Procedure for establishing a change of domicile

It used to be possible for an individual to submit their arguments concerning a change of domicile, and ask the Revenue to rule on whether they had satisfied the tests. This is no longer the case.

Where an individual comes to the UK from overseas, he is advised to complete form P86 which also incorporates a section on domicile. This 'helps the Revenue to determine if domicile is relevant in computing the taxpayer's liability' (SE 5032/SE 41060).

Where domicile status is unclear from the information provided on the P86: for instance, if the individual was born in the UK but is claiming a domicile of choice elsewhere, he is likely to be sent a longer, more detailed form (DOM1). However, the fact that an individual has completed a P86 and a DOM 1 and sent it to the Revenue does not mean that they have accepted his claim, even if he has heard nothing further from them.

When the worker claiming to be non-domiciled comes to complete his self-assessment form, one of the questions is whether his domicile status has been examined in the last six years. If he answers 'no' to this question, the Revenue warn that this 'will prompt a review of an individual's domicile which may lead to the issue of a TMA 1970, s9A enquiry' (*Tax Bulletin 29*, June 1997).

However, if the claim to be non-domiciled does not affect the tax due, the Inspector will decline to examine the claim (IM 5032).

Non-domiciled status will be agreed without further investigation by the Revenue if *all* the following are satisfied:

- The claimant was born outside the United Kingdom;

- The claimant's father was domiciled outside the United Kingdom at the time of his/her birth;

- The claimant came to the United Kingdom for the purpose only of an employment and intends to resume residence abroad on the cessation of that employment (IM 5032).

17.12 Consequences of being non-domiciled

17.12.1 Tax advantages

Being non-domiciled in the UK has important income tax implications for those within the personal services regime. This is because a non-domiciliary is not taxed in the UK on work done overseas for an overseas employer unless he remits the money earned (the 'foreign emoluments') to the UK (s192(2) ICTA 1988).

Note that this is a narrower definition of the remittance basis than that which applies to those who are not ordinarily resident, see **17.5.2**. The non-domiciliary is only within the remittance basis if the work has been carried out abroad for an overseas employer; the individual who is not ordinarily resident is within the remittance basis in respect of all work carried out overseas, see **17.13** below.

In addition, being non-domiciled can have major inheritance tax advantages, but these are outside the scope of this book.

17.12.2 Personal services implications of being non-domiciled

The legislation, quoted in full at **17.2** above, indicates that a worker will not be taxed on his overseas earnings if he:

> 'Would not be chargeable to tax under Schedule E if the client employed the worker, the worker performed the services in the course of that employment, and the deemed Schedule E payment were a payment by the client of emoluments from that employment.'

Thus if a personal service worker can establish that he is not domiciled here, and is working wholly overseas for a client who is 'resident outside, and not resident in' the UK, he can exclude from IR35 money received by the service company as long as it is not remitted here. Considerable care is needed with regard to what constitutes a 'remittance', see **17.13** below. If the money is subsequently remitted, a deemed income calculation needs to be performed, see **17.13.5** below.

17.12.3 Foreign emoluments

The following points should be noted as regards the definition of foreign emoluments:

(a) To qualify for the exemption, the duties must be performed 'wholly' outside the UK, apart from duties which are 'incidental' to the work done overseas. The concept of merely incidental is discussed at **17.8.2**;

(b) If some of the work is to be performed in the UK and some overseas, then two separate contracts should be considered, see below;

(c) Earnings from the Republic of Ireland are not foreign emoluments (s192(1) ICTA 1988), see **17.13.6**;

(d) If the overseas concern has a branch or agency in the UK, it could be argued that it does not satisfy the condition of being 'resident outside, and not resident in, the United Kingdom'. However the Revenue do not take this point, see SE 5013/SE 41010;

(e) Where the overseas concern is a branch or agency of a UK company, the payment however will be from a company which is resident in the UK. Amounts received from the branch or agency are thus not foreign emoluments. However, where the client is an overseas *subsidiary* of a UK company, it is not resident here, and thus the emoluments qualify for the exemption;

(f) Where a worker is engaged by an overseas client, he should endeavour to establish the residence status of his engager in order to determine whether the amounts paid into his service company can escape the deemed Schedule E computation. The question of a company's tax residence is discussed at **19.2**;

(g) It is worth noting that Inspectors are instructed as follows:

> 'If the emoluments do not fall within Case I . . . this might mean there is a big reduction in the amount chargeable, so you should examine the facts closely before accepting that emoluments fall within (the foreign emoluments) exception. In particular you should find out whether the employer has any place of business in the United Kingdom. If you can trace an accounts file for the employer, ask the accounts Inspector for instructions on the employer's residence status.

Dual contracts

Where an individual works for a UK client partly here and partly abroad, apportionment will not protect the earnings for the work carried out overseas. It may be possible to have two contracts, so that one of them falls within the rules for foreign emoluments, see **17.12.3**. However if the engagements are 'associated', relief may be restricted to that which is:

> 'Reasonable having regard to the nature of and time devoted to the duties performed outside and in the United Kingdom respectively and to all other relevant circumstances.' (Sch 12, para 2 ICTA 1988)

'Associated' is defined in s416 ICTA 1988, and includes companies one of which controls the other, or where both are under common control. Thus an attempt to split a contract with, say, a multinational, so that the amounts charged to the overseas subsidiary are much higher than those charged to the UK company, are likely to fail.

Dual contracts are discussed in the context of non-residence at **17.8.5** above.

17.12.4 Travel expenses

If a worker within the scope of the personal services rules is non-domiciled, he may be able to claim travel expenses in relation to journeys to the UK under s195 ICTA 1988. The main benefit of these rules is that they give relief for travel by members of the individual's family, as well as for journeys made by the worker himself. The latter would be allowable in any event under the travel rules set out in **11.6**. To qualify for the relief, the following conditions must exist:

- The worker must be non-domiciled and satisfy the requirements set out at (a) and (b) below;
- He must be taxable under Schedule E in respect of duties performed in the United Kingdom;
- The travel expenses must be borne by the intermediary, not by the individual.

The journeys relieved must be those:

- From his usual place of abode to any place in the United Kingdom in order to perform duties there, and the return journeys; and/or
- If he is in the United Kingdom for a continuous period of 60 days or more to perform duties, journeys undertaken by his spouse or child (under 18) to accompany or visit him in the UK. This is limited to two outward and two return journeys for any one individual in any one tax year;
- Unlike the normal travel rules, see **11.6**, there is no relief for any associated accommodation and subsistence.

Thus a personal service worker who was in the UK for a relevant engagement of at least 60 days could deduct from his deemed income calculation the costs of his spouse or children accompanying him, or coming to visit him in the UK. The cost must actually be borne by the intermediary, though reimbursement by the service company is sufficient for this condition to be met. The expenses are deducted at Step Three of the deemed income calculation, see **11.3.1**.

Relief is available under these rules for a period of five years from the date of the employee's arrival in the United Kingdom, provided that:

(a) He was not resident in the United Kingdom in either of the two years of assessment immediately preceding the year of assessment in which he arrived; or

(b) He was not in the United Kingdom for any purpose at any time during the period of two years ending with the day immediately preceding the day of arrival. In practice the Revenue usually accept that attendance at interview in order to obtain the engagement does not disqualify the worker.

17.13 Remittance basis

17.13.1 Outline of issues

Workers with a foreign domicile, and those who are not ordinarily resident in the UK, are on the remittance basis. A number of issues arise:

(a) There is a difference between the remittance basis for those not ordinarily resident and that applied to non-domiciliaries, see **17.13.2**;

(b) Care is needed where money is remitted out of 'mixed funds', only part of which derive from overseas earnings, see **17.13.3**;

(c) Ensuring that earnings are not remitted is complex; it is relatively easy to transfer funds to the UK inadvertently, see **17.13.4**;

(d) The remittance basis also gives rise to certain calculation issues for corporation tax and partnership tax computations, see **17.13.5**;

(e) Work carried out in the Republic of Ireland is not regarded as overseas for the purpose of the remittance basis, see **17.13.6**.

17.13.2 Meaning of remittance

Although both non-domiciliaries and those who are not ordinarily resident in the UK are on a remittance basis, the rules are not the same.

The Schedule E earnings of non-domiciliaries only qualify for the remittance basis if they are 'foreign emoluments', see **17.12.3**. They must thus be from an overseas employer and relate to work carried out wholly overseas. In the personal services context, this means that the client must be overseas and the work wholly overseas.

In contrast, the personal services worker who is not ordinarily resident in the UK can protect foreign earnings whether or not they are paid by an overseas client, and there is no requirement for the work to be carried out wholly overseas: the part relating to the overseas work can be sheltered from IR35 as long as it is not remitted here.

17.13.3 Remittances out of mixed funds

The Revenue take a different approach to remittances out of mixed funds, depending on whether the taxpayer is:

* Not ordinarily resident, and remitting money from a single engagement, part of which is carried out overseas; or

* On the remittance basis for another reason, such as because he is non-domiciled.

However this distinction in treatment is almost certainly unfounded, see below.

Not ordinarily resident with a single engagement

Where an individual who is not ordinarily resident has a single engagement, part of which is carried out overseas and part of which is carried out in the UK, it can be difficult to establish whether the former has been remitted to the UK.

The Revenue have a generous and relaxed attitude to this problem. SP5/84 states that where employees:

'(a) are resident but not ordinarily resident in the UK;

(b) perform duties of a single employment both in and outside the UK, so that they are potentially liable under both Schedule E Cases II and III, in respect of emoluments from that employment; and

(c) receive part of their emoluments in the UK and part abroad,

(then), provided the emoluments assessable under Case II are arrived at in a reasonable manner . . . the Revenue are prepared to accept that Case III liability will arise only where the aggregate of emoluments paid in, benefits enjoyed in, and emoluments remitted to, the UK exceeds the amount assessable under Case II for that year; and to restrict the Case III assessment to the excess of the aggregate over the Case II assessment.

In other words, where the employee has a 'mixed' employment, he will be deemed to have remitted first his non-taxable income, and only be subject to

UK tax on any balance. This is based on the decision in *Sterling Trust Ltd v IRC* [1925] 12 TC 868.

In the context of the personal services regime, this means that a worker who is not ordinarily resident will be deemed to have remitted taxed money before untaxed money, and can thus relatively easily protect his overseas earnings from the remittance basis, subject to the other tests at 17.13.4 below.

Other remittances

Where the ESC does not apply, the Revenue take a much stricter approach. This would therefore impact the earnings of non-domiciled personal services workers.

If earnings subject to the remittance basis are combined with other money, such as capital, within a 'mixed fund', the Revenue take the view that *taxable* amounts are remitted first, followed by any capital in the fund.

Their Inspector's Manual explains the position as follows:

> 'Where a person maintains abroad a fund (for example, a bank account) containing income assessable on the remittance basis, a capital lodgement to the fund is normally considered to lose its identity in the fund. . . . A subsequent remittance from such a mixed fund, therefore, represents income up to the full extent of the income content of the fund. Only when the income content of the fund is exhausted will any balance remitted be regarded as capital.' (IM 1567)

This view is based on the decision in *Scottish Provident Institution v Allan* [1901] 4 TC 409 where the judge held that 'no prudent man of business will encroach upon his capital for investment when he has income uninvested laying at his disposal.'

It is arguable that the Revenue view here is incorrect, and that the more correct view is that the taxpayer can choose whether to remit income or capital. The case for this was well made by David Williams and Gary Morris in *Taxation*, p422, 16 January 1997.

However it remains prudent, where the individual has capital overseas, to hold it separately from any income, whether interest or earnings. Having separate bank accounts for income and capital allows the latter to be remitted to the UK without having to dispute with the Revenue as to whether further tax should be paid.

Where this separate accounts approach has not been adopted, the arguments set out by Williams and Morris may be successful in protecting the individual from UK tax.

Further remittance problems arise where an overseas asset produces a capital gain, but these are beyond the scope of this book.

17.13.4 'Received in the United Kingdom'

Overseas earnings are treated as received in the United Kingdom if they are paid, used or enjoyed in, or in any manner or form transmitted or brought to, this country (s132(5) ICTA 1988). They remain earnings, even if they are subsequently invested in capital assets, see *Walsh v Randall* [1940] 23 TC 55.

The following therefore count as a remittance of Schedule E income into the UK:

• Payment abroad for goods or services supplied in the United Kingdom;

• Using a UK cheque or credit card to purchase goods or services, and the settlement of the debt out of overseas earnings, see IM 1569. A card issued by an overseas financial institution should thus be used in preference where it is intended to settle the bill out of unremitted funds;

• Purchasing an asset abroad out of overseas earnings, selling it, and then repatriating the proceeds;

• Bringing an asset into the UK which has been purchased abroad out of overseas earnings, and selling it here;

• Where money is borrowed overseas and brought to the UK and the loan is then repaid out of overseas earnings, this is a 'constructive remittance' (s65(6)–(9) ICTA 1988). This applies to non-domiciliaries but not to those who are not ordinarily resident.

However, where money is borrowed overseas and then brought to the UK, or alternatively used to purchase an asset here, and the *interest* on the loan is repaid out of overseas earnings, there is no remittance.

In addition, the mere transfer to the UK of assets purchased with overseas earnings does not itself constitute a remittance, see *Scottish Widows' Fund Life Assurance Society v Farmer* [1909] 5 TC 502.

17.13.5 Deemed income calculation issues arising from remittance basis

If an individual is on the remittance basis for services performed abroad he will not be chargeable under the rules of Schedule E. Thus he will not be within the personal services rules, see **17.2** above.

However, the calculation cannot be ignored, because if the amounts are remitted, they will become chargeable at that time (s19(1) ICTA 1988). Thus an individual could have a liability under the personal services rules several years after the work had been carried out, see Example 17C.

Example 17C

Marcin was born in Poland but moved to the UK several years ago. He has retained his Polish domicile. He has a personal service company providing IT services both in the UK and overseas. In 2000/01 he has income from relevant engagements of £50,000, of which £20,000 relate to engagements with overseas clients. His 2000/01 deemed income calculation is based on £30,000 of UK income.

In May 2003 he and his wife buy a house, and he remits the £20,000 relating to his 2000/01 overseas work. This is then added to his other income from relevant engagements in that year, and included in his deemed Schedule E computation for 2003/04.

There is no deduction in the partnership or corporation tax computation for the deemed payment until it is 'treated as made' (Sch 12, para 17 FA 2000). Thus, if the sums are remitted at some future date, a deduction can then be claimed in the partnership or corporation tax computation.

17.13.6 Republic of Ireland

Where an individual is non-domiciled, or not ordinarily resident, income from the Republic of Ireland is taxable here, whether or not it is remitted. This is the case whether or not:

- The worker's domicile/place of ordinary residence is the Republic of Ireland, or whether it is a third country. (This may be particularly relevant for those working on IT projects in the Dublin Docks area);

- The income is from employment, self-employment, or other amounts such as interest (s68 and s192(1) ICTA 1988).

17.14 Partners

Where a partner carries on a relevant engagement, he will be taxed on the deemed Schedule E income received by the partnership from that engagement. He must thus determine his residence, ordinary residence and domicile status, and then follow the Schedule E rules for determining the taxation of his income, as follows:

- If he is resident, ordinary resident and domiciled, he will be taxed on the full amount calculated under Sch 12 FA 2000;

- If he is resident and ordinarily resident, but non-domiciled and the engagement is carried out wholly overseas for a foreign client, he will be taxed on the remittance basis;

- If he is resident and domiciled, but not ordinarily resident, earnings related to overseas work will be taxed on the remittance basis;

- If he is non-resident he will be taxed on work done here unless it is 'merely incidental', see **17.8.2** or is covered by a double tax treaty, see **17.8.3**.

The interaction between the taxation of partnerships generally, and the personal services rules, is covered in Chapter 14.

18 Overseas implications – National Insurance

18.1 Introduction

The basis of liability to social security contributions varies considerably across the world. It may depend on the individual's nationality, his employer's place of business, or his residence, ordinary residence and domicile. The rules of the country where he lives and those where he works both need to be considered, together with overriding laws such as those of the European Union.

The National Insurance implications of an overseas posting are therefore already complex. IR35 adds a further level of difficulty. NIC is due where a worker would have had a liability had he been an employee of the client. The interaction of this hypothesis with international social security treaties is far from straightforward.

This chapter looks first at the position of UK workers going abroad, and then at overseas workers taking up UK engagements. It does not consider the position of partners. It concludes that international treaties may sometimes override the PSC legislation to eliminate the IR35 charge, so that there will be no attributable earnings. The worker may, however, still have a deemed income calculation, as the tax and NIC rules diverge. In other circumstances an individual may have an attributable earnings calculation but no deemed income.

These regulations are as yet untested and may be subject to different interpretations. However IR35 will prove particularly challenging for cross-border personal service workers.

18.2 Interaction with the personal services rules

Where a personal service worker carries out a relevant engagement abroad, or an overseas individual carries out a relevant engagement in the UK, the payments and benefits received by the intermediary from that engagement must be included in the attributable earnings calculation, and charged to UK employee NICs, if:

'The circumstances are such that, had the arrangements taken the form of a contract between the worker and the client, the worker would be regarded for the purposes of Parts I to V of the Contributions and Benefits Act as employed in employed earner's employment by the client.' (SI 2000 No 721 Reg 6(1)(c))

In other words, it is necessary to imagine that the worker was an employee of the client, and then ask if he would have been 'employed in employed earner's employment' by the client. If the answer to that question is yes, then his attributable earnings will be subject to employee NICs.

Furthermore, where this occurs, the service company will be the secondary contributor in respect of those attributable earnings. The Regulations say that:

'The intermediary, whether or not he fulfils the conditions prescribed under section 1(6)(a) of the Contributions and Benefits Act for secondary contributors, is treated for those purposes as the secondary contributor in respect of the worker's attributable earnings.' (SI 2000 No 721, Reg 6(3)(b))

This means that, where a liability for employer contributions exists, it falls upon the personal service company or partnership, whether or not it would have this responsibility under normal NIC rules.

However, this NICs liability relates only to the attributable earnings calculated under the personal services rules. Where a worker does not have attributable earnings, he may still be within UK NICs in respect of his actual salary and benefits. To the extent that IR35 does not apply, UK clients may also have a liability under existing legislation.

18.3 NICs and individuals working abroad

18.3.1 Outline of existing NICs rules

The rules for deciding whether someone who is working overseas has a liability to UK NICs can be summarised as follows:

(a) The basic rule is that where all the work for a particular employer is performed overseas, the employee is not in 'employed earner's employment' because that requires at least some of the work to be performed in the UK (s2 SSCBA 1992), and thus no NICs are due;

(b) There is an exception to this rule, even where the work is carried out wholly overseas, if:

(i) The employer has a place of business in the UK; and

(ii) The employee is ordinarily resident in the UK; and

(iii) Immediately before the commencement of the employment, the employee was resident in the UK.

In this case the employee is treated as in 'employed earner's employment' for the first 52 weeks of that employment (SI 1979 No 591 Reg 120). He is thus subject to Class 1 NICs, and his employer is a secondary contributor;

(c) The basic rule in (a) above is also overridden by various social security treaties, under which certain overseas employments are treated as if they had been carried out within the home country, see **18.3.3–5.**

18.3.2 Personal service workers overseas

If the rules set out in 18.3.1(a) and (b) are translated, so that they take account of the new regulations applicable to personal services, they read as follows:

(a) If all of the work for a particular *client* is performed overseas, then the *engagement* is not 'employed earner's employment' because that requires at least some of the work to be performed in the UK;

Since there can be no attributable earnings if there is no 'employed earner's employment', the PSC rules fall away. There is thus no attributable earnings calculation, and no liability to NICs. There might however be a deemed Schedule E liability because of the individual's tax residence status, see **18.4.5** below;

(b) There is an exception to the rule in (a), even where the work is carried out wholly overseas, if:

(i) The *client* has a place of business in the UK; and

(ii) The *worker* is ordinarily resident in the UK; and

(iii) Immediately before the commencement of the *engagement* the *worker* was resident in the UK.

In this case, the *worker* is treated as in 'employed earner's employment' for the first 52 weeks of that employment. Under the personal services rules he will thus be subject to Class 1 NICs, and his service company will be the secondary contributor.

It is interesting to note that where a worker is not within (b) above, e.g., because the client has no place of business in the UK, there is no liability to NICs under the PSC rules. However, in the 'real world', the worker is employed by an employer who has a place of business in the UK – namely his service company. He is thus within reg 120 and subject to UK NICs on his actual earnings, even though he has no attributable earnings.

18.3.3 EEA treaty arrangements

General rule

The EEA countries are Austria, Belgium, Denmark, Republic of Ireland, Finland, France, Germany, Greece, Iceland, Italy, Liechtenstein, Luxembourg, Netherlands, Norway, Portugal, Spain, Sweden and the UK. These countries operate under the Social Security law of the European Union. Its fundamental principles are as follows:

(a) A person should not have to pay contributions in more than one Member State at the same time;

(b) He should normally be subject to the contribution law of the state where he is employed or self-employed;

(c) This is the case even if he resides in another state or his employer has a place of business or a registered office in another state (EC Reg 1408/71, Art 13).

Where a person leaves the UK to work for an employer in another EEA country, he will no longer be liable to UK NICs because he is not in 'employed earner's employment' in the UK. This is the case even if his employer has a place of business in the UK – it thus overrides Regulation 120 (see 18.3.2(b) above).

Short-term posting

There is an exception to the general rule set out above, which covers short-term postings to other EEA states. Where a worker is employed in the UK, and is sent by his employer to work in an EEA state, he remains within UK NICs, provided that:

(a) The posting to the EEA state is not expected to last for a period in excess of 12 months; and

(b) He is not being sent to replace another person who has completed his term of posting (EC Reg 1408/71, Art 14(1)(a)).

If this short-term posting rule does apply, and the job overseas lasts longer than 12 months, although it was not expected to, the employee may remain in the UK scheme for a further 12 months, as long as the foreign social security authority agrees.

18.3.4 Application to personal services workers

General rule

Translating this to take account of the personal services regulations, the general rule would read as follows:

- A personal service worker who takes up a relevant engagement with a client in an EEA state would not have been an employed earner for UK NIC purposes if he had been an employee of the client. He will thus be outside the PSC rules;

- As a result he has no attributable earnings from his overseas engagement, no liability to employee NICs, and his service company has no secondary liability. However, he may still be within the scope of UK tax and have a deemed income calculation, see **18.4.5** below.

Once again, in the 'real world' he will still be employed by his service company, not the overseas client. He should thus be subject to UK NICs on his actual salary and benefits as he was before IR35.

Short-term posting

The short-term posting rule, rewritten in the context of personal services, would be as follows:

- Where a *worker* has a relevant engagement with a *client* in the UK, and is sent by that *client* to work in an EEA state, he remains within UK NICs, provided that:

  (a) The posting to the EEA state is not expected to last for a period in excess of twelve months; and

  (b) He is not being sent to replace another person who has completed his term of posting.

- If the short-term posting rule does apply, and the engagement overseas lasts longer than 12 months, although it was not expected to, the *worker* may remain in the UK scheme for a further 12 months, if the foreign social security authority agrees.

A PSC worker sent overseas by a UK client whose posting met these conditions would have remained within UK NICs had he been an employee of the client. He will thus remain within the PSC rules. His earnings from the relevant engagement will be included in his attributable earnings calculation, and his service company will be the secondary contributor.

Summary

One can attempt to summarise these complex rules by saying that:

- If a worker goes to work for an overseas client in an EEA country, he will be outside the PSC rules. He may, however, remain within UK NIC, which will then apply only to his actual salary and benefits;

- If a worker is sent overseas by a *UK client* and the engagement meets the short-term posting requirements, he remains within the PSC rules, as well as being within UK NIC generally;

- Even if he falls outside the attributable earnings calculation for NICs, he may remain within the Schedule E tax rules.

It should be possible to structure arrangements so that a worker is not sent abroad by a UK client, but takes up a separate overseas engagement. This would prevent the short-term posting rule coming into effect.

18.3.5 Bilateral Social Security Treaty countries

The provisions of each social security treaty are not identical, but the following general points can be made:

- Many social security treaties allow UK employees to remain within UK NICs if they are working in the overseas country for a limited period of time. Where a worker would have remained within UK NICs had he been an employee of the client, he will remain within the personal services rules, and his income from the engagement will form part of the attributable earnings calculation;

- However it is not always the case that a person who takes up a job overseas will have remained within UK NICs – it depends on the treaty provisions. If a worker would not have remained within UK NICs had he been employed by the client, he will also be outside the PSC rules;

- He may, nevertheless, remain within the provisions of the treaty because he is legally an employee of his service company. He will then be within UK NICs in respect of his actual earnings, but will have no attributable earnings.

18.4 NICs and individuals coming to the UK to work

18.4.1 Establishing whether the individual has a NIC liability

When an individual with a personal service company comes from overseas to take up a relevant engagement in the UK, the first question is whether there would have been a NICs liability had the worker been employed by the client. The answer to this question may be different depending on whether the individual has come from:

- An EEA country;

- A country with which the UK has a bilateral social security treaty; or

- From a country which is neither of these.

18.4.2 EEA countries

General rule

The basic EEA rules are set out at **18.3.3** above. Where a person comes to the UK from an EEA country to take up employment here, he is liable to UK NIC, unless he falls within the short-term posting exemption. Thus a personal service worker who lives in an EEA state, but takes up a relevant engagement with a client in the UK, would have been regarded as an 'employed earner' if he had been an employee of the client.

As a result he will be within the personal services legislation. He has to calculate his attributable earnings on the basis of the Regulations, and pay over the NIC arising on or before 19 April following the fiscal year. However, this is subject to the short-term posting rule.

Short-term posting

This is also discussed at **18.3.3** above. When this rule is translated into 'personal services speak', in the context of someone leaving the UK to work in another EEA country, it reads as follows:

'Where a *worker* is engaged to carry out a relevant engagement by a *client* in an EEA state, and is sent by that *client* to work in the UK, he will not have to pay UK NICs, provided that:

(a) The posting to the UK is not expected to last for a period in excess of 12 months; and

(b) He is not being sent to replace another person who has completed his term of posting.

If this short-term posting rule does apply, and the engagement overseas lasts longer than 12 months, although it was not expected too, the *worker* may remain outside the UK scheme for a further 12 months, if NICO agrees.'

A PSC worker sent to the UK by an overseas client, whose posting met these conditions, would have remained outside UK NICs had he been an employee of the client. Thus he passes the test set out in the Regulations, and remains outside the PSC rules.

This is fine if he is sent by his client to work in the UK and he is within the short-term posting rule. But what happens if he 'sends himself' as an employee of his service company, to work for a UK client? The personal services legislation does not allow him relief – he would not have been entitled to the short-term postings rule if he had been an employee of his UK client.

However, as a question of fact, he is an employee of his service company, and has been sent to the UK to take up an engagement with a client. Article 14 of the EC Regulations states that a worker on a short-term posting 'shall continue to be subject to the legislation of the first Member State'. This suggests that the PSC worker in this position will not fall within UK NIC laws at all, and thus will not come within the personal service regulations.

Assuming this is correct, the worker who comes to the UK and is within the short-term posting exemption will not be within IR35 for NICs, whether he is posted here by a client or by his own service company. He will thus be exempt from paying NICs on his UK personal service earnings, but may have tax liability, see **18.4.5** below.

As a practical point, where a personal services worker is covered by this exemption, he should bring with him Form E101. This will indicate that he is still paying social security contributions in the other country and give him exemption from UK NICs.

18.4.3 Bilateral Social Security Treaties

If an individual is:

(a) Paying social security contributions in a country with which the UK has a bilateral Social Security Agreement covering NICs; and

(b) Sent by that employer to work temporarily in the UK;

he may exempted from UK NICs, depending on the terms of the treaty.

Translated into 'PSC-speak' this means that if a worker is:

(a) Paying social security contributions in a country with which the UK has a bilateral Social Security Agreement covering NICs; and

(b) Has a contract with a client there, who sends him to work temporarily in the UK;

then, assuming he would have been outside UK NICs if he had been employed by the client, he will also not be within the personal services legislation.

As discussed in **18.4.2** above, if he is 'sent' by his own service company to work for a client in the UK, he is not within the same exemption. The terms of the treaty would have to be considered to see if they protect him from all UK NICs legislation (as does the EC Treaty) or not.

Where there is an exemption, the usual evidence is a certificate issued by the foreign social security institution, confirming that he continues to contribute to the overseas scheme. Again, although there is no NIC liability under the personal services rules, there may be a tax liability, see **18.4.5** below. The client may have a liability under existing NICs legislation, see **19.5.3**.

18.4.4 Other countries

If an employee is sent to work in the UK by an employer located overseas, he is not liable to UK NICs for the first 52 weeks while he is in the UK (SI 1979 No 591 Reg 119). Applying the personal services rules to this, if a worker is sent to work in the UK by an overseas client, he should likewise not have to pay NICs for the first 52 weeks.

This is, at least, what the regulations are probably intended to achieve. However, the PSC rules operate if an individual is an 'employed earner'. Regulation 119 does not say that the individuals cease to be employed earners for the first 52 weeks, merely that they do not have to pay NICs. Hopefully, the Revenue will take a purposive approach to this part of the Regulations, and treat the worker carrying out the engagement for the overseas client in the same way as if he had been employed by the client.

Assuming this is the case, there will be no attributable earnings calculation for the first 52 weeks, but there may be a deemed Schedule E payment, see **18.4.5**. Both employer and employee NICs will be payable from the 53rd week by the service company in respect of any attributable earnings. The client, however, remains the secondary contributor in respect of his actual salary and benefits, see **19.5.3**.

18.4.5 Consequences of being within the PSC rules for tax but not for NIC

Because the rules for establishing a NIC liability for overseas workers are different from those which determine the Schedule E tax liability, income can be included in the deemed Schedule E calculation for income tax purposes, but without a charge to NICs arising.

Despite the fact that no NIC is payable, it would appear that the deemed Schedule E calculation allows a notional deduction. Steps Eight and Nine of the deemed Schedule E calculation are as follows:

> 'Step Eight: Find the amount which, together with employer's national insurance contributions on it, is equal to the amount resulting from Step Seven
>
> . . .
>
> Step Nine: The result is the amount of the deemed Schedule E payment. (Sch 12, para 7 FA 2000)

Step Eight doesn't say 'together with employer's national insurance *payable* on it. . .'. This is in contrast to the NICs regulations, which read:

> 'Find the amount that, together with the amount of secondary Class 1 contributions *payable in respect of it*. . .'. (SI 2000 No 727 Reg 7)

It is thus reasonable to assume that the difference is deliberate, and that the deemed income calculation will produce the same tax charge whether or not the worker is subject to UK NICs. This would be fair, since if he is exempt from UK social security taxes, this is almost certainly because he is paying the equivalent in another country.

19   Offshore companies and partnerships

19.1 Introduction

Some of those affected by the personal services legislation have sought to distance themselves from it by setting up an offshore company. This chapter looks at what makes an intermediary 'offshore', and considers the implications of operating via an offshore service company or partnership within the context of IR35.

19.2 Corporate tax residence in the UK

19.2.1 Scope

A company which is tax resident here is subject to UK tax on its worldwide earnings. It is also required to operate PAYE and NIC in respect of employees who are themselves within the scope of UK tax. It was held in *ex parte Blain* [1879] 12 Ch D 522 that:

> 'All Acts of the United Kingdom Parliament must be construed as subject to territorial limitations, i.e., they operate only in regard to persons who are resident in the United Kingdom.'

Although the territorial limitations of some UK laws have since been stretched, the *Blain* case is respected authority for the fact that residence brings companies within UK laws, including those relating to the operation of tax and National Insurance. A UK resident company is thus required to deduct PAYE and NIC from a deemed Schedule E payment.

A company is tax resident in the UK if it is either incorporated here (s66 FA 1988), or is managed and controlled here (*Calcutta Jute Mills Co Ltd v Nicholson Ex D* [1876] 1 TC 83) However, double tax treaties may override this, so that if a company is resident in more than one jurisdiction, a tie-breaker clause in the treaty may determine that the company is tax resident in the other territory.

19.2.2 Management and control

The management and control test has been established by over a century of case law. In *De Beers Consolidated Mines v Howe* [1906] 5 TC 198 Lord Loreburn said that:

'A company resides, for the purposes of income tax, where its real business is carried on . . . I regard that as the true rule; and the real business is carried on where the central management and control actually abides.'

It is therefore necessary to work out what is meant by the place of 'central management and control'. The courts have held that this is the location where the highest level of control is exercised over the business, which may or may not be the same as the place where the operations are carried out. The Commissioners' summary of the facts in the *De Beers* case provides a nice illustration of the concept:

'The head office is formally at Kimberley, and the general meetings have always been held there. Also, the profits have been made out of diamonds raised in South Africa, and sold under annual contracts to a Syndicate for delivery in South Africa upon terms of division of profits realised on re-sale between the Company and the Syndicate. And the annual contracts contain provisions for regulating the market, in order to realise the best profits on re-sale. Further, some of the Directors and Life Governors live in South Africa, and there are Directors Meetings at Kimberley as well as in London.

But it is clearly established that the majority of Directors and Life Governors live in England, that the Directors' Meetings in London are the meetings where the real control is always exercised in practically all the important business of the Company, except the mining operations. London has always controlled the negotiation of the contracts with the Diamond Syndicates, has determined policy in the disposal of diamonds and other assets, the working and development of mines, the application of profits, and the appointment of directors. London has, also, always controlled matters that require to be determined by the majority of all the Directors, which include all questions of expenditure except wages, materials, and such like at the mines, and a limited sum which may be spent by the Directors at Kimberley.'

The place of central management and control is thus often, but not invariably, the place where the directors meet. The Revenue say that:

'Where doubts arise about a particular company's residence status, the Revenue adopt the following approach –

(i)   they first try to ascertain whether the directors of the company in fact exercise central management and control;

(ii)   if so, they seek to determine where the directors exercise this central management and control (which is not necessarily where they meet);

(iii) in cases where the directors apparently do not exercise central management and control of the company, the Revenue then look to establish where and by whom it is exercised.' (SP 1/90)

340

19.2.3 Application to personal service companies

In a one-man company, management and control rests with the single director. If he controls the company from the UK, the company will be resident here. Although in theory it is possible to control a company from overseas, even if the director is based in the UK, in practice it is very difficult. Business decisions cannot always be deferred until the director can reach a convenient offshore location.

In this context the Revenue say:

> 'Where ... it appears that a major objective underlying the existence of certain factors is the obtaining of tax benefits from residence or non-residence, the Revenue examine the facts particularly closely in order to see whether there has been an attempt to create the appearance of central management and control in a particular place without the reality.' (SP 1/90)

Thus purchasing an 'offshore' company from a jurisdiction such as Bermuda or one of the Channel Islands does not prevent it from being UK resident. If the director makes key decisions about the company from the UK, it will be managed, controlled and thus resident here.

19.3 Non-resident companies with a UK trading presence

The PAYE collection provisions, contained within s203ff ICTA 1988, state that:

> 'On the making of any payment of, or on account of, any income assessable to income tax under Schedule E, income tax shall ... be deducted or repaid by the person making the payment.'

In *Clark v Oceanic Contractors Incorporated* [1982] 56 TC 183 the Revenue argued that because this phrase included no territorial limitation, any employer could be required to deduct PAYE from his employees' emoluments, whether or not the employer was UK resident. However, the Lord Chancellor dismissed this:

> 'If the Crown is right, the garb of logicality which it claims for its submission conceals extraordinarily far-reaching and anomalous consequences. How can the PAYE duties be enforced? How can the system be made to work? How can it be supervised? How can the necessary documents be obtained for inspection by the Revenue, unless the foreign corporation is compliant? It all adds up to a practical impossibility of enforcing or monitoring the system against an uncooperative employer outside the United Kingdom making payments outside the United Kingdom.'

341

Nevertheless, by a 3:2 majority the House of Lords held that, if they can be made effective, the PAYE tax collection provisions can be applied to a non-resident company. For that purpose a 'trading presence' of the company in the United Kingdom is sufficient.

Thus, even where a company is non-resident, it can be required to deduct PAYE from a Schedule E deemed payment if it has a trading presence here. The same rules apply to NIC (SI 1979 No 591 Reg 119(b)).

This PAYE obligation does not depend on the company's residence, and so cannot be avoided by using the 'tie-breaker' provisions of a double tax treaty. These simply determine a company's residence for tax purposes, if it is resident in more than one country. The PAYE and NIC rules are determined by 'trading presence' not residence.

19.4 Non-residents with no trading presence in UK

19.4.1 PAYE

Where a company has no trading presence in the UK, it cannot be required to deduct PAYE from the Schedule E earnings of its workers under normal UK tax law. However, special rules have been introduced for deemed Schedule E payments, see **19.5** below.

The normal requirement, where a worker is assigned or seconded from an overseas employer to a UK-based business, is that the UK client becomes responsible for deducting the tax on the worker's emoluments (s203C ICTA 1988). This obligation applies automatically unless the overseas employer agrees voluntarily to deduct the PAYE.

The position is different if (a) the employer is non-resident, and (b) the worker is either non-resident, or not ordinarily resident. In this situation:

- The UK-based business is responsible for deducting PAYE on at least a proportion of the earnings (s203D ICTA 1988);

- But this only applies if a direction is given to the UK company by the Revenue;

- In practice the Revenue and the UK company will come to an agreement as to how much of the earnings should be taken into account.

19.4.2 National Insurance

The rules for National Insurance are similar. The UK client, or 'host employer' becomes the secondary contributor if a worker is employed by a foreign company and:

> 'In pursuance of that employment the personal service of the person employed is made available to a host employer; and the personal service is rendered for the purposes of the business of that host employer.' (s7(2)(b) SSCBA 1992, SI 1978 No 1689 Sch 3(9))

19.5 Special rules for offshore personal services companies

19.5.1 PAYE

Normally, the s203C provisions mean that where a worker operates from an offshore service company, but works in the UK for a client based here, responsibility for operating PAYE rests with the client, see **19.4**.

In the context of IR35, this would make the client responsible for deciding whether the engagement was 'relevant' within the meaning of Sch 12, FA 2000, and, if it was, require him to operate PAYE on the deemed Schedule E amount. This would have represented a reversion to the original personal services proposals set out in April 1999 (see **2.3.2**), under which the burden of complying with IR35 lay with the client.

In order to ensure that responsibility for IR35 rests with the intermediary and not the client, special deeming rules have been included in the personal services legislation. They apply where:

(a) The worker is resident in the United Kingdom;

(b The services in question are provided in the United Kingdom; and

(c) The client or employer carries on business in the United Kingdom.

In these situations 'the intermediary is treated as having a place of business in the United Kingdom, whether or not it in fact does so.' (Sch 12, para 11(6) FA 2000)

The effect of this paragraph is that, providing the worker is resident here and provides services here to a UK client, the service company is deemed to have a trading presence here, whether or not this would otherwise be the case. The company is thus brought within the PAYE legislation.

19.5.2 Interaction with s203C ICTA 1988

The IR35 deeming provisions take priority over s203C ICTA 1988, because the latter are only operative if 'PAYE regulations do not apply (either) to the person making the payment ... or to the employer'.

Thus, if a UK client engages a worker from an offshore service company, the obligation to deduct PAYE from the deemed Schedule E amount remains with the service company rather than with the client. However, this IR35 deemed trading presence rule has two important limitations:

(a) It applies only to the deemed Schedule E payment. Clients are still within the scope of s203C if the worker receives salary or benefits. The implications of this are discussed at **21.3.2**;

(b) It does not apply if the worker is non-resident, and thus section 203D ICTA 1988 remains in force, see **19.4.1**.

19.5.3 National Insurance

A similar approach has been taken for National Insurance. The service company rather than the client is responsible for the NIC on attributable earnings from relevant engagements. The regulations say that:

> 'The intermediary, whether or not he fulfils the conditions prescribed under section 1(6)(a) of the Contributions and Benefits Act for secondary contributors, is treated for those purposes as the secondary contributor in respect of the worker's attributable earnings.'

Thus the intermediary and not the client becomes the secondary contributor. However, once again this applies only to the IR35 attributable earnings and not to any salary or benefits.

19.6 Enforcement

19.6.1 Options

If the company is non-resident, and does not comply with its PAYE and NIC obligations in respect of the deemed payment, the Revenue have indicated that they will seek to enforce the liability at the UK address of the worker. They have also warned that:

> 'Action to recover employer's NICs not paid by an offshore company could also include action against any assets of that company located in the UK.'
> (IR175: *Supplying services through a limited company or partnership*)

The Revenue may also be able to make the worker personally liable for the outstanding tax and NICs, see **19.6.2** below. However, it has also been suggested that the IR35 deemed trading presence rules may be unenforceable and thus ultra vires, see **19.6.3**.

19.6.2 Transferring responsibility to the worker

If a company should have deducted tax and NICs, but has not fulfilled its obligations, the Revenue have general powers to collect the overdue amounts from the worker.

However, as discussed at **16.8.2**, these powers may be defective in the context of IR35, and thus the Revenue may be unable to transfer responsibility for the PAYE on the deemed Schedule E amount to the individual. However, the NIC regulations *are* effective, and collection of outstanding NICs can be therefore be enforced on the worker.

19.6.3 Is the legislation ultra vires?

If the intermediary has no trading presence in the UK, is the legislation unenforceable and thus ultra vires?

In *Clark v Oceanic* (see **19.3**) the House of Lords held that the PAYE rules could be applied to the company because it had a trading presence in the UK. It was thus able, at a practical level, to make the required deductions from employees' salaries. The concept of *deeming* a trading presence therefore seems to contradict the logic of the court, which was based on practical capacity to comply with the legislation.

But the IR35 deeming provisions are effective only if the *worker* has a UK address. Given that in most cases there is substantial identity between the worker and the company, the presence of the worker in the UK could be considered as a practical equivalent to a 'trading presence', and thus the provisions are likely to be enforceable along the same lines as the decision in *Clark v Oceanic*.

Even if this were not the position, it is doubtful that they are ultra vires. Lord Wilberforce, speaking in the same case, said that 'an unenforceable obligation is still an obligation which may be onerous.'

19.6.4 Investigations and information

The Revenue's various sources of information are summarised at **16.9**, along with comments on the type of investigation which might take place.

Deliberate use of a company registered offshore in order to disguise liability to IR35 is likely to be treated as at least avoidance and possibly evasion.

19.7 Partnerships

19.7.1 Residence

The official Revenue view is that because an English partnership is not a legal person, it has no residence. However they acknowledge that:

> 'There has been some nibbling away of the principle that a partnership does not have a residence (because) the concept of residence and partnerships appears in . . . sections of the Taxes Acts.' (ITH 1609)

In practice they seem to accept that a partnership is resident where it is controlled and managed, and this approach was supported by *Padmore v CIR* [1989] 62 TC 352.

When considering where a partnership with both United Kingdom and overseas partners is controlled and managed, they say that:

> 'We would usually regard as significant such factors as the comparative seniority of the partners in age and experience (a simple head count will not do of course), the extent of their interests in the firm, the source and control of the finance, the places of decision on policy and major transactions, the places and locations of partners' meetings and what was done at those meetings. The place of meetings incidentally is not a conclusive factor any more than it is – or ought to be – for companies. So the nature of the business done at the meeting is important. Is it really about control and management or just part of a facade to mislead us about the place of actual control and management?' (ITH 1612)

If a partnership is controlled and managed wholly abroad, and the UK partner is either not domiciled or not ordinarily resident, he will be taxed on profits earned in the UK and only on overseas profits if they are remitted (s112 ICTA 1988), see 17.13.

Where there is uncertainty as to whether or to what extent control and management is exercised in the UK, the position becomes complex and beyond the scope of this book. However, the Revenue's International Tax Handbook at paragraph 1617ff has an interesting discussion of the technical issues.

19.7.2 PAYE and NIC obligations

A partnership which is controlled and managed in the UK is regarded as within the UK Taxes Acts and so must apply PAYE and NIC to the deemed payment.

A partnership which is controlled and managed wholly overseas may still have a trading presence in the UK and thus be within ss203ff ICTA 1988, see **19.3** above. If there is no trading presence, the deeming provisions of Schedule 12, para 11(6) FA 2000 set out at **19.5** above come into play, as they apply to 'intermediaries' not simply to companies.

Thus a partner or employee of an overseas partnership, who is himself resident in the UK and carries on a relevant engagement here, will bring the partnership within the PAYE and NIC deduction rules as far as the deemed Schedule E payment is concerned.

The same issues regarding client responsibilities, and enforcement of the regulations, apply to partnerships as they do to companies, see **19.5.2, 19.5.3** and **19.6** above.

19.8 Summary

The position of an overseas company in the context of IR35 can be summarised as follows:

(a) Most PSCs with UK resident directors will themselves be UK resident, because they are managed and controlled here, even if they are registered overseas. They will thus be legally required to operate PAYE and NICs on any salary and benefits as well as on the deemed payment;

(b) If the company is non-resident, but has a trading presence here, it is obliged to operate PAYE and NICs as if it were UK resident;

(c) If the company has no trading presence, it will be treated as having such a presence for the purposes of the PAYE and NICs on the deemed payment, but only if the client is in the UK and the worker is resident here;

(d) In any other situation responsibility for PAYE or NICs rests with the client.

20 Particular businesses

20.1 Introduction

IR35 applies to all businesses, but bears more heavily on some than others. The opposite is also true – some service companies have a window of opportunity which is not available to all.

This chapter summarises some of the key issues affecting the provision of personal services by these specialised businesses. It should be read in the context of the general rules discussed in the rest of this book.

20.2 Actors and entertainers

20.2.1 General

Personal service companies are widely used in the media and performing arts. However IR35 only applies to those who would be employees if they did not have the 'wrapper' of a company or partnership. Thus the first question is whether the actor or entertainer would have been self-employed had he operated as an individual rather than via an intermediary. The answer may not be the same for tax as it is for National Insurance, because of the existence of NIC provisions deeming certain actors to be employees.

20.2.2 Tax: employed or self-employed?

Actors and entertainers have for many years fought the Revenue on issues of status. The Revenue succeeded in the case of *Fall v Hitchen* [1972] 49 TC 433, but the taxpayer won the right to be taxed as Schedule D in *Davies v Braithwaite* [1933] 18 TC 198.

In 1989 the Revenue announced that it was recategorisng actors who had standard Equity contracts as employees, with an amnesty for those who had been Schedule D for the previous three years (ESC A75). This blanket recategorisation was successfully challenged by Alec McCowen and Sam West in 1993, who convinced the Special Commissioners they were self-employed.

After this defeat the Revenue retreated, and have now accepted that 'Schedule D assessment of a performer's/artist's earnings will normally be appropriate

... (they) will generally be assessable under Schedule D as a matter of law rather than concession' (IM 1810; SE 7335/ESM 4121-2). The Revenue have also accepted that the same treatment should be accorded to stage managers, who usually have Equity contracts, see SE 7351/ESM 4124.

Most actors and musicians should therefore fall outside the personal services rules on first principles – they would not be employees if the intermediary did not exist.

However the Revenue have not completely abandoned the old case of *Fall v Hitchen*. They state that they continue to believe that Schedule E applies:

> 'Where a performer/artist is engaged for a regular salary to perform in a series of different productions over a period of time, in such roles as may be from time to time stipulated by the engager, with a minimum period of notice before termination of the contract, as was Mr Hitchen in Fall v Hitchen. This would apply for example to permanent members of some orchestras and permanent members of an opera, ballet or theatre company.' (SE 7333/ESM 4121)

If such individuals work via an intermediate company or partnership, they should consider whether they are within the personal services rules. In particular, where some members of a theatre company are paid via PAYE, and others operate through service companies, failure to apply the personal service rules is likely to be challenged.

20.2.3 National Insurance: employed or self-employed?

Historically, the DSS took a more aggressive line than the Revenue over the status of actors, and considered that almost all were 'employed earners'. However, after the case of *McCowen and West*, see **20.2.2** above, the DSS finally admitted in Press Release 98/202 (15 July 1998) that its view that actors and musicians are always employees could not be sustained.

Despite this, under SI 1998 No 1728 (followed by SI 1999 No 3) actors who are paid 'wholly or mainly by salary' were deemed to be employees for the purposes of employee Class 1 contributions from 17 July 1998. This begs the question of what is meant by 'salary', as the fees paid to many self-employed theatre actors are commonly called 'salary'. However this deemed status as employed earners for NICs has generally been welcomed by the acting profession as it allows them to continue to claim jobseeker's allowance when they are 'resting'.

Where an actor who uses a personal service company is deemed to be an employed earner for National Insurance purposes because he receives a 'salary', he will have to carry out an attributable earnings calculation to work out the Class 1 employee NICs on those earnings. There will also be secondary contributions due from the intermediary. However, if he is not regarded as an employee for tax purposes, he will have no deemed Schedule E payment. Having a liability for NICs but not for PAYE is discussed at **12.7.2**.

For simplicity, the attributable earnings calculation continues to be referred to in the following paragraphs as the deemed Schedule E calculation.

20.2.4 Expenses and other reliefs

The purpose of the new legislation is to subject the worker to tax and NICs on income from his relevant engagements broadly on the basis that it is employment income. As a result, the tax reliefs for employee expenses are applicable, rather than the more generous Schedule D legislation. Chapter 11 discusses the expenses and reliefs available under the personal services rules.

Actors and entertainers who are used to the 'wholly and exclusively' corporation tax rules for expenses will find that some costs are not deductible against their earnings from relevant engagements. These will of course continue to qualify for relief in the corporation tax computation, but this will be small comfort, as profits are likely to be negligible and losses are possible, see **13.7**.

Because of the narrowness of the Schedule E expenses rules, it is much more tax efficient if the costs are borne by the theatre or other engager, rather than by the service company. This is on the assumption that they represent genuine business costs for the engager and do not constitute a benefit to the worker.

Allowable expenses

Expenses which are allowed under the personal services rules include:

(a) *Genuine business expenses borne by the engager.* Business expenses borne by the theatre are likely to be allowable as wholly and exclusively for the purposes of the engager's business. Such costs might include make-up, clothes, props and laundry;

(b) *Agents' fees.* Where income is paid to the service company net of agents' fees, the fees are automatically excluded from the deemed Schedule E calculation, see **21.2.1**. Where they are paid by the worker, they must meet the criteria for tax relief set out in s201A ICTA 1988 that:

- They are paid to an employment agency under a contract with the worker, or to a co-operative society which acts as agent for its members;

- The fee is calculated as a percentage of the income from the engagement;

- It is deducted from earnings in the same fiscal year as those earnings are brought into tax;

- The maximum deduction is 17.5 per cent (inclusive of VAT) of the fees earned in the fiscal year.

(c) *Travel expenses.* Actors are often reimbursed their home to work travel, and this continues to be allowable under Schedule E. The travel rules are discussed in detail at **11.6**. There may also be reliefs for travel abroad, or for overseas entertainers coming to the UK, see **17.10.3** and **17.12.4**;

(d) *Pensions.* The personal services rules allow a deduction from relevant income for employer contributions to an approved pension, see **12.2**. The deemed Schedule E amount qualifies as net relevant earnings for pension purposes. In calculating net relevant earnings, it should be remembered that fees to artists' agents do not reduce NRE (s646(2) ICTA 1988).

20.2.5 Expenses disallowable in the deemed Schedule E computation

Expenses which actors currently obtain as deductible in their service companies which are not allowed against their deemed Schedule E income include:

- Make up, hairdressing, wardrobe and props, though under standard Equity contracts these are generally provided by the engager;

- Costs of attending interviews and auditions;

- Advertising, photography and tuition;

- Laundry, gratuities and postage;

- Professional publications such as *The Stage*;

- Equity subscriptions;

- Scripts, theatre and cinema tickets;

- Compact discs and cassettes.

20.2.6 Overseas issues

Chapter 17 discusses the effect of IR35 on workers who come to the UK from abroad and the consequences of taking up overseas engagements. Actors and entertainers are, however, subject to special rules.

Most workers are taxed on the basis of their residence, and double tax treaties prevent them suffering tax in more than one jurisdiction at a time. However most agreements provide that income derived by entertainers may be taxed in the country where the activities are exercised, rather than in the country where they are tax resident (see OECD Model Agreement, Article 17). Because of the difficulties in assessing and collecting the tax, withholding regimes are commonplace.

Overseas entertainers working in the UK

In the UK a withholding regime deducts basic rate tax from any payments made to a non-resident entertainer for performance, recording or promotional purposes (ss555–7 ICTA 1988; SI 1987 No 530).

This withholding applies whether or not the payment is made to a self-employed individual or to a service company. The legislation requires the payer to withhold tax 'where a payment is made to whatever person' (s555(2) ICTA 1988).

Where an overseas entertainer is subject to this withholding regime, he is exempted from the personal services legislation (Sch 12, para 6 FA 2000).

UK entertainers working overseas

A withholding regime also operates in many overseas countries, and it is generally a final tax, so that it discharges any fiscal liability the individual may have in that territory. Where the actor operates via a service company, withholding taxes may still be levied, though this varies depending on the territory.

Any tax deducted relates to income which legally belongs to the service company, not to the individual. In the UK, credit for the foreign tax withheld is thus due against the corporation tax payable by the company on its profits, rather than against the income tax on the salary or on the individual's deemed Schedule E payment.

However, the Inland Revenue have agreed that relief may be given against the individual's Schedule E income, although a specific claim to Revenue Head Office is required. They say that this may apply where:

> 'The foreign tax is imposed in a personal capacity on the entertainer etc. notwithstanding that the performance payments are made to the service company . . . If it is possible to directly link the performance in the overseas country and the income arising to the performer in the form of remuneration

from the service company then it may be that the remuneration derived by the entertainer can be identified with the income taxed by the foreign tax authority.'(DTRM 905)

A version of this double tax relief is now available to all those with personal service companies, but it applies only where the service company has insufficient UK corporation tax to absorb the foreign tax withheld, see **17.10.2**. It is unclear whether this narrower relief will henceforth apply to entertainers within the personal services regime, or whether they will still be able to take advantage of the more generous practice set out in the DTRM.

20.3 Directors and temporary executives

20.3.1 Social changes

In recent years the number of temporary executives, directors and consultants operating via service companies has grown considerably. This is partly a consequence of corporate restructuring, 'de-layering' and cost-cutting. More positively, there has also been a shift towards 'portfolio careers' in which individuals combine a number of non-executive directorships with some consultancy work.

20.3.2 Employed or self-employed?

A director is an officeholder, and by definition chargeable under Schedule E (s19(1) ICTA 1988). If the intermediary did not exist, the individual would clearly fall within Schedule E in respect of director's fees received. He is thus within IR35 for NICs. This is because the regulations apply where:

'The worker would be regarded for the purposes of Parts I to V of the Contributions and Benefits Act as employed in employed earner's employment by the client.' (SI 2000 No 727 Reg 6)

Under s2(1)(a) SSCBA 1992 an 'employed earner' means a person who is 'gainfully employed in GB either under a contract of service, or in an office with emoluments chargeable to income tax under Schedule E'. An attributable earnings calculation must thus be carried out for directors. There is however an exception for certain fees received by professional partnerships, while in other cases it may be possible to split the contracts so that only part is subject to NICs. These are both discussed below.

However the tax position is less clear. The IR35 tax legislation only applies if 'the worker would be regarded for income tax purposes as an *employee* of the client' (Sch 12, para 1(c) FA 2000, the author's italics); it does not apply to officeholders as such.

It is thus necessary to look at the hypothetical contract between the individual and the client. If the individual would have been a director, but not an employee, if the intermediary did not exist, then he will not be within Schedule 12. This suggests that someone who provides services as a non-executive director to a client will be within IR35 for NICs but not for tax. Other examples of this scenario are discussed in **12.7**.

The position for an executive director is more complex. He may of course be fully within IR35 for both tax and NICs. However he may be able to argue either that all the work is provided as a director, or that he is operating in a dual capacity.

All work carried out as a director

An individual may seek to argue that all his services are provided to the client in his capacity as a director, and not as a worker or employee. A similar approach has been accepted by the DTI in respect of the National Minimum Wage (NMW), see **22.2.2**. They have agreed that where a director does not have an explicit contract of employment he is not a worker, and is thus outside the NMW.

However, since IR35 is concerned with hypothetical contracts and not actual contracts, the NMW solution is not available. Each individual must thus consider whether he would have a hypothetical contract of employment with the client in addition to his directorship, if there was no intermediary. If there would have been such a contract, then IR35 will apply for both NICs and tax.

Dual capacity

If the individual's work for the client can be divided between his role as a director and that as a consultant, and he can show that he would be self-employed as a consultant if the company did not exist, then NICs (but not PAYE, see above) will apply to the fees received as a director but not to those received in a consulting capacity. For example, an accountant who is a non-executive director of a client company may also supply advice to that client as he does to others, and he would thus not be within IR35 in respect of the consultancy work.

Where this is the situation, it is recommended for simplicity that the consultancy work be severed from the directorship so that two contracts are set up between the service company and the client, one of which describes the director's duties and associated remuneration, while the second describes the other services to be provided, along with the fees to be charged.

Professional partnerships

Where directors' fees are received by partners, Extra-Statutory Concession A37 may allow them to be excluded from Schedule E. The concession applies where:

- The partners have received the fees as a normal incidence of their profession;

- The amounts are small in the context of the firm's business; and

- The fees are brought into the firm's profit pool

This is discussed further at **14.3**. Exemption is also available from National Insurance on the same basis (SI 1979 No 591 Reg 19B).

Although there is a Revenue practice (SE 1226/SE 03001-3, see **14.3**), which allows sole traders as well as partners to treat a small amount of employment income as if it were Schedule D, this concessionary treatment is specifically not extended to directors' fees. Only professional partnerships are accorded this particular privilege.

20.3.3 Pre-IR35 status issues

Before IR35, a number of challenges were raised by the Contributions Agency and the Revenue concerning the status of directors operating via service companies. The CA and the IR argued that the office of director is filled by the individual, not the service company, and thus the fees were taxable under Schedule E because they were earned by the directors and merely redirected to their companies.

It should be possible to resist this attack, providing the contractual arrangements have been set up as follows:

- The service company supplied the individual to take up the office of director;

- The contract for the supply of services is with the company, not the individual;

- Payment for these services is contractually due to the service company.

Thus, although the individual fills the office of director, payment for the services he provides has correctly been made to his service company.

20.3.4 Lump sums from pension schemes

When an individual retires, he is entitled to commute part of his pension as a tax free lump sum (s635 ICTA 1988; s590(3) ICTA 1988).

However, if he returns to work for his employer on a consultancy basis, or retains a non-executive directorship, the Revenue have argued that he has not retired, and have thus sought to tax the lump sum, see for example Adrian Waddingham's article in *Taxation* 18 May 2000. To protect their pension position, some individuals have set up PSCs through which they supply services to their former employer.

There are two questions: Was the service company effective before April 2000, and what is the position under IR35?

Pre-April 2000

As discussed at **20.3.3** above, the Revenue should not be able to 'look through' the contractual arrangements if they have been set up so that the contract is with the service company and payment is made to the company.

Furthermore, IR35 was implemented partly to deal with 'Friday to Monday' companies, see **2.2.3**. A retiring executive who returns to his former employer is a classic Friday to Monday situation. The fact that IR35 was necessary is itself evidence that the PSC route was generally effective in not creating an employment between the individual and his former employer, and that the Revenue's powers prior to 6 April 2000 were inadequate to deal with the situation. See also **4.1.2**.

Under IR35

The personal services legislation does not deem the worker to be an employee of his client, but simply reclassifies the income as Schedule E, see **10.4**.

A one-man company should thus continue to be effective in protecting the retiring executive from attacks that he is still an employee, and has not 'retired'. It should therefore safeguard his lump sum.

If the point continues to be taken by the Revenue, the individual should remind the Inspector that the same approach is not taken in the public sector, where the return of individuals to their previous jobs after 'retirement' has not been attacked. It is believed that for public policy reasons (such as a shortage of serving police officers) the Revenue have been discouraged from attacking their pension arrangements. The police are a particularly useful example, as they themselves hold offices and not employments, see *Dale v IRC* [1954] AC 11. A quotation from the Taxpayers Charter may then conclude the matter.

20.4 IT contractors

20.4.1 Political pressure

Led by Andy White and the Professional Contractors Group (PCG), IT contractors have been unrelenting in their attacks on IR35. Articulate, well-organised, independent and highly computer-literate, their campaign has been both formidable and unprecedented.

However, like other workers, they will only escape IR35 if they can show that they would not be employees of their clients if they were not working via service companies.

20.4.2 Employed or self-employed?

Some contractors, reviewing the status tests set out at Chapter 6, will find it difficult to avoid the conclusion that they fall within the new legislation. They work fixed hours on an open-ended contract under the direct control of the company's IT manager, and are indistinguishable from employees except for their higher rate of pay and lack of employment rights. An example of such a worker is Gordon, Example 1 in *Tax Bulletin 45*, see **24.2.2**.

At the other end of the scale are individuals with a business organisation, who work on a project basis, and have a highly marketable skill. They might be specialist designers of web sites, or operate 'computer hacking' programs as part of a security review programme. They probably fall outside the personal services rules. Henry is the Revenue's model of a self-employed IT contractor, see **24.2.3**.

A third group of individuals are in the 'grey area' between employment and self-employment. An example is 'Charlotte' in *Tax Bulletin 45*, see **24.2.4**. Some will adjust to IR35, while others will change the way they work, so they fall outside the legislation. Ideas as to how this might be done are given in Chapter 9. Some particular points are highlighted below.

Standard contracts

The Revenue have reviewed the standard contracts used in the IT industry, and have concluded that those who work in the manner required by these contracts will usually be within IR35. This is covered in more detail at 7.7 above.

Working as a professional

Some IT contractors may be able to argue for self-employment on the basis that they are a professional, exercising a skill. Despite the fact that they generally do not take financial risk, are employed on an hourly basis, are subject to some degree of control by the client, and provide little, if any equipment, they may still be within Schedule D, see **8.2** above.

Advice and solutions

It is recommended that individuals in the 'grey area' between Schedule D and Schedule E take advice on their status, either from the Revenue or from a tax adviser. The latter may also help the worker review ways of improving his position. An assumption that one is 'in the clear' may be dangerous, and prove costly if the company experiences an employer compliance review, with attendant interest and possibly penalties, see **16.9**.

20.4.3 Expenses

Where IT contractors fall within IR35, the expenses they can claim against their deemed Schedule E income are more restricted than those which are allowable in a company, see **11.3**. However, they remain entitled to a number of deductions and reliefs. These are discussed at **11.4** and are briefly summarised below.

Disallowable costs

Disallowable costs include:

(a) *Secretarial support.* Many contractors with service companies previously paid their spouse or partner a small salary for keeping the business records and taking client bookings. If the worker carries out only relevant engagements, and continues to pay his spouse, the salary will effectively be paid out of taxed income, see FAQ 40. However, there may be minimum wage issues if the spouse is not paid, see **22.2.2**. If, on the other hand, the work involved in managing the contractor's work-flow, liaising with clients and dealing with invoicing/bad debts is significant, it may indicate that the contractor is in business on his own account, and can thus escape IR35;

(b) *Training.* This is only allowable if, improbably, it is borne by the client, see **11.8**;

(c) The issue of equipment is discussed fully at **7.4.5** and **6.6.2**. The Revenue have set out their view on computer equipment owned by IT workers as follows:

'A deduction will only be given for capital allowances in working out the deemed payment where the plant or machinery is necessarily provided for use in the performance of the duties of the relevant engagement. This is a strict test and means that relief will only be given where the duties of the engagement meant that the company had to provide the equipment in question. If the company purchases the equipment out of choice then no deduction will be given. For example, where an IT contractor is required to use the client's computer equipment then no relief will be due for expenditure on computers owned by the service company. Neither will any relief be due where the client makes all the equipment necessary to do a job available but the worker uses his or her own computers, out of choice.' (FAQ Computation 10)

Note, however, that an IT consultant who 'must work exclusively at home using the worker's own computer equipment' may be self-employed and thus fall outside IR35 altogether (*Tax Bulletin 45*);

(d) *Home as office costs.* Contractors have traditionally claimed part of the costs of heating, lighting and furnishing their homes on the grounds that their company is based there. These expenses will only be allowed against their Schedule E earnings if they meet the stringent s198 ICTA 1988 test, see **11.5**. Such costs will be subject to critical examination by the Revenue, whose position has long been that:

'Very few employees . . . will be able to show that their home is, in a real sense, a place of work. It is not enough for an employee merely to carry out some aspect of his duties there. Usually this is a matter of personal choice rather than reflecting objective requirements of the job. The (client) will normally provide all the facilities necessary for the work to be carried out at the business premises.' (SE 4376/SE 32370, adapted for IR35)

The revised Schedule E Manual discusses this area in greater detail, and with specific reference to one-man service companies, see SE 32795 and 32800. In general they argue that case law, particularly *Miners v Atkinson* [1997] 68 TC 249, does not permit such deductions, and say that 'it will usually be possible to demonstrate that the work that the director or employee carries on at home is not the substantive duties of the employment'. They do however say that 'in very unusual circumstances, there may be exceptions.'

If the worker has only relevant engagements, the allowability of such costs in the corporation tax computation may also be questioned, see **11.3.6**.

Allowable costs

(a) *Travel.* Contractors' travel to the clients' sites is allowable for tax, assuming it meets the conditions described in **11.6**. This remains the case whether or not the expenses are reimbursed by the client.

However the service company should reimburse the costs rather than them being borne by the worker personally, as this will allow them to be deducted in the deemed Schedule E computation and thus reduce the NIC due, see **11.3.3**;

(b) *Subsistence.* The tax treatment of subsistence follows that of travel. Where travel is allowable, so to is the cost of food, drink and accommodation taken during the journeys, see Example 20A (adapted from IR 490 1:11).

Example 20A

Austin is an installation engineer who works at the premises of various clients throughout the United Kingdom. One week he travels between his home in Dover (where his service company is based) to a client's office in Gloucester, staying in a hotel for four nights and, then returning to Dover. The cost of the return journey is £130. The cost of subsistence (four nights in the hotel plus meals) is £300. Austin is entitled to relief for the full cost of his business travel, £430.

(c) *Overseas travel.* Where a UK resident and ordinary resident contractor goes overseas for an engagement lasting at least 60 consecutive days, tax relief is available not only for the costs of his travel and subsistence, but also for two return journeys made by his spouse and children, see **17.10**. This relief applies whether or not the family's journeys are reimbursed by the client. To be allowable the costs must be borne or reimbursed by the service company;

(d) *Call-out costs.* Where an IT specialist is on stand-by and he is reimbursed his travel costs when called out, this will be allowable on the same principle as other travel costs;

(e) *Professional indemnity insurance.* This is an allowable expense under s201AA ICTA 1988, see **11.10**;

(f) *Personal incidental expenses.* An amount of £5 a night (£10 for overseas engagements) when the individual is away from home overnight, is allowed to cover minor personal costs such as laundry and mini-bars. If reimbursed costs exceed this, they are however taxable in full, see **11.7**.

20.5 Musicians

20.5.1 General

Much of **20.2** above on actors applies also to musicians, who are equally likely to have personal service companies. In addition musical groups are sometimes considered to be a partnership for tax purposes, and these may also fall within the new rules.

20.5.2 Employed or self-employed?

The engagement may be under any of the following arrangements:

(a) Musicians engaged under 'first call' or 'guarantee' contracts. These give the orchestra the right to call on the musician's services, but then limit this demand so that they may undertake other work. The musicians are paid separately for each performance. These contracts are accepted by the Revenue as self-employment (SE 7364/ESM 4140);

   This follows *Addison and others v The London Philharmonic Orchestra Society Limited* [1981] ICR 261 and *Midland Sinfonia Concert Society Limited v The Secretary of State for Social Services* [1981] ICR 454. In both cases the court held that the workers remained essentially freelance musicians pursuing their own professions as instrumentalists with individual reputations even when playing for an orchestra. They were thus self-employed even though they did not have their own business structure or risk their own capital, see **6.7.6**;

(b) Musicians who are shareholders in the major London orchestras are self-employed. This is because these orchestras are run by the members themselves, who are thus co-operating in the business;

(c) The Revenue accept that orchestral players who are paid separately for each performance and are not guaranteed a minimum amount of work by an orchestra are self-employed (SE 7364/ESM 4140);

(d) Musicians who are engaged under standard Musicians Union contracts to play at concerts, pantomimes and musicals are treated as self-employed, in the same way as actors under Equity contracts, see **20.2.2** above;

(e) Musicians who are permanent members of major orchestras are generally taxable under Schedule E on the authority of *Fall v Hitchen* [1972] 49 TC 433, see **20.2.2** above. See also *Warner Holidays Ltd v Secretary of State for Social Services* [1983] ICR 440, where two musicians were held to be employed earners because (in contrast to session musicians) Warners had full and exclusive control over them and paid them fixed salaries.

However it should be noted that, like actors, see **20.2.3**, musicians who are self-employed for tax purposes may be employed earners for NICs. Thus a musician with a PSC who falls outside IR35 for tax purposes will nevertheless be required to carry out an attributable earnings calculation if he receives a 'salary' (SI 1978 No 1689 Reg 1(2)). Having a liability for NICs but not for PAYE is discussed at **12.7.2**.

20.5.3 Royalty companies

Groups of musicians sometimes operate through a two tier structure, where each musician has his own PSC, and the PSCs jointly own a royalty/management company. All group engagements are obtained through the management company, which also collects and distributes royalties relating to the group's records. The PSC contracts with the royalty company to supply the services of the musicians.

If the services were being supplied by the PSCs directly to the end-users, the musicians would be outside IR35. However, the interposition of the management company may create a technical problem as follows:

(a) The musicians are supplying services to the management company, and the contract they sign may contain elements which are characteristic of employment. For instance, the musicians may work exclusively for the management company and be subject to its direction and control;

(b) The personal services rules take effect if workers are contracted to supply personal services for the business of another. It is arguable that they are supplying services for the business of the management company, and are thus within the scope of Sch 12, FA 2000.

This would be an anomalous result, as the musicians would be outside IR35 if the PSC provided services to the end-user. It is hoped that the Revenue will not take the technical point. However, it is nevertheless recommended that the contractual arrangements between the PSCs and the management company should be reviewed to ensure they do not represent an 'employment' relationship.

20.5.4 Other points

The same issues concerning expenses and double tax reliefs apply to musicians as they do to actors, see **20.2**. For partnerships, see Chapter 14.

20.6 Oil and gas workers

20.6.1 General

Few North Sea oil and gas operators have many employees. Instead, they use flexible teams of workers each of whom has his own personal service company. Mr Doran MP described their position as follows:

'A large proportion of people now employed *(sic)* in the oil industry are contracted. The industry uses them to provide flexibility for the bad times. For example, at the beginning of last year, when the oil price almost halved overnight . . . the redundancies were almost invisible because contractors were simply shaken out of the industry. Their contracts were terminated. All the contractors who stayed . . . were forced to take substantial cuts, some as high as 20 per cent, which were imposed by the oil companies across the board with no questions asked. That was the requirement if people wanted to keep a contract. Contracts are written in a way that ensures oil companies have the power to do that. It gives the oil industry flexibility and that is the price that people who work in the oil industry have to pay.' (*Hansard*, 3 May 2000, Col. 197)

20.6.2 Employed or self-employed?

Service companies became ubiquitous in the oil and gas industry after the Revenue won the case of *Clark v Oceanic Contractors Incorporated* [1982] 56 TC 183, in which the House of Lords held by a 3:2 majority that Oceanic had sufficient presence in the UK to be required to operate PAYE. This applied not only to the remuneration of employees working within the UK sector of the Continental Shelf, but also to employees working from barges in other non-UK sectors. As a result the operators' PAYE responsibilities were significantly extended.

Service companies were thus established at least in part to avoid PAYE, and many of the workers are therefore likely to fall within IR35. The standard contracts supplied by the operators or agencies have many elements which make them similar to employment contracts.

However, in some cases the standard industry contract has been accepted as a matter of convenience by the worker, and may not reflect the reality of the relationship between the service company and the client. This is particularly the case where an individual is engaged for a relatively short period to carry out specialist skilled work.

Specifically, divers and diving supervisors are accepted by the Revenue as self-employed where they work as individuals (s314 ICTA 1988), and thus will fall outside the personal services legislation if they operate via a company.

20.6.3 Residence status and personal services rules

Summary of residence rules

The normal rules for tax residence are discussed in Chapter 17, and can be summarised as follows. An individual who is:

- Resident and ordinarily resident, is taxed in the UK on all his earnings, wherever the work is performed;

- Not resident, is taxed on work 'performed in the United Kingdom' (s19(1) ICTA 1988), but may be able to argue that it escapes tax either because it is 'merely incidental' to the overseas work, or because of a double tax treaty;

- Resident, but not ordinarily resident is taxed on work carried out in the UK, but earnings from work done elsewhere is not within the scope of UK tax unless the earnings are remitted here;

- Resident and ordinarily resident but not domiciled, is taxed on all work carried out in the UK, and on work carried out overseas for a UK employer. Earnings from work carried out wholly overseas for a foreign employer are taxed on the remittance basis.

Extended boundary of UK to include continental shelf

Most drilling work takes place outside the UK's territorial waters, and oil and gas workers operating in the North Sea are thus likely to be classified as not resident or not ordinarily resident. Under the normal rules for the taxation of earnings set out above, they would thus escape UK tax. To prevent this, s830(5) ICTA 1988 extends the boundary of the United Kingdom so that it covers any 'UK designated areas of the Continental Shelf'.

Interaction between extended boundary and residence rules

This extension operates only to tax the earnings of oil or gas contractors from work in the designated area as if they were resident and ordinarily resident in the UK. It does not actually change the workers' residence status. As a result the taxation of any other earnings, income, gains or assets is unaffected.

In particular the extended boundary rule does not affect the test of whether a person is absent from the UK. If he or she is outside the 12-mile limit at the end of a particular day that day is a day of absence (SE 4522/SE 33034). This is important because, in establishing whether an individual is resident, non-resident or not ordinarily resident, the number of days spent in the UK can be critical, see **17.6**.

As a result, where workers have earnings from non-UK sources, they may be able to protect these earnings from UK tax in general, and the deemed income computation in particular, as follows:

- Earnings from the UK, including the designated areas, are subject to tax either because the worker is UK resident and ordinarily resident, or because of the operation of s830 ICTA 1988;

- If the worker is either not resident in the UK, or not ordinarily resident, earnings from outside the designated areas which are not remitted to the UK will fall outside the deemed income computation;

- If the worker is resident and ordinarily resident, but not domiciled, he can similarly exclude his unremitted overseas earnings from his deemed income computation as long as his contract is with an overseas company and his work for that company is wholly outside the UK (including the designated areas). Where income is excluded from UK tax, however, it may be taxable in another territory, possibly at a higher rate.

National Insurance

The worker may thus be outside the deemed income calculation for tax, but he does not necessarily escape the NIC charge. An attributable earnings calculation may be required on his foreign source earnings, see Chapter 18.

20.6.4 Foreign tax and double tax relief

A worker from overseas who operates both in UK territorial waters and in those of his home country may be exempted from UK tax because a double tax treaty deems him to be resident in his home country rather than in the UK. Where this is the case, he will also fall outside the Schedule E provisions of the personal services legislation, which say that:

> 'The worker is not chargeable to tax in respect of the deemed Schedule E payment if, or to the extent that the worker (is) resident, ordinarily resident or domiciled outside the United Kingdom.' (Sch 12, para 11(3) FA 2000)

However, care is needed. Some double tax treaties do not include the Continental Shelf in their definition of the UK, and thus the workers may remain within Schedule E, see SE 7745/SE 67125. For the NIC position, see Chapter 18.

Where foreign tax is suffered on income which is brought into the deemed Schedule E computation, the tax may be allowable against the PAYE on the deemed salary, see **17.10.2**.

Norway

Where a UK resident and ordinarily resident worker operates in Norwegian territorial waters, the UK/Norway double tax treaty provides that he is taxable only in Norway on earnings derived from that work. These earnings will thus be excluded from the deemed income calculation, but at the price of paying Norwegian taxes.

The UK resident worker is, however, unlikely to be within the Norwegian social security system (see EPM 8321). Although his Norwegian earnings are excluded from the deemed income calculation, they need to be included when calculating his attributable earnings, see **18.3.5**.

Conversely, where a Norwegian is working in UK territorial waters, he is within the scope of UK tax, and thus the personal services regime applies to him. However, he is likely to remain within his home country social security system. He thus has a deemed Schedule E calculation, but no attributable earnings, see **18.4.5**.

20.6.5 Reporting requirements

The oil companies submit quarterly returns to the Revenue's Oil Taxation Office under Sch 15, para 2 FA 1973. The Revenue's *Oil Taxation Office Section 830 Manual* says, at paragraph 7.7.1, that:

> '(These) returns are the Oil Taxation Office's primary source of information about payments made to persons not resident in the United Kingdom which may give rise to a liability to corporation tax under ICTA 1988 s830.'

If it appears that there may be an undisclosed PAYE liability, relevant data from these returns is passed to Special Compliance Office. It could also be used in the future to help police IR35.

20.6.6 Travel expenses

Travel is a major cost for oil and gas workers, because their home base is often far from their place of work. A concession relieves them from tax on the cost of travel from the mainland to the rigs (ESC A65). It was expected that the travel rules introduced in 1998 (now included in s 198(1A)(b)(ii) and Sch 12A ICTA 1988) would ensure that workers obtained relief for their home to work travel for the part of their journey not covered by ESC A65, provided the standard two year/40 per cent tests were met, see **11.6.3** and *Tolleys Practical Tax* 29 July 1998. It was also accepted by the Revenue that if the rig itself moved, this amounted to a change of location, see *Tolleys Practical Tax* 23 September 1998.

However Sch 12A, para 5(3) ICTA 1988 says that there is no tax relief if a change in location 'does not have . . . any substantial effect on the employee's journey, or expenses of travelling, to and from the place where the duties fall to be performed'.

Some inspectors have been reluctant to accept that a change of location from one rig to another, even one a hundred miles distant from the last, was 'substantial' in the context of the worker's total journey. This has been challenged by those affected, on the basis that:

- Substantial is an absolute as well as a relative term; and

- Tax relief is given for changes in location of other taxpayers, where the distances involved were tiny in comparison. Equity between taxpayers is a relevant factor here.

If the Revenue succeed, oil workers will be disadvantaged when compared to other personal service workers.

Where the worker travels to a rig outside the UK's continental shelf, he will however be going 'abroad' and thus may qualify for the reliefs set out in ss193-4 ICTA 1988, see **17.10**. He will then be able to claim the cost of all his travel from the UK to the rig, even if it is not allowed under normal rules, and this will be deductible at Step Three of his deemed Schedule E calculation.

Similarly, a non-domiciled worker from abroad who satisfies the requirements of s195 ICTA (**17.12.4**) may be allowed relief in his deemed Schedule E calculation for the costs of his travel to and from a rig in the Continental Shelf, as this is regarded as part of the UK for Schedule E purposes, see SE 4720/SE 35080.

Other expenses

The Revenue accept that protective clothing worn as a matter of physical necessity because of the nature of the job, such as oil workers' overalls, are allowable under s198 ICTA 1988, see **11.5**.

20.7 Sportspeople

20.7.1 General

From a tax perspective, sports men and women have much in common with actors and entertainers, see **20.2**, particularly when they work overseas. However, there are some significant differences. In particular, some cannot be employees of their service companies in respect of their main activity, because the regulations of their sport require them to have a contract of service with their club. They can thus only use a service company or partnership for sponsorship and similar activities.

20.7.2 Employed or self-employed?

Schedule E income

Professional footballers are required by Football League rules to sign a contract of personal service with their club, and the income from this contract is invariably Schedule E.

However, other amounts may be paid into the player's personal service company by the club for services provided in addition to those supplied under his employment contract. Before IR35 these payments were often challenged by the Revenue on the basis that they formed part of the player's remuneration. In future the Revenue may instead attack such arrangements under the PSC rules.

Signing-on and transfer fees, payments for winning matches and loyalty bonuses all come within the scope of s19(1) ICTA 1988, see SE 7420ff/SE 64100ff. Benefit and testimonial matches may be outside the scope of Schedule E if they are not contractual (SE 7425/SE 64120). However if the testimonial or benefit match is 'expected or promised' the Revenue will hold that it is an implied term of the player's employment with the club and taxable under Schedule E. Monies from testimonials are not usually paid into a service company, as they are either outside the scope of tax, or taxable in any event under the player's employment contract.

Amateur players are not bound by the Football League rules, and thus are not required to have employment contracts with their clubs. The Revenue may nevertheless argue that they are employees. The Manual says:

> 'Where a payment or series of payments to a non-contract player appears to include a clear element of remuneration, for example appearance money, you should consider whether there is an oral or implied contract which makes the player an employee of the club. . . . You will also need to consider whether the terms of engagement of the player are similar to those applying to contract players. Other matters, such as the obligations imposed on keeping fit, training, availability for selection, times of reporting for matches, taking of instructions from managers and other officials, discipline and club rules and regulations generally may also be of relevance.' (SE 7420/SE 64145)

If a player had sought to protect himself from this sort of attack by using a service company, he will probably now fall within IR35, on the basis that he would have been an employee had he not operated via the company.

Professional cricketers and other sportspeople are also commonly under contract to their clubs, and their rewards from this contract are within Schedule E. Again, testimonials may be non-taxable, see SE 7800/SE 68400.

Sponsorship and promotional income

A sportsperson may have both an employment contract with his club, and an 'Image Contract' with his personal service company. The service company's objective is to exploit the player's name and likeness, and to collect fees for sponsorship and promotional activities. It may also own copyrights or trademarks relating to the player's activity.

In the context of IR35, the key question is whether the services provided under the Image Contract would be employment if the intermediary did not exist. In most cases the answer must be no. The service company is promoting the sports personality, not supplying quasi-employee services to a sponsor. Income received by the intermediary will therefore generally be outside the scope of the personal services legislation.

However, where the worker supplies regular services via his PSC to a single client, such as spending three days a week coaching for a university team, this may be a relevant engagement and the income received may be within the scope of IR35.

20.7.3 Overseas issues

Most individuals are taxed on the basis of residence, and are protected by international treaties from suffering tax in more than one jurisdiction at a time. Sportspeople are however treated differently, and may be taxed in the country where the activities are exercised. In general, the rules applying to sportspeople are the same as those for actors, see **20.2.6** above. Relief is also available for foreign travel as described in **17.10**.

If an overseas sportsperson with a service company plays in the UK, he will be subject to the existing withholding tax rules under s555 ICTA 1988 and not to IR35 (Sch 12, para 6 FA 2000).

20.7.4 Pension schemes

As with other service companies brought within IR35, a deduction is available for pension contributions made by the intermediary in respect of the worker, see **12.2**. The contributions thus reduce the amount of PAYE and Class 1 NICs paid by the service company.

Many sportsmen and women are allowed to make accelerated contributions into their pension scheme because their working life is shorter than that of the average person. In the context of the personal services legislation, the value of this may be substantial. The age at which retirement can be taken is as follows:

Age	Sport
30	Downhill skiers.
35	Athletes; badminton players; boxers; cyclists; dancers; footballers; National Hunt jockeys; real tennis players; Rugby League players; squash players; table tennis players; tennis players; wrestlers.
40	Cricketers; golfers; motorcycle riders (motocross or road racing); motor racing drivers; speedway riders; trapeze artistes.
45	Flat racing jockeys.

20.8 Subcontractors

20.8.1 Introduction

Building industry subcontractors used to be treated as self-employed if they held a SC60 certificate allowing them to be paid gross by the main contractor. However, in the mid-1990s the Inland Revenue and the Contributions Agency launched a major assault on subcontractors, reclassifying many as employees. Some set up service companies in an effort to avoid recategorisation.

20.8.2 Recategorisation: the history

The first sign of an attack came with the publication in October 1995 of the booklet IR148/CA69: '*Are your workers employed or self-employed? A Guide for Tax and National Insurance for contractors in the Construction Industry.*' This was followed by new instructions to Inland Revenue and Contributions Agency auditors.

On a piecemeal basis, and subject to the randomness of the auditors' visits, many formerly 'self-employed' workers were recategorised as employees. However this scatter-gun approach was widely criticised, and the IR/CA finally announced that businesses would be given until 5 April 1997 to review the employment status of their workers (IRPR 19 November 1996).

An article in *Tax Bulletin 28* gave comfort by stating that, if properly managed, a service company would be an effective way of avoiding recategorisation. It confirmed that:

> 'A valid contract between two companies is not a contract of employment. However, IR and CA may want to check that the agreements are validly

made, that they do in fact achieve the legal result that the parties intended and that the parties have acted in accordance with those agreements.'

In some cases clients and agencies, unsure of whether their subcontractors were inside or outside the rules for Schedule E, encouraged them to form limited companies. They thus avoided both responsibility for PAYE and the risks of a later recategorisation.

The final round: personal services?

The personal services legislation will now catch those service companies established a few years ago in order to avoid Schedule E recategorisation. Those set up because of uncertainty about the worker's status can no longer avoid the issue.

Individuals with service companies should first review whether they would be employed or self-employed if they did not have a company, see Chapters 5 to 9. If they are within the personal services regime, they should consider closing down the company. This is because of the harsh cashflow effects for subcontractors who fall within the PSC regime, see **20.8.5**.

20.8.3 Employed or self-employed?

The tests to establish whether an individual is an employee are discussed in detail at Chapters 5 to 9. In particular, the case of *Lee Ting Sang v Chung Chi-Keung* [1990] 2 AC 374, in which the Privy Council decided that a subcontractor was an employee, should be reviewed, see **8.3.1**, as well as the Revenue worked examples at **24.3**. The new Employment Status Manual at para 4323ff further expands the Revenue position.

20.8.4 Use of partnerships

In their article on subcontractors the Revenue indicated that partnerships set up to avoid recategorisation could be ineffective:

> 'The existence of a contract between a contractor and a bona fide partnership will be a pointer towards self-employment. But the mere fact that a worker is a member of a partnership does not mean that he cannot be an employee. If the true nature of the contract between the worker and the contractor is one of employment, the contractor must account for PAYE and NICs on the remuneration paid. The fact that the worker may also be a member of a partnership is irrelevant.' (*Tax Bulletin 28*)

However where the contract is between the partnership and the client, rather than between the contractor and the client, the Revenue's legal advice is that it is not possible to redesignate the contract as one of employment. This type of arrangement would thus be effective in avoiding recategorisation as an employee.

Partnerships thus had to be brought within IR35, if only to prevent them replacing companies as the new tax-efficient vehicle – not only for subcontractors, but for all those who use personal service companies. The implications of IR35 for partnerships are discussed in Chapter 14.

20.8.5 Subcontractor tax deductions and the deemed income calculation

Subcontractors have their own tax arrangements under s559 ICTA 1988. In some cases they are paid net of tax by the main contractor, and this is then set against their tax liability for the year.

Where the subcontractor is a partnership or service company, the deduction is taken into account within the company's or partnership's computation. If too much tax has been deducted, this can be recovered once the computation for the year is final.

An individual working via a partnership or service company may be within both the personal services legislation and the subcontractor regime. However the tax already deducted under s559 ICTA 1988 is not taken into account when calculating the tax due on the Schedule E deemed payment:

> 'Where section 559 of the Taxes Act 1988 applies . . . the intermediary is treated for the purposes of Step One of the calculation in paragraph 7 as receiving the amount that would have been received had no deduction been made under that section.' (Sch 12, para 8 FA 2000)

Subcontractors are thus likely to suffer a serious cashflow effect, as 18 per cent will be deducted from their income before receipt, and both income tax and NICs will subsequently be deducted on the same money because of the personal services rules, see Example 20B. The Revenue are aware of the unfairness of this tax charge, and have said that they have it under review.

Example 20B

Dylan is a subcontractor working through his own limited company. He has two relevant engagements during the fiscal year 2000/01, and invoices his main contractor £100,000 in total, including materials of £6,000 and travel of £4,000. He also has a further £5,000 in costs which are not allowable either under Schedule E or the subcontractor scheme, but are deductible for corporation tax. Dylan is paid under deduction of tax by the main contractor. He has paid himself £18,000 in salary during the year. His corporation tax year end is 5 April. There is no difference between his accrued and received income or expenses. His subcontractor position and deemed income calculation are as follows:

Part A: Subcontractor income

	Notes	£
Total invoiced		100,000
Less: materials	1	(6,000)
		94,000
Less 18%		(16,920)
Net receipt		77,080

Notes

1. Section 559 does not allow a deduction for travel.

Part B: Deemed Schedule E calculation

	Notes	£
Step One: Income received		100,000
5% allowance		(5,000)
Step Three: Allowable expenses	1	(10,000)
Step Six: Employer's NIC on salary paid	2	(1,661)
Step Seven: Salary paid		(18,000)
Income after expenses, salary and NIC on salary		65,339
Step Eight: NIC on deemed payment	3	(7,105)
Deemed Schedule E payment		58,234

Notes

1. It is assumed that the materials would be eligible for relief under s198 ICTA 1988

2. £18,000 − 4,385 = 13,615 x 12.2% = 1,661

3. £65,339 x 12.2/112.2 = 7,105

Part C: Income tax and NIC calculation

	Notes	£	£
Salary			18,000
Deemed salary			58,234
Gross income			76,234
Personal allowance		4,385	
Tax at 10% on		1,520	(152)
Tax at 22% on		26,880	(5,914)
Tax at 40% on balance of		43,449	(17,380)
		76,234	52,788

Part D: Corporation tax computation

	£	£
Turnover		100,000
Less: Travel	4,000	
Materials	6,000	
Employer's NIC	8,766	
Other costs	5,000	
Salary and deemed salary	76,234	
		100,000
CT position		NIL

Part E: Tax and NIC suffered

	£
Tax on subcontractor s559 deduction	16,920
Tax on salary and deemed salary	23,446
Employer's NIC on salary and deemed salary	8,766
Employee's NIC on salary and deemed salary	2,387
	51,519
Tax rate on net income after expenses of £85,000	60.6%
Tax recoverable when corporation tax computation agreed	£16,920
True tax + NICs payable (23,446 + 8,766 + 2,387)	£34,599
True tax + NICs rate	40.7%

Conclusion

Example 20B shows that Dylan has paid 20 per cent more in tax than is necessary, with consequently serious effects on his cashflow position. The actual shortfall will vary from case to case, because of the interaction between the amounts allowable under s559 ICTA 1988, and those deductible in the deemed Schedule E and corporation tax computations.

Although the money will be recovered once the corporation tax computation has been agreed, in the meantime the subcontractor may have difficulty meeting existing commitments such as mortgage payments. The cashflow effects also forces the subcontractors into the deemed payment regime. Most workers have the choice between paying themselves sufficient salary during the year and so avoiding the deemed payment, and suffering the deemed payment and withdrawing the funds as dividends, see **13.5**. However, if the subcontractor tries to pay himself enough salary to take himself outside the deemed payment requirement, he will find that he has insufficient funds to pay both the tax on the salary and the salary itself.

Subcontractors within s559 should thus consider whether they want to wait for a Revenue solution, or whether they should close down their companies, see **13.8**. However, closing the company may have commercial implications, as some agencies and clients have been unwilling to deal with subcontractors unless they had their own service companies.

20.9 Teachers and lecturers

20.9.1 Introduction

Service companies have become increasingly common among teachers and lecturers, particularly where they are 'supply teachers'. As with all service companies, the key question is: what would be their employment status if they did not have a company?

20.9.2 Employed or self-employed?

A full time teacher or lecturer with a permanent position in a school or university is almost certainly an employee. However the position is less clear with part-time or supply teachers. A full discussion of contract law and the status tests is in Chapters 5 to 8, and the Revenue view is set out at ESM 4501ff. In the context of teachers and lecturers some factors to be considered include:

1. How much *control* the teacher has, for instance over the course content and the times the lessons are delivered. The more control, the less likely the worker is to be an employee;

2. Does the teacher supply any necessary *equipment* at his own expense, such as a PowerPoint projector or photocopied handouts?

3. Whether the lecturer can send a *substitute*. This might be thought an easy condition to meet when a school is simply looking for a supply teacher – i.e., someone who broadly meets the requirements in order to fill a gap caused by absence. However in practice the educational establishment will revert to the agency to provide a substitute, not the lecturer. This will not

satisfy the substitution test, because the right to send a replacement must rest with the worker;

4. Does he satisfy the *Lorimer* test? In other words, does he have many short-term lecturing engagements with a variety of engagers; is there a common intention to create self employment as between the school/college and the lecturer; does he have a business-like approach to obtaining and organising his engagements? A more detailed discussion of the *Lorimer* case can be found at **8.2.1**.

5. What is the intention of the parties? The Revenue accept that this can be can be 'of fundamental importance in some instances' (ESM 4502).

Even where the worker can pass the self-employment test for tax purposes, he may not do so for NICs, see **20.9.3**.

Case law authority

Teachers or lecturers have, on a number of occasions, succeeded in arguing that they are self-employed. Many were National Insurance cases decided before the special regulations were introduced in 1978. Teachers should assess their own position against the decided cases, both those in their own field and the other decisions discussed in Chapter 8.

In *Argent v Minister of Social Security* [1968] 3 AER 208, Argent was a teacher of acting. The DSS argued that his engagement with the Guildhall School of Music and Drama constituted an employment, but the court held that he was self-employed because he had significant other acting work, was given no guidance on his teaching methods, was paid by the session and had no administrative duties. The judge said:

> 'When one looks at all the facts found one has a picture of a man skilled and experienced in his own profession, of the services of whom the corporation, as the owners of the Guildhall School of Music, were anxious to obtain for the benefit of their students. They give him a fairly free choice of what he teaches and an entirely free choice how he teaches. They do not prescribe his syllabus. They leave to him the actual manner of his teaching as the expert in that field. They impose no administrative duties on him. They leave him free to pursue the artistic side of his work for the benefit of the students whom he is there to teach and train for their later careers on the stage. To say that in those circumstances when a man is so employed at a rate per hour or at a particular fee for a particular job that he is employed under a contract of service seems to me, with all respect, to be quite unreal.'

This followed a similar case involving a professional lawn tennis coach (M51 [1956]). He was held to be self-employed since he was not controlled as to his methods of teaching, was not obliged to accept engagements, and was remunerated by a fee for each session.

However, these cases should be contrasted with *Sidey v Phillips* [1987] STC 87. Mr Sidey was a barrister who lectured part-time for both Thames Polytechnic and the Inner London Education Authority. Although the arrangements for his engagements were exceedingly casual, Mr Sidey knew that there were standard terms and conditions for part time teachers, and he was thus treated as having entered into contracts under those standard terms, and thus an employee. The same point was significant in the poorly argued case of *Fuge v McClelland* [1956] 36 TC 571. The lesson here is that arrangements should be clearly documented, or the standard terms may apply by default. In the case of the hypothetical IR35 contract, the other 'circumstances' have also to be considered, see **5.1.1**.

In the Privy Council case of *Narich Pty Ltd v Commissioner of Payroll Tax* [1984] ICR 286, lecturers who were contracted to conduct weight watchers classes were held to be employees of Weight Watchers International Inc. because they were 'tied hand and foot' with regard to how they had to perform the work.

20.9.3 National Insurance position

There are special NIC rules for teachers and lecturers, and these take precedence over the case law on employment/self-employment (SI 1978 No 1689 Sch 1, para 4). A teacher or lecturer will be regarded as an employed earner for NICs unless:

- The lectures are open to the public; or

- The number of days on which instruction is given has been limited, by prior agreement, to three days or less in three consecutive months; or

- Their earnings are paid by someone other than the body providing the education, such as directly by the students themselves; or

- The lecturers do not teach in the presence of those who are to receive the instruction, but do so by some 'distance learning' method, such as correspondence or video tapes. Open University teachers are an exception here – they have been brought within the NIC rules by special provisions (SI 1978 No 1689 Sch 1, para 4).

Thus a teacher or lecturer could be regarded as self-employed for tax, but an employed earner for NICs. He would therefore have to carry out an attributable earnings calculation, but not a deemed income calculation, see **12.7.2**. The intermediary would be liable for secondary NICs.

20.9.4 Overseas issues

Visiting teachers or lecturers may qualify for special double tax reliefs. Most UK treaties exempt teachers from tax if they come here to work for two years or less. Since this applies to income subject to PAYE, it will also apply to deemed income calculated under the personal services rules and thus these teachers will be outside IR35 for tax. However some agreements only exempt the income if it is 'subject to tax' in the home country, and the Revenue may thus ask for proof that the personal services income has been taxed abroad, see DTRM 1936.

Teachers going overseas are subject to the same rules in reverse, so that their earnings may remain within Schedule E and the deemed income computation even though they are working overseas.

20.10 TV and film industry workers

20.10.1 Background

Personal service companies are commonplace in the media. The Revenue Manual says somewhat testily:

> 'To avoid PAYE many film and video workers in Schedule E grades have set up limited companies. Normally the worker is the majority shareholder and a director. It is alleged that the service company supplies the services of the individual to a film or video production company. An examination of many such cases has shown that such arrangements often fail. The worker remains an employee of the production company. Tell the Film Industry Unit about any service companies of this kind that you find.' (SE 7324/ESM 4104)

In fact the Revenue's guidance notes to companies engaging workers is more pragmatic, simply saying, 'you may pay a service company gross where you are satisfied the service company is properly incorporated and you are actually engaging and paying the service company not the individual.' The pre-IR35 position is discussed in a similar context at **20.3.3**.

Now that Schedule 12, Finance Act 2000 is on the statute book, the Revenue will no longer need to argue that the company is a sham and should be 'looked through', see **4.1.2**. But the underlying point remains the same: would the individual have been employed or self-employed had he been working without the 'wrapper' of the company?

20.10.2 Employed or self-employed?

In March 1983, the Inland Revenue announced that it had carried out a review of workers within the film and allied industries and had concluded that:

> 'A number of workers engaged on "freelance" terms within the industry are engaged as employees under contracts of service, either written or oral.'

Re-categorisation of these workers began on 6 April 1983, and by the end of 1983 over 7,000 had been classified as employed earners (*Hansard* 16 January 1984 Vol. 52 Col. 14).

Following this exercise, the Revenue began issuing a list of the types of 'behind camera' workers it considers to be self-employed, and the list is updated annually. Workers who exercise a special skill on a production-by-production basis, or who provide special effects, form most of the Revenue's Schedule D group. A listing of jobs (or 'grades') which are accepted as Schedule D is available on application from the Revenue's Film or TV and Radio Industry Units.

In addition to the approved list, the Revenue also accept that an individual is self-employed if he has very many short-term contracts with a number of engagers, so that the facts of the case are on all fours with the vision-mixer in *Hall v Lorimer* [1993] 66 TC 349, see SE 7323/ESM 4103 and **8.2.1**.

Regular reporting of payments made 'to individuals or for the services of individuals' under s16 TMA 1970 is required on an annual basis of companies in the industry (TV Industry, Guidance Notes in respect of Freelancers).

21 Agencies, clients and umbrellas

21.1 Introduction

The original personal services proposals made the client responsible for deducting PAYE and NIC from the earnings of personal service workers, see **2.3.2**. In response to representations, the government subsequently transferred responsibility for complying with IR35 to the intermediaries. However, neither clients or agencies can ignore the personal services legislation, which has significant legal and commercial consequences.

The impact of the new regime on umbrella companies is discussed at **21.4** below. These composites were one of the triggers for IR35, see **2.2.3**, and they remain significantly affected.

21.2 Agencies

21.2.1 Areas unaffected by the personal services legislation

Agency rules

Existing legislation deems individuals supplying personal services to clients via an agency to be employees of the agency for the purposes of both tax and NICs (s134 ICTA 1988; SI 1978 No 1689 Reg 2; Sch 1, para 2; Sch 3, para 2). These rules currently exclude services provided via companies, and this continues to be the case under IR35.

A service company worker operating via an agency will thus not be within the agency rules (Sch 12, para 24 FA 2000; SI 2000 No 727 Reg 12). This is confirmed by FAQ General 13:

> '*Will the legislation for agency workers need to be rewritten?*
>
> This measure will do nothing to disturb the existing agency legislation at Section 134 Income and Corporation Taxes Act 1988. This is because Section 134 only applies to individuals. It does not apply to service companies.'

Fees

The deemed Schedule E calculation is based on the income *received* by the intermediary. Fees deducted by agencies en route to the service company do not form part of the income included in the calculation.

However, where fees are paid to an agency by the worker or the intermediary, there is no relief for these payments in the deemed Schedule E calculation. The exception is for agency fees paid by actors, providing they fall within s201A ICTA 1988, see **20.2.4**.

Relevant intermediaries

The legislation is aimed at 'relevant intermediaries'. An agency, although clearly an intermediary, will not normally be a *relevant* intermediary because it does not come within the conditions set out in Schedule 12, paragraphs 3–5 FA 2000. As a result, it is not jointly and severally liable for the service company's PAYE and NIC liability: that responsibility only attaches to relevant intermediaries (Sch 12, para 16 FA 2000, see **4.5.5**).

21.2.2 Contracts

The Revenue have reviewed the standard IT industry agency contracts, and concluded that they fall within IR35, see **7.6**. Since similar terms are generally included in other industries' standard contracts, these are also likely to be within the personal services legislation.

Agencies have been placed under considerable pressure to amend their contracts to help contractors escape IR35. How contracts may be changed is discussed in detail at Chapter 9. However, agencies should remember that:

- Liability under IR35 is based on the content of a hypothetical contract between the worker and the client. If clauses are inserted in the contract between the service company and the agency, but not in the contract between the agency and the client, the Revenue (and ultimately the courts) will try and establish the actual arrangements, see **5.5.2**. A contractual term which contradicts that reality, or is unsupported by the facts, is likely to be ignored or set aside;

- If the clauses are a sham, the Revenue will look through them. If the insertion of such clauses was a deliberate policy on the agency's part, it might attract unwelcome Revenue attention. At an extreme, it could be investigated by Special Compliance Office or attacked under s99 TMA 1970. This says that:

'Any person who assists in or induces the preparation or delivery of any information, return, accounts or other document which (a) he knows will be, or is or are likely to be, used for any purpose of tax, and (b) he knows to be incorrect, shall be liable to a penalty not exceeding £3,000.'

- The introduction of certain clauses into client contracts, while increasing the likelihood that the worker will be treated as outside IR35, also increases the level of risk for the agency. If the worker can send a substitute (see **9.3**) and the substitute is unsatisfactory, the client's right of action is against the agency, not against the service company. Similarly, if the worker has moved to a project basis (see **9.4**) and does not complete the project on time, the agency may be held responsible. The commercial consequences of changing contracts must therefore be considered along with their tax effects.

21.2.3 Other consequences

Workers who are within the personal services legislation may:

- Seek to put up their rates, to recover the extra costs of IR35, and this will have consequences for agencies. However, the additional tax and NIC suffered varies considerably, depending on the extent to which the service company previously took advantage of the various tax planning opportunities available;

- Move into employment, either with the client or with an agency. Their new employer will thus have all the normal employment law obligations as well as the secondary NIC cost. In consequence the worker's remuneration is likely to be lower.

21.2.4 Reporting to the Revenue

The Revenue have given notice that they will use their existing powers to obtain from agencies details of service companies to which payments have been made, and the amount and nature of the payments (s16 TMA 1970). The legislation is as follows:

(a) A business can be required, by notice from the Revenue, to provide a return of payments made 'for services rendered by persons not employed in the trade or business' of the payer;

(b) The return can be for any period, but the period will be specified in the notice;

(c) The return must give the name and address of the person(s) to whom payments were made, and this may include 'any business name and any business or home address';

(d) It should state the amount of the payment, and a payment includes 'the giving of any valuable consideration';

(e) Other particulars, such as the period over which services were rendered and the type of services which were provided, may also be required.

There are penalties of up to £300 if the return is late, and up to £3,000 for fraud or negligence (s98 TMA 1970).

Section 16 gives the Revenue very broad powers which are likely to be used extensively, especially in the early years of the personal services regime.

21.3 Clients

21.3.1 Outline

Many of the issues which are relevant to agencies also affect clients. In particular:

• Contractual changes and their implications for clients and agencies are discussed in Chapter 9 and **21.2.2** above. For example, if there is no notice period (**9.14**), is there a danger that the project will grind to a halt while a replacement is found?

• If there is a dispute with the Revenue as to whether a clause is valid, and thus what the true 'circumstances' of the arrangements are, the client may be required to give evidence in court;

• The commercial issues concerning pricing and the PAYE alternative are similar to those for agencies, see **21.2.3** above;

• Clients, like agencies, may be asked for information from the Revenue under s16 TMA 1970 (see **21.2.4**). However, complying with that obligation may be more difficult for a large multinational than it is for an agency. The agency is likely to be able to extract a list of payments made to service companies with relative ease; the client may have contractors working in many parts of its business, recorded under numerous different headings. Their invoices may have been absorbed within an overall project cost and be difficult to identify. Where a Section 16 return is required, clients should thus seek to negotiate a reasonable time-frame for its delivery to the Revenue.

21.3.2 Overseas service companies

Where a worker is supplied to the client by an overseas employer, the client can be required to operate PAYE and NIC on any salary paid to the worker, see **19.5.2** (s203C ICTA 1988; s7(2)(b) SSCBA 1992; SI 1978 No 1689 Sch 3(9)).

However, if the employer is a personal services company within Schedule 12 FA 2000, the obligation to deduct tax and NIC in respect of the deemed Schedule E payment rests with the service company. However, s203C continues to apply to payments of salary actually paid to the worker.

The client is thus in a difficult position, as he cannot know for sure what actual salary has been paid; he knows only what he has paid the service company. IR35 has not caused this problem, but has not made it disappear either. He has four options:

(a) To require the overseas company to supply the information. In practice he may only be prepared to rely on this if the overseas company is a connected party, such as a subsidiary or a joint venture partner;

(b) To deduct tax from the amount paid to the service company. This would, however, leave him open to an action from the worker, as he would be acting beyond his authority;

(c) Argue that although s203C is a legal obligation, it is unenforceable, as he does not have the information necessary to comply with the requirements. Since the overseas company is outside the scope of UK tax, it cannot be compelled to provide the client with the information. If the client takes this approach, the Revenue are likely to institute formal proceedings to obtain the PAYE (SI 1993 No 744 Reg 42). This process is discussed in the Revenue Manual under the heading 'Corresponding with reluctant employers' (EPM 9178);

(d) Not use workers supplied by overseas service companies.

Option (d) is probably the most common response, unless the client can satisfy himself under (a). Many reputable agencies take the same approach, refusing to place workers operating via overseas service companies because of the s203C issues for their clients.

Although the personal services legislation has shifted some of the onus onto the service company, sufficient burden remains on the client to make the use of overseas service companies very unattractive.

21.3.3 Third-party reporting

Where cash or other benefits are paid or supplied directly to the worker by the client, there may be a PAYE or other reporting obligation on the client. The circumstances in which this can occur are discussed at **10.5.4(5)**.

21.3.4 Freelance consultants

Where a client uses freelance consultants in his business, there is a risk that they could be recategorised as Schedule E by the Revenue's Employer Compliance Unit. The client may then be liable for up to six year's back PAYE and NICs.

Where there is doubt about the Schedule D status of a freelance consultant, clients might choose to take advantage of the IR35 provisions by insisting that new contracts are only made with personal service companies and not with individual freelancers. By so doing the client will have transferred the compliance burden to the service company. If the freelancer is confident of his Schedule D status, using an intermediary should not significantly increase his tax liability, as he will fall outside IR35.

21.4 Umbrella companies

21.4.1 Structure

Before IR35 most composites were structured as follows:

- The shares were held by the shareholders/workers, with each shareholder having a separate class of stock as well as one or more normal shares;

- The company's day-to-day business was carried out by an independent administrator;

- Earnings were subject to an administrative deduction which covered the costs of running the composite;

- Expenses relating to the engagements were commonly charged through to the company by the worker;

- Each shareholder earned a small salary, with the balance of his net earnings streamed through to him via the dividends on his personal class of shares.

21.4.2 Umbrellas and IR35

Composite companies gave individuals the benefits of their own service company, without the administrative burdens. It thus opened up the tax benefits of PSCs to a much wider group of workers, including secretaries, teachers and train drivers. The tax reliefs meant that running umbrella companies was profitable for the administrators, while the 'take-home pay' of the workers was higher than if they had remained as employees.

The Revenue clearly had umbrella companies in their sights when they announced IR35. In answer to Frequently Asked Question number 25. 'Will the new rules apply to people working for "composite" or "umbrella" companies?' the reply was a terse 'Yes'.

Most, if not all, composites come within IR35 because:

(a) The worker has a material interest in the intermediary, because he, and/or his associates, own 5 per cent or more of the shares in the composite, see **4.5.2**; or, more commonly,

(b) He receives from the company 'a payment or benefit . . . that can reasonably be taken to represent remuneration for services provided by the worker to the client' (Sch 12, para 3 FA 2000); and

(c) He either receives, or is entitled to receive, a payment or benefit which is not taxable under Schedule E, or has rights which would entitle him to such a payment or benefit (Sch 12, para 2(b) FA 2000).

In most cases the streaming of income to the worker via dividends will be caught by these provisions. See **9.15** for a brief discussion of schemes which have purported to avoid this requirement.

However, not all composites were set up for tax avoidance reasons. Some had as their primary aim the provision of administrative assistance to contractors. The post-IR35 world still has a need for this sort of service.

21.4.3 Composites post-IR35

Those umbrella companies which have survived so far tend to have the following characteristics.

Taking non-relevant engagements on trust

Most composites attempt to distinguish between relevant engagements and those within IR35. However, this usually involves obtaining a simple signed statement from the worker. If the worker is wrong, the income from the engagement has been incorrectly excluded from the deemed income calculation. Responsibility for carrying out this calculation and paying over the tax and NICs rests with the composite, not the worker: the composite is the relevant intermediary under the personal services legislation.

Workers entering into arrangements with composites should thus check:

• Whether the company can recover from the individual any PAYE, NICs and penalties which may arise if an engagement is subsequently recategorised by

387

the Revenue as within IR35, and if so, are any funds being retained to protect the company against this risk?

• What information has to be provided, and by whom, in order to establish whether the Revenue's recategorisation of the engagement as 'relevant' is correct? Who will remain in control if there are negotiations with the Revenue? Who will provide, and who will pay for, any professional advice?

• If a worker incorrectly certifies that his engagements are outside the scope of IR35, will other workers' income be used to settle the PAYE and NIC liability?

Using the 5 per cent allowance

To the extent that the workers are carrying out relevant engagements, the composite can access the 5 per cent round sum allowance. However, in many composites this is effectively used up in dealing with the company's administration. Since this is largely what the allowance was designed to cover, this may be a reasonable approach. But it bears more heavily on those who earn large sums than on those who are less productive.

Deemed income calculation versus dividends

The administrators are likely to distinguish between relevant and non-relevant engagements, and then pay out the earnings derived from the former as salary. This is simpler than using the dividend route. Despite paying the income out as salary, the composite still has to carry out a deemed income calculation to ensure that it comes to 'nil or a negative amount' (Sch 12, para 7, Step Seven FA 2000).

In some cases the administrators may seek to exploit the small cashflow advantage achieved (see **13.5.3**) by using the deemed income calculation and then paying the money out as dividends. However, this is administratively more complex and unlikely to be worthwhile.

Policing the expenses

The composite is also responsible for ensuring the correct identification of Schedule E allowable expenses. In practice this is achieved by allowing only certain costs, such as travel to the client's site, to be passed directly through the company, with other expenses being claimed on the individual's self-assessment return. However, excluding allowable costs from the deemed Schedule E calculation means that the PAYE and Class 1 NIC paid is higher than it need be. Although tax relief can be obtained via the self-assessment return, it is not possible to recover the NIC, see **11.3.3**.

22 National Minimum Wage, Working Families Tax Credits and Student Loans

22.1 Introduction

The National Minimum Wage (NMW) came into force on 1 April 1999. Its implementation is a matter of employment law rather than tax legislation, and this chapter will therefore only discuss the NMW in outline and consider how it affects the position of personal service workers.

The Working Families Tax Credit (WFTC) was first introduced in September 1999. It is a more generous replacement for family credit, awarded to low-paid workers with children. Despite its name, it is not a reduction in tax, but a government-provided earnings top-up. Entitlement to WFTC depends on the worker's income and assets, the number and age of any children, and childcare costs. From a personal services perspective, the key issues are how the deemed Schedule E payment, and any associated dividends, are treated for the purposes of WFTC.

There is also an interaction between student loans and IR35. Since 1 September 1998 students in England and Wales have been entitled to a student loan. After graduation the loan is recovered once income exceeds £10,000 a year. If the former student is employed, the student loan repayment (SLR) operates by way of deduction from salary. This chapter looks at how the deemed Schedule E amount and related distributions are regarded for SLR purposes.

22.2 National Minimum Wage

22.2.1 Outline

All workers are now entitled to the National Minimum Wage. The amount payable is £3.60 an hour until 1 October 2000 and £3.70 thereafter. Lower rates apply to workers under 21 and to those on accredited training.

Paying a worker the minimum wage is a legal obligation. There is no relief from the obligation simply because an individual chooses not to receive the money; and if the worker has an entitlement to the payment, then PAYE and NIC inevitably follow.

In the context of the personal services legislation, the key questions are:

(a) Who is a 'worker' for the purposes of the legislation?

(b) What is a 'wage' and does it include the deemed Schedule E payment?

(c) What is the position of a client or agency in the context of the NMW?

(d) How will it be enforced?

(e) What are the tax and NIC implications?

22.2.2 Definition of a worker for NMW purposes

A worker is anyone working under:

* A contract of employment, whether express or implied, and including an oral contract;

* A 'worker's contract' under which the individual agrees to perform work personally for someone, but is not an employee (s54 NMWA 1998).

Directors

There has been considerable confusion as to whether a director falls within the definition of 'worker'. If he does, he would be obliged to pay himself a salary at least equal to the NMW. However, the DTI have now confirmed to the ICAEW that their legal advice is as follows:

> 'If a person is a director and he does not have an explicit employment contract, then he will not be subject to the NMW legislation even when he carries out a wide variety of activities. These might include working in the company's shop: such duties will be done in his capacity as an office-holder (director) and not as an employee. Only if a director has an explicit employment contract as well as being a holder of the office of director will he be within the NMW.' (*TAXline*, April 2000)

They go on to say that 'the foregoing is a simplification: there will be complexities in certain circumstances'. A more detailed note is, at the time of writing, under preparation and will available on *TAXline*.

The foregoing is the DTI's opinion, and has not been tested by the courts, but it is arguable that a person who can ultimately control whether or not he is dismissed cannot be an employee. Support can also be found in the case of

Parsons v Albert J Parsons & Sons Ltd [1979] ICR 271, where the Court of Appeal held that a director who worked full time in the family business:

- Was not an employee;

- Had no implied, oral or written contract of employment; and

- His remuneration wholly related to his fees as a director.

While a court in the future could of course hold that the NMWA definitions are wide enough to include directors, for the present service companies should be able to rely on the DTI guidance. This means that directors do not have to pay themselves the minimum wage provided they have no formal employment contract with their companies.

Partners

Partners do not have a contract of employment with their partnership and the partnership cannot therefore be required to pay them the minimum wage.

Other family members

There is an exemption from the minimum wage for family members working in family businesses, but this is limited to workers in *unincorporated* businesses where the individual:

- Is a member of the employer's family;

- Resides in the family home of the employer; and either

- Participates in the running of the family business; or

- Shares in the tasks and activities of the family, and the work is done in that context (SI 1999 No 584 Reg 2(b)).

There is a similar exemption for people who live in the family home and are treated as a member of the family 'in particular as regards to the provision of accommodation and meals and the sharing of tasks and leisure activities'. (SI 1999 No 584 Reg 2(a))

Despite these exemptions, someone who works in a family business still has a right to make a claim for payment of the NMW. However, if there is no claim, the Revenue will not enforce the right.

This exemption clearly applies to family members working in partnership businesses, but does not extend to those working within limited companies. It is not possible for a family member working in a PSC to renounce entitlement to the minimum wage: there is no parallel in the NMW legislation to the Working Time Directive's opt-out clause, under which individuals can agree to work longer hours than the statutory maximum. Indeed the NMWA specifically provides that 'any provision in any agreement . . . is void in so far as it purports to exclude or limit the operation of any provision of this Act' (s49 NMWA). Thus family members must be paid the NMW if they are not directors and the business is incorporated.

22.2.3 Pay for NMW purposes

Pay for minimum wage purposes is the worker's basic salary, plus items such as incentives and bonuses. Extra sums such as overtime or shift work premiums do not count. All benefits in kind except accommodation are also excluded (SI 1999 No 584 Reg 5). Thus, if the company uses income from relevant engagements to provide benefits for the worker instead of paying him in cash, this will reduce the deemed Schedule E payment, see **12.4**, but will not meet the minimum wage requirements.

Status of deemed payment and associated dividends

Under IR35 a worker may have a deemed salary payment at the end of a tax year. This deemed salary is Schedule E for income tax purposes, and attributable earnings for NIC. The after-tax amount may be paid out as dividends.

However, neither the deemed Schedule E payment nor the associated dividends are wages for NMWA purposes. So workers who are within both the NMW and the personal services rules need to be paid an actual salary which is at least equal to the minimum wage.

Pay periods

The pay reference period for the NMW is the worker's actual pay period, *up to a maximum of one calendar month*. Workers who are paid less frequently than once a month will still have a pay reference period of one calendar month (SI 1999 No 584 Reg 10). The employer should thus ensure that salary is paid at least monthly; it is not enough simply to pay a cash bonus once a year.

22.2.4 Position of the client

As discussed at **22.2.2** above, a director of a PSC is not a 'worker' as regards the services he provides to his company and a partner in a partnership is not a worker in the context of the services he provides to his partnership. However, what is the position of the client? Could the individual who is supplying services to the client, either directly or via an agency, be regarded as operating under a 'worker's contract' in respect of the services he provides to the client?

Exemption

There is an exemption from the NMWA where 'the individual undertakes to do or perform personally any work or services for another party to the contract' and the status of the individual performing the services is 'by virtue of the contract that of a client or customer of any profession or business undertaking carried on by the individual'(s54(3)(b) NMWA 1998).

The exemption is thus defined by reference to the contract between the parties, and the contract under which the services of the PSC worker are provided to a client will normally state that it is between supplier and customer. This should thus protect clients from having the NMWA applied to their relationship with personal services workers.

'Looking through' the contract

It could however be argued that the true relationship between the parties is not that of customer and supplier, but a quasi-employment relationship to which the NMWA does apply. A court might be encouraged towards this approach if the worker was within the personal services legislation, since IR35 identifies those relationships where the intermediary is a mere 'wrapper', and thus where the worker would be an employee of the client if he was contracting directly.

However, if the contract were to be ignored in this way, one would also expect that payments made by the client/agency to the service company would be characterised as wages for NMWA purposes. It would be strange to look through the contractual arrangements in order to identify the status of the worker, and not also to recharacterise the payments made.

Conclusion

There is some risk that the NMWA could apply to payments made to PSC workers by the client or agency, and this risk may be increased by the tax legislation. The pragmatic solution is that amounts paid to contract workers should at least equal the minimum wage.

22.2.5 Enforcement

The Revenue, and not the DTI, enforce the minimum wage. Their guidance to employers states that:

'We may undertake an enquiry to check that you are paying at least the minimum hourly wage if one of your workers has contacted us, or as part of our programme of visits to employers to make sure you understand your obligations in relation to the National Minimum Wage.'

The service company or partnership could thus have its adherence to the NMW rules reviewed, even if no worker had made a complaint. Non-compliance can be a serious matter. The legislation makes it a criminal offence to:

• Refuse or wilfully neglect to pay the national minimum wage;

• Fail to keep adequate records;

• Keep false records; or

• Obstruct an enforcement officer.

If the NMW officers discover an underpayment, they can issue an enforcement notice. If this is not complied with, there may be a daily penalty of £7.20 in respect of each worker. The DTI's publication, *A Guide to the National Minimum Wage*, states comfortingly that 'Officers will give employers every chance to comply before considering any penalty'. However the maximum fine is £5,000, not to mention the criminal record.

PAYE and NIC implications

Non-payment of the minimum wage causes a further problem: unpaid tax and NIC. This is because, if there is a legal right to payment, the amount will be 'treated as received' and therefore within PAYE (s202B(1)(b) ICTA 1988).

Because of the pay period rules, see **22.2.3** above, entitlement to NMW subsists at the end of each month and interest will run from that date. The Revenue have confirmed to the ICAEW that arrears of tax will normally be sought from the employer by means of a settlement and interest will be due in the normal way. Penalties will not be sought. They have also pointed out that since the NICs legislation differs from that for tax, NICs should be accounted for in the normal way at the time of actual payment of the arrears.

Exchange of information

The Finance Act 2000 introduced exchange of information provisions under which data collected for NMW purposes could be made available to other Inland Revenue departments (s143 FA 2000). Similar rights had already been given to NMW teams allowing them to access tax information (s39 Employment Relations Act 1999).

The Revenue have confirmed that if, during the course of an inspection, a PAYE auditor had reason to believe that there was a failure to pay NMW, then the relevant information might be passed to a NMW enforcement officer. They have also said that an NMW officer might similarly pass information to a PAYE auditor.

22.2.6 Conclusion

Directors and partners are not normally within the scope of the NMW, and family members working for a partnership may also be exempted. Other employees *are* included, and neither the deemed Schedule E payment nor dividends counts as wages. A salary of at least the NMW must be paid to them on a monthly basis or more frequently. Otherwise the company or partnership may face overdue PAYE and NIC, plus interest and NMW penalties.

22.3 Working Families Tax Credit

22.3.1 Background

The government introduced the Working Families Tax Credit (WFTC) on 5 October 1999. It is an earnings top-up and, despite its name, effectively a rebadged social benefit. It replaces the earlier Family Credit but reaches more people. The Government's Red Book, *Budget 2000*, issued in March 2000, stated that the WFTC was being claimed by over one million families, and that this was expected to grow to 1.4 million.

The WFTC can be claimed by low-income families with children, where at least one adult is in paid work for at least 16 hours a week. The amount of the credit increases with each child, and is higher for older children. There is a further top-up if the adult works 30 hours a week or more.

Disabled Persons Tax Credit (DPTC) is similar to WFTC. A person is eligible for DPTC if he has an illness or disability which puts him at a disadvantage when getting a job.

Where someone qualifies for the WFTC or DPTC, a childcare tax credit (CTC) is also available. This covers 70 per cent of the cost of approved childcare, with the total spend capped at £100 a week for one child, and £150 a week for two or more children. For simplicity, in this chapter the WFTC, DPTC and CTC will normally be referred to as the WFTC.

Once a worker's earnings are above a given threshold, the WFTC is withdrawn at the rate of 55p for every pound earned. It is also tapered away where capital greater than £3,000 is held, see **23.3.3** below.

Most of the legislation dealing with WFTC has been pieced together out of the old Family Credit legislation, and is somewhat inaccessible. The tax credits are thus being administered using the Revenue's *Decision Maker's Guide for WFTC* (DMG) which is based on earlier guidance for Family Credit, and has no legal force. The rules are complex, and what follows is only an outline.

22.3.2 Earnings for WFTC

The main issue for personal service companies and partnerships is whether either the deemed Schedule E payment and/or dividends paid by the service company count as 'earnings' for WFTC purposes. If they do not, the worker may be entitled to WFTC.

Remuneration

Where a WFTC applicant is a director of his service company, the Revenue state that they will take into account as earnings both remuneration actually received and that 'to which a director is entitled but decides not to receive' (DMG 26026).

Unsurprisingly, the DMG does not yet deal explicitly with the deemed Schedule E payment and whether it is earnings to 'which a director is entitled but decides not to receive.' But it looks at a similar issue when it considers whether amounts advanced to a director ahead of his legal entitlement are earnings (the author's italics):

> 'It is not uncommon for directors who are voted remuneration (at the annual general meeting) to draw from their own current or loan accounts during the accounting year in order to have an income. These drawings are *neither earnings nor income other than earnings* because the directors are drawing money from the company in anticipation of future earnings or income.' (DMG 26034)

This means that the tax legislation set out in s202B ICTA 1988 (see 10.2) on the recognition of earnings for tax purposes has no parallel for WFTC. On the contrary, even access to cash by the director does not accelerate recognition of the earnings. This would suggest that a deemed salary which the director has no legal entitlement to receive is not remuneration.

Whether a director would be 'entitled to receive' his deemed Schedule E payment is likely to be a matter of law. If the money has not been voted to him as remuneration, he will have no entitlement. Assuming that the board understands how the PSC legislation works, they will not vote him the net Schedule E amount remaining after deduction of PAYE and NICs, because this will simply be taxed again as an actual salary payment, see **13.5.2**. He will thus have no legal entitlement and the amount should thus not be taken into account as earnings for WFTC.

Dividends

Dividends received by a director are treated as capital for WFTC purposes. The DMG says that:

> 'The decision maker should disregard a share dividend because it is income from capital but take it into account as capital from the date it is normally due to be credited.'(DMG 26031)

Since in most cases the money which has been taxed as a deemed Schedule E payment will be withdrawn as a dividend, this suggests that neither the deemed payment nor the dividend will count as earnings for WFTC.

Notional earnings

The Revenue say that 'the decision maker may treat an applicant as having income that is not actually received' (DMG 25001). It instructs the decision maker to try and establish whether the applicant (or partner) has received less pay than is normal for the work done (DMG 25083). If the answer is yes, then the ability of the person to whom the services were provided to pay a higher amount should be considered. A person 'includes a limited company or other corporate employer as well as an individual' (DMG 25089).

It is thus possible that the decision maker could take the view that the service company should have paid a higher salary for the work done, and indeed the existence of a deemed Schedule E payment might support this contention.

If notional earnings are ascribed to the applicant, a deduction is allowed for income tax, employee's NIC, and 50 per cent of a pension contribution paid by the individual (DMG 25106). Thus the worker will have a further deemed income calculation, on a different basis from that in the personal services legislation!

However, as the deemed payment will almost certainly be withdrawn as dividends, and these are specifically treated as capital by other provisions of the WFTC regulations, it is uncertain whether notional earnings would be ascribed to the worker.

Summary

Thus, from an earnings perspective it would appear that:

- The deemed Schedule E amount is not taken into account as remuneration;

- When dividends are withdrawn from the company they are treated as an addition to capital rather than as earnings;

- It is possible that 'notional earnings' would be ascribed to the worker on the basis that the salary paid by the company was lower than 'normal'.

22.3.3 Capital for WFTC

Even if a personal service worker's earnings are low enough to qualify him for WFTC, he may fail the capital test. The rules for recognition of capital are complicated, but in outline:

(a) To the extent that adults in the family have capital in excess of £3,000, the worker is credited with notional income of £1 a week for each £250 of capital. WFTC is withdrawn entirely once the family's capital reaches £8,000 (£16,000 for DPTC);

(b) 'Capital' for these purposes excludes the family's home, car, furnishings and certain other items, see DMG Chapter 44;

(c) Also disregarded are 'any assets of a business owned wholly or partly by the applicant or partner who is actively self-employed in that business' (Sch 3, para 6 FCA (Gen) Regs; DMG 43008(4)). Thus a partner's share of his business is excluded from the capital assets which are taken into account for WFTC;

(d) Similar treatment is granted to the director of company 'if the share-holder's interest in the company is similar to that of a sole trader or partner' (DMG 43020).

Dividends

Because dividends are counted as capital (**22.3.2**), a worker will have no entitlement to WFTC if his dividends, plus other capital assets, come to £8,000 or more. If dividends plus other capital assets are less than £8,000 but more than £3,000, 'tariff income' of £1 a week is deemed to have been earned on every £250 of assets. A PSC worker who has a deemed Schedule E payment will generally have received dividends in excess of £8,000, and certainly in excess of £3,000, over the course of a year.

However entitlement to WFTC is based on the worker's position 'at the date of application' (DMG 11005). The Guide says: 'An award of WFTC or DPTC is payable for 26 weeks. It is not normally affected by any changes of circum-stances during that period' (DMG 14063). The award may only be adjusted if the applicant dies, a young person stops full-time education, or there has been a duplicate award (DMG 14071–14122).

Thus entitlement to WFTC may exist on a particular date even if the director expects to receive regular future dividends from the company (see DMG 26031).

22.3.4 Mechanism for receiving WFTC payments

Initially WFTC was paid by the Inland Revenue directly to recipients. From 6 April 2000 employee recipients have been paid their credits via their wage packets. Where one of the adults is not in employment, he or she can elect to receive the WFTC directly. However this option is not available where both parents are in employment or to employees who are single parents.

Where a worker is entitled to WFTC, it will normally be paid to him by his employer. This applies to personal service companies as it does to other companies. In most cases the credit is funded out of the tax and NIC deducted from the payroll. However, in the case of a service company, particularly one relying on dividends to extract funds, the payroll is likely to be small or non-existent. If the worker's entitlement to WFTC exceeds the company's expected PAYE and NIC deductions, the Revenue will fund the tax credits directly by making a credit transfer into the company's bank account (SI 1999 No 3219 Reg 8).

22.3.5 Conclusion

The main assets owned by a personal services worker – his home, his car, and his company – fall outside the definition of capital for WFTC, and his dividend entitlement for the next period may not yet have crystallised. He may thus be able to pass the capital test. The decision maker may take the view that there are no notional earnings because the company's profits are being fully distributed as dividends, which are then taken into account as capital.

If the worker can satisfy the other conditions for WFTC entitlement, such as number and age of children and hours worked, the deemed Schedule E calculation and associated dividends may allow him to claim the tax credit while regular payments of salary might not. He may thus find, perhaps to his surprise, that he qualifies for the tax credits.

22.4 Student loan repayments

22.4.1 Outline

The student loan system was introduced on 1 September 1998, and applies to all students starting full-time higher education or teacher training after that date. Interest is charged on the loan at no more than 1 per cent above base rate.

Student loan repayments (SLR) are made from the April following graduation, or from April 2000 if later. No repayments are required if the individual's gross income is less than £10,000 a year. Unearned income of less than £2,000 per annum is ignored.

Where the individual has income of £10,000 or more, repayments equal to 9 per cent of the excess is due annually. If the worker is employed, deductions are made via the payroll; if he is self-employed, they are collected by self-assessment.

An employer must deduct SLR from salary:

• Once he has received a 'start' notice from the Revenue to this effect; or

• If the employee has a 'Y' in the relevant box of his P45.

If no start notice has been received, and there is no indicator on the P45, there is no obligation to deduct.

SLR will be policed by the Revenue's employer compliance department, and thus will be audited along with PAYE and NIC, see **16.9**.

22.4.2 Interaction with personal services legislation

Deemed Schedule E amount

The SLR definition of earnings is the same as that for secondary Class 1 NICs. Benefits in kind and other non-cash payments are therefore not taken into account. The National Insurance aggregation rules apply for SLR as they do for personal services, see **4.8.3** (SI 2000 No 944 regs 27ff and SI 2000 No 727 Reg 8(2))

Since the SLR obligation is based on the NIC definition of earnings, and the deemed Schedule E amount counts as earnings for NICs, see **10.1**, it will also be earnings for SLR purposes. If a worker with deemed Schedule E payment is within the SLR regime, the employer must pay over to the Revenue the SLR on the deemed Schedule E amount, along with PAYE and NICs, on 19 April following the end of the fiscal year.

There are penalties if the annual return is late, or if it is either fraudulent or negligent, on the same basis as for PAYE. The Revenue can also levy a maximum penalty on the employer of £3,000 per employee per year; this is greater than the amounts normally chargeable under the PAYE/NIC penalty legislation, see **16.6** (SI 2000 No 944 Regs 21–26).

Dividends

Dividends in excess of £2,000 a year are unearned income for SLR purposes, and the worker is required to repay an amount equal to 9 per cent of the dividend using his self-assessment form.

However, where the dividends relate to the deemed Schedule E payment, a student loan repayment has already been made on what is effectively the same income. To the extent that the dividend is covered by the deemed Schedule E payment, it is ignored for tax purposes and will not need to be entered on the SA return (Sch 12, para 13 FA 2000 and see **15.3.6**).

The Education (Student Loans) (Repayment) Regulations 2000 say that:

> 'In calculating a borrower's total income for the purposes of paragraph (1) there shall be excluded . . . income on which the borrower could not become liable to tax under a self-assessment made under section 9 of the 1970 Act for that year.' (SI 2000 No 944 Reg 15(5)(b))

Since it is understood that the dividend will not be included on the self-assessment return, it will also be ignored for SLR. This would be an equitable result, as otherwise two repayments will be required out of what is effectively the same funds.

Partners

Where the worker is a partner, the deemed Schedule E payment will likewise be earnings for SLR purposes. However, because partners are not employees, the partnership is unlikely to have received an SLR notice in respect of a partner with relevant engagements.

In most cases partners will therefore be required to deduct the SLR from income on their SA return, assuming this is more than £10,000 in total, and remembering that unearned income of less than £2,000 is ignored. The deemed Schedule E amount will be included as earnings on the self-assessment form, see **15.3.10**.

22.4.3 Conclusion

The deemed Schedule E amount will count as earnings for SLR purposes, but it is anticipated that any associated dividends will be ignored. Service company workers will have the amount deducted by their employer, partners will make the SLR via their self-assessment form.

23 Tax planning after IR35

23.1 Introduction

Chapter 3 set out the tax advantages available to service companies in the halcyon days before IR35. It pointed out that these remain accessible to those companies which fall wholly or partly outside the personal services legislation.

This chapter identifies the opportunities which remain available to companies and partnerships within IR35, and summarises the risks and opportunities discussed at greater length elsewhere in this book.

23.2 Status and contracts

The fundamental tax planning requirement following IR35 is a review of the worker's contractual arrangements. If the individual would not have been an employee of the client had there been no intermediary, IR35 will not apply. This issue is discussed in detail in Chapters 5 to 9. Particular questions to consider include:

- Is there mutuality of obligation? If there is no mutuality, there can be no employment (see **5.3**);

- Can the worker argue, as in *Lorimer* (see **8.2.1**), that he is providing his skills to a succession of engagers?

- What similarities are there between the worker's position and that of other taxpayers who have disputed their status in the courts (see Chapter 8);

- Can a fundamental change be made to his contract, so that it includes substitution, the right to hire others to carry out the engagement, or significant risk (see **6.5; 9.3–9.5**)? If he can, he is unlikely to be employed;

- Are other, more minor changes possible to his contractual arrangements that, taken together, would allow him to escape the personal services legislation (see **9.16–9.14**)?

- Does the worker want the certainty of a Revenue ruling on his contract (see **7.7**)?

23.3 Managing the deemed income calculation

The complexities of the deemed income calculation, including the choice between salary and dividends, are discussed in Chapter 13.

23.3.1 Dividends versus salary

* The intermediary will normally choose between either (a) paying salary, or (b) paying the tax and NICs on the deemed income calculation, and then distributing the net amount as dividends, see **13.5.1**;

* If the company has a 31 March accounting period, and is planning to take the deemed income/dividend route, it should almost certainly change its year end, see **13.4.6**. Otherwise it may never obtain full tax relief for the deemed payment;

* Where some shareholders have no relevant income, dividend waivers may be needed so that the individual with the deemed payment receives the appropriate distribution, see **13.6.2**;

* A claim needs to be made to exempt the dividends from tax, see **13.6.2**;

* Those who receive a dividend which is 'covered' by a deemed payment should be made aware of the self-assessment treatment, see **15.3.6**.

23.3.2 Paying the tax and NICs

* PAYE and NIC on the deemed payment is due on the following 19 April. In order to reduce or eliminate the interest payable, the calculation should be completed as soon as possible after the end of the tax year, see **16.4.2**;

* Clearly, any interest cost will be reduced where the salary route has been taken, as the PAYE and NIC due on 19 April will be small;

* If the dividend route has been selected, a shadow deemed income calculation during the year on a monthly basis will allow the final calculation to be carried out relatively quickly.

23.3.3 Keeping appropriate records

Careful record keeping is essential, as the deemed Schedule E calculation is based on cash rather than accruals basis, and fiscal years rather than accounting periods. Specifically:

* The income in the deemed Schedule E calculation is on a received not an accruals basis, see **10.2**;

- Expenses, pension contributions and salary are all deductible when paid, rather on the accruals basis used for the accounts, see **11.3.2**, **12.2.3** and **12.4.2**;

- Where more than one worker carries out relevant engagements, the invoicing and record-keeping process should identify the income and expenses relating to each person's work. This is simpler than trying to apportion it later;

- Apportionments will also be required between relevant and non-relevant income, see **10.3**, if this hasn't been achieved via the invoicing process;

- The expenses deductible in the deemed calculation are those which relate to the relevant engagements. If the company has a mixture of relevant and non-relevant engagements, separate records will be needed on an engagement-by-engagement basis. A reasonable apportionment is probably acceptable as an alternative, although not specifically provided for in the legislation.

23.4 Expense reliefs

Although reliefs for expenses deductible in the deemed Schedule E calculation are much less generous than those available under the rules for corporation tax (see **11.4**), nevertheless they should not be overlooked. They are discussed in detail in Chapter 11. Points to note include:

- Expenses should be borne by the intermediary rather than directly by the worker. They then reduce the deemed Schedule E amount and thus the NICs payable. If allowable expenses are borne by the worker, he obtains tax relief but no NICs relief, see **11.3.3**;

- The same is true of capital allowances – the assets should be owned by the intermediary, not the individual, see **11.11.1(c)**;

- Personal service workers should be fully conversant with the generous travel and subsistence reliefs, see **11.6**;

- Travel costs can be claimed in the deemed Schedule E computation even if they are not reimbursed by the client;

- Care should be taken when negotiating a contract of more than two years, or an extension to an existing contract which would take it beyond the two year point, as this will result in travel or subsistence expenses being disallowed from the date the contract *was expected* to exceed two years, see **11.6.3**;

- Taking a second contract which is geographically close to the first may cause the two year limit to be exceeded, if the change in location does not make a substantial difference to the travel costs, see **11.6.3**;

- The 5 per cent allowance may compensate for part or all of the inter-mediary's running costs. Since the allowance is related to income received, the higher the income within the intermediary, the greater the tax relief;

- The allowance is only effective for the purposes of the deemed Schedule E calculation. It has no effect on the corporation tax or partnership compu-tation. If there are insufficient actual expenses to use up the allowance, a payment to a family member might be contemplated, see **3.4**, bearing in mind the caveat that this may be challenged by the Revenue if unsupported by work done;

- Relocation costs paid by the client are tax free providing they are within the limits set down by legislation, see **10.6.10**.

23.5 Losses

The combination of the deemed income calculation and the rules for corpo-ration tax expenses means that corporation tax losses are likely, see **13.7**. Ways of using these losses are summarised at **13.7.2** and **13.7.3**. They include:

- Carrying them back against the previous year's profits so as to obtain a repayment of tax suffered;

- Group relieving them against the profits of another company;

- Introducing income into the company so as to shelter it from tax, though the Revenue may challenge this.

23.6 Pensions

Pension contributions paid by the employer are deducted from the deemed Schedule E amount. They thus reduce both the tax and the NICs payable.

Personal service companies are still in the privileged position of being able to use a Small Self Administered Scheme (SSAS) or an EPP (Executive Personal Pension) as the vehicle for their pension arrangements. As discussed in **3.6**, this type of pension often allows higher contributions than would be possible under a personal pension, as well as providing other tax planning oppor-tunities.

Practical steps which should be taken in the context of pensions include:

- Reviewing the worker's current pension arrangements and taking advice on whether an EPP or SSAS should be considered;

- Ensuring that, where possible, pension contributions are made by the company, not by the individual, as otherwise no NIC relief is obtained;

- Considering whether there is scope to use earlier years' pension capacity under the carry-forward, carry-back rules (s625, s641 ICTA 1988). These contributions have to be made by the individual personally and will not therefore affect either the deemed income calculation or the NICs payable. Tax relief will however be obtained at the individual's marginal rate.

23.7 Overseas issues

The interaction between IR35 and concepts such as residence, ordinary residence and domicile is complex, see Chapters 17 and 18. A personal services worker going overseas or coming to the UK should obtain individual advice in relation to his specific position.

Planning points include:

- The rules for tax and NICs are not identical, and an individual can be non-resident (and outside the deemed income calculation) for tax, but remain an employed earner for NICs (and thus have to complete an attributable earnings calculation), or vice versa, see Chapter 18 and 12.7.2;

- If an individual works overseas for a whole tax year, he will normally be non-resident and not within the scope of UK tax in respect of amounts earned that year, see 17.9.3;

- It may be possible to establish or retain a foreign domicile (see 17.11). This allows earnings from work carried out wholly abroad for an overseas client to escape UK tax in general, and the deemed income calculation in particular, provided they are not remitted to this country;

- A remittance basis also applies where the individual is resident but not ordinarily resident. This allows *all* earnings for work done overseas, not only that for an overseas client, to escape UK tax as long as it is not remitted here, see 17.5.2.

- Workers coming to the UK should ensure that they retain their 'not resident and/or not ordinarily resident' status for as long as possible, to protect overseas earnings from the deemed income calculation. Care is needed, because intentions as well as actions can trigger both residence and ordinary residence, see 17.5.1;

- Dual contracts should be considered by non-domiciliaries where engagements involve some overseas work, see 17.12.3. Dual contracts may also be appropriate for those who are not ordinarily resident, see 17.8.5;

- Workers may obtain relief for overseas tax suffered on their foreign earnings against the PAYE on their deemed income calculation, but only if the overseas tax cannot be offset against corporation tax on the company's profits, see **17.10.2**;

- A deduction may be available in the deemed income calculation for the cost of family members travelling to visit a PSC worker overseas. This is the case even if the client does not reimburse the costs, see **17.10.3**;

- Family travel expenses may also be allowable where an overseas worker is carrying out a relevant engagement in the UK, see **17.10.4**;

- If an individual is seeking to establish permanent residence abroad, but is not working there full-time, care is needed with the 90 day rule. It is possible to be outside the UK most of the time but still remain resident and ordinarily resident here and thus within IR35, see **17.9.4**;

- Where work is to be carried out in an EEA state other than the UK, it is better to have a separate engagement with an overseas client rather than being sent overseas by a UK client. This should prevent the short-term posting rule coming into effect, and ensure the worker escapes the PSC NICs charge and is liable only on his normal salary and benefits, see **18.3.4**;

- Where the director is working in the UK, his service company is likely to be tax resident here, even if it is registered overseas, see **19.2.3**. If the company *is* offshore, IR35 deems it to have a place of business here, providing the worker and the client are both resident in the UK, see **19.5**. In both cases the company is required to apply PAYE and NICs to the deemed payment, and failure to do so may incur penalties.

23.8 Partnerships

Although many of the problems and opportunities arising from the new legislation apply to all intermediaries, some points are particular to partnerships. They include:

- Partners should consider whether it is possible to escape IR35 altogether, by carefully reviewing the legislation and other exemptions, see **14.2** and **14.3**. It may be possible to exclude the partnership from the personal services legislation by taking in new partners, such as brothers-in-law or sisters-in-law, see **14.2.2**;

- Expenses should be borne by the partnership rather than by the partner directly, because this reduces the deemed Schedule E amount and thus the NICs payable. If allowable expenses are borne by the worker, tax relief can only be obtained via the partnership computation. There is also no Class 1 NICs relief, see **14.5.4**. Reimbursement of expenses by the partnership achieves the correct result;

- The same is true of capital allowances – assets should be owned by the partnership, not the partner, see **14.5.5**;

- There are strict rules for deducting expenses in the partnership return, and also for losses (see **14.6.3**). Partnerships need to be fully conversant with this part of the legislation to ensure that their self-assessment form is correct.

23.9 Clients and agencies

- Workers need the co-operation of clients and agencies if they are to restructure their contractual arrangements so as to fall outside IR35, see Chapter 9;

- In restructuring a contract, the and risks for the client and the agency should not be ignored, see **21.2.3** and **21.3.1**;

- If the tax status of freelance consultants is uncertain, clients may wish to reduce their own PAYE and NIC exposure by engaging only service companies and not individuals, see **21.3.4**;

- If the service company is offshore, the client still has to deduct PAYE and NICs from any salary due to the worker, although responsibility for the deemed payment rests with the intermediary, see **21.3.2**;

- Engaging a worker supplied by an overseas service company can thus be administratively burdensome, and may create liabilities to PAYE and NICs which are not discovered until the client has a PAYE audit;

- Both clients and agencies may have to provide the Revenue with detailed information about payments made to service companies, see **21.2.5**. Establishing in advance how this data is to be collected will simplify the compliance process.

23.10 Penalties and investigations

- If the PAYE and NICs on the deemed payment are late, there will be an interest charge but no penalty, as long as the procedures set out at **16.4.2** are complied with;

- IR35 is likely to be policed by the Revenue's Employer Compliance Unit. If a company has misunderstood the rules, it should be able to rely on Dawn

Primarolo's promise that the penalty regime will be applied with a light touch, see **16.7.2**;

- In other situations, the normal pleas for mitigation may be accepted, see **16.7.4**.

23.11 Other possibilities and risks

- It may be possible to retain surplus funds within the company in order to take advantage of the low corporate tax rates, see **3.8**;

- Capital gains tax planning, using taper relief rules and annual allowances, should be investigated where the intermediary has some intrinsic value;

- Tax reliefs are available against other income for interest on money borrowed and then invested in the company, see **3.7**;

- The deemed Schedule E payment does not count for minimum wage purposes, and workers other than partners or directors will thus need to be paid an appropriate salary, either on a monthly basis or more frequently, see **22.2.3**;

- IR35 does not apply to engagements with householders, so a service company could be used for domestic help, such as nannies or gardeners, see **4.3.1**;

- The possibility that the worker may be entitled to WFTC can be examined, see **22.3**;

- Student loan repayments are due on the deemed income amounts, see **22.4**, and failure to operate the SLR can cause interest and penalties to arise;

- The reasons for and against liquidating the service company are given in **13.8**.

24 Case studies

24.1 Introduction

The Revenue have provided six cases studies showing how the status tests apply to particular situations. *Tax Bulletin* 28, April 1997 covered subcontractors in detail, while the more recent Tax Bulletin in February 2000 focused on IT contractors. But the general points in both are relevant to all personal service workers. The background to these case studies is discussed at Chapters 6 and 7.

24.2 Case studies for IT contractors with service companies

24.2.1 Outline

The Revenue's case studies show how the status tests apply to a worker who is:

(a) Within the personal service rules (Gordon);

(b) Outside the personal service rules (Henry); and

(c) Balanced on the line between the two (Charlotte).

24.2.2 Example 1: Gordon, an IT contractor working through his own service company

Facts	Comments
Job description/Control	
Client is a large retail concern. The contract was obtained through an agency. The terms and conditions of the engagement are set out in the contracts between the client and the agency and the agency and Gordon's company.	The fact that the engagement has been obtained through an agency has no bearing on whether Gordon would have been an employee or not.
Gordon works as part of a support team for the client's payroll system. The team leader (another IT contractor) tells Gordon what work he is to carry out at any particular time (e.g., help-desk work, specific maintenance tasks, etc.).	The extensive right of control that exists here is a very strong pointer to employment. The more important features are the client's ability to shift Gordon from task to task and to specify how the work should be done – but in addition the client can control where and when the work is carried out.
The client has the right to tell Gordon 'how' the work should be carried out – although in practice such control is not normally necessary.	
Gordon must work a regular 40-hour week on the client's premises.	The company is paid an hourly rate for Gordon's services and the only financial risk comes from invoicing. There is no opportunity to profit from sound management of the work covered by the contract. Overall this points to employment.
Payment basis/risk	
Gordon's company is paid an hourly rate for Gordon's services. Any extra hours worked (by mutual agreement) are paid at 1.5 times the normal hourly rate. The client makes payment monthly following submission of an invoice by the agency. Gordon's service company invoices the agency.	The engagement runs for six months and holiday pay/sick pay might be expected had there been a direct engagement. But both parties see the actual company/client contract as a contract for services and this is probably why no such payments are made. A minor pointer to self-employment.

Holiday pay/sick pay

No sick pay or holiday pay paid under the terms of the inter-company contract.

Length of contract and personal factors

The contract is for six months.

Gordon uses a computer, telephone, fax, etc., at home to seek and negotiate contracts for his company.

Gordon has worked through his company for two other clients in the last two and a half years – one for three months and one for two years. Prior to that he was a direct employee of another engager.

Gordon's company has a limited 'business organisation' consisting of an office and associated equipment at his home. This is a pointer to self-employment – but not an overly important one in the context of a six-month contract of this sort.

Other points

Neither side can terminate the contract early.

Neutral factor (no right to terminate is common in engagements of this length – whether employment or self-employment).

There is no restriction imposed by the contract that prevents either Gordon or his company providing services to others during the engagement.

Mild pointer towards self-employment.

Both parties never intended Gordon to be an employee.

Pointer to self-employment, but will only be relevant if the other factors are neutral.

Overall picture

The engagement is fairly long term and there is an extensive right of control over Gordon. He must carry out the services personally. The client provides equipment and accommodation and there is no significant financial risk to the company.

The only pointers to self-employment are the minimal financial risk (from invoicing), the ability to work for others (again, a minor point) and the existence of a business organisation/work for other clients.

Standing back from the detail therefore the engagement is one which would have been an employment had it been direct between Gordon and the client. The common intention for self-employment does not alter that. Whilst it would have proved decisive in a 'borderline' situation a review of other factors points strongly to employment here. The new rules would apply to the engagement.

413

24.2.3 Example 2: Henry, a consultant engineer working through his own service company

Facts	Comments
Job description/Control	
Client is a large manufacturing company. Under a previous contract Henry has undertaken a broad review of a 15-year-old production line and established that significant improvements could be made to the line to increase productivity. Under the current contract Henry is to produce a further report with detailed and costed proposals on the improvements and how they might be carried out with minimum disruption to production.	A specific task has been agreed and the client cannot shift the worker to another task. Henry has the major say over how the work is carried out and when. The client does have some right to ongoing control over the work in that regular reports are required and changes in Henry's proposals can be sought.
Henry has a free hand over how his work is carried out and when (although there is a deadline of three months for completion). However, Henry is required to keep the client fully informed about progress and the client can require Henry to modify proposals if any aspect seems unsuitable to them.	Overall, control is limited.
Payment basis/risk/opportunity to profit	
Henry is paid £70 an hour but there is a ceiling of 300 hours on the work. If Henry takes longer than this he will only be paid extra if unforeseen difficulties arise or the client insists on unreasonable changes. If the work takes less than 300 hours Henry is only paid for the hours worked.	Henry is being paid an hourly rate and there is no real prospect of his making a loss. Nevertheless he is subject to a ceiling and must complete the work in the time allowed for otherwise he will have to finish the work in his own time without further payment. This is a mild pointer to self-employment.
Holiday pay/sick pay	
No sick pay or holiday pay paid under the terms of the inter-company contract.	Pointer to self-employment.
Length of contract and personal factors	
The contract has a deadline of three months.	

Henry has worked through his company as an engineer for many years and it is accepted that the company is 'in business'. The company has had many engagements similar to the current one and is generally engaged to provide an 'expert' service by clients with little engineering expertise.

The company has a business organisation and many different clients. This is a significant pointer to self-employment.

Henry has an office and computer at home which he uses for work extensively.

Equipment

Henry visits the client's factory regularly to examine the production line and processes. The only significant equipment he uses is his own computer (to prepare the report). 70 per cent of the work is done in his office.

Significant and fundamental equipment is provided by the company as is office accommodation. This points to self-employment.

Other factors

Engagement cannot be terminated 'early' other than following a breach of contract.

Neutral factor (no right to terminate is common in engagements of this length – whether employment or self-employment.)

There is no restriction imposed by the contract that prevents either Henry or his company providing services to others during the engagement.

Mild pointer towards self-employment.

Both parties intend that the company is engaged to carry out the work and that Henry is not an employee of the client.

Pointer to self-employment, but will only be relevant if the other factors are neutral.

Overall picture

Henry is a skilled worker who has been engaged to carry out a specific task and control over him is limited. He is paid based on an hourly rate but there is an over-riding limit within which the work agreed must be completed. There is a contract deadline of three months and the company has many other clients. Some important equipment is supplied by the company and the work is mainly carried out away from the client's premises.

Henry would have been self-employed if engaged directly by the client and the new rules will not apply. Even if the contract had been expected to last for a longer period – say, nine months – the other factors would still have led to a conclusion of self-employment.

24.2.4 Example 3 – Charlotte, an IT consultant working through her own service company

Facts	Comments
Job description/Control	
Charlotte's client for this engagement is a software company. She has been engaged for her programming skills to work on a specific project as part of a team developing a new piece of software. She works to the client's project manager who allocates particular sub programs to Charlotte that she writes. The client expects the project to last for around three months.	There is an extensive right of control over Charlotte. The more important features are the client's ability to shift Charlotte from task to task and to specify how the work should be done. In addition the client can control to some extent where and when the work is carried out. But control is not total. Charlotte is engaged to work on a specific project so cannot be told to work on something completely different – and she cannot be required to work elsewhere. Overall, this is a strong pointer to employment.
The manager specifies the way in which the sub-program is to be structured and can require changes to be made to make the work fit in with other parts of the program as it is developed, to rectify overall design faults, etc.	
Charlotte works a set number of hours but actual working times are flexible in line with the company's flexi-time arrangements for its employees. She is required to work at the client's premises.	
Payment basis/risk/sick pay/holiday pay	
Charlotte is paid £3,600 every four weeks in return for working a 40-hour week. Extra payments are made at the equivalent hourly rate for any additional hours agreed. Payment is made 14 days after the company has invoiced the client.	It is the arrangements between the service company and the client that are important here. The company is paid the equivalent of a salary – with overtime payments – but no sick pay or holiday pay. Although the invoicing arrangements result in a small financial risk this is minor. Overall there is no significant financial risk

No sick pay or holiday pay is paid, under the contract Charlotte has with her company. She is paid an on-going, but much lower, salary which includes provision for holiday pay and sick pay.

and no opportunity to profit from sound management of the task. This points to employment.

Length of contract and personal factors

The contract is for 12 weeks – but there is provision for an extension if the project over-runs and all parties agree to the extension.

Charlotte does some work for another client at weekends and has worked for various clients in the past – always through her company and often through employment agencies. Her contracts have usually lasted for between one and three months. Most have been similar to this one but some have involved her in specific tasks for a fixed fee using her own equipment and working at home.

Charlotte and her company have a 'business organisation' – including an office and associated equipment based at Charlotte's home. She has a variety of clients and all her contracts have been fairly short term.

Charlotte has an office at home and a computer and other office equipment that is used for some of her other work. These contribute to her company's business organisation – which she uses to obtain work, keep records, prepare invoices, etc.

This is a strong pointer to self-employment.

Other factors

The company is contracted to supply Charlotte to do the work personally.

Both point to employment.

All equipment is supplied by the client.

The engagement cannot be terminated 'early' other than following a breach of contract.

Neutral factor (no right to terminate is common in engagements of this length – whether employment or self-employment).

There is no restriction imposed by the contract that prevents either Charlotte or her company providing services to others during the engagement.

Pointer to self-employment.

417

| All parties intended that the company/client engagement would be self-employment. | Pointer to self-employment, but will only be relevant if the other factors are neutral. |

Overall picture

This is a borderline case. On balance, given all the facts, Charlotte would have been self-employed had she been engaged directly by the client. The new rules will not apply to the engagement.

The following point towards self-employment:

• Existing business and a variety of different engagements, some of which would clearly count as self-employed if she had been engaged directly by her client.

• Overall business organisation (office and equipment at home, businesslike approach to obtaining engagements and carrying them out, etc.). Charlotte would clearly be regarded as being 'in business on her own account' for those engagements where she carried out a specific task for a fixed fee using her own accommodation and equipment.

• Risk from invoicing.

• The lack of an exclusivity clause.

Other factors point to employment:

• There is fairly extensive control over Charlotte. The client can dictate 'what' work is carried out on the project and 'how' the work is done. But control is not total. Charlotte cannot be directed to work on another project or undertake some quite different work. Nor is there control in other areas (e.g., she is subject to the client's normal staff rules/disciplinary procedures).

• There is virtually no financial risk in the engagement and no opportunity to profit from sound management of the task.

• Charlotte must carry out the work herself.

• All equipment and accommodation is provided by the client.

What can then have more significance is the extent to which the individual is dependent upon, or independent of, a particular paymaster for the financial exploitation of his or her talents (see *Hall v Lorimer*). The fact that Charlotte's company is also engaged in contracts which involve carrying out a specific task for a fixed fee, using her own equipment, suggests that it is a genuine business and neither she nor her company rely on a single client for the exploitation of her talents. These factors balance the control and other employment factors that exist in this particular context and put the matter near the borderline where the mutual intention for self-employment becomes decisive.

However, the overall picture would have been rather different had the engagement been longer. For example, had the engagement been for twelve months the 'personal factors' would have been far less significant and the employment pointers would have predominated. Just because a person has an established business does not automatically make them self-employed for all engagements (see *Fall v Hitchen* (49 TC 433) – also referred to in *Hall v Lorimer*). Also, if she had not also had contracts of a type which would clearly have fallen within the definition of self-employment, employment pointers would have dominated and the contract at issue would have been one of employment. The same could apply to shorter contracts.

24.3 Case studies for subcontractors

24.3.1 Context

These were not aimed at subcontractors with service companies, as the publication of these case studies pre-dated the PSC rules. Instead they applied the status tests to individual subcontractors, asking whether they would be self-employed or employees. However, since the IR35 rules depend on the same status tests, these case studies remain highly relevant.

24.3.2 Example 1 – General labourer

Facts	Comments
Job Description/Control	
Undertakes a variety of unskilled and semi-skilled work (e.g. digging footings, assisting craftsmen, etc.). Engager moves him from task to task as necessary. Can be told how to do a particular task but this is generally unnecessary in view of his experience.	Strong control exists here. The more important features are the engager's ability to move the worker from job to job as priorities change and to have the ultimate say in how the work should be carried out.
Payment basis/risk	
Paid a weekly wage plus overtime.	No financial risk or opportunity to profit from sound management points to employment.
Holiday/sick pay	
No sick pay paid (has been sick twice over last 12 months). No holiday pay but has been allowed three weeks off (unpaid) for holidays during over the last the last 12 months.	The engagements run to some months and holiday pay/sick pay might be expected. But to take both parties think the engagement is self-employment and this is probably why no such payments are made. A minor pointer towards self-employment.

Length of engagement and personal factors

Taken on for the expected duration of the engager's building project – usually weeks or months with the actual length depending on how well the project progresses. Has worked for the same engager almost exclusively for three years – but with two periods of 'unemployment' of three weeks and two months during the same time.	Not a 'permanent' employment, but a series of fairly lengthy separate engagements with one engager. No evidence of working for several engagers. Overall, the pattern of work suggests employment.
Does odd jobs for private householders at weekends with payment 'by the task'. Earned £600 from this over the last 12 months.	Is to this extent 'in business'. But small part-time earnings of this nature will not be the key factor when measured against a full time engagement running to weeks or months.
Worker keeps an 'office' at home. He has a home computer which he uses to record income and expenses. He also has a phone which he uses to arrange weekend work and new contracts.	Has an office and is fairly business-like in the way he organises and runs his engagements. This points towards self-employment.

Other factors

All equipment and materials provided by the engager except for working clothes and boots.	Point to employment
Hired personally to do the work.	Point to employment
Engagement can be terminated by either side on 1 week's notice.	Point to employment
Both parties clearly intend that the engagements amount to self-employment	Pointer towards self-employment and important in borderline situations. Not conclusive where – overall – other factors point to employment.

Overall picture

The picture which emerges is of a weekly paid worker carrying out unskilled and semi-skilled work with the engager having strong control. These are strong pointers towards employment. Other factors also point to employment (equipment, lack of financial risk, period of notice). Although some personal factors point to self-employment taking all factors into account the engagements amount to employment. The mutual intention for self-employment would only be decisive where the other factors were borderline – and here they point to employment.

The result would be similar even if personal factors were stronger (e.g., regular working for many engagers). Other factors (particularly the strong right of control) would outweigh such factors.

24.3.3 Example 2 – Plasterer

Facts	Comments
Job Description/Control	
Contracted to plaster walls and ceilings of a two classroom school extension. Cannot be told 'how' to do the work but it must be completed satisfactorily. Work to be done during normal working hours at the site.	Little or no control over 'what' is to be done and 'where' (fixed by the contract) or how it is to be done. Limited control over when the work is to be done. Points to self-employment.
Substitution	
May choose to pay and send a substitute or use assistants. Engaged and used an assistant to help throughout the contract.	Strong pointer towards self-employment.
Equipment and materials	
Provides only equipment needed (hand tools and shovel/container for mixing). Materials supplied by engager.	No significant equipment required. The fact that the engager supplies materials points towards employment.
Payment basis/risk	
Paid per square metre plastered. Worker is responsible for completing entire job within time allotted.	There is opportunity to maximise profit from the sound management to the task. Worker must complete the contract so this is not pure piecework and there is real financial risk. E.g., were the worker to fall ill he would be responsible for hiring others to complete the contract (even at a loss).
Three-week deadline for completion with a penalty of £100 per day for failure to complete the work on time.	Further risks arise from the penalty clause for failing to meet the deadline and the requirement to rectify work at his own cost (including materials).
Must rectify faulty work in own time and own cost (including supplying extra materials needed).	All pointers to self-employment.

Other factors

Length of contract – three weeks	A minor pointer to self-employment.
Works for many engagers (20 in past 12 months). All contracts of less than six week duration.	Has a pattern of working under short-term contracts for many different engagers. Pointer to self-employment.
No holiday or sick pay. No right to end contract unless serious breach of terms.	Not significant in the context of a three week engagement.
No office at home. Prepares accounts from record book recording all receipts and expenditure. Has a phone which he uses to arrange new contracts.	Little in way of 'business organisation' (e.g., yard or office etc.). Not a significant pointer either way.
Both parties intend that the engagements amount to self-employment.	Pointer towards self-employment in borderline situations.

Overall picture

The picture painted is of a self-employed individual carrying out skilled work and genuinely accepting the risks of being in business on his own account. The worker.

• Is subject to little control.

• Faces real financial risk.

• Engages and pays an assistant to help perform the contract.

• Works for a variety of engagers on fairly short-term contracts.

24.3.4 Example 3 – Bricklayer

Facts	Comments
Job Description/Control	
Engaged solely as a bricklayer. Engager moves him from task to task as necessary. He is provided with helpers who mix mortar, carry bricks, etc. Engager cannot tell him 'how' he wants the work done but expects competent workmanship and a reasonable level of output.	Control over 'what' is to be done – but limited to the extent of what bricks should be laid and cannot be diverted to quite different work. Little control over the manner in which the work is to be done. An employment pointer but not as strong as in Example 1.
Substitution	
Hired personally to do the work	Points towards employment

Equipment

All provided by engager except for working clothes, boots and trowel.

Worker providing own 'small tools'. Engager supplies other equipment and all materials. Pointer to employment.

Payment basis/risk

Paid a weekly wage plus overtime.

No financial risk or opportunity to profit from sound management. Points to employment.

Length of contract

Taken on for the expected duration of the engager's building project (usually weeks or months at a time). Has worked for the same engager almost exclusively for three years but with three periods of 'unemployment' of one week, three weeks and 1 month during that time.

Not a 'permanent' employment but a series of fairly lengthy separate engagements with one engager. No evidence of working of several engagers. Overall, the pattern of working suggests employment.

Right of dismissal

Engagement can be terminated by either side on one week's notice.

Pointer towards employment.

Holiday/sick pay

No sick pay paid (has been sick once over last 12 months). No holiday pay but has been allowed to take a total of three weeks off for holidays (unpaid) during engagements over the last twelve months.

The engagements run to some months and holiday/sick pay might be expected. But both parties think the engagements are self-employment and this is probably why no such payments are made. A minor pointer towards self-employment.

Personal factors

No office at home. Records income and expenditure in a notebook. Has a phone which he uses to arrange weekend work and new contracts.

Little in the way of a 'business organisation' (e.g., yard or office, etc.) Not a significant pointer either way.

Does odd jobs for private householders at weekends with payment 'by the task' – earned £600 from this over the last 12 months.

Is to this extent 'in business'. But small part-time earnings of this nature will not be a key factor when measured against a full-time engagement running to weeks or months.

Prior to first working for this engager had been an apprentice bricklayer with another firm.

No evidence of existing full time business prior to working for this engager.

Has had a 714 certificate for the last three years – which expires in two years time.	Not a relevant factor.

Overall picture

The picture painted is of a skilled worker who is told what is to be done at any particular time but with little control over how it is to be done. 'Control' points towards employment but not as strongly as in Example 1. Other factors also point towards employment (e.g. weekly wage, lack of financial risk, period of notice).

Of those factors pointing to self-employment:

• Lack of holiday and sick pay are not conclusive.

• Mutual intention will only be decisive where other factors put the engagement near the borderline.

• There are no significant personal factors pointing to self-employment. There is not, for example, a clear pattern of regular working for many engagers or regular working under very short-term contracts. Further there is no evidence of an established pattern of working and business prior to the series of engagements with this engager.

Overall, the terms and conditions alone point towards employment and personal factors do not significantly affect this. The contracts are therefore considered to be contracts of employment. But the case is not far from the point where mutual intention would be decisive. If there had been a single ongoing contract or holiday pay/sick pay had been paid, the argument for employment would be much stronger.

On the other hand, if significant personal factors had existed (e.g., regular working for many engagers under short-term contracts), or there had been task based payment, the picture overall would probably be sufficiently borderline for mutual intention to decide that these SEPARATE engagements amounted to self-employment.

Index

References are to paragraph number.

accommodation
 benefit 10.6.1
 travel, subsistence and, *see* **travel**
accounting periods, changes to
 companies 13.3,13.4.
 partnerships 14.6.4
actors and entertainers
 employment status
  for NICs 20.2.3
  for tax 20.2.2
 Equity contracts 20.2.2
 expenses
  agents' fees 11.4, 20.2.4
  allowable 20.2.4
  disallowable 20.2.5
  travel 20.2.4
 overseas issues 20.2.6
 pensions 20.2.4
Advance Corporation Tax (ACT) 3.2.1,
 3.2.4
agencies
 as clients 5.6
 contracts with 5.5.1, 5.5.2, 9.3.6, 21.2.2
 Revenue, reporting to 21.2.4
 tax planning, post-IR35 23.9
 training paid by 11.8.2
appeals process 7.8
apportionment
 expenses for IR35 11.3.5
 income for IR35 10.3
 income for non-residents 17.8.4
assets
 annual value 10.6.2
 benefit charge 10.6.2
associated companies 4.5.2
associates 4.5.2, 14.2.2
attributable earnings calculation
 allowable expenses, for 11.4.2
 generally 10.1
 no deemed Schedule E 12.7
 see also **deemed Schedule E calculation**
avoidance schemes, IR35 9.1.5

benefits
 reason of employment, provided by
  10.5, 10.6, 12.4.3
 self-assessment, reporting of 15.3.3

specific
 accommodation 10.6.1
 assets 10.6.2
 cars 10.6.3
 chauffeurs 10.6.4
 conferences 10.6.5
 entertaining 10.6.6
 fuel 10.6.7
 generally 10.6
 gifts 10.6.8
 loans 10.6.9
 relocations 10.6.10
 staff functions 10.6.6
 telephones 10.6.11
 third parties, provided by 10.5.4,
  10.6.6, 12.4.3
 travel and subsistence *see* **travel**
business structure: status test
 changing contractual arrangements 9.12
 generally 6.7.6
 Lorimer case 8.2.2
 Revenue view 7.4.11

capital allowances
 company 11.11
 partnership 14.5.5, 14.6.3
 self-assessment 15.3.4
 tax planning pre-IR35 3.5.2
capital gains tax planning pre-IR35 3.9
cars
 benefit charge 10.6.3
 business mileage 11.6.8
 capital allowances 11.11.3, 14.5.5
 fuel 10.6.7
casual workers 5.3.2, 5.3.6
chauffeurs, benefit charge 10.6.4
childcare tax credit (CTC) 22.3.1
clients
 agencies as 5.6
 agency/client contracts 5.5, 9.3.6
 contracts with 5.4
 end-users, as 4.3.2
 number and variety of 6.6.4, 7.4.7, 8.2.2
 overseas service companies 21.3.2
 PAYE, obligation to deduct 10.5.4
 substitution clauses 6.5.2, 9.3.3
 tax planning post-IR35 23.9

clients—*cont.*
  third party reporting 21.3.3
  training paid by 11.8.2
close companies
  definition 3.7.2
  loans to participators 3.10.4
commuting, ordinary 11.6.3
companies
  cessation 13.8
  insolvency 13.7.4
  intermediaries, as 4.5.2
  liquidation 13.8.5
  retention of funds in 3.8
  sham 4.1.2
  share options 9.9.1
  see also **corporation tax; dividends; offshore companies; umbrella companies**
composites
  'captive' 4.5.2
  defined 2.2.3
  see also **umbrella companies**
conferences, benefit charge 10.6.5
continental shelf 20.6.3, 20.6.6
contractors, *see* **IT contractors; subcontractors**
contracts
  agencies 21.2.2
  changing contractual relationship
    business structure 9.12
    consequences 9.2
    control tests 9.6
    equipment 9.8
    exclusivity 9.13
    fundamental changes 9.2
    holiday pay and benefits 9.9.1
    hourly rates 9.9.2
    insurance 9.7
    intention of parties 9.10
    notice 9.14
    project-based work 9.4
    staff, hiring of 9.5
    substitution clause 9.3
    tax clauses 9.11
    termination of contract 9.14
  clients 5.4
  dual 17.12.3
  Equity 20.2.2
  'first call' 20.5.2
  global 5.3.1, 5.3.5, 5.3.6, 5.6
  'guarantee' 20.5.2
  hypothetical
    general principles 5.1
    interaction with contract law 5.2

national minimum wage 22.2.4
of or for service 4.4
standard 7.6, 20.6.2
tax planning post-IR35, 23.2
umbrella 5.3.1, 5.3.5, 5.3.6
control: status test
  contractual changes 9.6
  generally 6.6.3
  Revenue view 7.4.6
  specialist, control over 9.6.2
  teachers 20.9.2
corporation tax
  5 per cent allowance, interaction with 11.2.3
  CTSA (Corporation Tax Self Assessment) 15.8
  expense disallowances 11.3.6
  generally 13.1
  losses
    CTSA 15.8.2
    expenses exceed 5 per cent of income 13.7.1
    generally 13.7, 23.5
    insolvency 13.7.4
    management of 13.7.3, 23.5
  planning in context of IR35 3.2, 13.9
  small companies' rate 3.2.2
  starting rate 3.2.2
  see also **accounting periods, companies, dividends, offshore companies**
Corporation Tax Self Assessment (CTSA) 15.8

deemed Schedule E calculation
  generally 10.1
  no attributable earnings calculation 18.4.5
  Step One
    5 per cent allowance 10.5.1, 11.2
    generally 10.5, 10.6
    partnerships 14.5.2
  Step Two
    generally 10.5, 10.6
    partnerships 14.5.3
  Step Three
    generally 11.3
    partnerships 14.5.4
    Step Seven, interaction with 12.4.5
  Step Four
    generally 11.11
    partnerships 14.5.5
  Step Five
    generally 12.2
    partnerships 14.5.6

deemed Schedule E calculation—*cont.*
Step Six
generally 12.3
partnerships 14.5.7
Step Seven
generally 12.4
partnerships 14.5.7
Step Three, interaction with 12.4.5
Step Eight
generally 12.5
partnerships 14.5.8
timing of payment 16.3
see also **attributable earnings**
calculation, NICs, partners
definitions
associated 17.12.3
associates 14.2.2
composites 2.2.3
domicile 17.11.1
fraud 16.6.3
Friday to Monday companies 2.2.3,
20.3.4
material interest 4.5.2
merely incidental 10.6.3
negligence 16.6.3
ordinary residence 17.5.2
personal service company (PSC) 2.2.1
remittance 17.13.2
status tests 6.3.1
travel expenses 11.6.1
worker for NMW purposes 22.2.3
directors
generally, including temporary
executives 20.3
national minimum wage 22.2.2
NICs 12.7.3
pension schemes, lump sums from
20.3.4
professional partnerships, income from
20.3.2
Disabled Persons Tax Credit (DPTC)
22.3.1
divers, employment status 20.6.2
dividends
double taxation 13.6
illegal 3.10.3
national minimum wage 22.2.3
NICs 3.2.3
non-residents 17.8.7
salary versus dividend 3.2, 13.5,13.6,
23.1
self-assessment
UK dividends 15.3.6
overseas companies 15.3.8

student loan repayments 22.4.2
taxation of 3.2.3
using to extract profits 13.6.1
see also **companies; corporation tax**
domicile status
changes of, procedures for establishing
17.11.5
choice, domicile of 17.11.4
concept 17.11.1
consequences of being non-domiciled
dual contracts 17.12.3
foreign emoluments 17.4, 17.12.1,
17.12.3, 17.13.2
personal services implications 17.12.2
tax advantages 17.12.1
travel expenses 17.12.4
married women 17.11.3
origin, domicile of 17.11.2
self-assessment 15.3.8
see also **remittance basis**
double taxation
CTSA 15.8.2
dividends 13.6.1
claiming relief 13.6.2
entertainers 20.2.6
intermediaries, payments/benefits paid
to worker by 10.5.2, 12.4.3
non-residents (double tax treaties)
17.8.3
offshore companies
corporate tax residence 19.2.1
non-resident with UK trading
presence 19.3
oil and gas workers 20.6.4
DPTC (Disabled Persons Tax Credit)
22.3.1
dual contracts 17.12.3

EBT (employee benefit trust) 4.5.2, 9.15
EET (employee's earnings threshold)
4.8.2, 12.3.2
emoluments, foreign 17.4, 17.12.1,
17.12.3, 17.13.2
Employer Compliance Unit 16.9
engagements, length and number of:
status test
case law examples 8.2.2, 8.2.4, 8.3.3
generally 6.6.4
Revenue view 7.4.7
enquiries by Inland Revenue
aspect 15.2, 15.5.4, 15.8.2
CTSA 15.8.2
disclosure 15.2
full 15.2, 15.5.4, 15.8.2

enquiries by Inland Revenue—*cont.*
  random 15.4.2, 15.5.4
  see also Inland Revenue investigations;
    penalties
entertainers *see* actors and entertainers
entertaining, benefit charge 10.6.6
EPP (Executive Pension Plan) 3.6.1, 3.6.5
equipment, provision of: status test
  case law examples 8.2.2, 8.3.1
  contractual relationship, changing terms
    of 9.8
  generally 6.6.2
  IT contractors 7.4.5, 11.11.2
  Revenue view 7.4.5
  teachers 20.9.2
exclusivity: status test
  generally 6.7.2
  contractual relationship, changing terms
    of 9.13
Executive Pension Plan, *see* EPP
executives, temporary, *see* directors
expenses
  disallowed 11.3.6
  generally 8.2.2, 11.4, 11.5, 23.4
  included in deemed Schedule E payment
    11
  NICs 11.4.2
  pre-IR35 3.5.1

family members, payments to 3.4
FAQs (Inland Revenue Frequently Asked
    Questions)
  5 per cent deduction 11.2.2
  accounting periods, problems with
    13.4.3
  generally 2.3.7
  overseas issues 17.10.2
  partnerships 14.1, 14.2.2
  penalties, concession on 16.4.2
  purpose of IR35 3.2.3
  round sum cash payments 10.5.4
  Schedule E calculation, deemed 11.2.2,
    11.3.2
  substitution status test 7.4.1
  travel expenses 11.6.3
  umbrella companies 21.4.2
  VAT 13.10
footballers 20.7
fraud
  generally 16.6
  self-assessment 15.6.4
Friday to Monday companies 2.2.3,
    20.3.4
fuel, benefit charge 10.6.7

gifts, benefit charge 10.6.8
'global' employment contracts 5.3.1, 5.3.5,
    5.3.6, 5.6.4

hire cars, benefit charge 10.6.3
hiring of staff *see* staff, hiring of
holiday pay 9.9.1
hourly rates 9.9.2

ILAs (Individual Learning Accounts)
    11.8.4, 15.3.5
income
  apportionments of 10.3, 11.3.5, 17.8.4
  recognition of
    corporation tax basis 13.2.1
    deemed Schedule E basis 13.2.2
Individual Learning Accounts (ILAs) *see*
    ILAs
individuals as intermediaries 4.5.4
Inland Revenue
  April 1999 paper 2.3.2, 2.3.3
  booklets and manuals 7.2
  concerns over tax advantages of PSCs
    2.2.3
  case studies 7.5, 24
  clearance process 7.7
  Employer Compliance Unit 16.9
  investigations 16.9
  mutuality, view of 5.3.7, 7.3.4
  self-assessment guidance 14.6.4
  September 1999 press release 2.3.4
  standard contracts 7.6
  status tests, view of 7.3, 7.4
  see also FAQs, penalties, enquiries by
      Inland Revenue
insolvency 13.7.4
insurance
  clauses, appropriate 9.7
  employer's liability 11.10
  Professional Indemnity (PII)
    generally 11.10
    IT contractors 20.4.3
    Schedule E expenses 11.4
  public liability 11.10
intention of parties: status test
  changing contractual arrangements
    9.10
  generally 6.7.5
  Revenue view 7.4.10
intermediaries
  generally 4.5
  companies 4.5.2
  partnerships 4.5.3
  individuals 4.5.4

intermediaries—*cont.*
  more than one 4.5.5
  sole traders 4.7
interest
  PAYE and NICs 16.5
  self-assessment 15.6
investigations 16.9
IR35 – purpose, development and scope
  generally 1.0, 2.2
  April 1999 Inland Revenue paper 2.3.2,
    2.3.3
  de minimis exemption 4.6.2
  scope of legislation 4.1.3, 4.2–4.8
  September 1999 press release 2.3.4
  treated as single employment 10.4
IT contractors
  case studies 24.1
  generally 20.4

lecturers *see* teachers and lecturers
loans, benefit charge 10.6.9
'locums' 5.3.2, 10.6.1
'long-term temps' 2.2.3
  losses *see* corporation tax: losses

'material interest' test 4.5.2
'merely incidental' test 10.6.3
musicians 20.5
mutuality of obligation
  generally 5.3
  Revenue view 5.3.7, 7.3.4
  status cases 5.3, 8.2.2, 8.2.3, 8.2.4

National Insurance Contributions *see*
    NICs
  national minimum wage 22.1, 22.2
negligence
  generally 16.6
  self-assessment 15.6.4
net relevant earnings *see* NREs
NICs (National Insurance Contributions)
  actors/entertainers 20.2.3
  administration/deductions 16.2.1
  agency workers 5.6.4
  aggregation of earnings 4.8.3
  annual earnings period 4.8.2
  business mileage rules 11.6.8
  calculating 12.5.2
  Class 1
    end of year returns 16.2.3
    generally 12.3.2, 12.5.1
    partnerships 14.7.1
    payment deadline 16.4.1-16.4.2

    see also penalties
Class 1A
  client/third-party responsibilities 10.5.4
  generally 12.3.3, 12.5.1
  Class 2 14.7.1
  Class 4 14.7.1
  dividends, illegal 3.10.3
  EET (employee's earnings threshold)
    4.8.2, 12.3.2
  individuals working abroad 18.3
  national minimum wage 22.3.5
  offshore issues 18, 19.4.2, 19.5.3
  oil and gas workers 20.6.3
  partners
    Classes 2 and 4 14.7.1
    directors' fees, relief for 14.3.4
    overseas issues 19.7.2
    payment deadlines 14.8
    small earnings exception 14.7.2
  payment deadlines 14.8, 16.4.1
  penalties *see* penalties
  personal pensions 3.6.3
  post-IR35 tax planning 23.3.2
  scope of legislation 4.8
  teachers and lecturers 20.9.3
  travel costs 11.6.8
  UEL (upper earnings limit) 4.8.2, 12.3.2
  unpaid
    collection from worker/director
      16.8.1, 16.8.2
    penalties for 16.6.4
  visitors to UK 18.4
  Working Rule Agreements 11.6.6
  see also attributable earnings calculation,
    offshore companies
NMW *see* national minimum wage
non-domicile *see* domicile
non-residents *see* residence status –
    individuals: non-residents
Norway, double tax treaty 20.6.4
NREs (net relevant earnings)
  deemed Schedule E calculation 12.2.4,
    12.2.5
  entertainers 20.2.4
  personal pensions 3.6.3
  small salary payments 3.3
  stakeholder pension schemes 3.6.4,
    12.2.5

'off-the-peg' solutions 9.15
offshore companies
  client's position 21.3.2
  corporate tax residence in UK 19.2

enforcement procedures 19.6
non-resident companies
offshore companies—*cont.*
no trading presence in UK 19.4
with UK trading presence 19.3
personal services rules 19.5
oil and gas workers 20.6
ordinary residence 17.5.2, 17.5.3

P11Ds
administration/deductions 16.2.2
deadlines 16.2.2
employers' obligations 10.5.4
generally 16.2.2
interaction with IR35 10.5.5
intermediaries, payments received by
workers from 10.5.2
partnerships, not applicable 14.8
personal service rules, common benefits
10.6
P60 forms 15.3.2
**part and parcel of the organisation: status
test** 6.7.7
partnerships
60 per cent test 14.2.2
associates 14.2.2
deemed Schedule E calculation
accounting dates 14.6.4
benefit received from client 14.5.3
capital allowances 14.5.5, 14.6.3
expenses 11.3.4, 11.3.6, 14.5.4, 14.6.3
fiscal year basis 14.5.2
interaction with partnership
computation 14.6.3
loss restrictions 14.6.3
other partners, effects on 14.6.5
pensions 14.5.6
receipts basis 14.5.2
Step One 14.5.2
Step Two 14.5.3
Step Three 14.5.4
Step Four 14.5.5
Step Five 14.5.6
Step Six 14.5.7
Step Seven 14.5.7
Step Eight 14.5.8
timing of 14.6.2
directors' fees, tax treatment 14.3.2,
20.3.2
employees within 14.4
exceptions to personal services
legislation
concessions and practice 14.3
no relevant engagements 14.2.1

statutory 14.2.2
generally 14.1
intermediaries 4.5.3, 16.3.1
national minimum wage 22.2.2
NICs
Classes 2 and 4, interaction with
14.7.1
directors' fees, relief on 14.3.4
overseas implications 19.7.2
payment deadlines 14.8, 23.3.2
small earnings exception 14.7.2
offshore partnerships
PAYE and NIC obligations 19.7.2
residence 19.7.1
overseas issues, remittance basis 17.14
PAYE
overseas implications 19.7.2
payment deadlines 14.8
personal services legislation 14.1
profit sharing arrangements 14.2.2
record keeping, importance for self-
assessment 15.2
relatives 14.2.2
reason for inclusion 4.5.3
reporting of personal services income
benefits 15.3.3
capital allowances 15.3.4
expenses 15.3.4
pension contributions, reliefs 15.3.5
residence status 19.7.1
Revenue practice (SE 1226) 14.3.3
Schedule E income received by partners
14.3.3
self-assessment
interim payments 14.6.4
record keeping 15.2
reporting of personal services income
15.3.3, 15.3.4, 15.3.5
requirements 15.3.10
single clients 14.2.2
student loan repayments 22.4.2
subcontractors 20.8.4
tax planning, post-IR35 23.8
PAYE (Pay as You Earn)
actors/entertainers 20.2.2
administration/deductions 16.2.1
annual return
clients, relevance to 10.5.4
coding notices 16.2.1
interaction with IR35 10.5.5
intermediaries
multiple 4.5.5
payments received by workers from
10.5.2

PAYE (Pay as You Earn)—*cont.*
  investigations, time limits for 15.4.2
  national minimum wage 22.3.5
  offshore companies
    enforcement 19.6.2
    non-resident with no trading presence
      in UK 19.4.1
    non-resident with UK trading
      presence 19.3
    special rules for personal service
      companies 19.5.1
  partners
    coding notices, lack of 16.2.1
    overseas companies 19.7.2
    payment deadlines 14.8
  payment deadlines 14.8, 16.4.1, 23.3.2
  penalties
    collection of unpaid tax from
      worker/director 16.8.2
    self-assessment 15.6.1
  post-IR35 tax planning 23.3.2
  PSA (PAYE Settlement Agreement) 10.7
  self-assessment 15.3.2, 15.6.1, 15.7
  unpaid
    collection 16.8.1, 16.8.2
    penalties for 16.6.4
payment in lieu of notice *see* **PILON**
payment terms: status test
  changing contractual terms 9.9
  generally 6.7.3
  Revenue view 7.4.9
PCG (Professional Contractors Group)
  20.4.1
penalties
  assets, confiscation of 16.6.1
  collection
    time limits for 16.8.1
    workers or directors, from 16.8.2
  concessions 16.4.2
  criminal 16.6.5
  fixed 16.6.2
  fraud 16.6.3–16.6.5
  imprisonment 16.6.1
  negligence 16.6.3–16.6.5
  reducing
    benefit of the doubt 16.7.2
    mitigation 16.7.4
    reasonable excuse 16.7.3
  tax planning, post-IR35 23.10
  see also **enquiries; investigations, self-
    assessment**
pensions
  actors and entertainers 20.2.4

  directors 20.3.4
  Executive Pension Plans (EPPs) 3.6.1,
    3.6.5, 12.2.5, 23.6
  executives, temporary 20.3.4
  lump sums from 20.3.4
  occupational schemes 3.6.5
  personal pensions 3.6.3
  self-assessment reliefs 15.3.5
  Small Self Administered Schemes
    (SSASs) 3.6.5, 12.2.5, 23.6
  sportspeople 20.7.4
  stakeholder schemes 3.6.4, 12.2.5
  tax advantages 3.6
  tax planning, post-IR35 23.6
personal factors *see* **engagements, number
  of**
personal incidental expenses 11.4, 11.7,
  20.4.3
PII *see* **insurance**
PILON (payment in lieu of notice) 6.7.4,
  9.14
professional workers and status tests
  generally 6.4.4, 6.6.3, 6.6.4, 8.2
  Revenue view 7.4.6, 7.4.8
professional subscriptions 11.4, 11.9
**profiting from sound management: status
  test**
  case law examples 8.2.2, 8.2.3
  generally 6.5.3
  Revenue view 7.4.3
project-based work 9.4
PSA (PAYE Settlement Agreement) 10.7

recategorisation of workers
  freelancers 2.2.2, 21.3.4
  partners 4.5.3
  sole traders 4.7
  subcontractors 7.2
receipts basis 10.2, 13.2, 14.5.2
record keeping 15.2, 23.3.3
relevant events 16.3.1
relocations, benefit charge 10.6.10
remittance basis 17.13
Republic of Ireland
  foreign emoluments 17.12.3
  remittance basis 17.13.6
residence status – individuals
  abroad 17.9.6
  days spent in UK 17.6
  generally 17.2, 17.5.1
  non-residents – individuals
    dividends received, tax treatment
      17.8.7

residence status – individuals—*cont.*
    double tax treaties 17.8.3
    dual contracts for 17.8.5
    full-time contract abroad 17.9.2
    generally 17.8.1, 17.9.1
    income apportionment 17.8.4
    'merely incidental' 17.8.2
    procedures for obtaining non-
        residence status 17.9.5
    tax allowances for 17.8.6
  oil and gas workers 20.6.3
  ordinary residence 17.5.2
  outline 17.4
  partnerships 19.7.1
  permanent residence abroad 17.9.4
  personal services 17.2
  procedure for establishing
    coming to UK 17.7.2, 17.7.3
    leaving the UK 17.9.5
  self-assessment 15.3.8
  UK residents working abroad
    relief for overseas tax suffered 17.10.2
    tax basis 17.10.1
    travel expenses 17.10.3
  see also **domicile, offshore companies**
risk, significant financial: status test
  court decisions 8.2.2-8.2.4, 8.3.2
  generally 6.5.3
  project-based work 9.4.1, 9.4.3
  Revenue view 7.4.2

salary
  deemed Schedule E calculation 12.4.2,
    13.4.4, 23.3.1
  self-assessment 15.3.2
  withdrawal of funds as 13.5
  see **dividends**: salary versus dividend
    comparison
self-assessment
  'aspect enquiries' 15.2, 15.5.4, 15.8.2
  changing the tax return 15.5
  CTSA (Corporation Tax Self
    Assessment) 15.8
  disclosure 15.4
  discovery rules 15.2, 15.4.1, 15.5.5
  'error and mistake' rules 15.2, 15.5.3,
    15.8.2
  'full enquiries' 15.2, 15.5.4, 15.8.2
  generally 15.1
  individual return 15.2
  interest 15.6
  interim payments 15.7
  partnerships
    generally 15.2

    interim payments 14.6.4
    record keeping 15.2
    requirements 15.3.10
  penalties 15.6
  random enquiries 15.4.2, 15.5.4
  records, retaining of 15.2
  reporting personal services income
    benefits 15.3.3
    capital allowances 15.3.4
    deemed Schedule E income 15.3.2
    dividends 15.3.6
    expenses 15.3.4
    notifying chargeability 15.3.1
    overseas aspects 15.3.8, 15.8.2
    partners 15.2, 15.3.3, 15.3.4, 15.3.5,
      15.3.10
    reliefs 15.3.5
    residence status 15.3.8
    salary 15.3.2
    self-employed individuals 15.3.9
    student loan repayments 15.3.7
  Revenue guidance 14.6.4
share options, provision of 9.9.1
shareholders, loans to 3.10.3
skill of workers
  mutuality and 5.3.4, 5.3.6
  status cases 8.2.2, 8.2.3, 8.3.1, 8.3.2
SLRs (student loan repayments)
  generally 22.4
  NICs 3.2.3
  self-assessment 15.3.7
Small Self Administered Scheme *see*
    SSAS
sole traders 4.7
sportspeople 20.7
  benefit matches 20.7.2
  employment status 20.7.2
  Football League rules 20.7.2
  Image Contracts 20.7.2
  loyalty bonuses 20.7.2
  overseas issues 20.7.3
  pension schemes 20.7.4
  signing-on fees 20.7.2
  sponsorship and promotional income
    20.7.2
  testimonial matches 20.7.2
  transfer fees 20.7.2
  winning matches, payments for 20.7.2
SSAS (Small Self Administered Scheme)
    3.6.1, 3.6.3, 3.6.5, 12.2.5, 23.6
staff, hiring of: status test
  changes to contractual arrangements 9.5
  generally 6.5.4
  Revenue view 7.4.4

status tests
benefits provided 6.7.3, 7.4.9, 9.9.1
business structure 6.7.6, 7.4.11, 8.2.2,
    9.12
control 6.6.3, 7.4.6, 9.6
dismissal, right of 6.7.4, 9.14
engagements
    length and number of 6.6.4, 7.4.7,
        8.2.2, 8.2.4, 8.3.3
    regular or long, with same client 7.4.8
equipment, provision of 6.6.2, 7.4.5,
    8.2.2, 9.8
exclusivity 6.7.2, 9.13
factors personal to worker 6.6.4
generally 6.1
'in business on your own account' 6.4
intention of the parties 6.7.5, 7.4.10,
    9.10
part and parcel of the organisation 6.7.7
payment methods 6.7.3, 7.4.9, 9.9
risk, significant financial 6.5.3, 7.4.2, 9.4
sound management, opportunity to
    profit from 6.5.3, 7.4.3, 8.2.2, 8.2.3
staff, hiring of 6.5.4, 7.4.4, 8.3.1, 9.5
substitution 6.5.2, 7.4.1
tax planning post-IR35 23.2
termination *see* **status tests**: dismissal
Steps 1–9 *see* **deemed Schedule E payment**
student loan repayments (SLRs)
generally 22.4
self-assessment 15.3.7
subcontractors
case studies 7.5, 24.3
generally 20.8
partnerships, use of 20.8.4
recategorisation 7.2, 20.8.1, 20.8.2
tax deductions 20.8.5
subscriptions, professional 11.4, 11.9
subsistence expenses 11.4, 11.6.5, 20.4.3
see also travel
substantial effect test 11.6.3
substitution: status test
changes to contractual arrangements
    9.3
generally 6.5.2
Revenue view 7.4.1
teachers/lecturers 20.9.2

TAS (Taxed Award Scheme) 10.7
tax payments
end of year returns 16.2.3
P11Ds 16.2.2
PAYE administration 16.2.1

Schedule E deemed payment, timing of
    receipt of income following relevant
        event 16.3.2
    relevant events 16.3.1
subcontractors 20.8.5
see also **PAYE (Pay as you Earn)**, **P11Ds**
tax planning post-IR35
agencies 23.9
clients 23.9
contracts 23.3
corporation tax 13.9
deemed income calculation, managing
    23.3.1–23.3.3
expenses 23.4
losses 23.5
overseas issues 23.7
partnerships 23.8
pensions 23.6
record keeping 23.3.3
reliefs 23.4
status 23.2
travel and subsistence 11.6.7
tax planning pre-IR35
capital allowances 3.5.2
capital gains tax 3.5.3, 3.9
dividend/salary comparison 3.2
expenses 3.5.1
family members, payments to 3.4
interest relief 3.7
National Insurance 3.2.3
pensions 3.6.
pitfalls 3.10
retention of funds 3.8
small salary payment 3.3
Taxed Award Scheme (TAS) 10.7
teachers and lecturers 20.9
telephones, benefit charge 10.6.11
television and film industry workers 20.10
third parties
clients, reporting 21.3.3
income and benefits from 10.5.4, 10.6.6,
    12.4.3
training expenses
agency, paid by 11.8.2
client, paid by 11.8.2
Individual Learning Accounts (ILAs)
    11.8.4, 15.3.5
IT contractors 20.4.3
limits of relief 11.8.3
self-employment, indicator of
    11.8.5
specific deductions 11.4
worker, paid by 11.8.1

travel expenses
40 per cent test 11.6.3
accommodation 10.6.1, 11.6.5
actors and entertainers 20.2.4
business mileage 11.6.8
cessation of business 11.6.3, 13.8.4
defined 11.6.1
IT contractors 20.4.3
legislation 11.6.2
NICs 11.6.8
non-domiciled status, consequences
    17.12.4
oil and gas workers 20.6.6
ordinary commuting 11.6.3
planning for 11.6.7
private travel 11.6.4
reliefs, requirements for 11.4
subsistence 11.6.1, 11.6.5
substantial effect test 11.6.3
temporary workplaces 11.6.3
two year rule 11.6.3
UK residents working abroad 17.10.3

vehicle running costs 11.6.8
wholly, exclusively and necessarily test
    11.5
Working Rule Agreements (WRAs)
    11.6.6
see also **subsistence expenses**

umbrella companies 21.4
see also **composites**
umbrella contracts 5.3.1, 5.3.5, 5.3.6

VAT (Value Added Tax) 13.10
visitors to UK
entertainers 20.2.6
NIC liabilities 18.4
sports people 20.4.3
tax position 17.5

working families' tax credit (WFTC) 22.3
working overseas 17.9, 18.3
WRAs (Working Rule Agreements) 11.6.6